Teaching Psychology

This volume provides thoroughly updated guidelines for preparing and teaching an entire course in psychology. Based on best principles and effective psychological and pedagogical research, it offers practical suggestions for planning a course, choosing teaching methods, integrating technology appropriately and effectively, developing student evaluation instruments and programs, and implementing ideas for evaluation of your own teaching effectiveness.

While research based, this book was developed to be a basic outline of "what to do" when you teach. It is intended as a self-help guide for relatively inexperienced psychology teachers, whether graduate students or new faculty, but also as a core reading assignment for those who train psychology instructors. Experienced faculty who wish to hone their teaching skills will find the book useful, too.

Sandra Goss Lucas received her bachelor and master's degrees (and a teaching certificate) in teaching social sciences from the University of Illinois in 1971 and 1972, respectively. She received a PhD from Indiana University, Department of Counseling and Educational Psychology, in 1984 with minors in psychology and women's studies. She taught introductory psychology in high school and at two community colleges prior to joining the Psychology Department at the University of Illinois (Urbana-Champaign) in 1984, where she became Director of Introductory Psychology in 1998. She retired as Director of Introductory Psychology in May 2009, but continues to teach psychology courses. Her teaching awards include the University of Illinois Psychology Department Teaching Enhancement Award, the University of Illinois Campus Award for Excellence in Undergraduate Teaching, the University of Illinois College of Liberal Arts and Sciences Award for Excellence in Undergraduate Teaching, the University of Illinois Psychology Graduate Student Organization Instructional Award for Excellence in Teaching and Advising at the Graduate Level, and the Alpha Lambda Delta Award for Outstanding Teacher of Freshmen. She has been a member of the National Institute on the Teaching of Psychology steering committee since 1986. She has written a book on teaching introductory psychology, *Teaching Introductory Psychology*, as well as several articles on the topic of teaching.

Douglas A. Bernstein completed his bachelor degree in psychology at the University of Pittsburgh in 1964 and earned his master's and PhD degrees in clinical psychology at Northwestern University in 1966 and 1968, respectively. From 1968 to 1998, he was on the psychology faculty at the University of Illinois at Urbana-Champaign, where he taught classes ranging from 15 to 750 students, and served as both Associate Department Head and Director of Introductory Psychology. He is currently Professor Emeritus at the University of Illinois and Courtesy Professor of Psychology at the University of South Florida. He is a fellow of the Association for Psychological Science. For 35 years he served as a member of the planning committee, and then as committee chairman, for the National Institute on the Teaching of Psychology. In 1994, he founded the APS Preconference Institute on the Teaching of Psychology. In 2001, he served on the advisory panel to the APA Board of Educational Affairs Task Force on Undergraduate Psychology Major Competencies, and he served for two years as the founding chairman of the Steering Committee for the APS Fund for the Teaching and Public Understanding of Psychological Science. His teaching awards include the University of Illinois Psychology Graduate Student Association Teaching Award, the University of Illinois Psi Chi award for excellence in undergraduate teaching, and the APA Distinguished Teaching in Psychology Award. He has coauthored textbooks in Introductory Psychology, Abnormal Psychology, Clinical Psychology, Criminal Behavior, and Progressive Relaxation Training, and has also contributed chapters to *Teaching Introductory Psychology: Theory and Practice, The Teaching of Psychology: Essays in Honor of Wilbert J. McKeachie and Charles L. Brewer,* and (with Sandra Goss Lucas) *The Compleat Academic: A Career Guide.*

Teaching Psychology
A Step-By-Step Guide

Second Edition

Sandra Goss Lucas and Douglas A. Bernstein

Psychology Press
Taylor & Francis Group
NEW YORK AND LONDON

Second edition published 2015
by Psychology Press
711 Third Avenue, New York, NY 10017

and by Psychology Press
27 Church Road, Hove, East Sussex BN3 2FA

Psychology Press is an imprint of the Taylor & Francis Group, an informa business

© 2014 Taylor & Francis

The right of Sandra Goss Lucas and Douglas A. Bernstein to be identified as authors of this work has been asserted by them in accordance with sections 77 and 78 of the Copyright, Designs and Patents Act 1988.

First published by Lawrence Erlbaum Associates 2004

Library of Congress Cataloging-in-Publication Data

Teaching Psychology: A Step-By-Step Guide, Second Edition / Sandra Goss Lucas and Douglas A Bernstein.
    pages cm
1. Education. 2. Psychology. 3. Teaching Methods & Materials. I. Goss Lucas, Sanda. II. Bernstein, Douglas A.
  BF575.P9N48 2013
  155.9'2—dc23   2012048031

ISBN: 978-1-138-79033-9 (hbk)
ISBN: 978-1-138-79034-6 (pbk)
ISBN: 978-1-315-76309-5 (ebk)

Typeset in Utopia
by Apex CoVantage, LLC

Printed and bound in the United States of America by Publishers Graphics,
LLC on sustainably sourced paper.

To Dave and Doris and Frank

Contents ● ● ● ● ●

Preface ● ● ● ● ●

Our motivation for updating this book is essentially the same as it was for writing the first edition, namely to share with you what we have learned about teaching psychology, and what others have learned through their research on effective teaching. Although we came to teaching from very different backgrounds, we both revere effective teaching and have spent our professional careers trying to achieve it.

Sandy always wanted to be a teacher, and fulfilled that dream by pursuing a teacher education program and earning a teaching certificate in social sciences. After completing student teaching at a junior high school and an internship at a high school, she earned a master's degree in teaching social sciences, then spent the next six years teaching psychology at two different community colleges. Married with two small children, Sandy decided her next step was to complete the PhD program in educational psychology (with an emphasis on teacher behavior) at Indiana University. Before being admitted to that program, she was told by members of the admissions committee to rewrite her goals statement that, in their view, placed too much emphasis on teaching and not enough on research. She did so, but throughout her graduate career she continued to find opportunities to teach.

Doug came to teaching through a very different route. His first course was introductory psychology, and he was assigned to teach it while still a graduate student at Northwestern University. Unlike Sandy, he had absolutely no preparation for teaching, and learned to teach as best he could, mainly through the school of hard knocks, as it were. After completing his doctorate in clinical psychology, Doug joined the faculty at the University of Illinois at Urbana-Champaign, where, except for a couple of sabbaticals and short leaves, he spent 30 years teaching graduate and undergraduate psychology courses.

In 1984, after Doug was appointed as director of the department's large, multisection introductory psychology program, he was looking for an assistant director, and Sandy applied for the job. Thus began a 30-year professional partnership that has evolved into a wonderful friendship.

The first thing we did was to revise the structure of the introductory course and reorganize the administrative structure through which it was taught. We each taught our own sections of the course, but part of our reorganization plan took the form of creating a training program for the graduate students who would be teaching most of the other sections.

After decades of offering teacher preparation programs, courses on teaching, and advice to these students, and eventually to all graduate teaching assistants in the department, we realized that we had collected a lot of material that might be of value to new teachers in other psychology departments, too. We found several ways to share bits and pieces of that material with our colleagues. For a number of years, we gave one-day workshops on the teaching of psychology at various locations around the country. And we continue to give talks on teaching, separately and together, at the annual National Institute on the Teaching of Psychology and elsewhere.

Then we began to write about teaching. In a chapter in Prieto and Meyers's *The Teaching Assistant Handbook,* Sandy described the orientation program we developed for psychology teaching assistants at Illinois. In 1997, Doug described his views on teaching introductory psychology in a chapter for Robert Sternberg's book, *Teaching Introductory Psychology: Theory and Practice.* And in 2001, Roddy Roediger asked Doug to write a chapter about teaching for the revised edition of *The Compleat Academic.* Doug invited Sandy to be his coauthor on that chapter, and while writing it, we realized that what we wanted to say about teaching psychology far exceeded our page limit.

The first edition of this book was a greatly expanded discussion of the topics covered in that chapter, and more. It was, and is, based on our own teaching experiences, as well as on the research and experience of other psychology faculty whose work we have read and whose advice we have taken. We obviously share a general set of values about teaching psychology, but we do disagree on some details of policy and procedure. These occasional disagreements gave us a chance to offer multiple options for dealing with various teaching situations.

We wrote, and have now updated, this book mainly with new psychology teachers in mind, but we know that seasoned teachers—including ourselves—too can benefit from exposure to new teaching ideas and techniques, and from occasionally reevaluating their teaching and its effectiveness. We think that our own teaching has improved as a result of writing this book and revising it into a second edition, and we hope that reading it will do the same for you, no matter how much or how little teaching experience you may have.

You will notice that our presentation focuses on the practical far more than the theoretical. There are already many good books about the educational and psychological theories underlying effective teaching at the postsecondary level, and much of the advice we offer is grounded in some of those theories. But our main goal was to create a research-based "how to" book on the teaching of psychology that can be read from beginning to end, but that can also serve as a quick reference and source of specific ideas for dealing with a wide range of teaching situations at a moment's notice. It is the kind of book that Doug could have used back in 1966 to help make his first teaching experience easier, less stressful, and more effective.

The chapter titles have not changed in this second edition, but the information you will find in each chapter has been rewritten to incorporate current research on effective teaching and the many changes in the landscape of teaching that have taken place since the first edition was published. The chapter sequence was chosen to present information in the order in which a new teacher might need it. So in Chapter 1 we describe some basic principles of effective teaching, the characteristics of today's students, and the expectations placed on today's teachers. Chapter 2 deals with such topics as developing course goals and how to plan a course, write a syllabus, establish a grading system, and choose a textbook. Chapter 3 presents a step-by-step guide to the first few days of class, from finding and exploring the classroom, to presenting a syllabus, to ending a class session. Chapter 4 focuses on the development of one's teaching style and on the many options psychology teachers have to express that style in the context of giving lectures, conducting demonstrations, asking and answering questions, leading discussions, and the like. In Chapter 5, we offer advice and suggestions for evaluating student learning and performance via exams, quizzes, and a wide variety of writing assignments. We also provide guidelines for developing and grading each type of evaluation method, and we suggest ways of matching evaluation options—and one's evaluation criteria—to course goals and objectives. Chapter 6 takes up the vital topic of faculty–student relations and how to manage them. Here you will find advice on how to create a comfortable and inclusive classroom climate, provide academic assistance, protect students' privacy, improve their motivation to learn, write letters of recommendation, and assist students with special needs or problems, as well as how to prevent and manage students' classroom misbehavior and deal with complaints, special requests, excuses, and academic dishonesty, all within the context of the highest standards of teaching ethics. Chapter 7 deals with the constantly changing world of educational technology. In addition to offering a classification of teaching technologies, the chapter points out that technology can enhance or interfere with teaching and can promote or impair learning, and urges teachers to think carefully about when and whether or not each of today's high-tech teaching methods will advance teaching goals.

In Chapter 8 we take up the topic of how to evaluate the quality and effectiveness of your teaching. We emphasize the importance of establishing a continuing process of self-evaluation and of relying on colleagues as well as students as sources of evaluative information. Finally, in Chapter 9, we discuss the need to integrate teaching into the rest of your academic life, including how to deal with the anxieties and stresses associated with teaching.

In every chapter, we offer checklists and/or other material that we think will be of use to new and experienced teachers alike, including forms for dealing with students' excuses and complaints about exam items.

We hope that you enjoy reading this book as much as we have enjoyed writing and revising it, and we look forward to hearing your comments on our efforts and your suggestions for improvement. You can reach us at gossluca@illinois.edu or douglas.bernstein@comcast.net.

Sandra Goss Lucas and Douglas A. Bernstein

1

● ● ● ● ●

Introduction

Some Characteristics of Effective Teachers
Basic Principles of Effective Teaching
Your Role as a Teacher
Teaching Online
Some Final Comments

It has been a decade since we wrote the first edition of this book, and we did so partly because national surveys and our own experience led us to believe that most teachers of psychology at colleges and universities, while experts in the content of their disciplinc, did not have strong backgrounds in educational techniques and technologies. Has the situation improved since then? To some extent, yes. A small-scale survey of 47 new psychology professors found that 82% of them had taken a course on teaching while they were in graduate school (Silvestri et al., 2012). Further, an analysis of information from 51 U.S. psychology departments found that all of them offered their graduate students teaching training courses, teaching supervision/mentoring, or both, and that this training was a requirement for teaching assistants in 84% of these departments (Beers, Hill, & Thompson, 2012; Buskist, 2013a). Still, too few new faculty are receiving extensive teaching training as part of their graduate education (Buskist, 2013a; Buskist et al., 2002; Prieto & Meyers, 2001). And for many, the training they do receive is little more than a one-shot seminar or orientation program offered by the psychology department or a campus faculty development unit. It is far less common to see one- or two-term courses that provide graduate students with didactic and practical training in all aspects of teaching.

As a result, too many teachers of psychology today are still entering their first classrooms having spent years as apprentices to expert mentors in research, but with little or no formal preparation for their role as a teacher (Buskist, 2013a; Buskist et al., 2002; Golde & Dore, 2001; Kennedy, 1997; Mervis, 2001). They have to teach by default, doing the best they can, relying on their guts and their wits and the (good and bad) examples set by their own teachers. The results can be mixed, at best. As one observer bluntly put it, "Many faculty are not effective in the classroom because they don't know what they are doing or why" (Weimer, 1988, p. 49). Adding to this problem is the fact that new psychology teachers seldom receive the kind of early feedback from peers or mentors that can help them identify their strengths and weaknesses and improve their teaching. As James Lang put it, "In jobs in other kinds of businesses, new employees will receive regular performance reviews to get them on track; in academia, we prefer to let our new employees flounder around on their own for as long as possible—the ones that survive, we figure, have what it takes to be a teacher" (2008, p. 266).

We don't think that any psychology teacher, novice or veteran, should have to "flounder around," and because the first edition of this book was well received, we thought it was time to offer a second one that includes the latest information on teaching methods and research and takes into account the significant changes that have occurred in the higher education landscape. Some of these changes are directly linked to difficult economic times for colleges and universities, and are reflected in larger classes and in more online classes, including massive open online courses (MOOCs). Other changes are linked to the explosion in the availability and use of educational technology such as student response systems ("clickers"), online presentation of basic course material ("flipped" classrooms), and sophisticated learning management systems (LMSs) that allow instructors to post information, grade assignments online, and provide online quizzing and testing, and that allow students to easily access course material and track their performance on course assignments (Pacansky-Brock, 2013). Still other changes reflect changing student demographics. Psychology teachers today are seeing more older students, minority students, and first-generation students (Hoover, 2013; National Center for Educational Statistics 2013a; U.S. Census Bureau, 2012). These changes have had an enormous impact on how we teach our classes and future changes will continue to do so.

Nevertheless, we love teaching, and we want you to love it, too, because despite its many challenges, it offers countless rewards. One observer captured the situation well when he described teaching as "the educational equivalent of white-water rafting" (Brookfield, 1990, p. 2). He was referring to the emotional ups and downs that college teachers typically experience, and most veteran psychology teachers know exactly what he meant. We have all had days when our classroom is alive with the excitement of effective teaching and eager learning, as well as days when planned demonstrations and activities don't work, when students are bored or mystified by even the most carefully crafted presentations, and when the process of handing back exams turns ugly. Actually, we would take Brookfield's metaphor a step further, because for most new psychology faculty, teaching is the equivalent of white-water rafting without a guide. This condition need not be permanent, however, nor are certain faculty doomed to swirl forever in the rapids. With enough planning, practice, and effort, virtually anyone who wants to become an effective teacher, or a more effective teacher, can do so. Our colleague Bill Buskist put it this way: "No one ever achieves excellence in teaching by accident. Excellent teachers are made, they are not born. Sure it may be true that some of us have natural propensities that lend themselves to good or even excellent teaching, but it is no less true that excellence in teaching requires extraordinary effort and hard work" (2013b).

In this chapter we briefly describe some of the most notable characteristics of effective teachers and then consider some of the specific teaching methods and behaviors that contribute to their effectiveness—and that can contribute to yours, too.

Some Characteristics of Effective Teachers

Hundreds of articles have been written about teaching excellence and teaching effectiveness, but there is still no general agreement about the definition of either. Our own view corresponds closely to that offered by Bill Buskist: "Excellent teaching is any form of instruction based on empirically supported or otherwise demonstrably effective pedagogy that produces meaningful, significant, transferable, and enjoyable student learning experiences" (2013b).

About 15 years ago, a meta-analysis of research relating teaching methods and student learning found three aspects of teacher behavior to be positively correlated with student learning: enthusiasm, clarity, and the ability to have good rapport with students (Murray, 1997). This finding is consistent with the results of other studies that related teacher characteristics and student learning (Feldman, 1998; Junn, 1994; Lowman, 1998; Marsh & Roche, 1997; McKeachie, 2001; Teven & McCroskey, 1996). More recent research, which relates students' learning outcome to their perceptions of teacher behaviors, has identified an additional group of characteristics seen in effective teachers of psychology or virtually any other discipline. These include "well organized and prepared," "clear," "expressive" (Pascarella, Salisbury, & Blaich, 2011; Pascarella & Terenzini, 2005), and "interesting" and "approachable" (Weimer, 2013a). Compilations of these and other studies of "expert teachers" found that such teachers have a well-articulated knowledge base; use instructional strategies that motivate students to learn; increase student engagement with and interest in subject matter; cultivate critical thinking skills; communicate learning goals and provide formative feedback; establish and maintain effective relationships with students; communicate high expectations for every student; use wait time (i.e., give students time to think about their questions before moving on); have an appropriate pace; demonstrate enthusiasm; are fair and ethical; demonstrate caring for and responsiveness to students; know about student interests and backgrounds, and relate that knowledge to course content (Feldman, 1998; Hativa, 2013b; Kusto, Afful, & Mattingly, 2010; Marzano, 2010; Moore, Moore, & McDonald, 2008; Onwuegbuzie et al., 2007; Orlando, 2013b; Pepe & Wang, 2012; Seldin, 1999a; Trudeau & Barnes, 2002; Weimer, 2013a).

A list like this can be inspiring, but perhaps also a bit overwhelming, especially for new teachers, so in the next section we describe 10 basic teaching principles that, if you adopt them, will help you to demonstrate many of the most important characteristics of effective teachers.

Basic Principles of Effective Teaching

The first seven of these principles come from the aptly titled article "Seven Principles for Good Practice in Undergraduate Education" (Chickering & Gamson, 1987, 1991). The last three were added by the Center for Teaching Excellence (now the Center for Innovation in Teaching and Learning) at the University of Illinois, Urbana-Champaign. Although focused on undergraduate teaching in general, we think that these principles apply perfectly to the teaching of psychology at any level. We describe each of them briefly here; we elaborate on them throughout this book.

1. Encourage Student–Faculty Contact

Frequent and fruitful contact between students and faculty inside and outside the classroom is important for establishing and maintaining students' motivation and involvement in the learning process. When students know that their teacher cares about their progress, they are more likely to persist at learning tasks, even when the tasks are difficult. Further, the experience of getting to know at least a few teachers as individuals can enhance students' intellectual and emotional commitment to learning and actually increase the likelihood that they will stay in school.

2. Encourage Cooperation among Students

Learning is enhanced when it occurs as part of a team effort. Like effective work, effective learning can often come through social collaboration rather than isolated effort in a competitive atmosphere.

Collaborative learning also offers the advantage of helping students develop social responsibility while interacting with others whose ideas and thoughts expand their own thinking and deepen their own understanding.

3. Encourage Active Learning

"Learning is not a spectator sport" (Chickering & Gamson, 1991, p. 66). Students learn, retain, and understand more course material when they actively engage it—by talking about it, writing about it, questioning it, debating it, applying it, and relating it to what they already know—rather than sitting passively as information washes over them in lectures, videos, or other prepackaged formats.

4. Give Prompt Feedback

To focus their efforts to learn, students need feedback about what they know and what they don't know. This feedback should be frequent enough to guide students' efforts; it can take the form of pretests on course material as well as all sorts of quizzes, examinations, papers, projects, and other assignments that help students reflect on how far they have come in accomplishing their learning goals and how far they still have to go.

5. Emphasize "Time on Task"

Some forms of learning can take place without conscious attention, but in psychology courses there is no substitute for paying attention and devoting time to the learning task. Teachers can play a vital role in promoting adequate "time on task" by focusing most of every class session on the material to be learned. They can also help students learn to use time wisely, both in terms of efficient and effective study skills and in relation to time management in general. Whether this assistance comes through personal advice or referral to campus counseling facilities, it can offer a vital aid to learning for those who need it most.

6. Communicate High Expectations

Expect a lot from your students and you are likely to get it. A teacher's high expectations can maximize the performance of all students—from those who are bright and motivated to those who are less well prepared or initially less eager to exert themselves. When students experience their teacher's high expectations as realistic, if challenging, their expectations of themselves tend to rise accordingly.

7. Respect Diverse Talents and Ways of Learning

Like other people, students differ in many ways, including what they know, what talents they have, and even their favorite ways to learn.

A student who shines during class discussion might be all thumbs during a lab session. Students who are used to dealing on their own with practical matters in the workplace might be less adept at or patient with assignments that focus on abstract theories or group problem solving. If possible, give students the opportunity to show their talents and learn in ways that work for them, but don't hesitate to challenge them to learn in new ways that do not come so easily.

8. Be Organized and Prepared

The organization and planning that go into your psychology course help determine what students will learn and how easily they will learn it. A well-planned and well-organized course also conveys to students that you care about teaching and about them. The perception of a caring teacher, in turn, is associated with higher student ratings of teacher performance.

9. Communicate Enthusiasm

Effective and highly rated teachers also tend to communicate enthusiasm, even love, for psychology and for the teaching enterprise. There are many ways to get this message across. Lively lectures, fascinating demonstrations, and other dramatic classroom activities certainly convey enthusiasm for the teaching enterprise, but so do high-quality, carefully chosen presentations and assignments, challenging exams, well-conceived grading systems, and the like. When students sense their teacher's passion for the course is authentic, the effect can be contagious.

10. Be Fair and Ethical

Fairness and the highest ethical standards—in presenting material, in dealing with students, and in evaluating them—is fundamental to effective, high-quality teaching. A related goal is to ensure that students deal fairly with one another in the classroom. Students thrive in learning situations where the teacher's integrity and their confidence in that integrity govern all aspects of the course. High ethical standards should be evident in classrooms that make all students feel welcome, in evenhanded grading, in unbiased consideration of students' requests, and in the avoidance of even the appearance of impropriety in faculty–student relationships. Discrimination, bias, or self-interested abuse of power have no place in teaching.

As we said, these are general principles, meaning that there are many ways to follow them. If you watch effective teachers in action, you will find that they don't follow a pre-established script; they have found their own unique way to pursue the principles of effective teaching within the framework of their own personalities. In other words, you don't have to conform to someone else's ideal of a "good teacher" to be an effective teacher. As you begin to develop your own teaching style, don't feel obligated to emulate a favorite teacher—unless that person's style and your own are truly alike. In the long run it is best to simply be yourself. If you have a humorous streak, don't try to suppress it in the classroom. However, if you don't normally make wry comments and engage in witty repartee, don't try to be a comedian in class. The truth is that students tend to like and respect teachers who display almost any interpersonal style as long as that style is authentic and as long as it is clear that the teacher cares about them and about teaching the course. By the same token, they tend to dislike even the flashiest, funniest, or most scholarly style if they see it as phony.

Being genuine is an essential part of developing your teaching style, but it is not sufficient in and of itself to guarantee success in teaching psychology. Similarly, although it is vital to care about your teaching and your students, you still have to find appropriate ways to communicate that caring. An important key to effective teaching, then, is to translate your motivation and good intentions into good practice. This means learning or honing a variety of more specific skills that can help you to be an effective teacher (Junn, 1994; Lowman, 1998; McKeachie, 2001; Svinicki & McKeachie, 2014). In the chapters to follow, we offer our advice on how to develop these skills.

Your Role as a Teacher

If you are like many new teachers of psychology, it was your interest in psychology itself, not the prospect of teaching it, that led you to pursue a graduate degree and an academic career. In fact, the realization that teaching is a major part of academic life might have dawned on you only slowly over your years of graduate study, and might have come into focus only as you contemplated a teaching assistantship or were discussing teaching assignments with prospective employers. Yet teaching has always been a part of professors' jobs, and in North America prior to about 1850, it was their only job. Around this time, the European university model, with its emphasis on research and graduate education, began to influence higher education in the United States. Especially at major universities, promotion and tenure came to be based more on research productivity than on the quality of undergraduate teaching or service to the community (Boyer, 1990). During World War II, research became even more firmly embedded in professors' job descriptions as the federal government funded research in many disciplines, including psychology, to aid in the war effort. That funding has continued in varying degrees ever since, as have the research activities of college and university professors. Surveys of college and university faculty in the 1990s found that more than 60% of all higher education faculty, including 21% of faculty at research universities, felt that teaching effectiveness should be the primary criterion for promotion and tenure (Boyer, 1990). This view is reflected in the tenure and promotion policies at some institutions, and teaching effectiveness is included in almost every professor's performance evaluations. More recent surveys have found that about 97% of faculty feel that teaching is an essential or very important part of their responsibilities (Berrett, 2012a; Hurtado et al., 2012). So even if your academic interests are focused on a research career, there is good reason to spend the time and effort it takes to improve the effectiveness of your teaching. Besides, "teaching skillfully may be less time consuming than teaching badly" (Svinicki & McKeachie, 2014, p. xvii).

What Is the Task?

The teaching task you face as a psychology professor depends mainly on the level, type, traditions, and orientation of the department and institution you have joined. If you are at a major research university, you might be asked to teach just two courses per term, and perhaps only one of these will be at the undergraduate level. You might at first be assigned only one course (perhaps a graduate seminar) so that you can get your bearings and establish your lab or scholarly work. If you are at a large community college, you were probably hired primarily or exclusively as a teacher. If you are not expected to engage in research, your teaching assignment might include two or more sections of two or more courses, for a total of four to six classes per term. Obviously, the heavier your teaching assignment, the more courses you have to prepare, the less experience you have in teaching them, and the less support there is to ease the burden, the more daunting and stressful the teaching task is likely to be.

Graduate and Undergraduate Teaching

As already mentioned, we believe that the principles of effective teaching, and most teaching skills, apply equally well at the graduate and undergraduate levels. You should be aware, however, that the characteristics and needs of undergraduate and graduate students in psychology differ enough that a slightly different approach is required for each group. Most notably, undergraduates, especially those in their first term at college, tend to need more support and socialization into the culture of higher education than do graduate students (Erickson, Peters, & Strommer, 2006; Erickson & Strommer, 1991).

Many undergraduates come to college from a high school culture where the rules and expectations are considerably different from those of the culture they are about to enter. For example, they might have grown accustomed to having small classes taught by teachers who knew them personally and who took time to remind them about upcoming assignments, quizzes, and exams and the need to prepare for them. Further, as college-bound members of their graduating class, they might have become used to being among the "smart" kids and performing well above average without having to exert all the effort of which they are capable. Finally, they might have depended on their parents to get them out of bed and off to class on time, not to mention ensuring that they were fed and dressed in clean clothes. Most of these familiar circumstances change in college. Students who live at home might retain some of the perks of childhood, but their college teachers are far less likely to track their progress or question irregular attendance or poor performance. They may be faced for the first time with large lecture sections and find themselves too intimidated to ask questions, even after class. They might have few friends on campus, and they might be distressed by the loss of the well-established social support system and the relatively high social status they enjoyed back home. With fewer hours in class to create structure for their day, they may have difficulty managing their time, especially when it comes to allocating time to complete long-term assignments such as term papers and projects. They might even get lost on campus from time to time. In many ways, then, they are starting over. If you will be teaching first-year students, keep in mind that they are in the midst of a stressful life transition. It will be up to you to decide how much to "nurture" these students, but be aware that they might want and need more support and assistance than those who are further along in their undergraduate careers.

By the time they enter a graduate program in psychology, your students will usually have well-honed academic skills, and their academic socialization is usually complete. If you teach at the graduate level, your role will expand to include mentoring as well as instruction. In addition to teaching course content, you will be helping students to conceive, develop, and design research projects; analyze the results of those projects; and clearly communicate those results in scholarly papers and presentations. In fact, a vital part of your role as a teacher of psychology graduate students is to act as a role model for the next generation of researchers, and because many of your graduate students will become faculty members themselves, you will also be a role model for the next generation of teachers.

In short, whether you are teaching at the undergraduate level, the graduate level, or both, the development of effective teaching methods will be important for your career, your sanity, and your academic legacy.

Most of the suggestions we offer to help you in this regard relate to teaching undergraduates, but keep in mind that virtually everything we suggest—especially the need to be prepared, organized, enthusiastic, and committed—applies to graduate teaching as well.

Who Is the Audience?

In the 1960s, the typical college student in the United States was a white, middle-class male who was enrolled for full-time study and whose expenses were paid primarily by his parents. He did not hold a job during the academic year, and he entered college with a B average. He expected to perform at an average level and his main goals probably included developing a meaningful philosophy of life (Astin et al., 1997). This profile has changed dramatically since then (Astin, 1990; Astin et al., 1997; Dey, Astin, & Korn, 1991; Erickson et al., 2006; Erickson & Strommer, 1991; Hansen, 1998; Higher Education Research Institute, 2002; Menges & Weimer, 1996; National Center for Education Statistics, 1999, 2001; Sax, Astin, Korn, & Mahoney, 1999, 2000; Sax, Bryant, & Gilmartin, 2003).

For one thing, more students than ever are taking courses on a part-time basis, usually because financial need forces them to hold a full- or part-time job. More than 40% of full-time students work at least part time, while more than 75% of part-time students are employed (National Center for Education Statistics, 2013a).

Today's college students also tend to be older than those of the past. In 1970 less than 28% of undergraduates were over the age of 25, but by 1999, that percentage had increased to 39% (National Center for Education Statistics, 2013b). Between 2000 and 2011, the enrollment rate for students over the age of 25 increased by 5% (National Center for Education Statistics, 2013c).

Beginning in 1980, female college students outnumbered males, and now comprise 58% of all undergraduates (National Center for Education Statistics, 2013c). The percentage of college students representing various ethnic minority groups has slowly increased, too. In 1971, 91.4% of new undergraduates were European Americans, 6.3% were African Americans, 0.5% were Asian Americans, and 1.3% were Hispanic Americans. By 2013 the figure for European Americans and other whites had dropped to 69.7%, whereas the others had risen: to 11.5% for African Americans and other blacks, to 10.7% for Asian Americans and Asians, and to 14.5% for Hispanic Americans and other Latinos/Latinas (Astin et al., 1997; Pryor et al., 2013; Sax et al., 1999). These trends are expected to continue such that, collectively, ethnic minority students will constitute the majority of U.S. college students by the year 2025.

The diversity of college students goes far beyond age, gender, and ethnicity. More students than ever before are entering college with less than adequate academic preparation and with special needs stemming from disabilities. Even the disabilities are more diverse than ever. In the past, most disabilities involved blindness, deafness, paralysis, or other physical problems that could be accommodated by minor changes in the way classes were conducted. Today's teachers are faced with more students with learning disabilities or other cognitive difficulties that might be more difficult to accommodate. One major university reported that 65% of students registered with the Division of Rehabilitation Services had been diagnosed with cognitive or psychiatric disabilities rather than sensory or physical disabilities (Collins, 2003). (We discuss the impact of diversity on today's students throughout this book because you are likely to encounter it in every class you teach.)

In 1967, almost 83% of incoming students chose "developing a meaningful philosophy of life" as their main goal in college; only 43.8% chose "to be very well-off financially." The size of the group choosing the "philosophy of life" goal declined steadily to just more than 39% in 1987, and rose to only 42% in 1997 (Astin et al., 1997). Today, being "very well-off financially" is the main goal of 81% of entering college students, and 74.6% said that "to be able to make more money" was their reason for attending college (Pryor et al., 2013).

Students also are displaying unrealistic expectations about how long their college education will take. According to one survey, more than 84% of students expect to graduate in four years, while statistics indicate that, on average, only a little more than 40% will do so (National Center for Education Statistics, 2013d). Students are also coming to college after having experienced grade inflation in high school (Astin et al., 1997) and expect their high grades to continue. In fact, like their counterparts in Garrison Keillor's fictional Lake Wobegon, most of today's college students tend to rate themselves as "above average" on both academic and interpersonal criteria, and more of them than ever expect to pursue advanced degrees (Astin et al., 1997; Campbell & Twenge, 2013; Pryor et al., 2013). These students tend to be surprised and resentful when the level of effort that once led to As or Bs now earns only Cs or Ds.

Students' reactions to grades depend partly on their mindset or beliefs about intelligence (Dweck, 1986, 2008, 2010; Gaultney & Cann, 2001; Grant & Dweck, 2003; Rattan, Good, & Dweck, 2012; Rattan, Naidu, Savani & Dweck, 2012; Svinicki, 1998; Yeager & Dweck, 2012). Students with a growth orientation tend to be interested mainly in developing skills and learning course content. They care about good grades, of course, but these students focus mainly on increasing their competence. They seek challenges that foster learning, they persist in the face of difficulty, and they do not attribute errors or failure to a general lack of ability; they believe that intelligence is fluid, not fixed, and that they can learn to do better. Students with a fixed mindset tend to be more interested in grades and in appearing "smart" than in actually acquiring skills and mastering course content. They tend to believe that they have a fixed amount of intelligence and if they have to work harder than other students, or have difficulty learning, it is mainly because they lack intelligence. Accordingly, they tend to be less persistent than their growth-oriented peers in the face of challenges and difficulties. In fact, although these students want to do well on evaluated tasks, their fear of failure and negative evaluation is such that they tend to shy away from challenges. When they perform well on a task, their pride stems mainly from having done better than others rather than from having accomplished something for its own sake (Svinicki, 1998). When they do not perform well, they tend to attribute their failure to their general lack of ability (Dweck, 2008, 2010; Rattan, Good & Dweck, 2012; Rattan, Naidu, Savani & Dweck, 2012; Svinicki, 1998; Yeager & Dweck, 2012). As described in Chapter 6, these differing mindsets can have significant implications for your students' responses to you and your course requirements, assignments, and grading system, as well as to your efforts to motivate diligent study habits.

In the 1960s, grades ranked high among students' main worries. Today, students are worried about many other things, including how to pay for their college education (Astin et al., 1997; Pryor et al., 2013). Many expect to work part time while attending college, especially during recently stressful economic periods when the availability and size of grants and scholarships have been slow to keep pace with demand and the rising cost of attending college. Students face other stressors, too. Between 1985 and 2013, the percentage of students who reported "being overwhelmed by everything I have to do" and "frequently feeling depressed" rose steadily from less than 20% to just more than 30% (Astin et al., 1997; Pryor et al., 2013; Sax et al., 1999). For females the latter figure has reached just more than 40%. Further, a longitudinal study of entering students has found declining levels of emotional health during the first year of college (Pryor et al., 2013; Sax et al., 2003). It has been suggested that students' stressors, including the economically based need for part-time study, are significant factors in lengthening the time it takes students today to complete their bachelor degrees (Pryor et al., 2013; Upcraft, 1996).

In summary, when teaching undergraduate courses in psychology, you will encounter students who represent a wide range of ethnic backgrounds, abilities and disabilities, interests, motivations, and expectations. Some will be diffident and frightened; others will be overconfident and unrealistically optimistic. Whether they are full- or part-time students, many will be trying to fulfill academic obligations while dealing with a job, financial pressures, family responsibilities, relationship problems, and other stressors. Preparing to deal with the diversity of today's students is one dimension of the task you will face as a psychology professor. In the remainder of this book, we address many others, beginning in Chapter 2 with what may be your first question: How do I start?

● ● ● ● ●

Teaching Online

When we wrote the first edition of this book, true online classes were a fairly new enterprise. They were often referred to as "distance learning" and were primarily the domain of community colleges, where commuter students needed more convenient access to courses. When people talked about "distance learning," they were typically referring to a "correspondence" course that, though using the Internet instead of the post office, presented content similar to the equivalent face-to-face version and whose teachers gave little thought to the unique characteristics of the distance learning format. How things have changed. During the 2000–2001 academic year, about 1.3% of college students were enrolled in fully online programs; by 2009, this figure was 12.1% (Shachar & Neumann, 2010). Today, online education (as it is now called) has exploded. At least 33% of all higher education students, or about 6.7 million people, are learning at least partly online (Allen & Seaman, 2013), and the rate of increase in the use of online courses has far outpaced enrollment in higher education in general. And although online instruction was originally designed to allow off-campus students to take college courses, many students today who live on or near campus enroll in online courses, too, primarily because of the schedule flexibility these courses allow. Some institutions are even requiring students to enroll in a certain number of online courses (Parry, 2010).

As you can see from Table 1.1, online education has evolved from a "learn anywhere" to a "learn anytime" to a "learn at any pace" method of delivering courses (Shachar & Neumann, 2010). At the same time, it has become increasingly clear that, compared to the face-to-face format, far more time and effort are required to develop and teach an online course. This may be one reason why, even though student learning outcomes appear about equivalent in online and traditional courses (Allen & Seaman, 2013; Shachar & Neumann, 2010; Ward, Peters, & Shelley, 2010), faculty support for the value and legitimacy of online education has decreased (Allen & Seaman, 2013; Liu, 2012). Some faculty and administrators point out that online education might not be for everyone

Table 1.1 Characteristics of Online Education

Type of Course	Percent of Content Delivered Online	Typical Description
Traditional	0%	No online technology used—content is delivered in writing or orally.
Web Facilitated	1–29%	Uses Web-based technology to facilitate what is essentially a face-to-face course. May use a course management system (CMS) or Web pages to post the syllabus and assignment.
Blended/Hybrid	30–79%	Blends online and face-to-face delivery. Substantial proportion of the content is delivered online, typically uses online discussions, and typically has a reduced number of face-to-face meetings.
Online	80+%	Most or all of the content is delivered online. Typically no face-to-face meetings.

(Allen & Seaman, 2013)

because it takes more self-discipline to succeed in an online course than in a face-to-face course (Allen & Seaman, 2013). This skepticism, as well as the typically lower student retention rates seen in online courses, has been cited as among the greatest barriers to the further expansion of online education (Allen & Seaman, 2013).

Nevertheless, online education is not likely to go away. And, while we address issues in online education in depth in Chapter 7, we have also supplemented our discussions of teaching methods in general with special "Online Considerations" sections that highlight what you might want to think about when applying these methods in online courses. As a case in point, let's review online considerations relating to the 10 principles of effective teaching discussed previously.

Online Considerations

1. Encourage Student–Faculty Contact

Online courses require a social presence from the instructor. Because students will often not have face-to-face contact with you, you will need to provide clear guidelines for interaction with students, including appropriate types of communication and timelines for responding (Graham et al., 2001). To make the course more personal, many instructors provide a picture and biography of themselves (VCU, 2013). Some have students create their own home pages providing their own biographical information and pictures (VCU, 2013). In addition, using virtual office hours and text chat, along with e-mail, creates the student–faculty contact (VCU, 2013).

2. Encourage Cooperation among Students

Most online courses will contain a discussion component and assignments that require group collaboration. The current trend in online course development has emphasized the online community and student cooperation above the individualistic, solo work that was typical of most distance learning and early online courses. Using wikis and Google Docs allows students to work together on projects and write in an asynchronous format. Using LMS chat rooms allows students to work synchronously on assignments (VCU, 2013).

3. Encourage Active Learning

An online course needs to encourage students to actively engage in the material, whether it is individual reflection or a group project. Assignments should be crafted so that students have to apply the concepts to information they already know—for example, relating a situation from their lives to one of the lesson's concepts. Merely asking students to watch online lectures or to take multiple choice quizzes and a couple of multiple choice exams does not promote active learning. Encourage students to develop online presentations or search the Web for new information. We discuss ideas for active learning assignments in Chapter 4.

4. Give Prompt Feedback

Just-in-time teaching can be used effectively in an online course. By polling students about what they know and don't know about a subject, and making the general information available, the teacher can let students know instantly how their knowledge base compares with that of their classmates. In addition, the teacher can tailor the upcoming lecture or discussion around areas of confusion (VCU, 2013). Graham and colleagues (2001) argue that there are two types of feedback: information feedback, which is often an answer to a question or a grade on an assignment, and acknowledgment feedback, which confirms that the teacher has heard a student comment or received an assignment. They believe that while it is difficult to provide individual feedback on every graded component, instructors should not neglect the acknowledgment feedback, for example, letting students know you have received an assignment—which occurs easily in a face-to-face class via eye contact or the actual handing in of the paper.

5. Emphasize "Time on Task"

Graham and colleagues (2001) sum this up succinctly—"Online courses need deadlines." Regularly distributed deadlines encourage students to stay on task. As we know from our face-to-face students, time management is often a big issue for them. This is accentuated in an online course if students are allowed to work totally at their own pace. Keeping online students on task is also helped by having discrete modules with deadlines and/or having a weekly schedule that students are expected to adhere to.

6. Communicate High Expectations

"Providing students with challenging tasks, samples cases, and praise for quality work communicates high expectations" (Graham et al., 2001). Providing students with rubrics can also communicate a teacher's high expectations (VCU, 2013). In addition, faculty should explicitly let students know about their expectations in regards to time requirements, professional communication, and so forth. "Online it is important to set the expectations on quantity and quality of work, degree of interaction, levels of communication and learning outcomes" (VCU, 2013).

7. Respect Diverse Talents and Ways of Learning

This might take the form of allowing students to choose project topics as well as encouraging students to express their diverse viewpoints (Graham et al., 2001). Students might also have an opportunity of choosing how they want to turn in assignment—for example, via podcasts or videos, as well as written format (VCU, 2013).

8. Be Organized and Prepared

As we discussed in the opening of this chapter, being organized and prepared is consistently recognized as a characteristic of effective teachers. This is even more critical in an online course. Without the scheduled communication afforded in a face-to-face class, it is easy for students to lose focus and "get behind" in the course work. By having your entire course planned and prepared, you enable students to work through the material in a coherent, organized manner.

9. Communicate Enthusiasm

This is definitely more difficult in an online course than in a face-to-face course. We believe the basics of communicating enthusiasm in an online course include demonstrating a concern for students. Videotaping a welcome message, sending students a welcome e-mail, interjecting positive comments in discussion, making it explicit that you value and will use student input, and being a consistent, positive presence on the Web site are all ways to communicate enthusiasm. One instructor asked students to post their favorite movies and music to a discussion board. He then linked song lyrics and movie clips to the topics of his online lectures (Dziuban, Moskal, & Brophy, 2007).

10. Be Fair and Ethical

In some ways, this is easier online than in a face-to-face class. Because you do not "see" your students when interacting, the subtle ethnic or gender biases that might be an influence in a face-to-face class tend not to appear. Because your course is prepared before it starts, you should announce your grading system at the beginning of the course, and alterations of it are less common than in a face-to-face course. In addition, by posting rubrics for your grading, you can grade without even knowing students' names, following an objective standard.

We hope that you find such applications of use, whether you are currently teaching an online course or have plans to teach one in the future.

Some Final Comments

In this chapter we have listed some of the most important principles of effective teaching, along with a description of some of the teacher characteristics that translate those principles into an effective teaching style. If you are just starting your teaching career, the prospect of trying to emulate these "master teachers" might seem daunting, but remember that today's master teachers were yesterday's novices, and no matter how well their personalities and content knowledge might have prepared them for their teaching role, they all faced doubts, fears, and uncertainties, and certainly all had a lot to learn. And they did. We hope that this book will help you do the same, and that your role as a teacher will bring to you the same enjoyment and satisfaction that it has brought to us.

2

● ● ● ● ●

Preparing Your Courses

Setting Goals
Choosing Course Materials
Creating a Syllabus
Setting Up a Grading System
Communicating with Your Students
Some Final Comments

We try to teach well, and we know that most of our colleagues do, too. Still, we are constantly amazed at how many students tell us about courses they have taken that were so disorganized as to leave students wondering whether they learned anything other than not to take another class with that instructor. These students describe courses in which instructors provided no syllabus (leaving students in the dark about reading assignments and even exam dates), took so long to grade and return exams that feedback came too late to be of much help, went off on so many tangents during class that relevant material was never covered, and even failed to explain how course grades would be determined. This is a shame, because most of the course organization problems that students complain about, problems that could well interfere with their learning, can be prevented simply by taking the time to prepare a course properly. In fact, one of the keys to effective teaching lies in careful planning (Svinicki & McKeachie, 2014; University of Illinois Center for Teaching Excellence, 1999).

● ● ● ● ●
Setting Goals

The first step is to establish your goals in teaching the course, because—just as when starting on a long trip—once you know where you want to go, it is easier to plan a route that will get you there. Your course goals will reflect both what you want your students to get out of a particular course and the purpose the course is designed to serve in your departmental and institutional curriculum.

To be honest, the main goal of many new teachers is simply to get through the course in one piece. This is understandable, but even experienced teachers might not have thought much about their teaching goals—mainly because it is so easy to ignore them. You can teach year after year without ever explicitly establishing goals that go beyond "doing a good job," "teaching the material," "being fair," or the like.

These are fine goals in general, but there are many other, more specific teaching goals that might guide the development of your course. One way to begin considering them, and the role they play in your courses, is to complete the Teaching Goals Inventory (TGI) (www.centeach.uiowa.edu/tools.shtml). Developed by Thomas Angelo and Patricia Cross in 1993, it is still the most comprehensive such inventory available. The TGI lists 53 student competencies and gives you the opportunity to rate the importance of each of them in each of your courses. Taking the TGI online generates an instant report that summarizes the goals that you rated as "essential," "very important," "important," or "unimportant." You can also compare your responses with those of thousands of other faculty members. The TGI can be useful in itself, but it might also stimulate you to think about additional goals that you consider important in your courses.

Once you have used the TGI and your own reflections to clarify what you want your students to get from each course, you will find it much easier to plan your courses to align with your goals. For example, if you think it is important for your students to develop critical thinking skills, you will probably plan a course that gives them the opportunity to, say, critique and debate the validity of research results. If you value collaborative learning skills, you might plan to have students work in teams to summarize research articles, solve course-related problems, or carry out other projects. If you simply want to ensure that students can define the terms and identify the concepts presented in the course, you will probably create exams and class activities that test those skills.

Your course goals should also take into account the role each course plays in your department and on your campus. Is it a prerequisite for other courses and, if so, what are they? What courses, if any, are prerequisites for yours? Is your course part of a specialized sequence? Knowing what your students are likely to know when they arrive in your classroom will help you establish a starting point and determine the appropriate level for your class presentations and reading assignments. Knowing what your department or college expects students to know when they finish your course will help you decide what material to cover (and not cover) and what level of detail is appropriate. Are students expected to leave your course with a detailed knowledge of, say, social cognition, with a general appreciation of the major themes in psychology, with improved skill at problem solving, critical thinking, writing, studying, or what? Your class presentations and other class activities would probably touch only on the basics of psychology if you are teaching an introductory course, but would focus on more subtle nuances in a capstone seminar for seniors in a psychology honors program. Answering these goal-related questions will help you to make these and numerous other decisions as you organize your courses.

It is not always easy, especially at the beginning of your teaching career, to keep personal, departmental, and institutional goals in mind as you plan your courses, so don't hesitate to ask for advice from more experienced colleagues who have taught the same courses. They can help you understand how the course has been taught in the past, what approaches have and haven't worked, the reputation the course has acquired, and the like. Correspond, too, with instructors who teach the same or a similar course on other campuses. There are listservs and e-mail groups dedicated to teaching psychology where discussion of appropriate goals and materials for courses is often illuminating, even to an instructor who has taught a particular course for many years. Among the best of these are *Teaching in the Psychological Sciences* (*TIPS*) (www.faculty.frostburg.edu/psyc/southerly/tips) and *Psychteacher* (http://teachpsych.org/news/psychteacher.php).

Finally, remember that course goals are not set in stone. As you gain experience with a particular course at a particular institution, your goals might change. One mark of effective teachers is the ability to adapt to changing curricula, changing campus demands, and other challenges while adhering to the goals and standards they consider most important.

Online Considerations

While some might disagree, we believe that pedagogical goals need not change just because a course is delivered online or partly online. What does change, obviously, is how you meet those goals (VCU, 2013). For example, if one of your goals is student collaboration, in the face-to-face classroom you would probably assign group projects and organize students into teams to work on them. In an online course, you could still use group projects, but you would probably have to think about those projects more carefully before assigning them. For example, you would have to decide if it is feasible to ask students to work synchronously via a chat venue (e.g., a Moodle student lounge) or whether it would be better for the final product to be a wiki that is created asynchronously by everyone in the group.

Further, because the emphasis in online course participation switches from the spoken word to the written word (Creasman, 2012), if you value—and wish to assess—students' participation, you will have to consider options such as monitoring students' postings to a discussion board or arranging for synchronous presentations via videoconferencing software.

* * * * *

Choosing Course Materials

Once you have established the goals for your course, the next task is to decide which learning materials you want your students to use. Typically, this involves choosing a textbook and additional readings. If you are solely responsible for choosing course materials, we suggest you begin the selection process by examining the materials chosen by colleagues who have taught the course recently. You can also check out the course materials being used by faculty at institutions similar to yours by visiting their departments' home pages, then following links to the relevant online syllabi. Contact these instructors for evaluative comments on their course materials, and perhaps send more general requests for recommendations to the psychology teachers' listservs mentioned earlier.

Most instructors assign a textbook and, in our experience, most students prefer this option. Once you have seen what others teaching the course use, we suggest that you create a short list of textbook candidates then request an examination copy of each by contacting their publishers' sales representatives (just type in the company name at google.com and follow links to local reps). Also ask to see any supplemental materials that might be available to accompany the books. These typically are housed on the textbook Web site and include an instructor's resource manual, a test item bank, PowerPoint presentation slides, video clips, a student study guide, case examples, supplementary readings, and the like. In most cases you will be able to evaluate these supplements after obtaining the relevant passwords to access the publisher's Web site.

Which is the right book for you and your students? We agree that "the first consideration in choosing texts is whether students are likely to read them, work with them, and learn from them" (Eble, 1988, p. 126). It is also important to choose a book that supports students' independent learning. This means that in addition to holding students' interest, the chosen book should be sufficiently clear, current, and accurate that you can rely on it to provide further details and a broader context for your class presentations. It also means that your students can rely on it as a guide to further reading and to help them learn on their own about important topics that you do not have time to cover in depth, or at all, during class.

Several textbook evaluation guides are available on university teaching center Web sites. One of the most comprehensive of these, at the University of Texas, El Paso, presents seven useful criteria to evaluate textbooks. These include (1) "looking for an intelligent use of headings and sub-headings within chapters"; (2) "previewing chapter outlines presented at the beginning of each chapter"; (3) "examining objective questions and review questions throughout a chapter"; (4) "evaluating end-of-chapter reviews"; (5) "connecting online resources to the textbook"; (6) considering the level at which the book is written; and (7) looking at visuals—chart, graphs, photos, and so forth. More details, as well as opportunities to practice comparing textbooks, are available at the UTEP Web site, http://reading.utep.edu/module14/module_flash.html. Barbara Davis (2009) provides another helpful list of relevant selection criteria.

Today's decisions about textbooks include the question of whether to assign an e-book. Some colleges have mandated a change to e-books (Young, 2010), but though this well-intentioned effort does save students money, most students—including those who are highly technologically literate—prefer print textbooks (Howard, 2013; Woody, Daniel, & Baker, 2010). In fact, students prefer "plus-print" packages that include a paper textbook that comes with electronic supplements (Howard, 2013). In short, in deciding on a print textbook or e-book you will have to consider the policies at your institution, the characteristics and preferences of your students, and the way your course is delivered.

If you want to use teaching materials in addition to, or perhaps instead of, a main textbook, there are plenty of options, including sets of readings that can be assembled in a custom-designed course packet (Davis, 2009). You might also consider assigning downloadable material for students to read, but before doing so be sure that you understand relevant copyright laws and restrictions that may apply to published materials (Davis, 2009; Hilton, 2003).

As you select your course materials, keep in mind a running total of the number of pages involved. We do not endorse expecting too little of your students or underestimating their abilities, but it is a good idea to make reading assignments that can be accomplished—with comprehension—in the allotted time, and in the context of the students' overall course load (Davis, 2009). Remember, your students will have to do the reading for your course while also satisfying the reading required by instructors in several other courses. Be selective and thoughtful in choosing what materials you assign. A comprehensive reading list looks great, and even reasonable, at the beginning of the term, but it will not serve the purpose of promoting student learning if the students never have time to cover what you have assigned, let alone think deeply about it.

Finally, we suggest that you put at least one copy of all materials on reserve at the library or on your LMS, again keeping in mind copyright laws. (We discuss LMSs in more detail in Chapter 7.) As textbook costs and economic pressures have risen, some students find it more difficult to purchase all the materials assigned in all their classes, and for them, the library is a vital link to your course. Even those who do buy all their assigned materials will find it useful to have access to course readings between classes and at other times when they find themselves with time to study, but without print copies of their books.

Online Considerations

Today, most academic resources can be found in an electronic format, including textbooks that can be downloaded to computers, tablets, smartphones, e-readers, and other mobile devices. Indeed, as technology becomes more sophisticated, we expect electronic resources to become the norm. So although the materials you choose for your course can be the same whether you are teaching face-to-face or online, how online students access the material may change. For example, if you are going to assign a textbook, make sure that everyone has the option of buying or renting it online (usually through the publisher's Web site), and if you are assembling your own packet of materials, make sure that off-campus students can access it electronically or have a way to purchase a print copy.

Creating a Syllabus

Most colleges and universities require that students get a course syllabus and most instructors provide one. A syllabus serves motivational, structural, and evidentiary purposes (Slattery & Carlson, 2005).

As a motivational document, it sets the tone of the course and conveys your enthusiasm for the course material. Reading your syllabus affects your students' perceptions of you as a person (Erikson, Peters, & Strommer, 2006; Saville et al., 2010), which is why some teachers include an "About Me" section to let students know a little about their background (Thompson, 2007). A detailed syllabus also creates the impression that you are organized and have other attributes of a master teacher, including being prepared, knowledgeable, open-minded, approachable, and enthusiastic (Saville et al., 2010). Its firm but friendly tone also shows you care about your teaching and want students to do well (attributes that are consistently associated with good teacher evaluations). A good syllabus can also serve as a model for professional thinking, planning, and writing (Parkes & Harris, 2002). Distributing a syllabus that is well organized, clearly written, and free of grammatical and spelling errors will not only give students a good first impression of you and your course, but will help create an expectation of the sort of product you will be expecting from them in their written assignments. In short, a well-constructed syllabus can help students learn more from your course (Parkes & Harris, 2002; Slattery & Carlson, 2005), partly by creating positive expectations. And when the syllabus provides a clear description of the course and your grading system, students find it easier to prepare for tests and other evaluations in a timely manner (Saville, 2012). A good syllabus can also help students make sense of a course by explaining why certain content is included and how the various course topics all fit together (Parkes & Harris, 2002). It can even help students to decide whether they can (or want to) handle your course's requirements in the context of their other courses and commitments. Those who are not prepared, academically or otherwise, to deal with your course can drop it without penalty, thus preventing problems for themselves and for you.

The structural purpose of a syllabus is to present the organization of the course and help students understand how to succeed in it (Habanek, 2005). It serves as a preview and road map of the course and as a guide to what your students can expect from you and what you will be expecting of them. Creating a course syllabus is a vital step in course planning because the process requires you to think carefully about many details—including class projects, exam and term paper dates and deadlines, make-up exam policies, and the like—that might otherwise slip through the cracks until students ask about them.

The third function of a syllabus is evidentiary, meaning that it can be used as evidence of your teaching style as well as of your competence in promotion and tenure decisions, so be sure to include all your syllabi in your teaching portfolio (Parkes & Harris, 2002; see Chapter 8). Syllabi also serve as evidence of departmental quality during accreditation reviews, of course content in relation to decisions about course transferability, and even as a legal document. On most campuses, your syllabus is a legally binding contract between you and your students. It provides the grounds for imposing penalties on students who fail to meet their responsibilities, and for students to file complaints against professors who don't follow announced grading procedures or who otherwise depart substantially from what they promised to do (Parkes & Harris,

2002). Accordingly, consider carefully what you say in your syllabus, say it clearly, and then stick to it. If you must make changes after the course begins, don't just announce them in class: distribute written notification to all students and make an announcement on your LMS.

By the way, the manner in which you present your syllabus in class can be just as important as the document itself (Thompson, 2007), and we discuss that point in more detail in the next chapter.

If creating a syllabus sounds daunting, remember that you don't have to start from scratch. Start by taking a look at the syllabi written for courses like yours by colleagues in your department and on psychology course Web sites around the country. In addition, the Society for the Teaching of Psychology (STP) offers help through its Office of Teaching Resources in Psychology (OTRP). Project Syllabus is a collection of syllabi for a variety of psychology classes: you can review them by visiting the OTRP Web site at http://teachpsych.org/otrp/syllabi/index.php. Your campus's instructional development center can also provide general advice and information on writing a syllabus.

The advice you find is likely to vary considerably. At one extreme are instructors like us who value a learning-centered syllabus that provides as much detailed information as possible, often including a statement of the instructor's teaching philosophy (O'Brien, Millis, & Cohen, 2008). These instructors argue that the more information students have about course goals, their responsibilities, and grading criteria, the more successful they will be (O'Brien et al., 2008). At the other extreme are teachers who describe the typical course syllabus as "rule-infested, punitive, (and) controlling" (Singham, 2007, p. 52). One study in support of this view (Thompson, 2007) found that most of the boldface text in syllabi is negative, leading students to perceive that the teacher is yelling at them before the course even begins. Other critics (e.g., Jones, 2011) complain of "syllabus bloat" and encourage instead the use of more interesting and creative electronic or print syllabi that students will actually read. (For examples, see the Carnegie Mellon Eberly Center Web site at www.cmu.edu/teaching/designteach/design/syllabus/samples-creative/.)

Whatever specific form your syllabus takes, and whether you hand it out in class or post it on your course Web page or LMS, we believe that it will be one of the most important documents in your course. Let's consider in more detail some elements of what we believe to be a good syllabus.

A Model Syllabus

The first step in construction of the syllabus is to look at a calendar and mark (and count) the number of class meetings you will have for the coming academic term. Don't forget to identify standard vacation days such as Thanksgiving or spring break, as well as any class days that coincide with religious holidays (e.g., Kwanzaa, Yom Kippur, Ramadan) that, even if not official vacation days, might not be the best times to schedule a quiz or other graded event. (You can find a list of all religious holidays at www. interfaithcalendar.org.) Next, mark any calendar dates on which your own commitments will require another instructor to stand in for you. Marking the calendar in these ways gives you an overview of your course and makes it easier to see the optimal placement and spacing of quizzes and exams. It will also help you see whether the submission deadlines for term papers or other projects you might be planning to assign will give you a chance to grade those assignments in a timely manner.

As already noted, it is up to you to decide how much information to include in your syllabus, but here are the top 10 items that long experience tells us should be on every syllabus:

1. **The name, number, and title of your course** (e.g., Psychology 100, Introduction to Psychology). You should also include a paragraph or so that describes what the course will cover, and perhaps a rationale for the topics included.
2. **The days, time, and location of class meetings** (e.g., MWF, 10 A.M., 101 Psychology Building).
3. **Your name, office address, and how to contact you,** for example, your e-mail address and/or your office phone number. We include our home or cell phone numbers because doing so demonstrates our concern for our students and because, in the decades during which we have provided them, few students have used them inappropriately. This policy also follows the first principle for good practice in undergraduate education, namely encouraging student–faculty contact. If you do offer a personal phone number, remember that students often keep late hours, so be sure to indicate the hours during which nonemergency calls will be welcome.
4. **The schedule of your office hours.** Later in this chapter we offer some suggestions for making office hours part of your overall faculty–student communication plan, but for now we just suggest this rule of thumb: schedule at least two office hours per week per course either face to face or online. Take your own schedule into account, of course, but when possible, set up your office hours so they do not match the likely scheduling of your students' other classes. Office hours at 9 A.M. on Monday, Wednesday, and Friday or at 11 A.M. Tuesday and Thursday will make visits impossible for students who have another class at those times. Setting up office hours that include, say, 9 A.M. on Monday and Tuesday might be a better plan. Be aware, too, that office hours in early morning or late afternoon (especially on

Friday) will probably not attract many visitors. In teaching a face-to-face class, you might wish to reserve the hour before class as preparation time, but the hour following class is an ideal office hour, as discussions begun in class can continue as you walk with students to your office. Avoid "to be arranged" (TBA) office hours. Students are more likely to stop by your office if you have established fixed times during which you will be available. In fact, many students perceive TBA office hours to mean "don't bother me." Whatever your schedule of formal office hours, be sure to let students know that you are available to meet with them at other times, too. You can easily do this by listing your regular office hours and adding the phrase "and by appointment." Taking this simple step will encourage students to contact you even if they cannot attend your standing office hours.

5. **The name(s), office location(s), phone number(s) or e-mail addresses, and office hour(s) of anyone who will be helping you teach the course,** along with a brief statement about what these assistants can and cannot be expected to do. If the TAs will be holding online office hours, be sure to include information about those hours as well.

6. **A statement about respect for individuals, including class conduct expectations and statements of accommodations for students with disabilities** (often copied from the university Web site). In our courses, this statement reads as follows: "Any student requiring special accommodations should notify the instructor as soon as possible. All accommodations will follow the procedures stated in the University Code of Policies that can be accessed at www.uiuc.edu/admin_manual/code/rule4.html."

7. **A list of all books, articles, and other readings that will be required or recommended** for the course, along with information about where these materials can be found (e.g., on reserve in the library or on the course LMS) or where they can be purchased.

8. **A description of exactly how students' performance in the course will be evaluated.** This description should begin with a statement about the number of exams and quizzes, the number and length of papers or mini-assignments, journal writing, laboratory work, and research or projects. Due dates for each of these items should be included.

9. **A detailed description of how final grades will be determined.** Whether you choose one of the grading systems discussed later or some other one, be sure to explain it carefully. The more clearly you do so in your syllabus, the less trouble and confusion you will have to deal with at the end of the term. Tell students how much each exam, quiz, or other assignment will count toward the final grade, whether attendance and class participation will affect the final grade, whether

and how missed exams or quizzes can be made up, and how missed deadlines will be handled. In addition, make it clear if students are or are not allowed to work together on various out-of-class assignments.

10. **A list of class rules and policies.** If attendance is important to you, say so. If you prefer that students who come in late sit in a particular area of the class (to minimize disruption) state that as well. Make your expectations for the class as clear as possible from the outset to avoid confusion and conflict later.

Beyond these top 10 items, we think that it is also worthwhile to include the following information:

1. **An outline of your goals for the course.** This can be as specific or general as you would like, but such a listing is more powerful if it uses action verbs such as "evaluate," "create," and "analyze" (Slattery & Carson, 2005). Also, each of your assignments should be associated with a course goal or goals. Some instructors prefer to concentrate on five to seven goals for the semester and state them as measurable outcomes (Barrick, 1998; personal communication, February 12, 2003). For example: *By the end of the course the student will be able to differentiate various types of learning and apply them to appropriate situations.* Others prefer to offer a more general overview of course goals, such as: *This course is an introduction to the field of psychology. Throughout the course, you will be encouraged to develop your ability to think critically about psychology and about topics outside of psychology. Your assignments will prompt you to apply the concepts to your own life. Your active participation in this course will enable you to use psychological concepts in your everyday interactions.*

2. **A list of the topics you plan to cover at each class meeting,** along with the book chapters or other readings or assignments that are to be completed before each meeting. This is a good place, too, to show the scheduling of all exams and quizzes, and the due dates of any other evaluated work, such as class projects, papers, and the like.

3. **A list of any special out-of-class activities,** such as field trips, lab visits, or departmental colloquia that are available or required. On some campuses, faculty are actually required to include this information in every course syllabus (Barrick, 1998; personal communication, February 12, 2003).

Keeping Track of It All

Students sometimes forget what the course syllabus says about when quizzes and exams are scheduled, when paper assignments are due, and the like, but they are not the only ones. In the day-to-day chaos of academic life, it is all too easy for teachers, too, to lose track of the assign-ments they made, the guest speaker they were to contact, or the quiz they were supposed to have prepared. To minimize the chances that you will forget to complete important course-related tasks on time, we suggest that you create for each course a master list of events and responsibili-ties, organized by date, to act as a "tickler file." We have used master lists for decades, and it is amazing how helpful they can be as one gets older and busier—or just older. A good master list can be a lifesaver because if you build into it enough lead time for each task, you will never find yourself in a last-minute frenzy to create PowerPoint presentations, write exams, or organize demonstrations. We review our master lists at the beginning of each week of each term to be sure that we are ready for the days ahead. A paper copy of your master list will work, but maintain-ing it in an electronic format makes it accessible and revisable from your Internet-connected devices. Most electronic calendar programs can be set to send you e-mail or other reminders when each task on the master list becomes imminent. Be sure to edit the content of each course's mas-ter list as the term proceeds. So if it took you a week, not a day, to write a 20-item quiz for your neuroscience course, adjust the dates on your mas-ter list accordingly. The next time you teach that course, any scheduling crunches that appeared last time should not occur again.

Online Considerations

The syllabus in online courses is especially critical because you will probably not have the luxury of presenting and explaining it in a live format. Accord-ingly, the online syllabus should be very detailed. To reinforce those details, consider creating and posting a short video in which you present the sylla-bus to your students and invite questions and comments via e-mail, text, or chat. A video, like a live presentation, will allow your students to see who you are and to begin to form their impression of you as a teacher. As for virtual office hours, they are a must. There is Skype, of course, as well as specialty software packages such as BlackBoard's Collaborate that allow students to see you as well as talk with you online. Be sure the syllabus includes clear instructions on how to access such software, how to make a virtual visit, and the like. The layout of the online syllabus will differ from the one you use in a face-to-face class. For example, the main topics of your syllabus might be presented as a menu, allowing students to easily navigate to the appropri-ate information. Students in your online course will be more likely to read and use the syllabus if for no other reason than that they will not always be able to quickly or easily clarify information face to face. So your online syl-labus should not only be clear and organized, but visually appealing and structured so that even the least technologically savvy student will be able to easily navigate it.

• • • • •

Setting Up a Grading System

Grading is often thought of as the mere process of placing a letter from A+ through F next to each student's name at the end of the term, but grading should be much more than that (Walvoord & Anderson, 1998). It should be an integral part of your courses and should reflect your goals for each course (Zlokovich, 2001). For example, if you want to promote your students' ability to critically analyze research on the effects of psychotherapy, or learn the names of neurotransmitters and psychoactive drugs, or synthesize information about various theories of motivation, your grading, as well as your teaching, should reflect these goals. Evaluated tasks that demonstrate achievement of critical analysis ability, knowledge of vocabulary, or content integration should count most heavily toward student grades.

Also, students prefer a grading system that allows them to earn points rather than lose points. In other words, frame your grading system so that students compile points rather than starting with a certain number of points that can be lost during the course. In one study, the "losing points" system was associated with poorer student performance (Bies-Hernandez, 2012).

Grades constitute the second of two kinds of feedback students receive regarding their progress in meeting the goals you have set for them. The first is *formative feedback*, performance-related information intended to guide students as they develop knowledge and skill in your course. Designed mainly to help students improve their performance, formative feedback is more assessment than evaluation. In contrast, grades constitute *summative feedback*, the final evaluation of a student's performance on a particular assignment or in a particular course. Because grades help establish students' credentials for graduation and admission to further educational and occupational opportunities, students want grades—especially good ones—and, at all but a few institutions, faculty members are required to give them. Assigning grades in a satisfactory way takes some doing, and, as always, some planning (Davis, 2009; Ory & Ryan, 1993; Svinicki & McKeachie, 2014; Walvoord & Anderson, 1998).

The Golden Rules of Grading

There is no "best" grading system, but in this section we describe a few golden rules for assigning grades (Davis, 2009; Ory & Ryan, 1993).

First, grading must be accurate, meaning that course grades must reflect each student's level of competency. Accuracy is best achieved through the development of thoughtful assignments tied to learning goals and relevant grading criteria (Davis, 2009).

Second, grading must be fair, and just as important, it must be perceived as fair by students. Therefore, it is imperative to set up a system that assures students that those who turn in equivalent performances will receive equivalent grades. The system should also make it clear that certain ranges of total scores, or percentages of available points, will result in certain grades. Ensuring fairness in your grading system is an important aspect of pursuing fairness in your overall teaching effort, a goal consistent with the final principle of good teaching practice listed in Chapter 1. In addition, students perceive grading fairness when they believe their instructor works to help them perform well (Gordon & Fay, 2010).

Third, grades must be dispensed consistently, meaning that the grading system described at the beginning of the term should not be subject to unannounced, unpredictable, or repeated changes. Your syllabus should list each and every way points can be earned (e.g., through tests, quizzes, papers, research projects, class participation, extra credit options, etc.), and how many points can be earned in each category (Davis, 2009; Saville, 2012). Assign points only on the basis of these categories, and don't make special arrangements with individual students, even when you wish you could. Don't base grades on how much you like particular students, how hard they are trying, or other factors that cannot be quantified and announced in advance. Similarly, base final grades on students' total performance, not on the degree to which they improved during the course. The latter option is unfair because an improvement bonus is unavailable to those whose performance is moderate but consistent, or who do well all along. Avoid basing final grades on just two or three assignments. The more graded components you can include—within the limits dictated by class time and grading time—the more representative of student performance those grades are likely to be (Davis, 2009; Ory & Ryan, 1993). Try to schedule graded assignments so that they are distributed relatively evenly throughout the term. And make sure that the first graded assignment is returned well before the course drop deadline (Davis, 2009).

Following these "golden rules" will make it easier to follow a final one, namely that grades must be defensible (Davis, 2009; Ory & Ryan, 1993). Your grading system should allow you to explain and justify—to students or anyone else who has a right to ask—how and why each student's grade was determined. If you heed all these basic rules, you will reduce grade-related stress, not only because your students will know what to expect and thus be less likely to argue about grades, but also because you will be far less vulnerable to charges of capricious grading. As you develop and refine your grading system, use it consistently, and learn to rely on its fairness, you will find that the grading process will become a relatively routine aspect of your job, allowing you to concentrate on your main task, which is teaching.

Choosing Your Grading System

Whatever you do, be sure to choose your own grading system; don't let it choose you. Trouble awaits the instructor who hopes that appropriate grades will make themselves obvious at the end of the term through natural gaps or break points in the final distribution of total points earned by students. Even if the teaching gods could be relied on to provide such gaps, using them to establish grades on an ad hoc basis would be defined as capricious grading at most institutions. Ad hoc grading is capricious, first, because you would not be able to explain on the first day of class how grades will be determined. It is capricious, too, because the gaps appearing in a distribution are likely to be caused in large part by random factors and measurement error, not by meaningful differences in achievement. If you were to administer an alternate form of your final exam, the gaps might appear in different places (Ory & Ryan, 1993). Also, in thinking about your grading scheme, don't try to reinvent the wheel. As with other aspects of teaching, consult with more experienced colleagues to learn about systems they have used successfully. These consultations will also help familiarize you with the grading system rules or norms that might apply in your department and on your campus.

Norm-Referenced versus Criterion-Referenced Grading

Norm-referenced grades can be assigned using a planned distribution, as when students whose total scores fall in the top 10% of the class distribution earn As, those in the next 20% get Bs, those in the next 40% get Cs, those in the next 20% get Ds, and those in the bottom 10% get Fs. Notice that, in this system, all possible grades will be assigned, but the actual number of points associated with each grade will vary from class to class, depending on how well the best students do.

Criterion-referenced grades are assigned individually, regardless of the performance of any other student or of the class as a whole. In the simplest form of criterion-referenced grading, an A is assigned to anyone who earns, say, 90% of the points available in the course or on a particular assignment. Those earning, say, 80% to 89% of the available points earn a B, and so on. The advantages of criterion-referenced grading are that (a) students are evaluated on an absolute scale determined by the instructor's definition of what constitutes mastery of course material, (b) final grades indicate the degree to which students achieved that mastery, and (c) because students are not competing against each other, they tend to be more cooperative (Ory & Ryan, 1993). Potential disadvantages of criterion-referenced grading include the fact that it can be difficult to determine what criteria are valid in a given course, especially when it is taught for the first time. For example, is it reasonable to expect students to achieve at the 90% level in a cognitive psychophysiology course, given the difficulty of the material? If no one reaches that level, will you be comfortable assigning no As? Answering these questions is easier after you have taught the same course more than once, which is why criterion-referenced grading might not be the best system for new teachers (Davis, 2009; Ory & Ryan, 1993).

Norm-referenced grading has the advantage of rewarding students whose academic performance is outstanding relative to the class (Ory & Ryan, 1993). It can also prevent grade distortions when, for example, even the best students perform poorly because a test or other assignment was flawed in some way. In such cases, the best of the poor performances would still earn As; under a criterion-based system, everyone might receive an F. Norm-referenced grading can lead to some unfortunate consequences, however, especially when there is little variability in the performance of a particular class. Under such a system, even if all your students earned at least, say, 80% of the points available, some of them would still receive Cs, Ds, and Fs. And even if none of your students scored above 50% on any graded assignment, some of them would still get As, Bs, and Cs. In these (thankfully rare) cases, anyone unfamiliar with the characteristics of the class in question could easily be misled about the meaning of norm-referenced grades (Ory & Ryan, 1993).

In general, educational researchers prefer using a criterion-referenced method of assigning grades (Davis, 2009; Svinicki & McKeachie, 2014). Some have gone so far as to say that "grading on the curve is educationally dysfunctional" (Svinicki & McKeachie, 2014, p. 129). We prefer a hybrid grading system that features the strengths of both criterion- and norm-referenced options while avoiding many of the pitfalls of each.

Hybrid Grading Systems

Our favorite hybrid system was developed by Frank Costin for a large, multisection introductory psychology course at the University of Illinois at Urbana-Champaign (see Davis, 2009). In this system, the instructor first computes the mean of the scores earned by the top 10% of all students on any graded assignment, whether it be a quiz, an exam, or total points at the end of the term. (If there were 50 students, for example, you would calculate the mean score of the top 5.) This mean becomes the benchmark for establishing letter grades. For example, to earn an A, students would have to earn at least 95% of the benchmark; earning a B would require

85% of the benchmark; a C would require 75% of the benchmark, and so on. Notice that this hybrid incorporates many of the advantages of both norm-referenced and criterion-referenced grading systems. It allows all students to earn an A if they do well enough; it does not penalize students for poorly designed evaluation instruments; and earning a high grade typically requires a high absolute level of achievement, not just a high relative standing within the class. Many students will be unfamiliar with this grading system, but we have found that they come to like it better than either strictly criterion-referenced or strictly norm-referenced systems.

A Mastery Approach

As an alternative to traditional grading systems, some instructors use a mastery approach to learning. Mastery learning systems gained popularity in the 1970s, stimulated by B. F. Skinner's work on programmed learning. He was horrified by the "lockstep" teaching methods used in his daughter's third-grade mathematics class and in traditional educational systems as a whole. He did not think it made sense to require all students to learn the same material at the same pace, and to be tested on it on the teacher's schedule and then graded based on the level of performance the students had achieved at some predetermined time (Skinner, 1954). He proposed instead a system whereby students could "teach themselves," at their own pace, using a teaching machine that presented increasingly difficult material on a particular topic and that tested their growing knowledge and mastery as they read by filling in the blanks in incomplete sentences (Skinner, 1968). Skinner's work on programmed instruction was directly responsible for the development of Keller's *Personalized System of Instruction* (PSI), which is still in use today on some campuses around North America (Beard & Hartley, 1984; Fuller, 2005; Keller & Sherman, 1974; Ruskin, 1974).

Using PSI, students engage modules of course material one at a time, and at their own pace, then take competency tests when they feel ready. If they can display mastery of one module, they are allowed to proceed to the next one. If not, they can study some more and take a new version of the mastery test.

This process is repeated as often as necessary with each module in the course until some level of mastery is demonstrated. In short, the PSI instructor establishes the level of knowledge or skill required to earn each letter grade, and it is up to the students to meet the criteria for whatever grade they wish to achieve. In some PSI systems, students must demonstrate mastery of a certain segment of text material before being admitted to lectures related to that material. This arrangement ensures that all students attending a lecture have read the material relevant to it.

Needless to say, creating a mastery course involves a lot of work. It requires developing modules of course content and an organized and accessible system for testing and retesting students' knowledge of course material. Accordingly, the mastery approach to teaching and grading is not the most popular one available. Still, it does have its benefits (Jacobs & Chase, 1992; Kulik, Kulik, & Bangert-Drowns, 1990; Kulik, Kulik, & Cohen, 1979; Svinicki, Hagen, & Meyer, 1996), and with the advent of today's computerized and online testing capabilities, mastery learning systems are now more feasible than ever (Brooks, Nolan, & Gallagher, 2000).

The Role of Extra Credit in Your Grading System

Regardless of the grading system you choose, you might consider offering students the option of earning extra credit points for work that goes beyond the standard requirements of your course. Extra credit can be granted for tasks such as writing an additional paper, participating in a research project, attending campus-wide lectures, engaging in course-related community service, or even taking a "second-chance" exam (Weimer, 2011). Some experienced instructors favor extra credit options as a way of helping students compensate for poor performance on standard graded tasks, or as a way of helping superior students enjoy the fruits of their motivation and ability. Others oppose the idea of extra credit, arguing that it is tantamount to capricious grading, or that it offers an undeserved opportunity for lazy students to save their grades at the last minute, thus rewarding both sloth and procrastination. One professor put it this way: "I've seen too many students squeak by on extra credit, students who have not learned the material or who have learned so little of the material that it is virtually useless. I can't help wondering, every time I read about a bridge collapsing or a building falling, whether the chief engineer was once a student who passed a structural course with extra credit" (Slay, 2005). As you might expect, students like to have opportunities for extra credit (Norcross & Dooley, 1993; Weimer, 2011), but it is usually the most able and highly motivated individuals, not the lazy ones, who take advantage of those opportunities (Hardy, 2001). Perhaps because they recognize this pattern, most psychology faculty do not see much value in making extra credit options part of their grading systems (Norcross & Dooley, 1993; Weimer, 2011).

Still, if you like the idea of extra credit, and want it to be more than a life raft tossed out to slackers, consider including the extra credit opportunities throughout the course, not just at the end. Further, be sure that your syllabus includes detailed information about extra credit and how to earn it. Discuss the extra credit options on the first day of class, too, and make sure students understand that extra credit is available to anyone who wants to do extra work. Mentioning or offering extra credit only to certain students on an ad hoc basis surely falls into the category of making special deals, which is another way of defining capricious grading.

Online Considerations

We see no reason to adapt your grading system or grading scale for online courses. The important thing is to construct your grading system carefully so that it can be explained in your syllabus, and also so that it can be consistently applied at the end of the course. And, as in face-to-face courses, be sure to reevaluate your online grading system when the course is over so that you can decide if it met your needs or requires modification. The method of delivery should not alter the basic foundations of your courses.

Communicating with Your Students

Clearly explaining your grading system is just one way of pursuing the first principle of effective teaching, establishing good student–faculty contact. Another communication channel is opened when you encourage students to ask you questions and discuss course-related problems and issues before, during, and after class, and at other times, too. The traditional format for out-of-class communication is the faculty office hour.

Establishing Office Hours

We have already suggested that you set up at least two office hours per week per course, and that you schedule your office hours at convenient times that are least likely to consistently conflict with your students' other classes. However, we suggest that you do more than simply make yourself available. Go out of your way to encourage students to visit you in your office. Remind them that they do not have to have a problem to meet with you, and that talking to an instructor is not "brown-nosing." Give them an agenda for an office visit by suggesting, perhaps, that it would be a good time to discuss questions they have about class presentations, prospects for careers in psychology, and the like. If your class is small enough, give a writing assignment early in the term, then ask each student to meet with you to discuss possible topics. Invite students who performed below average on the first graded assignment to stop by to discuss their understanding of the material and possible ways of improving their performance.

Above all, be in your office during your office hours. If you must be gone for a few minutes, be sure to leave a note on your door telling visitors when you will return. If you have to cancel an office hour session, leave a note about that, too, and if possible, notify your classes via e-mail. Failure to appear at scheduled office hours is often mentioned by students as being among their pet peeves about faculty, and can contribute to negative teaching evaluations. So, when scheduling your office hours, don't forget to make them convenient for yourself as well as for the majority of your students.

When a student is in your office, we suggest that you leave the door at least partly open, unless the student requests that you close it before discussing a private matter. This simple step provides an important measure of comfort and protection for you and your students.

Electronic Office Hours

Electronic office hours are becoming increasingly popular alternatives or supplements to face-to-face office meetings. Using e-mail, Skype, or videoconferencing software (such as Collaborate), students can contact you at their convenience from wherever they have Internet access. Using that same access, you can offer virtual consultation from wherever you are. E-mail gives you the luxury of responding at your convenience and after you have had time to formulate thoughtful replies. Skype and videoconferencing allow students to ask questions and receive immediate feedback. Students appreciate online office hours partly because they know you are readily available. They are more likely to ask a quick question about a homework problem or a writing assignment online than if they had to wait for a scheduled office hour. Further, some of your more reticent students will feel freer to ask their questions and to present their ideas electronically when they might not have done so in class or during an office visit (McKeage, 2001).

Still, when students are experiencing an academic problem, or if they need information about where to turn for a personal problem, they might want to talk to you in person. Also, because e-mail does not allow students and teachers to see or hear each other, such communication can result in misunderstandings. Finally, the apparent remoteness of e-mail sometimes leads people to make ill-advised comments that would not have occurred in person. So although students are receptive to virtual office hours (McKeage, 2001), a mixture of electronic and face-to-face communication is probably ideal.

A class mail group, which allows you to contact all of the students in your class at once, is useful for announcements (upcoming deadlines, for example) and for general follow-ups to questions raised in class. One instructor we know e-mails "virtual lectures" to her students following any class sessions during which time ran out before she could present important material. You can also post information easily in your LMS—including lecture slides, additional resources, or supplemental readings. Be aware, too, that new technologies such as Cel.ly allow you to text students without having to reveal phone numbers (Franz, 2013).

Online Considerations

The videoconferencing software that is of use in a face-to-face class is, of course, the essence of faculty–student communication in an online environment. Office hours will necessarily need to be "virtual" and thus the videoconferencing software you use will be important. As already noted, your syllabus should include specific details about how to use that software. Many online classes offer this information through a video; some of these videos are developed by those who provide technical support of the online course and include screenshots of the various sites and pages that students will encounter. Because many students who take online classes work full time or have less flexible schedules than traditional students, some of your virtual office hours should be in evening and weekend time slots.

Remember, too, the more general role that e-mail plays in an online environment. It is a substitute for the face-to-face communication that would occur in a traditional classroom. This means that many online students will be impatient to hear from you once they have e-mailed their questions or comments. To guide their expectations, be sure to specify in your syllabus your normal response times. Many online teachers promise to reply in 48 hours. To keep up with the e-mail traffic, you will have to check your e-mail many times a day—perhaps more than you ever have before. But don't rush your replies. As already noted, rapidly written messages can be easily misunderstood, especially if what you intended as a simple response or a bit of gentle humor is read as a brush-off or an insult. If e-mail is the only type of interaction students have with you, they will base their evaluations of your course solely on the content of those messages.

Some Final Comments

In this chapter we have offered advice on setting goals for your course, choosing a textbook, developing your syllabus, grading your students, and communicating with them about it all. Once you have done all these things, it is time to think about the next question you have to address, namely, what you should do during the first few days of class to get your course off on the right foot. This is the subject of the next chapter.

3

● ● ● ● ●

The First Few Days of Class

Exploring Your Classroom
Establishing Yourself as a Teacher
Presenting Your Syllabus
Learning Your Students' Names
Setting the Stage for Group Work
Ending the First Class
Some Final Comments

You have established your goals for teaching your course, selected your teaching materials, set up your grading system, and created your syllabus. It is now time to prepare for the first few days of class. These days will be important because the way you present yourself and the way you use your time during your first few classes will set the tone of your teaching, telling your students a lot about what they can expect from you and your course, and about what will be expected of them (Davis, 2009; Kelly, 2010). It is normal to feel some anxiety on the first day of class; even many experienced teachers experience some nervousness that day. Once you and your students get to know each other and form a working relationship, you will probably find teaching much less stressful and a lot more enjoyable, but be aware that there are several things you can do to minimize that first-class anxiety. These include checking out your classroom in advance, planning the first day so that it focuses on your students as well as yourself, and beginning with information that is easy for you to talk about (Kirk, 2009).

● ● ● ● ●

Exploring Your Classroom

At least a week before the new term begins, visit each of your classrooms and familiarize yourself with their layouts and systems. Pay attention to all the details. If a room is normally locked, be sure you have a key or know whom to contact to open the door. Locate the switches and controls for lighting, projection screens, temperature, window shades, and other aspects of the classroom environment that you will need to control during class. Does everything work properly? Is there a table for your notes and other teaching materials and equipment? If you plan to use a chalkboard or dry-erase board (some teachers still do so!), confirm that chalk or felt-tipped pens are available, and just in case, plan to bring your own. If anything is missing or malfunctioning, report it to the appropriate office so that the problem can be solved before your first day of class. Be especially careful to ensure that you know how to operate all aspects of classroom teaching technology. Is yours a "smart" classroom with a computer-based teaching station, or will you perhaps have to bring your own laptop and connect it to an installed projector and amplifier? If you will have to wheel in a departmental computer/projector setup on a cart, find out where it is housed and how you can access it. If you are going to use "old technology" such as videocassettes, be sure there is a VHS player in the room and that it works. Especially if you will be bringing your own projector, laptop computer, or other equipment, check the location of the electrical outlets you will need and whether an extension cord will be required. Will you want to connect to the Internet through a campus network during class? Be sure you have all the cables or wireless network information you need for doing so—including the correct passwords. If possible, try out your PowerPoints, videos, audios, and the like to be sure that no hidden problems will interfere with your presentation on the first day of class.

And, just as important, be sure that there are enough seats to accommodate the number of students enrolled in your class. If in doubt, contact the campus office that manages classroom seating. Consider, too, how well the room's seating accommodations fit your instructional style (Chism & Bickford, 2002). For example, many psychology teachers feel that, in small classes, a circular seating arrangement is the most conducive to student–faculty communication, especially when the teacher occupies a different seat during each class period (Billson & Tiberius, 1998). If you plan to create a seating circle, be sure that your classroom's chairs can be arranged this way. Even if you are only planning to have think-pair-share or small-group discussions from time to time, figure out how you will set up chairs during these activities. If the seats in your classroom are connected in rows or attached to the floor (as they often are in large lecture halls), think about how you will arrange for students to engage in these or other active learning strategies (Eberly Center, 2013). (We discuss active learning strategies in detail in Chapter 4.)

Online Considerations

Although a physical classroom plays no part in online classes, think of your Web site or LMS as your virtual classroom. So before the course begins, try navigating through the site. Check that all important aspects of the course appear in the menu and can be accessed easily. Be sure that all dates and other information are correct. Double check the settings for any assignments or quizzes or exams that will be taken online. For example, be sure that students can access the appropriate material when they need to and that if an assignment is timed, the timing is set correctly. In other words, you should "walk through" your course as if you were one of your students, and do it far enough in advance so that if you do find problems and you have to rely on campus technical support for solutions, the problems can be remedied before your course goes "live."

Establishing Yourself as a Teacher

It has been suggested that students arrive on the first day of class with many unspoken questions in mind, including: Will this class meet my needs? Is the teacher competent? Will the teacher be fair? Will the teacher care about me? What should I call you? Will I have to say anything out loud in the class? How tough are the exams? How will I know what material is most important? (Davis, 2009; Ericksen, 1974; Forsyth, 2003; Lieberg, 2008; Scholl-Buckwald, 1985).

It is vital to begin to address these unspoken questions, through word and deed, during the first class session. Some instructors make the first day of class a short day by just distributing a syllabus, making a reading assignment, and letting the students leave. Often these are the teachers who are the most anxious about teaching (Lang, 2008; Svinicki & McKeachie, 2014). But what message would you be sending about yourself, your course, and your approach to teaching if you did this? Although you might not have intended to create this impression, students might well get the idea that you don't consider class time particularly valuable, that you might not care much about teaching (or them), that they can expect you to do most of the talking, and that they should sit passively and listen. Once those perceptions and expectations have coalesced over the first several classes, they are unlikely to change much (Emmer, Everston, & Anderson, 1979; Kelly, 2010).

Managing Students' Expectations

Here are some tips about verbal and nonverbal behaviors that will help you to establish a more desirable set of student expectations on the first day of class.

Dress Professionally

Dressing professionally is especially important if you are new to teaching, young, or female (Eberly Center, 2013; Lang, 2008; Lieberg, 2008). Remember that you can always go from more formal to less formal attire as you get to know your class and establish yourself in students' eyes, although trying to gain students' respect by suddenly dressing more formally is not likely to have much effect other than to signal desperation (Eberly Center, 2013).

Arrive Early

Get to class early and bring with you all of the materials that you will need, including copies of the syllabus (if you are distributing print versions) and sample copies of the reading materials you will be assigning. Be prepared to tell students where they can get these reading materials and which items are on reserve in the library (Davis, 2009). When students arrive, they should see your name and the name and number of your course displayed on the chalkboard/whiteboard or on a PowerPoint slide. These simple things send the message that you care about your teaching and are fully prepared (Kelly, 2010; Scholl-Buckwald, 1985).

Be Friendly

While waiting for class to begin, greet and make small talk with students as they enter the room. This is another simple step, but one that begins the process of establishing mutual respect and the good faculty–student contact that serves as the first principle of good practice in teaching (Billson & Tiberius, 1998; Boice, 1998a; Delaney, 2009; Carnegie Mellon, Eberly Center, 2013; Kirk, 2009; Svinicki & McKeachie, 2014).

Be Human

When it is time to begin the class, introduce yourself, say a few words about your background, your academic and scholarly activities, and maybe even some of your outside interests. In deciding how you introduce yourself, think about what students are likely to want to know about you. Remember, though, that you don't have to tell students everything, so they don't necessarily need to know intimate details about your life, that this is your first time teaching, that this is your least favorite course, or that you are feeling nervous (Eberly Center, 2013; Svinicki & McKeachie, 2014; Wright, 2012). On the other hand, it is a good idea to tell students about your deep interest in psychology and why you enjoy teaching this particular course. Remember that enthusiasm for course material and for teaching in general is a characteristic typically associated with instructors who are rated as effective by students and peers (Andersen, 1986; Billson & Tiberius, 1998; Davis, 2009; Eble, 1988; Kirk, 2009; Murray, 1997; Scholl-Buckwald, 1985; Timpson & Bendel-Simso, 1996; Wright, 2012).

Invite Contact

We mentioned that one of most students' unspoken questions is about what they should call you (Lieberg, 2008). This is especially true among first-year students who are used to addressing their high school teachers as Mr. or Ms. So give them a hand. Let your students know right away how you would prefer them to address you—as Dr., Mr., Mrs., Ms., Professor, Doug, Sandy, or whatever (Davis, 2009). The easiest way to do this is to put the information on that first PowerPoint slide or blackboard display; this also helps students learn how to spell your name. One of the authors writes Dr. Sandra Goss Lucas (Sandy) on the board to show that she indeed has the PhD credential, but prefers the class to use first names. It is important to remove any doubt or ambiguity about this small but important matter, because some students will avoid contact with teachers, even if they need help, simply because they are not sure how to address them.

Develop a Sense of Community

Six qualities have been identified as essential in establishing a sense of community in the classroom. They are connection, participation, safety, support, belonging, and empowerment (McKinney et al., 2006; Svinicki & McKeachie, 2014). Your first class should begin to promote these qualities.

For example, when students introduce themselves to each other it creates connection and addresses the second principle for effective teaching, student cooperation. So, in a class of 50 or fewer, have students give their name (you can check attendance as they do so) and any nickname or abbreviated name they prefer. You can also ask students for information that will help you remember them, for example, "Tell us something unique about yourself, or "Tell us a reason you are glad to be in class today." In larger classes, you can simply ask students to introduce themselves to those seated nearby.

If you plan to include various kinds of group activities in your course, you might set the stage through more elaborate introduction methods. Some instructors ask pairs of students to interview each other for a few minutes during class, or in a longer conversation outside of class, and then introduce their partner to the class (Davis, 2009; McGlynn, 2001; Scholl-Buckwald, 1985).

You can also use various "icebreaker" activities to help students become more comfortable with each other and with you on the first day of class (Billson & Tiberius, 1998; Davis, 2009; Eberly Center, 2013; Lang, 2008; Scholl-Buckwald, 1985; Svinicki & McKeachie, 2014). One instructor asks students to form groups of three or four to write a course-related question they would like the instructor to answer. The instructor then collects the cards, responds to some, and saves the rest for later in the course. Like briefer introduction strategies, this one helps students to meet each other while encouraging cooperative learning (Erickson, Peters, & Strommer, 2006). Other instructors use "First Day Graffiti" in which students move around and complete incomplete sentences that have been posted throughout the classroom, such as "I am most likely to participate in classes when . . . " or "Students in courses help me learn when they" . . . (Weimer, 2013c). One of the authors (SGL) uses a list of 10 statements pertaining to the content of her introductory psychology course. For example, one statement is, "I slept 8 hours last night." Students then move around the room looking for someone who can truthfully sign one of the statements listed. Because a student can only sign one statement on each sheet, this exercise guarantees that every student will meet at least 10 fellow students. In addition, the instructor can introduce topics in the course (e.g., stages of sleep and sleep deprivation) through the statements. You could also list attributes such as "lives in ____ dorm" or "prefers to study early in the morning"; the commonalities students find might help you to create study groups. You could even simply ask students to raise their hands if they fit these descriptions; then have students with raised hands pair up to discuss other things they might have in common. Other icebreakers and first-day activities can be found in *Successful Beginnings for College Teaching: Engaging Your Students from the First Day* (McGlynn, 2001).

If nothing else, after introducing yourself, get some information about your students simply by distributing index cards and asking students to write their name and provide other information you would like to gather about things such as their major, their e-mail address, the psychology courses they have taken, and topics they want to learn about in your class (Carnegie Mellon, Eberly Center, 2013; Kirk, 2009). Reading over these cards after the first class will give you a better idea of who your students are, how well they are prepared, and the range of their interests. Spend a few minutes at the next class session discussing some of the interests expressed and how those topics will fit into the course. Taking time to do this provides yet another way to show your commitment to teaching and your interest in students.

Online Considerations

Unless you are appearing in live or recorded video feeds, your manner of dress is a nonissue in an online course. However, it is still important that you introduce yourself to your students and that your students get an opportunity to begin building a sense of community. The easiest way to present yourself is to post a short welcome video (dress appropriately!) that students can access even before they begin the course. The video should convey your enthusiasm for teaching the course and for teaching it online and should give students a sense of who you are as a teacher and as a person. So address the same questions that are of interest to students in your face-to-face classes—including how to contact you and the form of address you prefer. This video should be separate from the one you might create to help students navigate the course. As in a face-to-face class, students need to get to know one another, and the easiest way to begin to promote community is through icebreaker activities similar to those mentioned earlier. You can do the same if you establish standing working groups. For example, you could give students a short survey on the first day, asking students about their preferences regarding times for group work (e.g., some students will prefer weekend time for class work; others might prefer to work in the evenings; full-time students might want to meet during the daytime). By providing the survey, you are maximizing the chances that the groups will be successful. You also might establish roles in each group (such as reporter, facilitator, timekeeper, etc.) and have students in the group choose their role. (Be sure to have more than one student in each role because there are typically more drops in an online course than in a face-to-face course.) Let students choose their group name (we ask them to create a name consisting of one noun and one adjective from the textbook).

Presenting Your Syllabus

Once introductions are accomplished, distribute your syllabus or ask students to follow along using the copy they downloaded from your course Web site (see Chapter 2 for ideas on syllabus construction). Remember that your presentation style tells students about your attributes as a person and as a teacher. An ideal presentation includes PowerPoint slides to highlight important aspects of the syllabus, and its tone should balance your role as a caring teacher who wants to help students succeed with your role as an authoritative presence who expects students to exert serious effort to learn and to take responsibility for themselves. Several tips are available for syllabus presentation, including being positive, selling the course, using inclusive language, and clearly outlining course rules (see Thompson, 2007, pp. 59, 62). Remember, too, that your students are probably seeing the syllabus (or its details) for the first time; they will not be able to absorb it all at once, so expect to answer questions about it during the next class. After covering its main points during the first class, some instructors make the syllabus the first reading assignment. During the next class they provide three-by-five cards on which students (perhaps working in small groups) can write syllabus questions, and the instructor then spends 10 minutes or so answering those questions (Brown, 2012; Erickson & Strommer, 1991).

Encourage your students to use the syllabus as a reference when they have questions about the course and its requirements. Be sure to post the syllabus on your class LMS or Web site so that students can access the information and print a copy for themselves if they desire. Start your discussion of the syllabus by listing your course goals. This strategy offers a natural lead-in to how class time will be spent (Davis, 2009; Erickson et al., 2006; Svinicki & McKeachie, 2014). For example, if one of your main goals is to promote critical thinking about abnormal psychology or team-work in problem solving, highlight the fact that the assigned readings are designed to support classroom activities that involve analysis of the validity of psychiatric diagnoses or small-group problem-solving tasks. In this connection, be sure to let students know if the reading assign-ments are to be completed before or after the class session covering that topic. Some students, especially first-year students, will be unsure about this matter, so state your preference explicitly in your introduction, as well as in the syllabus.

Students will be particularly interested in how they will be graded in your course, so be sure to discuss the number and types of graded assign-ments there will be and how final grades will be determined.

Encourage Instructor–Student Interactions

Reviewing the syllabus offers a perfect opportunity to continue demon-strating your commitment to the first principle of good practice in teach-ing, promoting student–teacher interaction. When you get to the part of the syllabus that lists your office address, make it clear that you are inter-ested in meeting with your students. Make it easy for them to find you by giving some details and landmarks that will help students locate your office. Encourage them to stop by to ask questions or simply to introduce themselves. Point out your schedule of office hours, but tell students that you will be happy to arrange additional meeting times by appoint-ment. This is also a good time to highlight your e-mail address and to give students an idea of how long it will normally take to get a reply to their e-mail messages. Let them know, for example, if you don't read e-mail after 10 P.M. or over weekends. If you offer virtual office hours, explain how students can take advantage of them.

Describe aspects of your schedule that will affect students' access to you. For example, if you have another class immediately before or after this one, explain why you will seem too rushed to chat when you arrive and/or depart. Otherwise, students might get the false impression that you are not interested in them. Finally, if you have listed your home or cell phone number on the syllabus, now is the time to point out that you also listed the hours (e.g., 9 A.M. to 11 P.M.) during which your students can call. If you explain the reasons for these rules—that you go to bed early, or that you live with small children or an ailing parent—students are unlikely to abuse the privilege of having your home number.

Discuss Learning Objectives and Your Expectations

If you have not already done so when presenting your syllabus, begin your discussion of the course content with a summary of your learning objectives. Tell students why those objectives are important and how you plan to achieve them (Carnegie Mellon, Eberly Center, 2013; Erickson et al., 2006). One very senior professor begins this discussion by presenting a list of 17 possible course goals and asking students to choose their top three. Then he compares their composite with his top three, which leads to a discussion of the course content (Svinicki & McKeachie, 2014).

Be honest with your students about the amount of work that will be required in your class. Assure them that it can all be accomplished, but don't underplay the effort that will be necessary to succeed in the course. Most students will rise to the challenge (Timpson & Bendel-Simso, 1996), but those who can't or don't wish to handle the workload are better off dropping your course before it is too late. This is also a good time to emphasize how important it is to read all the assigned material when it is due. Not every student will follow this advice, but it is worth offering.

Display a copy of each of the required books, articles, and other assigned materials; note where the materials can be purchased and where the reading assignments can be found (e.g., on the syllabus, in handouts, on the LMS, in the library). Offering this information not only demonstrates that you care about your students, but also makes it more likely that they will have the correct materials on hand when they need them. Tell the students, too, a little bit about the texts and other readings you have chosen and how they relate to your course outline and your course goals (Boyd, 2003; Eble, 1988).

Unless you are the world's fastest talker and your students are the world's best note takers, you won't have enough time in class to cover all the important information in the assigned readings. Mention this fact and point out that, as a result, your students will be responsible for doing a lot of learning on their own. It is vital that students understand this, especially if you plan to test them on material that is not covered in class.

If you are using a textbook, explain the meaning of pedagogical features such as boldface print, italicized or highlighted text, critical thinking exercises, chapter summaries, self-tests, review tables, and the like (Boyd, 2003). Demonstrate how to access the resources available on the course Web site or LMS. This orientation can be especially important for first-year students and those whose academic preparation has been less than ideal. If they don't know what to look for in their readings, they might not recognize the importance of pedagogical features, and might fail to use them as they read and study.

Spend some time too on the course guidelines and expectations (these should be listed in the syllabus as well). Tell students, for example, that attendance matters, that they should raise a hand and be recognized before speaking, that eating or drinking is not permitted in class, that you hate it when students start packing up to leave before class time has ended, or whatever rules and regulations regarding student behavior are especially important to you (Carnegie Mellon, Eberly Center, 2013; Wright, 2012). And mention the rules that will govern *your* behavior. For instance, we always tell our students that we will start each class on time and that we will never extend a class beyond its scheduled ending time. (This information helps get students to class early and assures them they will not have to rush to their next class.)

In laying out ground rules for your course, be explicit. Do not assume that students will already know these rules, even the ones that seem intuitively obvious to you. Your rules might be utterly new to some students, especially those who have operated under different rules (or few rules) in other college classes or in high school.

Ask for Questions

Once you have covered the course basics, be sure to ask for questions (Wright, 2012). Do so in a way that lets students know that you expect them to have questions and that you are happy to answer them. Murmuring "Any questions?" as you gather your materials to leave the room is not the way to get this message across. Instead, say something like "OK, I know I have hit you with a lot of information. What questions do you have for me?" If no one immediately asks a question, take some time to scan the classroom. This, too, demonstrates that you really want students to respond. Be sure to wait long enough for students to work up the nerve to raise their hands (believe it or not, some students will be more nervous about addressing you in class than you are about addressing them). If no questions are forthcoming, have a few in mind to get the ball rolling. You could say, for example, "You might be wondering if the exams are cumulative (or whether attendance is mandatory, or what to do if you have to leave class early, or how to choose a paper topic, or where the lab is)." Then give the answers in a friendly way. In short, if you want your students to feel free to ask questions throughout the course, offer them genuine opportunities to do so on the first day and then reward them when they respond.

Present Some Course Content and Establish Class Structure

One of the most important things that you will do the first day is to teach some course content (Eberly Center, 2013; Kelly, 2010; Svinicki & McKeachie, 2014). Do so in a way that whets students' appetite for the material you will be covering during later classes. You might want to pose some questions for students to answer (perhaps in small groups), or maybe even administer a short quiz designed to test students' knowledge of or misconceptions about the content of your course. In ours, we often hand out a brief true-false test with items that seem quite easy and obvious (e.g., "schizophrenia is a form of multiple personality" or "it is easier to get help in a crowd"), but that all represent common misconceptions about behavior and mental processes. Students are surprised and curious when the quiz is scored in class and they discover that many of the things they thought they knew about behavior and mental processes turn out to be wrong. This experience helps to motivate students to begin their reading and to come back to the next class. Whatever option you choose, it is good to give students a taste of the course material to come, so that they leave that first class with something to think about.

Think, too, about the features of your ideal class and try to incorporate those features into the first day's content. So if you want students to participate, you need to structure the first day to include student participation. If you want students to work in pairs or groups, include such an activity the first day. Student expectations about how a course is conducted are set very early—so be sure that their expectations include behaviors that you value.

● ● ● ● ●

Learning Your Students' Names

There are four main reasons we think it is important to learn as many of your students' names as possible, and as early in the term as possible (Billson & Tiberius, 1998; Davis, 2009; Erickson et al., 2006; Leamnson, 1999). First, it is less stressful to teach people you know rather than a group of strangers. Second, your effort to learn names—even if you don't learn them all—clearly demonstrates that you care about your students as people, an attribute that is likely to have a positive impact on your teaching ratings. Third, learning names can help your students feel less anonymous and less disconnected from their instructors. Being seen as an individual, not a number, can be especially important to first-year students, who might find themselves in relatively large classes for the first time. Finally, feeling a closer connection to faculty can help students to do better in their classes, and it certainly makes them more likely to seek help and advice when they need it (Erickson et al., 2006; Leamnson, 1999). Learning students' names can be a daunting task, especially in large classes, but there are ways to make it easier.

Collect Flash Cards

One psychology instructor we know asks each of her 200 students to paste a photo of themselves to the back of the three-by-five information card she hands out on the first day of class. She carries these cards with her for the next couple of weeks, using them as flash cards to test herself as she learns students' names at odd times, such as while riding the bus, while waiting for meetings to begin, and even just before bed. (To ensure that she gets these cards back on the second day of class, she makes it a course requirement to turn them in and gives points for doing so.)

Create a Context

Another instructor capitalizes on the principles of cognitive psychology to create a context for remembering students' names (Bailey, 2002). He finds that the more information he gathers about students, the easier it is to remember their names. Accordingly, he asks students to include on their information cards such items as the names of their pets or something about themselves that they consider unique. He also creates location cues by asking students to sit in the same seats throughout the term. Further, as students ask or answer questions or make comments during class, he jots down information on their cards—such as hair color or voice characteristics. He then engages in elaborative rehearsal, creating a "funny, weird, or meaningful association with some information about each student" (Bailey, 2002, p. 184). He organizes the cards in an order that duplicates the students' location in the classroom, and even uses chunking by creating a story that links the students in each row. Finally, he tests his memory by trying to fill in the correct names on a blank seating chart. Eventually, he can call on students by name in class and as they turn in assignments or enter the room.

Practice, Practice, Practice

In relatively small classes, you can practice learning names simply by calling the roll each day. We tell our students (truthfully) that the roll call is done only so we can learn their names, and that there is no penalty for missing class, but we find that taking attendance actually seems to boost attendance. Whether you call the roll or find other excuses to use your students' names, you will find that practice eventually helps you to remember many more names than you thought you would. And don't be afraid to make mistakes. Tell your students that you want to get to know their names, that you will try to call them by name, and that you would appreciate it if they correct you when you make errors. They will not be insulted if you call them by the wrong name, and they will help you to get it right.

Name Tags

Having students wear name tags for the first couple of weeks of class can also help you learn names. Students are happy to comply when you explain that you are working to remember their names and that the tags will help. Name tags with adhesive backs are relatively cheap and easily disposed of after class. Just having a pile of blank name tags and markers as students come into class prompts them to make and wear a name tag.

⬤ ⬤ ⬤ ⬤ ⬤

Setting the Stage for Group Work

If you plan to ask your students to work together in groups or teams, either inside or outside of class, set the stage for collaborative learning by assigning students to their working groups during the first few days of class. By creating the groups yourself rather than allowing students to do so, you can ensure that each group is as diverse as possible in terms of gender, ethnicity, and year of study. By establishing these groups early in the term, you create the immediate opportunity for students to form a supportive network of classmates. Students who are in the same work group for class discussions might end up studying together when the time comes to prepare for quizzes and exams.

Forming working groups is easy. On the first or second day of class, send around a sign-up sheet on which the students can record their name, year in school, campus phone number, e-mail address, and campus address. (If you have already handed out and collected student information index cards, this step is unnecessary.) Later, you can assign students to groups based on gender, ethnicity (if you know it), seniority, and address (those who live close to one another might be more likely to meet outside of class). At the next class, announce the composition of the groups you have formed. Then ask the members of each group to get together during that session to work on a problem or answer a question and make a group report to the class. A few sessions before your first quiz or exam, give the groups a few minutes in class to arrange a time and place to get together to study.

Having students work together periodically in class and encouraging them to study together outside of class not only helps them to get to know, like, and depend on one another, but also helps create a friendlier and more supportive classroom environment for you as their teacher. We discuss group learning activities in more detail in Chapter 4.

Online Considerations

There is not truly a "first day" experience in an online course, but a welcome video and information on how to navigate the course (whether in an additional video or voiceover screen shots) should be available before the first day of the term. Further, it is important that students feel that you "know" them personally in some way. We have students post pictures of themselves on the LMS so that we can associate names with faces. In addition, we have an applied concepts journal assignment throughout the semester, in which students choose concepts from the class materials and provide personal examples of each (e.g., how they operantly conditioned their younger sister to make her bed). These examples are then posted and not only do other students comment on them on the discussion board, but the instructor provides individual, private feedback, being sure to always address each student by name. This often results in students sharing more information online than they would in a face-to-face class. Thus, we get to know our online students in a different, and sometimes more personal, way than those in our face-to-face classes. However, it is vital that these instructor–student and student–student connections occur very quickly in an online course because much of the routine activity in an online course is fairly solitary.

Ending the First Class

There is a lot of administrative work to do on the first day of class but, as we mentioned earlier, it is also important to cover some course content as well (Carnegie Mellon, Eberly Center, 2013; Kelly, 2010; Scholl-Buckwald, 1985; Svinicki & McKeachie, 2014). And don't forget to remind students of their reading assignment for the next class, as well as any other homework you have set for them—including the return of information cards or other material you have asked for.

Bringing class to an organized conclusion is important for every session, not just the first one. As the end of class approaches, don't just let time run out. Reserve a few minutes to summarize the main points you have covered and to say a few words about the material you will address the next time (Billson & Tiberius, 1998). You might even consider using the final two minutes to have your students jot down and turn in their reactions to the day's lecture. This little exercise not only shows that you care what your students think, it also provides you with immediate feedback on how the class went (Svinicki & McKeachie, 2014). One instructor ends every class by asking small groups of students to engage in a review. He provides two conceptual questions for group members to discuss, then randomly calls on two or three groups to summarize their discussion aloud. He finds that these reviews increase students' understanding of the concepts discussed, and also help to develop a sense of community in the classroom (Love, 2013).

Some Final Comments

Just as you will do on the first day of class, this chapter has presented too much material for you to absorb all at once. We hope the summary and Checklist 3.1 will serve as a useful reminder when you meet your class for the first time and that it will act as a stimulus for adding your own individual items. The checklist also includes items discussed in Chapter 2 that are especially relevant to keep in mind on the first day of class.

Online Considerations

Again, because there really is no one "first day" of class in an online environment, the important issues we have discussed in this chapter will need to be addressed before the course begins. In addition, we can't emphasis enough how important teacher–student interaction and student–student interaction will be in setting the tone for your online class. So, posting questions to a discussion board for students to contemplate as they begin the class and setting up student groups is an important priority for the beginning of an online course.

Checklist 3.1 Some Points to Remember about the First Day of Class

Before the first class meeting:

1. Become thoroughly familiar with the required resources (textbook, Web assets, etc.) so that you can easily answer questions about them.
2. Visit your classroom before the term begins to check on its physical layout and characteristics. Do you need a key to enter? Where are the light switches? Are there enough student desks? Is there an instructor desk? If you will use a chalkboard, is there chalk available, or do you need to bring your own? If you will need to darken the room to make PowerPoint or videos more visible, are there shades at the windows— and do they work? Is any of the audiovisual or computer equipment locked in cabinets or closets for which you will need keys or lock combinations? Is there any missing or broken equipment?
3. Write a syllabus that includes:
   a. The course number and title.
   b. When and where the course meets.
   c. Your name, office address, and how to contact you. (If you decide to provide your home or cell phone number, include rules for its use).
   d. Your scheduled office hours.
   e. Information about anyone who will be helping you teach the course (e.g., TAs).
   f. A list of course goals and, possibly, how you plan to meet those goals.
   g. A statement about respect for individuals along with expectations of the class.
   h. A list of all required and recommended materials.
   i. A description of all evaluation procedures, including exactly how the final grade is computed and an explanation of every graded component.
   j. A list of class rules and policies.

4. Plan a course content "teaser" for the first day of class—a question, a group project, a problem, or a dilemma for students to deal with that will help them begin to think about the material to be covered in the course.

Some First-Day Dos and Don'ts

Do:

1. Arrive early with all of the materials that you will need. Write the course name and number and your name on the blackboard or have it visible on a PowerPoint slide.
2. Chat with students as they enter the classroom before class starts. Treat your students with respect.
3. Introduce yourself. Tell your students a little about your background, interests, and so on. Tell them how they should address you.
4. Go over the important points of your syllabus, including course ground rules. After covering the basics, ask for questions, then scan the room as you give the class plenty of time to work up the courage to speak. If no questions are raised immediately, be ready with some of your own.
5. Encourage students to come to your office hours with additional questions or just to get acquainted.
6. If you want to create an early active learning experience, do a course-related demonstration or set up a brief group activity. For example:
   a. Assign students to small groups and give them five minutes to agree on a course-related question that they would like the instructor to answer and then write that question on an index card you have provided.
   b. Present a problem or case study for students to solve or analyze.
   c. Ask students to tell you what course topics they are most interested in learning about. List these topics on the board or on a PowerPoint slide, and note which ones will be covered in which course content areas.
   d. Ask students to write a paragraph about what they hope and expect to get out of your course.

Don't:

1. Arrive late and ignore students.
2. Distribute the syllabus and dismiss class.
3. Let students sit through the entire class without giving them the opportunity to meet even one other student in the class.

The first day of class is a challenge, but once it is over, you will soon realize that the rest of the term remains, and you have a lot of psychology to cover. How can you present that material in the most effective way and in a manner that matches your teaching style? We consider these questions in the next chapter.

4

Developing Your
Teaching Style

So what should you actually do in the classroom? How should you allocate class time? How can you structure learning opportunities for your students outside the classroom? Which face-to-face teaching techniques are most effective and which can be adapted for use in an online course? In this chapter we explore the answers to these questions, beginning with traditional teaching methods and moving to more recent techniques.

Preparing for Class

Your first task is to decide what content you want to cover in a particular class and how you want to deliver it. You will want to have class notes, but don't try to write out everything that you want to say. Script-like narrative notes can be a lifesaver early in your teaching career, especially if you want or need a lot of help in remembering the details of course content, but they can also create a tendency for you to read them aloud. As a result, you may not make enough eye contact with your students and your presentation may sound stilted (Svinicki & McKeachie, 2014).

Consider organizing your notes as an outline that contains enough information to remind you what you want to say and what activities you want to incorporate, but that is not a word-for-word script. We have found that this format will help keep your presentation style and tone of voice conversational, not droning. Your outline can include concept examples, cases that you might want to mention, and cues about when to start video clips, visit Web sites, use a learning activity, and go to the next PowerPoint slide. Some instructors use their PowerPoint slides as their class notes (Svinicki & McKeachie, 2014), but don't let them become text-heavy scripts that you end up reading to the class (Davis, 2009).

We suggest that you create a file for each class session into which you can place new information for use the next time you teach it. That information can include concept examples (especially those good ones you get from students), research studies, URLs for videos, or news items that are relevant to a particular topic. You might not use all of this material, but it will be there for you, and reviewing it allows you to decide whether to use it and how. Remember, though, that you cannot just keep adding more "good stuff" because if you try to cover it all, you will run out of time and the class will feel too rushed, for both you and your students. So when you add something new, recognize that something old might have to go.

⊙ ⊙ ⊙ ⊙ ⊙

Effective Lecturing

Lectures have a bad reputation nowadays; many people view them as old-fashioned, potentially boring, and relatively ineffective for promoting discussion, critical thinking, and hands-on application of course material. Nevertheless, if you are like most psychology teachers, and certainly like most new teachers, you will spend some, or even most, of your class time giving lectures (Benjamin, 2002, 2013; Smith & Valentine, 2012). Some teachers rely on lectures for the wrong reasons, such as that it is the only way they know how to teach or that it is the easiest way to teach. One survey of 744 teachers found that they believed the two most effective ways to teach were hands-on activities and practical exercises, yet when asked to report which teaching technique they had used during their past 10 teaching sessions, 90% of them said that they had lectured for about half of their class sessions, and 50% said they had lectured during all class sessions (Smith & Valentine, 2012).

Actually, there are good reasons to lecture. Lectures serve to present up-to-date information; to summarize information from a variety of sources; to adapt material to meet the needs of students; to provide scaffolding for students' reading; and to focus on the key ideas of the course (Svinicki & McKeachie, 2014). In addition, a well-organized, well-presented lecture by an enthusiastic teacher can motivate students to read and learn on their own. Lecturing has also proven cost-effective when teaching a large number of students (Short & Martin, 2011).

We don't have a simple prescription that will guarantee your success as a lecturer, but we can offer some tips and guidelines.

Planning Your Lectures

As with all teaching activities, planning is key. We suggest that you prepare an outline for each class session so that it includes more material than you can cover in one class period. Having extra material offers two advantages. First, it ensures that you will not run out of content even if nervousness causes you to move through it faster than you thought you would, or if you decide to skip parts of a lecture that, in light of how the class is going, now seem too complex, too simple, or not likely to work as well as you had expected. Second, having extra material gives you a head start on preparing for the following class session.

As mentioned earlier, though, the fact that you have prepared a lot of material doesn't obligate you to cover all of it in any particular session (Zakrajsek, 1998), or even to cover it at all. There will inevitably be topics that you will have to leave out, or that you will have time only to touch on, if you are going to keep reasonably close to the schedule of topics, reading assignments, and exams and quizzes advertised in your syllabus. We don't worry too much about leaving a topic without fully addressing it in class, because we know that students don't learn from lectures alone. They also learn—and are responsible for learning—from their assigned reading, from talking to teachers and fellow students, and from computer labs, class projects, papers, and other activities discussed later in this chapter. So don't rush to cover everything you wish you could cover. If you do, you will be exhausted and your students will be overwhelmed.

To make planning easier, keep track of where you had to stop at the end of each class session. This simple procedure creates a record of your intended and actual pace of progress through the course. You can then use this information to do a better job of planning your coverage of the same content the next time you teach the course.

When planning your lectures, remember that there are limits on your students' attention span and information-processing capacity. Traditional wisdom and some research suggest that student attention is usually highest during the first 10 minutes of a lecture, after which it tends to wane. In fact, some research suggests that students retain 70% of the material during the first 10 minutes, but only 20% during the last 10 minutes; that most students listen attentively only 40% of the time during a 50-minute lecture; and that if you lecture at about 150 words per minute, students will only hear about 50 of those words (Jones-Wilson, 2005; Lang, 2008). Other researchers do not find this particular pattern, but they do find that attention wanes throughout the lecture, depending on the students, the lecturer, and the course material (Bunce, Flens, & Neiles, 2010; Davis, 2009; Johnstone & Percival, 1976; Wilson & Korn, 2007).

With this in mind, plan to engage periodically in activities that will recapture student attention, especially during classes in which you expect to spend a significant portion of time in straight lecturing. These activities might involve one of the active learning methods described in more detail in the next section, or they might simply provide an unusual way to introduce a new topic or subtopic—perhaps by telling a story, posing a problem, framing a dilemma, describing a mystery, or asking a question. For example, reading an excerpt from the case of "H.M." or showing a "Mr. Short-Term Memory" sketch from old *Saturday Night Live* shows are just two attention-getting ways of introducing a lecture segment on the formation of long-term memories. One of the easiest methods to reengage students is to use student response systems ("clickers") to answer questions that you pose. You might also use a quick think-pair-share activity (discussed later in this chapter), or simply let students stand up and stretch (Svinicki & McKeachie, 2014). Many experienced instructors have found that the best way to maximize student attention throughout a given class period is to present a series of 10-minute lecturettes, followed by some type of active learning opportunity. This mixing of lecture and active learning techniques has become far more common these days, except perhaps in the very large lecture sections discussed later (Erickson, Peters, & Strommer, 2006).

Research suggests that, perhaps because of limitations on attention, the average student can absorb only about three to five major points during any particular lecture (Lowman, 1995). Accordingly, the most effective lecturers plan to concentrate on those few major points (Tozer, 1992), presenting information about each of them in several ways to maximize the chances that everyone understands the material. This might mean, for example, presenting and giving applied examples of three main theories of prejudice rather than trying to describe in detail every theory listed in the textbook.

In summary, the compulsion to try to cover "everything" during class leads to what some observers have called "the nonstop fifty-minute lecture" (Erickson et al., 2006). We agree with Erickson and colleagues that, beginning in their first year of college (if not before), students should "be weaned from their conviction that material cannot be important if it is not covered in class" and that we as teachers need to be weaned from our "belief that students cannot learn it unless we say it" (Erickson et al., 2006, p. 91).

Delivering Your Lecture

Easily perceived stimuli help to hold students' attention, so when it is time to walk into the classroom and deliver your carefully planned class presentation, remember that the first step in keeping your students with you mentally is to be a clear presence physically.

So be sure that all your students can see you. This might mean that you have to move around the room a bit as you talk, perhaps even walking among the students if you are comfortable doing so. A certain amount of movement—along with whatever characteristic hand gestures you might use while speaking—creates visual variety that helps hold your students' attention—but don't overdo it. Students tend to find it distracting, even annoying, when teachers pace frantically or engage in certain other repetitive actions such as endlessly capping and uncapping a pen. (See Chapter 8 for some tips on getting evaluative feedback on your class presentation style.) If an injury or disability does not allow you to move around or requires that you sit as you interact with your class, try to position yourself on a platform or other elevated location, especially in classrooms where seats are not arranged on risers. In these flat classrooms, students in the back might be especially likely to lose focus if you let yourself become a disembodied voice.

You can also increase your students' attentiveness by constantly scanning the room and making eye contact with everyone from time to time. Some students will look back at you with more interest than others, so there is a natural tendency to spend more time looking at those who are "with you." However, if you can resist letting your scanning pattern be shaped by this kind of operant reinforcement, you will find that even the less involved students will stay at least marginally interested if you use your eyes to let them know that you are talking to them, too.

Be sure, also, that all your students can hear what you are saying. If you are teaching in a large classroom, or if you have a soft voice, you might need to use a microphone. (As described in Chapter 3, you should determine this need while you are exploring your classroom and its facilities before the new term begins.) Once you are sure it is audible, use your voice to attract attention. Speaking too softly or too rapidly or speaking in a monotone are surefire ways to lose students' interest. If you are not sure how you sound in the classroom, record yourself as you deliver a mock presentation, then listen to it and try to be objective about the volume, clarity, and quality of your voice (ask a friend or colleague to comment on the recording, too). If you are not happy with what you hear, work on speaking louder, more distinctly, and with more variations in pitch to help keep students interested and awake (McKeachie, 2001).

Incorporate Multimedia Materials

Multimedia materials help hold students' attention, so use them whenever possible. If you are describing the results of the Milgram experiment, or the structure of the eye, or various categories of memory, for example, don't depend on your words alone to keep students interested. Show a video clip from Milgram's original study, present an Internet image of eye anatomy or a PowerPoint slide listing the memory components you plan to cover. You might also want to present some of this material on handouts on which students can take notes as you present the material.

Define Your Terms

Remember, too, that it is easy for your students to lose interest if they don't understand the vocabulary you are using. In addition to speaking audibly, clearly, and in an organized way, be sure to define and display the spelling of every psychological term that is likely to be unfamiliar to students. There are a lot more of these unfamiliar terms than you might think. If you are like most psychology teachers, you have come to adopt a specialized vocabulary that is easily understood by your colleagues but that could mystify, confuse, or mislead the average student, especially those taking their first psychology course. For students new to psychology, the course-specific meaning of terms such as *reinforcement, correlation, fMRI, attribution,* and perhaps even *cognition* will probably require some explanation, and terms such as *priming, negative reinforcement,* and *interposition* surely will! Even in upper division and graduate courses, there will undoubtedly be terms that students will be encountering for the first time. The more often you use such terms without defining and displaying them, the harder it is for students to follow the thread of your narrative, and the easier it is for them to lose interest in the lecture.

Ask for Feedback

How will you know if students don't immediately understand the terms you use? If you have previously invited students to raise a hand when they don't understand something in your presentation, a few might actually do so and ask for a definition or a spelling, but most will not. If you wonder whether students have understood a particular term, be on the safe side and take a moment to define and spell it. Be proactive in heading off misunderstanding and confusion about other things, too. Pause now and then to ask if anything you have said so far—including new terms—is unclear. When you see a few frowns, furrowed brows, or heads resting on palms, students are probably confused or are losing interest, so that would be a good time to stop and ask for more explicit feedback. (We say "when" you see these signs because even the most effective and experienced teachers have a few students who are likely to be bored, fall asleep, or leave class early; don't be too hard on yourself when you see these things in your own classroom—unless the entire class leaves!)

Don't just ask the perfunctory "Are there any questions?" question, however. Show your students you truly care how the class is going. Ask something like "OK, what terms have I used that you don't understand?" or "What questions do you have at this point?" or "Is all this making sense to you?" or "Am I going too fast? Too slow?" Or ask a "clicker" question about the content. You could pair this with think-pair-share, by having students choose an answer, then discuss their answer with a neighbor, and answer the question again. "Unless we succeed regularly in inviting students to reveal their misunderstandings and confusion, we are likely to overlook their lapses in understanding. Feedback from students is crucial to improving their learning, our designs, and our teaching" (Wiggins & McTighe, 1998, p. 175).

Provide Plenty of Examples

In addition to defining and spelling key terms, concepts, principles, and phenomena, be sure to illustrate them with at least one, and preferably several, examples or analogies. So if you are presenting material on homeostasis, give a couple of examples of homeostatic processes, such as the body's efforts to maintain constant levels of temperature or blood sugar. Then, to make the concept even clearer, you could point out that the homeostatic process is similar to the action of a thermostat-and-furnace system that maintains constant temperature in a house. By including lots of examples, analogies, metaphors, and similes, you not only hold your students' attention; you make the material easier to understand. This is particularly true if the examples, analogies, metaphors, and similes are vivid, offbeat, funny, and relevant to students' life experiences (Center for Teaching Excellence, 1999; Tozer, 1992; Zakrajsek, 1998). One instructor we know told his students about a line of ants marching along his kitchen floor and used the image as a memorable example of the common fate principle of perceptual organization. The instructor's resource manuals that accompany most psychology text-books usually offer excellent examples that you can sprinkle into your lectures to clarify and enliven even the most difficult concepts.

Incorporate into each class session at least one example or demonstration that you truly enjoy (Davis, 2009). Students will respond to your enthusiasm; many former students have told us that it was our "weird" examples that stuck in their minds and helped them to understand and remember important material and retrieve the information during exams.

Emphasize Linkages

It is easier for students to pay attention to what you are saying if they can easily see how the topic you are covering is related to the rest of the material and to the rest of the course (McTighe, 2010). Help them to see the "big picture" by displaying a brief overview of each day's presentation on a blackboard, PowerPoint slide, or a handout so that students can easily refer to it throughout the session. The overview need be no more than a list of the main topics in your class outline. See Chapter 6 for a discussion of how such advance organizers can be used to help students link new information to what they have already learned.

Emphasize linkages in your class presentations, too. Point out how each new topic you discuss is related to those covered previously or to topics yet to come. To take just one example, a lecture on brain chemistry is likely to be a lot more interesting to the average student if you describe its role in creating the effects of drugs ranging from alcohol and caffeine to marijuana and cocaine as well as of drugs for treating mental disorders. Highlighting linkages in every class session can help students to perceive your class presentations—and your course—as a coherent whole rather than a laundry list of unrelated topics.

Practice, Practice, Practice

We would all like our lectures and other class activities to come across to students as smooth and fascinating, full of spontaneous stories, memorable examples, and elegant transitions, delivered by a professor who uses notes as a reminder, not a script. Approximating this ideal can take years of experience, but even one dry run can improve your performance considerably (Davis, 2009). As your audience, use a video camera or a willing friend or relative. If you make a video, review it and focus on any mannerisms, vocal patterns, dysfluencies (e.g., uhmmms and ahs), or repetitive words or phrases (e.g., "ya know?" or "OK?") that might be distracting or annoying to listeners. Then try it again and see if you can improve on the things you didn't like the first time. You might never get yourself to stop saying "OK?" but the practice won't have been wasted. You will be amazed at how much easier it is to present information in class when it is not the first time you tried it.

Ending Your Class

Keep track of time as you teach, and when about five minutes remain, bring each class to an organized end by summarizing its key points or asking the students to do so (Davis, 2009). Don't hesitate to generate some curiosity about your next class by offering a "teaser" about something it will contain. When students hear that "Next time, we'll find out how many of you are colorblind," or "On Friday you'll have a chance to figure out which parenting style you grew up with," you can be sure a lot of them will be in class.

In other words, organize the end of class as carefully as you organize the rest of it. Otherwise, you might be in the midst of presenting important material just as the class ends, when few students are likely to be paying much attention. They watch the time, too, and many will already have started packing up to leave. You can minimize this tendency, and the noise it creates, by nipping it in the bud. The first time you encounter the beginnings of "anticipatory departure behavior" (ADB), get everyone's attention and explain that ADB is annoying to you and disruptive to other students. Explain, too, that there is no need for ADB because you promise never to continue lecturing beyond the end of class period. Gentle reminders about this plan in the next class or two are usually all it takes to eliminate the problem.

Lecturing Styles: Presentation versus Performance

Some teachers draw a distinction between lecturing styles focused on presentation versus performance (Short & Martin, 2011). The goal of the presentation style is to impart the maximum amount of information, whereas the performance style is designed to engage and motivate the audience. The two styles differ in terms of visual and oral presentation, degree of audience interaction, personal references, humor, and controversy. In one study of these two styles, students were exposed to lectures in each format. In the presentation-style lecture, PowerPoint slides were full of information, the instructor behaved in a formal manner, and the only audience participation occurred at the end, when the instructor asked for questions. The instructor provided no personal examples or anecdotes, used no humor, and avoided controversial topics. In the performance-style lecture, the same instructor was informal, put only a few key points on each PowerPoint slide, provided personal examples, led activities that created student–instructor interaction, used humor when appropriate, and presented controversial topics designed to grab students' attention. Afterward, students were asked to give ratings of their interest in the topics presented and later were tested over the concepts. The performance lecture not only engaged the students more, but the students actually learned more. The results of this study highlight the fact that the value of lectures can depend on how they are delivered; they can be effective pedagogical tools or gateways to boredom.

Online Considerations

Most online courses contain a lecture component—in fact, we would argue that the lecture component in an online course is more important than in a face-to-face class. Some synchronous courses require students to be online during the lecture component of the course so they are able to ask questions and make comments as the lecture proceeds. Unfortunately, many online courses offer no more than lectures that have been recorded during the teacher's face-to-face class, or a voiceover that accompanies PowerPoint slides. While some type of lecture component is usually necessary to impart basic information, it should not be the only way teachers teach online students.

Some blended courses have students come to class only for the lectures and engage in the other aspects of the course on their own. In the "flipped" classroom, the lectures are presented online and are to be viewed before the students come to the face-to-face component of the course. This system allows students to more knowledgably participate in active learning opportunities in class. Harvard physics professor Eric Mazur has used this system for many years and has found that it results in up to twice as much retention of course material compared to standard classroom lecturing (Renner, 2013). Other institutions have reported similar results (Berrett, 2012b; Gray Wilson, 2013; Loftus, 2013). In fact, online lectures allow the professor to "lecture better," because those lectures can be edited and polished to improve their quality (Hill, 2013).

Each module in our totally online course includes three 10-minute mini-lectures. They are short because we know that our students have limited time and attentional resources, and that they might not retain as much information if they were to listen to a 30-minute lecture without the opportunity to interact. Regardless of length, the lecture aspect should be only part of the course. There should also be activities such as group projects, journal writing, and other ways to encourage students to actively engage with the material and each other.

Promoting Active Learning

The concept of active learning gained popularity in the early 1990s following publication of Bonwell and Eisen's (1991) seminal book by that name. While the term is used less frequently today, the basic idea remains, that is, that instructors should incorporate into the classroom ways for the students to engage with the material rather than just passively listening to lectures. "There is a big difference between hearing and learning" (Svinicki & McKeachie, 2014, p. 191). Bonwell and Eisen (1991) described active learning as anything in which students (a) do something other than watching and listening, (b) work on skill development rather than just try to absorb information, (c) are required to engage in higher-order thinking about course material (e.g., "What does it mean?" rather than just "What am I supposed to remember?"), and (d) have a chance to explore the ways course material relates to their own attitudes and values. In other words, classes that incorporate active learning focus on students' learning, not the teacher's teaching (Cherney, 2011).

Many books and articles describe research evidence for the effectiveness of active learning techniques and provide suggestions for how teachers can incorporate them into their classrooms. You can promote active learning in a virtually endless number of ways. Some of the most common and basic examples include assigning small-group problem-solving tasks; setting up classroom debates; asking students to write and discuss "one-minute essays" about a particular topic (e.g., "What would the world look like if you lacked depth perception?"); and having students respond to a "clicker" question based on the main point of the previous 15 minutes of your lecture (Heward, 1997).

Students tend to enjoy active learning experiences and show special interest in courses that incorporate them (Davis, 2009; Moran, 2000; Murray, 2000). Active learning methods help students to go beyond memorizing isolated facts, think more deeply about course material, consider how new material relates to what they already know, and apply what they have learned to new and different situations. This kind of more elaborate thinking about course material also makes it easier to remember that material. Studies of students in elementary schools, high schools, community colleges, and universities have found that active learning methods are followed by better test performance and greater class participation as compared with passive instructional techniques (Brelsford, 1993; Cherney, 2011; Chu, 1994; Davis, 2009; Hake, 1998; Kellum, Carr, & Dozier, 2001; Kerr & Payne, 1994; Meyers & Jones, 1993; Short & Martin, 2011; Svinicki & McKeachie, 2014).

Some active learning techniques, such as "think-pair-share," are relatively easy to incorporate. You simply pause after presenting new material and pose a problem or multiple choice question related to that material. Students first choose the answer they think is correct and then compare their answer—and the reasoning behind it—with that of the person sitting next to them. This consultation process helps more students discover which answer is correct and also to understand why the correct answer is correct when you reveal and discuss it.

Other techniques, such as in-class debates or role-playing activities, are more time consuming and might be more difficult to organize and carry off successfully. Our advice is to start slowly, trying out short, easy active learning activities at first, then progress to more elaborate ones as you gain experience and confidence in using them.

We present ideas for active learning methods later in this chapter, but there are other valuable resources, as well, including a journal titled *Active Learning in Higher Education,* instructor resource manuals that accompany most major psychology textbooks, and a number of activities handbooks for psychology (Benjamin & Lowman, 1981; Benjamin et al., 1999; Buffington, 1996; Makosky et al., 1990; Makosky et al., 1987; Slife, 2001; Ware & Johnson, 2000a, 2000b, 2000c). Ideas for active learning that other psychology instructors have used with success in their classrooms are also available in *Teaching of Psychology* (the official journal of the Society for the Teaching of Psychology) and in "Teaching Tips" (a regular column featured in *The Observer,* the official newsletter of the Association for Psychological Science). Blogs and forums focused on teaching psychology, such as Psychwatch (www.psychwatch.com/), PsychTeach (psychteacher@list.kennesaw.edu), and the Society for the Teaching of Psychology Web site (http://teachpsych.org/), have discussions and/or resources on active learning techniques for specific courses. You can also consult other, more detailed presentations on active learning (e.g., Bean, 2011; Bonwell & Eison, 1991; Meyers & Jones, 1993; Silberman, 1996).

Remember that active learning techniques need not totally replace your traditional teaching approaches. Instead, as suggested earlier, you can use them to create variety and a change of pace so that every class session features portions in which students become participants, not just spectators (Shulman, 2003). In accordance with the segmented lecture format discussed earlier, some instructors organize their lectures into 10-minute "lecturettes" (Jenkins, 1992), each of which is separated from the next by some type of active learning experience, such as a few minutes of small-group or individual work on some problem or task. As the students work, the teacher walks around the classroom, answering questions, making comments, and the like, before reconvening the whole group for the next "lecturette."

In the flipped classroom discussed earlier, the active learning aspects of the course become the focus of the classroom time, because students are expected to have watched or listened to lectures or presentations on their own beforehand (Fulton, 2012; Khan, 2012; Wilson, 2013). Remember, though, that employing active learning techniques does not guarantee that students will learn the material. The teacher has to make sure that students know the purpose of each activity and become engaged in making connections between that activity and what they have already learned (McTighe, 2010).

Some students may at first resist active learning methods because these activities violate their expectations about what is supposed to happen in the classroom, but as noted earlier, most come to enjoy them, and are likely to learn and retain more from them than from more passive educational experiences (Bonwell & Eison, 1991; Cherney, 2011).

Conducting Memorable Demonstrations

Classroom demonstrations offer a particularly useful way to illustrate a wide variety of psychological concepts, principles, and phenomena. For example, a video of children failing a conservation task can make the principle of conservation come alive for students, just as seeing or hearing an interview with a hospitalized patient can give bipolar disorder a human face and voice. Although demonstrations can be vivid and dramatic, they do not automatically promote active learning. Many demonstrations, such as those just mentioned, are fascinating, but they leave students in the role of passive observers, so they might not be as memorable as they could be.

With some creative adjustments, however, almost any demonstration can become an active learning opportunity. In fact, we think that demonstrations are among the easiest and most enjoyable of all active learning techniques. Consider that interview with a mental patient. Instead of telling students that they are about to hear someone who has been diagnosed as bipolar, you could preview the tape by telling students that they will be asked to decide, based on their DSM-5 handout, which diagnosis they think the patient should receive and why. At the end of the interview, the class can vote on a diagnosis, and in the following discussion, students can describe the specific behaviors that led to their decision. Compared to simply presenting the interview, this procedure is virtually guaranteed to produce deeper cognitive processing of the interview content and more elaborate consideration of what it conveyed. Similarly, if you are lecturing on obedience, you could demonstrate its power by asking a student to make a funny face or take off a shoe. But how much more memorable it would be if you asked the entire class to stand, turn in a circle, jump up and down, or engage in some other pointless activity! This version of the demonstration is not only more memorable for having given everyone a personal experience with obedience, but makes it impossible for anyone to think, "I wouldn't have done that."

There are more opportunities than you might think to use active learning demonstrations. Web sites associated with many psychology textbooks are filled with ideas and detailed instructions for conducting active learning demonstrations. The APA and the APS have Web sites devoted to ideas for use in specific psychology courses, and many of the references mentioned earlier in relation to active learning provide information for classroom demonstrations. More general tips for using active learning demonstrations can be found in journals such as *Active Learning in Higher Education, College Teaching, The Teaching Professor, The National Teaching & Learning Forum,* as well as the Society for the Teaching of Psychology's journal, *Teaching of Psychology.* Finally, don't forget to ask your more experienced colleagues to tell you about the active learning demonstrations that they have found useful.

A word of caution, however: always practice every demonstration before you try it in class for the first time. Even procedures that seem simple and foolproof on paper can be complex and tricky in practice, and it is much less costly (and embarrassing) to discover this in the company of friends and colleagues than to squander time and a teaching opportunity in the classroom. This point was underscored some years ago when an introductory psychology teacher we know tried to present an unusually vivid demonstration of the application of stimulus control, an operant conditioning principle. The plan was for a police officer from the local canine unit to bring his dog to class and put the animal through its paces, including obeying commands to "attack" and "stop." Unfortunately the officer's work schedule left no opportunity to rehearse the demonstration. So when the officer stood on one side of the stage of our colleague's lecture hall and commanded his dog to attack a student "suspect" who had volunteered to stand on the other side of the stage wearing an arm protector, there was, shall we say, a chance for unforeseen complications. The plan was for the officer to give the "stop" command before the dog reached the "suspect," and though the dog tried to stop, he slid across the polished hardwood stage, reached the frightened student, and began to gnaw violently on the arm protector until he was called off. A dry run of this demonstration would have revealed the slippery floor problem; as it was, the demonstration was memorable, but for the wrong reasons.

Online Considerations

Many blended classrooms and flipped classrooms make use of class time to incorporate demonstrations of course content. Though such interactive demonstrations are not possible in an online environment, instructors who teach both face-to-face and online can videotape classroom demonstrations in their face-to-face class and use it in their online course. Students can also be asked to try out some demonstrations on their own. Unfortunately, though, the online teaching environment does not normally allow for real-time classroom demonstrations that involve all students.

Answering and Asking Questions

Another easy and obvious way to promote active learning in the classroom is to ask students questions and to encourage them to ask questions of you. Yet, in the average college classroom, regardless of course level or section size, little class time is devoted to the important process of asking and answering course-related questions (Weimer, 1989). Many psychology teachers are so focused on covering a certain amount of material during each class session that they are hesitant to interrupt their lectures by asking students questions. Further, these teachers' verbal and nonverbal behavior tends to send the message that they don't have time to stop for questions from their students, either. Even those who do pose questions, and who invite students to ask questions, might not generate the kind of lively exchange they are after. Usually, the problem lies in how they question their students and how they respond when students question them. In this section, we highlight ways you can handle both of these processes in ways that can enliven the classroom atmosphere and help students learn.

Answering Students' Questions

The way you deal with your students' questions can solidify or undermine your relationship with them. If you respond with impatient or perfunctory answers, students will get the message that you don't care much about their learning and that they shouldn't ask any more questions. Assuming that this is not what you want to convey, we suggest that you let students know, on the first day of class and frequently throughout the term, that you are happy to answer their questions. Then, when someone raises a hand to ask a question, recognize the person (calling the student by name, if possible) and listen carefully to the entire question to be sure you understand it. Don't interrupt with an answer that presumes you know what the student is getting at; you might end up answering the wrong question!

Provide verbal and nonverbal reinforcement during the question. Establish eye contact, nod with understanding as the question is asked, and perhaps move closer to where the student is sitting so as to hear better. Don't look at your notes or fiddle with the computer or gaze out the window. Let the student and the rest of the class know that the question has your full attention (Goodwin et al., 1981).

Next, repeat or paraphrase the question (Davis, 2009). This step is crucial not only to ensure that you have understood the question, but especially in larger classrooms, that everyone else has heard and understood it, too. Students will lose interest in the proceedings if you are answering questions—or responding to comments—that they did not hear. Like listening to one end of a cell phone conversation, this experience can be frustrating and annoying.

If the question is particularly interesting or thoughtful, say so, and thank the student for asking it (Davis, 2009). Finally, if you can answer the question, do so. When you are finished, ask if the answer was clear and offer students the opportunity to ask follow-up questions.

Be prepared, too, for questions you can't answer. All psychology teachers get such questions, and how you respond when you are stumped can be just as important to good student–faculty relations as when you have a ready answer. Above all, relax. Your students do not expect you to have a full and complete answer to every possible question about every aspect of psychological knowledge, especially if you are at the beginning of your teaching career. Stay calm, don't demean students for stumping you, and don't try to make up an answer. If you do, your students will eventually see through the pretense and lose respect for you. (One of us had a professor whose students occasionally entertained themselves in class by asking questions about nonexistent psychological theories, just to listen to the answers he would fabricate.) We suggest that, instead, you deal with tough questions in four steps.

First, admit that you don't know the answer (or don't have much of an answer), and reward the questioner for asking the question (Davis, 2009). We typically say something like "Wow, that's a great question. I don't think I know the answer to that one." Second, ask if anyone else has any idea what the answer might be. This step conveys respect for your students, in that it suggests that someone in the room might know more about a particular topic than you do. (In some cases, this is actually true!) Third, promise to research the question and report back to the class during the next session, via e-mail, or on the course Web site. Fourth, keep your promise. Post the results of your research or begin the next class with a summary of what you have found. Your students will appreciate your efforts more than you can imagine.

You might also want to respond to particularly intriguing questions with the suggestion that the entire class should seek answers, too. However, we advise against making this a formal assignment because students tend to perceive such assignments as punishment for asking questions.

Asking Questions

We have suggested that you pose questions during your lectures—beginning on day one—as a way of creating variety and promoting active learning, but what if no one responds? If this possibility is a worry, you can minimize the problem by phrasing your questions clearly and carefully and then giving your students enough time to (a) come up with their answers and (b) work up the courage to raise a hand. Like teachers in general, most psychology faculty tend to allow only a second or two of "wait time" before answering their own question. Waiting any longer creates what seems to them to be an awkward silence. However, such a short wait time can be counterproductive. It implicitly tells students that you don't really expect them to answer your questions, and eventually they might not even try (Andersen, 1986). If you give students about five seconds to think about your questions—maybe six or seven seconds for especially profound or complex questions—they are far less likely to view your questions as rhetorical and far more likely to come up with good answers (Tobin, 1987). Even some of your "slower" students might participate more, simply because you have given them sufficient time to think of an answer.

While silently counting off the seconds during the waiting period, let your students know you want to hear from them by scanning the room with a hopeful look and making eye contact all around. If no hands go up, be ready to call on those whose facial expression indicates they might want to reply. (Say something like, "Margo, you look as though you might want to answer this one.") If you have no takers after 7 to 10 seconds, it is probably time to rephrase or simplify the question.

Sometimes it is the way we pose a question that makes it so hard to answer. Questions that are clear and straightforward tend to draw the quickest and most interesting replies. So ask "How might we apply Bandura's ideas about modeling to teach social skills to autistic children?" rather than "What do you think of Bandura's idea about modeling?" In other words, give your students a clue about the focus of your question rather than asking them to figure out what you are driving at. If you ask "What is the most telling criticism of evolutionary theories of human social behavior?" the students have to guess what you think it is. If you want them to think about the issue, ask something like "What do you see as the biggest problem with using evolutionary theory to explain human social behavior?"

Overall, the more questions you sprinkle throughout the lecture, the more carefully you phrase them, and the more patient (up to a point) you are in waiting for answers, the more responsive your students are likely to be. It will not take many class sessions of such questioning techniques before your students will be comfortable with your questions and willing to answer them.

Online Considerations

One of the drawbacks of the online-only classroom is that it does not allow for spontaneous questions and comments from students. True, an online course must allow students to ask questions, often in a Q & A forum posted on the home page, and it should encourage students to answer questions posed by fellow students. But the answer to questions such as "Where can I find instructions for the group project?", an answer that could be quickly and easily provided to every student in a face-to-face classroom, can become a communication problem in an online course. Thus, navigation of the online course must be made clear to students and instructors must be diligent in monitoring the Q & A forum to make sure that student questions are answered quickly. Also, students who ask questions in face-to-face classes may not do so in online classes, often because they feel more isolated than they do even in a very large face-to-face classroom. This problem can be addressed by creating small groups in which all students have to interact. Many instructors find that they must work harder in the online environment to encourage comments and questions among students and from students to teachers.

Stimulating Class Discussions

Ideally, your class presentations will encourage students to think more deeply about course material and make them want to discuss it with you and their classmates. Many students feel more connected to the course when they are given an opportunity to engage in class discussions. Stimulating beneficial class discussions requires accomplishing five main tasks (Svinicki & McKeachie, 2014). These include (1) helping students prepare for discussion, (2) eliciting and maintaining participation in the discussion,

(3) facilitating the discussion so as to make it productive for learning, (4) helping students learn and practice the process of civil discourse, and (5) listening to the students supportively to make the class a safe place to express ideas. With these tasks in mind, we offer the following guidelines for setting up and conducting successful class discussions (see also Brookfield & Preskill, 1999; Davis, 2009; Forsyth, 2003; Neff & Weimer, 1989).

First, students must be prepared for class discussions. Although spontaneous discussion is often a good indication of student interest, students need to learn something about the material and think about it enough to avoid having "discussions" become an exercise in sharing ignorance. Let your students know about a planned discussion during the previous class session, and remind them about the required pre-discussion readings, Internet research, or other assignments that they should complete. Completing these assignments will make it much easier for students to participate in and get the most out of the upcoming discussion. You might also hand out a list of questions or issues that will frame the discussion scheduled for the next class. Reading through this list allows students to begin considering their views on the discussion topic and to see the relevance of what they are being asked to do in preparation. Some instructors even ask students to organize their thoughts in a "one-minute paper" or other brief in-class writing assignment immediately before the discussion begins (Davis, 2009; Lang, 2008; Svinicki & McKeachie, 2014). Interteaching, which we discuss later in this chapter, uses a more structured version to prepare students for discussion.

It goes without saying that when it comes to scheduled discussions, you should be way ahead of your students (Cashin & McKnight, 1989; Ewen, 1989; Lang, 2008). Develop a plan for jump-starting the discussion (Davis, 2009; Svinicki & McKeachie, 2014). One instructor we know asks students on the first day of class to silently reflect on two questions: "What makes a great discussion?" and "What kills a discussion?" (Multhaup, 2008). Students then pair up to discuss their responses, after which the whole class has a general discussion. This activity effectively begins the course with a class discussion and acts as a gateway to discussions during later class sessions (Davis, 2009; Lang, 2008).

One way to begin a discussion is to create a classroom experience, such as showing a short course-relevant video (e.g., a TED talk) and focus discussion on that video (Svinicki & McKeachie, 2014). One of the authors uses TED videos in her positive psychology class and they never fail to start a lively discussion. To help students focus on particular aspects of a presentation, provide a handout that lists a few questions about the important content.

You could also focus discussion on a case study that you have asked students to analyze. Another way of stimulating discussion is to ask students to engage in a short role play in which they illustrate a course-related topic such as a particular personality trait, interview method, leadership style, parenting practice, or whatever. Still another effective discussion starter is to ask a provocative question or describe an extreme position about a course-related topic (e.g., "What would happen if we outlawed all tests of mental ability for college admission?" or "What would you say to a state governor who proposed that people should have to take parenting classes and get a license before they could legally have children?"). Students are usually eager to respond to such hypothetical questions (Davis, 2009; Svinicki & McKeachie, 2014).

In fact, discussion starters like these might be so successful that your main problem will be to ensure that the discussion remains focused and productive. To facilitate the discussion without letting it degenerate into a classroom version of the *Jerry Springer Show,* let your students know in advance about whatever rules you intend to apply. For example, will students have to raise a hand and be recognized before speaking? You also need to decide what role you will play in the discussion. Will you be the moderator? Will you take a position on topics? Your role will depend on the type of class you teach, the academic level of your students, their experience with discussion, and your personality.

For students to engage in a genuine discussion, they need to feel that your classroom is a safe place to express their ideas and convictions (Saville et al. 2012; Svinicki & McKeachie, 2014). Much will depend on your demeanor in class and students' level of interaction with their class-mates. However, students should be aware that there is no place in your class for racist, sexist, homophobic, or other ad hominem remarks. You should always be prepared to intervene to put a stop to any such remarks, but try to do so in a constructive way. Unless the remark is simply too extreme to tolerate, we suggest that you not directly punish the offending student. Instead, try to use the incident to move the discussion forward. For example, you might say to the class, "You know, X probably wasn't aware of it, but that comment was actually a pretty good example of the kind of (say) homophobia that makes life more difficult for gays and lesbians. Given the prevalence of those views, what do you think it says about sexual orientation as a choice versus a biological predisposition?"

Whether a discussion was planned or arose in response to something you or a student said in class, encourage all your students to participate by rewarding those who speak first. Maintain eye contact and nod your head as they talk, rephrase what they have said so that the entire class can hear, and then ask the class to react to what they say. Now and then, you might also want to offer interim summaries of what has been said so far as a way to generate further comments and reactions (Cashin & McKnight, 1989; Davis, 2009; Ewen, 1989). Once things get rolling, though, don't feel obligated to respond to every student's comment—or at least leave plenty of wait time before doing so. If you don't dominate the situation, your students will eventually begin to talk directly to each other. If you seek to fill brief silences with a mini-lecture, your students will soon get the message that this is entirely your show, and the discussion might dry up (Brookfield & Preskill, 1999; Cashin & McKnight, 1989; Ewen, 1989).

As one teacher put it, your ideal role in a discussion is to discreetly employ initiating, clarifying, and probing questions rather than make authoritative statements or ask rhetorical questions, to guide the flow of the discussion toward its intended purposes and to enhance the value of the experience for members. You also should "generate a non-evaluative, non-threatening environment conducive to a free and open interchange of ideas" (Fisch, 2001, p. 6). In other words, challenge your students during discussions, but don't make them feel threatened (Cashin & McKnight, 1989; Svinicki & McKeachie, 2014).

We have talked about organizing discussion sessions for the class as a whole, but it is sometimes easier to get all students involved if discussions take place, or at least begin, in smaller groups (Davis, 2009; Erickson & Strommer, 1991; Lang, 2008). Indeed, some research suggests that students see small-group discussions as stimulating the highest level of critical thinking (Hamann, Pollock, & Wilson, 2012). Ask students to spend some time discussing a topic, question, case, or issue in groups of three to six, and then ask a representative from each group to summarize for the entire class that group's answer, position, or conclusions. You can then invite reactions from other groups via individual comments or their own representatives' reports, which might support or conflict with what has already been said.

When it is time to end the discussion, bring it to a close a few minutes before the end of the class period. This will give you time to summarize the most important points raised, to clear up any misconceptions or misinformation that might have been created, and to suggest additional reading or Web-based research that will help students follow up on what they have learned.

Online Considerations

A good online course incorporates student discussion. In fact, students report that online discussions provide a better forum than face-to-face discussion for expressing their thoughts (Hamann et al., 2012). There are other advantages to online discussions, too. They "overcome barriers of time and space; provide a risk-free environment that encourages a frank exchange;

minimize the potential for confrontation; neutralize status indicators and social distractors; and broaden the range of feedback by incorporating peer-to-peer exchange" (Warren Trufant, 2003, p. 2).

Some online discussions consist of nothing more than having students post to a discussion board and requiring or encouraging other students to respond. You can facilitate such small-group discussion by organizing course "peer groups" made up of four to six students that respond to each other's posts. (For a discussion of rubrics to evaluate online asynchronous discussions, see Penny & Murphy, 2009.) Because some students might plagiarize material in these discussions by cutting and pasting their responses from other sources, it is important to stress that all posts need to be original (Jones, 2013a).

Threaded discussions centered around a specific topic can encourage critical thinking when instructors "start where students are—choose topics that relate to their knowledge level and experience; start with non-threatening topics that will not discourage participation; acknowledge the development of "group" personalities and dynamics; model diagnostic questions, appropriate comments and prompt feedback; create scenarios that relate the topic to real circumstances; combine discussion with peer-editing activities to enhance collaboration; and encourage students to view postings as "works in progress" rather than final products" (Warren Trufant, 2003, p. 4).

Some online courses require students to meet synchronously to discuss course content. This is possible because most online courses include student chat rooms (through Collaborate or other conferencing software) and/or social forums. The chat rooms allow students to meet synchronously to discuss course material and group projects. The social forum is for non-academic interactions—allowing students to express outside interests and talk with each other, much as they would before or after a face-to-face class.

● ● ● ● ●

Assigning Student Presentations

Many psychology teachers presume that they are the main source of knowledge in the classroom, but there are many ways students can learn on their own and from each other. Classroom presentations not only serve as an alternative source of course information, but stimulate students to delve more deeply into a topic than they might otherwise have done. Student presenters also get practice and develop skill at public speaking in a relatively nonthreatening atmosphere (Ashcroft & Foreman-Peck, 1994).

To help your students do the best job possible, you might want to provide a set of grading standards similar to the paper-grading rubrics discussed in Chapter 5. If you distribute the rubric when you announce the student presentation assignments, it will be more likely to create the kinds of presentations you are after. Typical rubrics include criteria such as the quality of the content presented, the effectiveness of the delivery style, degree of audience involvement, and appropriate use of multimedia resources. The rubric should provide specific illustrations of exemplary, minimally acceptable, and unacceptable presentations. On the audience involvement dimension, for example, an unacceptable performance in one rubric was defined as "put class members to sleep," whereas an exemplary performance was defined as "related the topic to the students' lives and used concrete examples, stories, quotes, and questions to involve the audience" (Wilson, 1999, p. 3). You can allow students considerable latitude in their choice of presentation topics, or you can create a more structured list.

In a large introductory psychology class, one teacher spends the first five minutes of a class session describing three concepts that the students have read about in their textbook (Bleske-Rechek, 2001). She then assigns one-third of the class to address each concept by forming small groups and spending some time coming up with a real-life situation that illustrates or demonstrates that concept. Each team then presents its results to the class. Instead of using a complex grading rubric, this instructor simply gives credit for student participation; the presentations themselves are ungraded. She reports that students put a lot of work into their presentations and that many of them are excellent.

●●●●●

Working with Small Groups

Small-group activities that lead to class presentations are but one example of collaborative and cooperative learning activities. *Collaborative learning* is a general term referring to group learning experiences that can range from peer tutoring and student–faculty research projects to short-term group work in class. *Cooperative learning* is a subtype of collaborative learning, and refers more specifically to activities in which 2 to 15 students work together toward a common goal (Cooper, Robinson, & McKinney, 1994; Halpern, 2000).

Here, we focus on the creation of cooperative learning groups, the collaborative learning format most commonly used by psychology faculty (Millis & Cottell, 1998). These groups can be formal or informal. Formal cooperative learning groups (sometimes called teams) spend all or part of an academic term working on an experiment, a survey, or some other long-term research or writing project. (For more information about using team-based learning (TBL), see Michaelson, Sweet & Parmelee, 2008.) Informal cooperative learning groups come together for shorter periods, sometimes for just a few minutes, to work together on a relatively simple assignment (Johnson et al., 1998b).

To be most successful, cooperative learning groups should have two main attributes. First, they should be structured so that the students must work together to do well on their assignment. This feature helps to promote an atmosphere in which there is no incentive for group members to compete with each other. Second, the groups should promote individual accountability, meaning that each member's contribution to the group's effort must be measurable. This second attribute minimizes the phenomenon known as social loafing.

It is also a good idea to constitute the groups so that they include members of both genders and are as heterogeneous as possible on ethnicity and other demographic variables (Halpern, 2000; Johnson et al., 1991; Millis & Cottell, 1998). When set up properly, cooperative learning groups give students the opportunity to address course material in a new and interesting way while providing valuable experience at working with others to achieve success. These groups also help students to develop the leadership, communication, and other social skills needed to function effectively in the context of a team. In this regard, encourage your students to discuss among themselves how the group is working (or not working), the nature of any problems they might be encountering, and how they can overcome those problems (Brown, 2000; Cooper et al., 1994; Halpern, 2000; Johnson, Johnson, & Smith, 1991, 1998a, 1998b; Millis & Cottell, 1998; Smith & MacGregor, 1998).

The effectiveness of cooperative learning in psychology classrooms is supported by hundreds of studies indicating that this teaching format results in higher achievement and more positive and supportive relationships among students than do competitive or individualistic learning (Fullilove & Treisman, 1990; Hsiung, 2012; Johnson et al., 1991, 1998a). A number of factors have been proposed to explain the apparent value of cooperative learning. For example, some students find it easier to learn when discussing course material with peers than when listening to a professor's lecture. Peers speak the same generational language, they are less threatening to each other in terms of power and status, and they might be more willing to reveal to one another what they don't understand. A supportive peer group atmosphere also offers a safe opportunity for students to check the validity of what they think they know, and to be corrected and taught by fellow students whose knowledge is more extensive.

These benefits do not magically appear simply because, like Linda Richman on *Saturday Night Live* shows of old, you ask students to "talk among yourselves" (Halpern, 2000; Johnson et al., 1991). To get the most from cooperative learning activities, you'll have to take an active role in planning and overseeing them. Here are some tips for doing so (Cooper et al., 1994).

First, if you are new to cooperative learning methods, start slowly. Make these methods just a small part of the total grade. For example, as described in Chapter 3, one of us typically sets up study groups on the second day of class and then asks these groups to get together that day to work on a simple, but graded, statistical problem. These same groups reconvene from time to time during the term to work on other graded assignments in class. These groups also make a presentation to the class in which they summarize and analyze a classic study in psychology, and for which group members receive a grade based on their part of the presentation.

Second, no matter how simple or complex the task you assign to groups, be sure to introduce it clearly. All too often, instructors think that they have described cooperative learning assignments in class only to be inundated afterward with requests to clarify the assignment. Worse, some groups think they understood the assignment, but did not, and so they work hard at completing the wrong task. To minimize both problems, we suggest that you describe each cooperative learning assignment orally, but also in a PowerPoint slide and/or handout that helps everyone understand precisely what they are to do, how they are to do it, what the product should be, and when the work is to be handed in or presented (Jenkins, 1992). Supplying your grading rubric should also help to explain your expectations. And be sure to link the group work to your course goals (Hansen, 2006).

Third, although some instructors see cooperative learning activities—especially those that occur during a class session—as an opportunity to take a break, the truth is that successful cooperative learning activities actually intensify student–faculty contact. As student groups work on their tasks, you should offer support by strolling around the room, answering procedural questions, monitoring progress, and keeping everyone on task (Halpern, 2000). Your hands-on involvement with cooperative learning groups increases the students' time on task and motivation, gives them more immediate feedback on progress, and provides a model for how to think about course material (Halpern, 2000).

Other sources provide further information on setting up effective cooperative learning activities and managing the problems that can arise from them (Brown, 2000: Hansen, 2006). One of the biggest of these problems is student resistance to the cooperative learning enterprise. For one thing, engaging in cooperative learning requires students to change their classroom role from passive observer to active participant. The same is true of other active learning methods, but cooperative learning groups also require students to prepare more extensively for certain classes and makes attendance at those classes less a personal choice than a community need. Moreover, participation in cooperative learning groups makes it difficult or impossible for some students to stay in the class background, as shyness or lack of interest might ordinarily lead them to do.

Cooperative learning activities also require students to abandon the idea that they are in competition with their peers; instead, they are expected to work with others for mutual benefit. Some highly competitive students find this aspect of cooperative learning especially distasteful. Although some students easily take to the idea of peer-to-peer learning and teaching, those who hold more traditional views of the teacher as the only source of knowledge in a course might find it difficult to accept the cooperative learning format as promoting real learning (MacGregor, 1990). With all this in mind, be sure that, in addition to carefully explaining to students what they are to do in each cooperative learning assignment, you describe the value of cooperative learning in general and why students are being asked to work in a group on this assignment. Let them know you understand that, for some, this will be a new and possibly jarring experience, but ask them to withhold judgment until they have tried working in a group format for a while. Also, be sure to let students know that students who study in cooperative learning groups outperform those who study individually on exams and homework (Hsiung, 2012).

Jigsaw

A special version of cooperative learning, called jigsaw, was developed by Elliot Aronson (1978) and later embellished by others (K. Smith, 2000). Its original purpose was to reduce racial prejudice by arranging for black and white students in newly integrated elementary school classrooms to work together and to create "mutual interdependence, where cooperation is required to earn an individual goal: good grades" (Perkins & Tagler, 2011, p. 195). In a jigsaw exercise, each member of a small work group gathers information that is needed by the entire group to solve a problem or complete some other task. As an "expert" in one particular area, each group member spends some time presenting information to the rest of the group, as well as listening as other members make their presentations. This arrangement makes every member of the group equally valuable, so the group's work cannot be dominated by any particular student or students. Further, even the quieter students must actively participate for the group to succeed.

For example, one of the authors assigns each of Stephen Chew's five study skills videos (www.youtube.com/playlist?list=PL85708E6EA236E3 DB) to five groups of students. In class, each group discusses the important concepts from the video they watched. Then the class reconvenes in *new* groups of five, each member of which had watched a different video. These new groups use information from all of the videos to decide on the important concepts necessary to develop good study skills. So for these groups to be successful, each member needs information from those who watched different videos, and each member must contribute his or her own knowledge. For more information about using jigsaw, visit www. jigsaw.org./.

Using Case Examples

Professors of business, law, medicine, and other professions have long used case examples as a main vehicle for helping their students learn and understand the implications of course material. Reading, analyzing, and discussing cases creates opportunities for students to engage in active learning and—when allowed to work in groups—in cooperative learning as well. Faculty in psychology use case studies, too, especially to illustrate material in personality and abnormal psychology courses, but cases are now also finding their place in many other courses. One introductory psychology instructor we know has incorporated case studies as an integral part of his class presentations on topics ranging from research methods and biological processes to learning, memory, and social psychology (Hendersen, 2002a). Some of these cases are really just standard lecture examples that he has expanded into "case-lets" or "mini-case studies." However, because they allow students to actively engage the example rather than just hearing about it in a lecture, these case studies can help make even large lecture sections more interactive (Hendersen, 2003).

Indeed, most psychology instructors use case studies to promote discussion of the topic a case illustrates, what it means, how representative it is, and what conclusions can (and cannot) be drawn from it. Case studies can be especially useful in the in-class portion of the flipped classroom (Herreid & Schiller, 2013). Some instructors read cases in class, then ask students to discuss them in a general session or in small groups. Others distribute a case study handout during one class session and ask students to be ready to discuss it during the next class. Some also include a list of study questions to help students think about the case, and might even require students to submit a memo summarizing their analysis of the case (Silverman & Welty, 1990). The memos can be collected and graded; doing so encourages students to spend the time necessary to read and analyze each case (Leonard et al., 2002). You will probably find that the more you ask students to do with cases, the more likely they will all have something to say when the cases are discussed in class.

To prepare yourself for these discussions, think about the case and recognize that you might have to summarize and synthesize differing interpretations of it. In fact, because students' views of a case can be so diverse, discussing cases in class has been described as "like bringing a scattered group of parachutists into contact from all the random places they have landed" (Boehrer & Linsky, 1990, p. 52). As with any class discussion, remember to encourage all students to participate. You can do this in relation to cases by asking open-ended questions and questions that do not have just one correct answer. Although you might begin by asking the class, say, how many employees worked at the factory described in a case study, if your ultimate goal is to help students understand differences among leadership styles, it might be more productive to ask questions such as, "Which of the supervisors did the maintenance staff like best, and why?" In other words, your questions should be designed to stimulate exploration of the meaning of the case, not just to demonstrate an ability to recall its facts (Silverman & Welty, 1990).

In deciding whether to use a case study activity at a particular point in your course, ask yourself, first, what the goal of the activity will be. Is it to familiarize students with a particular concept, principle, or phenomenon, to explore the causes of some phenomenon, or what? Once you have decided what student competencies you want to promote, it will be easier to decide on the structure and details of the case study activity (Leonard et al., 2002). For example, if your goal is to help students to think more deeply about theories of prejudice, you might ask them to read about the background of someone who has been convicted of a hate crime and then perhaps write about the biological, cognitive, and social factors that might have contributed to the person's attitudes and behaviors. If the goal is simply to underscore differences in parenting styles, you could read transcripts of interviews with parents then ask the class to say whether the parents are permissive, authoritarian, authoritative, or uninvolved, and why.

Select cases that seem most appropriate for meeting your objectives. You will find such cases included in instructor's resource manuals that accompany various psychology textbooks, and in many other sources, as well—including scholarly publications, newspaper articles, films, books, and, of course, the Internet (see also Dziegielewski, 2013; Meyer & Weaver, 2013; Oltmanns et al., 2012; The National Center for Case Study Teaching in Science Case Collection: Psychology, 2013; Rosenthal, 2002; Sacks, 1970, 1996). If no appropriate case studies are available, you might consider developing your own. For example, to help him conclude his introductory psychology course, the professor mentioned earlier created his own case study for use on the last day of class. It presents a science fiction writer's view of what psychology courses will look like in 50 years. The professor uses it to show students that psychology is a dynamic, constantly changing discipline. He also uses the case as a springboard for a class discussion about whether the discipline of psychology as we know it today will even exist in 50 years, and if so, what questions will have been answered and what questions will remain or emerge. Finally, to demonstrate how quickly psychology changes, he reads outdated information about human behavior and mental processes as presented in 50-year-old introductory psychology textbooks (Hendersen, 2002a).

You can even create fictional cases from your imagination or from bits and pieces of real cases. If you do fabricate any cases, or alter the details of real ones, be sure to let your students know about it. Case examples need not be real to be realistic or to illustrate and help students understand course material, but it is vital that students know whether they are reading about real examples, composites created from real examples, or fictional accounts that typify real phenomena. Be sure also that the cases you choose (or create) are short enough and sufficiently focused to permit your students to read and analyze them in the class time allotted. Finally, the cases should be written at a level that is appropriate for your students; that is, challenging, but not too complex (Leonard et al., 2002).

Finding, creating, and using case studies in class takes time and energy, but the results can be well worth the effort. Faculty who have done so report a wide range of benefits, such as helping students to identify and think about problems, evaluate possible solutions, and appreciate general principles that can be applied in other situations. Dealing with cases also enlivens the classroom atmosphere and enhances students' involvement with course material and with each other, all of which is especially valuable in large classes (Boehrer & Linsky, 1990; Hendersen, 2002a; Silverman & Welty, 1990).

Just-in-Time Teaching

The goal of linking students' out-of-class and in-class activities can be facilitated through *just-in-time teaching* (JiTT), also known as *preflights*, using preparatory Web-based assignments (Novak & Patterson, 2010). JiTT typically involves the instructor posting questions on the course Web site about the material to be presented during the next class session. Ideally, these questions are linked to the learning objectives for that unit, and rather than just asking for recall of memorized facts, the questions should require students to relate and apply course concepts and phenomena to their own experiences. The students are to post their responses on the Web site, thus providing the instructor with information about how well they have understood the concepts that are about to be discussed during the next class. The responses are usually due a few hours before the class meeting, providing instructors with enough time to alter or "tweak" their presentation to include more information about concepts that are still unclear to students while downplaying or deleting content that students already seem to understand well.

JiTT not only helps teachers tailor classroom presentations, but provides students with a measure of how well they understand the material, personalizes the information, and provides a link between new, upcoming information and previously presented concepts (Novak & Patterson, 2010).

To be truly effective, information compiled from JiTT assignments should be presented in class, with good responses displayed and acknowledged. Student responses to the posted questions should also account for a small portion of their total grade, because non-graded assignments often are not completed.

Interteaching

Research suggests that student engagement is a key to success in academic endeavors (e.g., Kahu, 2013; Kuh et al., 2008; Miller et al., 2011; Taylor & Parsons, 2011 see also the *Journal for Student Engagement in Higher Education*). Engagement is defined by what students actually do—that is, how much time is spent on academic activities—rather than by their attitudes toward academics. Three types of engagement appear to have a positive impact on student success, namely time on task, interaction with peers, and interaction with faculty (Saville, 2011) (see our discussion of these topics in Chapter 6). All three can be affected by your teaching style, and one way to adjust that style to promote engagement is to adopt a set of procedures known as *interteaching* (Boyce & Hineline, 2002).

Interteaching involves creating a preparation guide for each of the assigned readings. The guide typically includes 8–12 items and one or more questions related to each item. The idea is to guide the students' reading and get them to think about the material before they come to class. During the first one-third of the next class session, the teacher delivers a "clarifying lecture" aimed at explaining anything that students might have found confusing during the previous class and providing supplemental information as well. Next, pairs of students go over the guides that they prepared for the class, comparing answers and discussing the assigned topic while the teacher walks around the classroom guiding discussion and answering questions. Toward the end of class the students fill out a record sheet in which they note how well the discussion went and what material is still unclear to them. The teacher collects these record sheets and uses them to create the clarifying lecture for the next class (Boyce & Hineline, 2002; Saville, 2011, 2013; Saville et al., 2011).

Interteaching also involves graded testing of students' knowledge at least five times per semester (often, the lowest score can be dropped). In some cases, teachers also award "quality points" based on how each student's discussion partner answered certain exam questions (Boyce & Hineline, 2002; Saville, 2011). This method is designed to increase cooperation among the partners.

Though relatively new, the use of interteaching has been associated with increased student engagement, higher academic performance, and greater student enjoyment of the course (Saville, 2011; Saville et al., 2011).

⬤ ⬤ ⬤ ⬤ ⬤

Problem-Based Learning

Yet another way to promote student engagement is to base at least some of your classes on problem-based learning (PBL). PBL is based on the assumptions "that human beings evolved as individuals who are motivated to solve problems, and that problem solvers will seek and learn whatever knowledge is needed for successful problem solving" (Svinicki & McKeachie, 2014, p. 208). In other words, PBL builds on students' natural curiosity when presented with a problem and takes advantage of self-directed learning. PBL differs from the use of case studies primarily in how the material is presented. Whereas case studies are presented in advance and students often have time to prepare, PBL presents a problem situation that students are immediately asked to solve. Specifically, they have to gather more information about the problem, analyze its important components, generate and evaluate a range of solutions, and recommend a course of action (Azer, 2011; Davis, 2009; Svinicki & McKeachie, 2014). Typically, students work in teams because there is some evidence that the collaborative aspect of the exercise is most vital for student learning (Yew & Schmidt, 2012).

So in a PBL exercise, students teach themselves and their peers as they grapple with the problem and decide what information they need and how to gather that information to solve the problem. The instructor's job is to support and guide the independent learning process. Some medical schools have organized their entire curricula around PBL, but for most psychology teachers, PBL is used as one of many alternative active learning techniques. It takes some effort to do so, because using PBL effectively requires that you identify and describe a problem that is clearly tied to course content and objectives and that can be solved in multiple ways with differing consequences, all in a reasonably short period of time.

Online Considerations

Many of the active learning techniques discussed here can be adapted for group projects in an online course. For example, in the personality unit in an online introductory psychology course, student groups can learn about projective tests by analyzing responses to a "Draw a Person" test. Alternatively, each group member can be assigned a different short reading that must be assimilated by the entire group in order to write a short paper or answer questions about a particular topic. Some online courses require student groups to make presentations via collaborative software, synchronously, so the entire class can comment on them. In other words, teaching an online course should not prevent you from incorporating active learning components. We discuss more specific online activities in Chapter 7.

● ● ● ● ●

Service-Learning

Service-learning is an approach to teaching that integrates community service with academic study to enrich learning, teach civic responsibility, and strengthen communities (Fiske, 2001; National Service-Learning Clearinghouse, 2003). Among the advantages attributed to service-learning are that it allows students to learn by joining theory with experience and thought with action; to see the relevance of an academic subject in the real world; to do important and necessary work while increasing civic involvement; and to encounter a richer context for learning—including cross-cultural experiences and preparation for careers (Brooks & Smith, 2011; Cooper, 2003; Enos & Troppe, 1996). Students still engage in typical academic activities—they go to class, take exams, and write papers, but they also work with members of the community in activities related to course content (Khanna, 2011). For example, one instructor had her introductory psychology honors seminar students work with members of the local Boys and Girls Club. The students observed or used the concepts discussed in class, so when they were studying learning principles, they tried to improve youngsters' behavior via positive reinforcement. In a psychology of aging course, the instructor arranged for students to visit homebound elderly people. He found that the service-learning experience resulted in far more positive attitudes toward the elderly and a more thoughtful orientation toward the students' own aging process (Marchese, 1997).

Service-learning is often a small component of a course, but it can be one of its core aspects. To be effective, though, service-learning components must be integrated into the rest of the course in ways that promote your course goals. This integration includes establishing criteria for the grading of students' performance in the service-learning component of the course.

If you plan to include a service-learning component in your course, be aware that there are many time-consuming logistical problems to address, including making the community contacts necessary to create service-learning placements and finding the time to supervise the students who occupy them (Hardy & Schaen, 2000). Arrangements must also be made to transport students to and from their placements, to ensure their safety, and to insure against liability claims in the event of accident or injury. In short, creating service-learning opportunities is a lot of work, and if you are new to teaching, it might be wise for you to postpone adding a service-learning component in your own courses. However, don't forget that the option exists, or that service-learning placements can create some of the most important and memorable aspects of a student's course experience.

You can find more information, resources, tips, and useful links relating to the use of service-learning in books (e.g., Bringle & Duffy, 1998; Cress et al., 2005), or at Web sites such as that of the UCLA Clearinghouse for Community Learning (www.uei.ucla.edu/communitylearning.htm) or the *Michigan Journal of Community Service Learning* (http://ginsberg. umich.edu/mjcsl/).

● ● ● ● ●

Encouraging Critical Thinking

Wade defined critical thinking as "the use of those cognitive skills or strategies that increases the probability of a desirable outcome. It is purposeful, reasoned, and goal directed. It is the kind of thinking involved in solving problems, formulating inferences, calculating likelihoods, and making decisions. Critical thinkers use these skills appropriately, without prompting, and usually with conscious intent in a variety of settings. That is, they are predisposed to think critically. When we think critically, we evaluate the outcomes of our thought processes—how good a decision is or how well a problem is solved. Critical thinking also involves evaluating the thinking process—the reasoning that went into the conclusion we have arrived at or the kinds of factors considered in making a decision" (1988, p. 93). The Foundation for Critical Thinking says that "Critical thinking is, in short, self-directed, self-disciplined, self-monitored, and self-corrective" (cited in Paul & Elder, 2001, p. 1). A list of critical thinking skills identified by Diane Halpern (2002) is presented in Table 4.1.

Students in your courses might already be familiar with the concept of critical thinking, and might also recognize the importance of employing critical thinking skills. However, just because people know how to think critically doesn't mean they will do so (Halpern, 2002). Using critical thinking skills on a daily basis takes time, practice, and the motivation to exert the additional effort required. Further, critical thinking is entwined with content; that is, to think critically about a topic requires that one has enough background knowledge to allow the person to apply critical thinking skills to it (Willingham, 2008). In other words, we can

Table 4.1 Halpern's (2002) Taxonomy of Critical Thinking Skills

The following skills not only help students to better understand, evaluate, and apply what they learn in psychology courses, but also help them to make more informed and logical decisions as consumers, employees, and citizens.

1. *Verbal reasoning skills.* These are the skills needed to comprehend and defend against the persuasive techniques embedded in everyday language. They include, for example, the ability to recognize that an individual's thoughts determine the language they use to express them.

2. *Argument analysis skills.* These include the ability to identify conclusions, recognize variations in the quality of reasoning in support of an argument, and determine the overall strength of an argument.

3. *Hypothesis testing skills.* These include the ability to accumulate observations, formulate hypotheses, and evaluate and use evidence to decide if it confirms or disconfirms those hypotheses.

4. *Skills for understanding likelihood and uncertainty.* These include, for example, understanding the meaning of statistical summaries and how statistics can be used to both represent and misrepresent facts. These skills also include the ability to recognize the importance of base rates in evaluating hypotheses, and to understand and appreciate the impact of cognitive biases about probability, gains and losses, and the like on judgments and decision-making processes.

5. *Decision-making and problem-solving skills.* These include the ability to properly define and represent problem statements; identify possible goals; generate, select, and try alternative solutions; and choose the best alternative given the purpose of the problem-solving or decision-making task.

be critical thinkers in a domain in which we have expertise, but may not have enough information to be a critical thinker in another domain.

Because psychology courses focus on various aspects of the behavior and mental processes that govern all human affairs, psychology courses are particularly appropriate venues for helping students to refine and practice their critical thinking skills. As a psychology teacher, you can be an active agent in motivating them to do so. There are many ways you can encourage and reward critical thinking as you teach, but as with other aspects of effective teaching, they will take some thought and some planning. One way is to use higher-order thinking questions on quizzes (Barnett & Francis, 2012). We discuss this and other applications of learning principles in Chapter 5.

Classroom Demonstrations and Critical Thinking

We have already suggested the importance of conducting demonstrations to create opportunities for active learning, but you can turn many of them into critical thinking exercises as well. To take just one example, suppose that, in a course on sensation and perception or introductory psychology, you plan to demonstrate the opponent processes involved in the visual system. A standard method for doing so is to spin a spiral pattern to generate afterimages that create the sensation of movement in the opposite direction (Holland, 1965). (If you spin the spiral to create the appearance of inward movement, the afterimage creates the impression that objects in the visual field are moving outward, or expanding.) By definition, this is an active learning experience, but there are a number of ways you can make it an opportunity for critical thinking, too. You can ask the class to predict—on the basis of lectures and readings (students must have information about the physiological aspects of vision to be successful)—what they will experience and why when they look at your face after seeing the spinning display. To make correct predictions, the students will have to recall what they have learned about feature detectors in the visual cortex; then apply that knowledge to a new situation. To make the demonstration more dramatic, get a pair of spirals and, with the help of assistants, spin them in opposite directions in opposite corners of the classroom. Ask half of the class to look at one spiral, the other half at the other one. If you then ask students to look at your face, half of them will see it appear to expand and the other half will see it appear to shrink. As students describe their differing experiences, ask them to propose ideas about what must have happened and why.

You can also incorporate critical thinking elements into other aspect of your courses. Students' "diagnoses" of psychiatric patients and case studies can not only illustrate a phenomenon, but can stimulate students to think critically about them. You might also use descriptions of, say, people with symptoms of neurological damage or impairment. After reading about each case, students could be assigned to hypothesize which brain areas are affected and whether the problem is likely to have been caused by brain damage or drugs and, if the latter, which drugs might be involved. Remember, though, that critical thinking exercises like these will be useful only if students have enough information about brain areas and the effects of psychoactive drugs to be able to analyze the problem.

You can even use the course textbook as a vehicle for critical thinking. We know of an instructor who asks his students to choose a page of the text that is of particular interest and to read one or more of the scholarly references cited on that page. The students then decide if the evidence in those references warranted the assertions made in the book. If not, the students are to rewrite the page as they think it should appear, given the evidence available. It is unlikely that many authors of psychology textbooks anticipate that their books will be used in this way, but many texts, especially those for the introductory course, incorporate a variety of other features designed to promote critical thinking. In the book we know best, each chapter contains a "Thinking Critically" feature that invites students to ask themselves five questions about a particular chapter-relevant topic or issue: What am I being asked to believe or accept? What evidence is available to support the assertion? Are there alternative ways of interpreting the evidence? What additional evidence would help to evaluate the alternatives? What conclusions are most reasonable? (Bernstein, 2014). Other books offer other features that can be used to reinforce your message about the importance of critical thinking. There are also excellent books that focus specifically on promoting critical thinking in every aspect of your teaching (e.g., Halpern, 2002, 2003). The Foundation for Critical Thinking publishes a guide to critical thinking that includes templates for analyzing the logic of an article and for problem solving, as well as a list of criteria for evaluating reasoning and a checklist for assessment (Paul & Elder, 2001).

⬤ ⬤ ⬤ ⬤ ⬤

Teaching Style and Class Size

The teaching methods you learn and the teaching style you develop can serve you well in any psychology classroom, but you might have to adjust them to accommodate classes of differing sizes (Cramer, 1999; Erickson et al., 2006; Gibbs, 1992; Smith & MacGregor, 1998; Svinicki & McKeachie, 2014). The current trend in higher education is toward larger classes, especially at the introductory level. These classes are full of first-year students, the ones who typically have the greatest difficulty in the kinds of large classrooms that one student has described as true "distance learning" (Parry, 2010). Because these students tend to feel anonymous they may decide that class attendance is unimportant, especially if their instructor offers nothing other than lectures (Erickson et al., 2006; Mulryan-Kyne, 2010). And indeed there is a strong temptation for instructors of large classes to spend most of their class time lecturing. This is understandable. Many instructors, especially newer ones, feel disconnected from their students in large classes. It is more difficult (maybe impossible) to learn and remember all the students' names or to keep track of how well each of them is doing. Many psychology faculty are overwhelmed by the demands of teaching large classes and uncomfortable in a role that makes them feel more like a performer than a teacher (Ward & Jenkins, 1992). The fact that larger classes tend to be noisier, more crowded and hectic, and less conducive to informal student–teacher interactions can intensify a teacher's (and students') sense of isolation from the educational process (Erickson et al., 2006; Schroeder et al., 2013). Under these circumstances, it is no wonder that many faculty tend to arrive at the last minute, deliver a lecture, and allow (and even encourage) students to listen passively.

Still, even in large classes it is possible to teach effectively and to promote active learning and critical thinking using specialized versions of the lectures, demonstrations, discussions, presentations, and other methods we have described in this chapter. To meet the challenges and compensate for the suboptimal conditions presented by larger classes, planning and organization are, as always, the keys to success.

It has been suggested that teaching large classes effectively involves two "strategic principles" (Erickson et al., 2006). The first is to bridge the gap between the teacher and the students. This means, for example, greeting students informally as they enter the classroom. Teacher greetings, even in a large classroom environment where the teacher often does not know the students' names, have been associated with higher student attendance and even increased academic performance (Schroeder et al., 2013). So use the minutes before class begins to chat informally with your students, perhaps even standing at the door as they enter (Mulryan-Kyne, 2010). In addition, any technique to relieve the anonymity of the students is worth pursuing. You can, for example, assign seats and then use a seating chart to get to know students' names or use clickers to let students know that their input is important to you (Erickson et al., 2006).

You also can move around the room, making eye contact with as many students as possible. If you are lecturing as you walk, carry your notes to remind yourself about when to advance to the next PowerPoint slide. If students are working on a small-group activity, walk among the groups, checking in to assess their understanding. Any movement that takes you away from behind a podium will increase your connection with your students.

The second strategic principle involves small-group discussion and activities. Dividing the class into groups of five to eight students improves their sense of involvement and their learning (Erickson et al., 2006; Mulryan-Kyne, 2010; Schroeder et al., 2013). Fruitful interactions among students can take place, even if theater-style chairs are fixed to the floor—for example, through think-pair-share activities. (For several "quick-think" activities in a lecture, see Nilson, 2014). The think-pair-share method also helps students in a large lecture hall to remain attentive, and might even improve their subsequent exam performance (Ruhl, Hughes, & Schloss, 1987). Incorporating in-class group assignments can alleviate the sense of anonymity and encourage attendance as well (Schroeder et al., 2013).

Remember, too, that students in a large, crowded room might be especially hesitant to raise their hands, so when you ask for questions, you might have to build in a little extra wait time or draw out the students in other ways. We tend to do this by saying something like, "OK, I know you have some questions about what I have been talking about—what are they?" or "Who's got a question but has been afraid to ask it in such a big room?" When students do ask questions, plan ways to amplify the rewards for doing so. For example, approach the student so that the interaction becomes more personal and friendly. Stroll around the room as further questions occur or as a discussion develops. Needless to say, it is absolutely essential to repeat every student's question, answer, and comment so that the entire class can hear it and follow the thread of events. If you use these simple methods, your students—who have cut their teeth on audience participation talk shows on television—should have little or no trouble accepting the idea that their teacher is walking among them with a microphone. In fact, our experience suggests that there is no reason why student–teacher interactions can't be as easy and as lively in large classes as they are small ones. So, if you are tempted to just lecture because you believe that larger class size is related to lower student achievement no matter what the teacher does, look at recent research showing that teacher expertise can be a more significant determinant of student learning than class size (Mulryan-Kyne, 2010).

Other adjustments to large classes revolve around administrative rather than educational problems. For example, instead of distributing a handout in a large class, you might want to just post it to the course Web page. And if you do distribute a paper handout, be sure to wait until everyone has a copy before referring to it. To minimize the delay, develop a standard strategy for distributing material, perhaps placing a table near the entrance where students can pick up the day's handouts as they arrive. If you don't have teaching assistants, recruit student volunteers to help you quickly get material to the entire class.

You will also have to think about how to collect quizzes and exams as your students complete them, and about how students will retrieve their graded work on the days you hand it back for the vital process of feedback and discussion. Will there be a box in which students should deposit exam forms, test booklets, and answer sheets? Will you have graded exams stacked in alphabetical order for students to collect when you call the first letter of their last name? These are the systems that we have found useful in classes of up to 750, but they must be set up carefully to keep students from seeing each other's results (see Chapter 6, where we discuss this and other legal and ethical issues in teaching). One colleague advocates stationing teaching assistants in various parts of the classroom where they hand back exams to students whose last names are in particular segments of the alphabet (Lowman, 1987). Whatever alternative you choose, if you have never taught a large class before, seek advice about your collection-and-return system from a more experienced colleague before making your final decisions. Remember that no matter how carefully you plan and organize your system for returning exams and quizzes, the scene will probably be somewhat chaotic and will probably take 10 to 20 minutes the first time you implement it. Once students learn the system, though, the process will become routine and will take less class time. This is especially true once students learn to come to class on time when graded assignments are being returned.

For further advice on how to adjust your teaching style and procedures to large classes, consult sources such as Davis (2009), Erickson and colleagues (2006), Gibbs and Jenkins (1992), MacGregor (2000), and Weimer (1987).

Online Considerations

Many administrators see the online course as the ultimate large classroom. Indeed, many online courses have no enrollment limits, so the problems and issues that occur in a large face-to-face classroom are exacerbated in an online environment. It is even easier for students in an online course to be disengaged from the content and the course and to feel anonymous. It is of vital importance, then, to maintain some type of personal contact with each student. This means that students in an online course have to receive feedback on assignments from an instructor in some format. Perhaps the LMS has a feedback component in the online grader allowing you to leave comments in the students' individual grade pages. If not, you might want to send a personal e-mail with your feedback. This adds to the effort required in online teaching, which is why, even though administrators may believe that the teacher–student ratio can be higher in online courses, most of those who have taught online suggest that it actually needs to be lower if the students are to be engaged in the learning process.

The Last Day of the Course

After all of your planning and all your effort, after many weeks of good and not-so-good classroom experiences, you will inevitably find yourself teaching the last class of the term. When you get there, you might find the experience bittersweet. You and your students will be sad to see the course end, especially if it has gone well, but also happy to have successfully completed yet another academic term. For many psychology faculty, the last day of class comes and goes without ceremony; they simply finish presenting content and/or review for the final exam. Yet the last day provides an opportunity to bring the student–teacher experience to a close in a way that students appreciate and enjoy. Remember that the last day of your class is also the first day of the rest of your students' lives (Eggleston & Smith, 2001; Keith, 2011; Maier & Panitz, 1996).

Some faculty use standard closing activities, including summarizing the course content, reviewing the course syllabus and discussing which course goals were and were not met, and having students create concept maps illustrating major aspects of course content. You might also collect and have students reflect on any course portfolios that had been assigned (Maier & Panitz, 1996). If you administered a pretest at the beginning of the course to assess what your students thought they knew about psychology, you might also spend part of the last class session reviewing their responses to that test and discussing how their ideas have changed since the first day of class (Eggleston & Smith, 2001).

You might consider giving students a small memento of the course. In a small class, these could be certificates of achievement that include a personal note for each student or an acknowledgment of some aspect of his or her accomplishments in the course. In a large class, the mementos could be "fortunes" containing a reminder of an important idea or lesson from the course or of something especially interesting that happened in class. Or perhaps just put some words of wisdom on the blackboard or computer screen (Eggleston & Smith, 2001). The memento provided by one instructor (Keith, 2011) consists of a one-page, single-spaced letter to his students conveying the core skills and perspectives he hopes that they have learned and how privileged he feels to have worked with them. He tells students, too, that he hopes they will be readers of at least one book a week, and he lists on the back of the page 50 books to get them through the next twelve months if they decide to follow his advice.

You might also consider asking students to spend some of the last day writing a letter that describes some of what they have learned from the course. To help them organize their thoughts, you might ask them to address a question such as "What is psychology?" or "Which studies or ideas do you think have been most important in shaping the development of (e.g., biological, cognitive, social, clinical) psychology?" One instructor we know asks students to make a list of the "Top 10 Things Learned in This Course" and to turn it in on the last day of class. Reading and discussing students' differing lists can lead to an interesting discussion. As mentioned earlier, another professor ends his course by asking students what they think psychology will look like in 50 years (Hendersen, 2002a).

You can invite current students to pass on their views of and experiences in your course by writing a letter to the students who will take the course next term. You can read these letters to help you improve the course, and also hand out copies of some of them to your next class (Maier & Panitz, 1996). One of us uses a more general version of this idea in a small honors section of introductory psychology for students who are fresh out of high school. At the end of the following spring semester, she sends these students an e-mail message asking them to tell her what they wish they had known about coming to college, but that no one told them. By passing that information on to new first-year students, she helps establish rapport with them, but a side benefit of this exercise is that it serves to maintain contact with her former students, too.

Remember to take time on the last day of class to invite your students to stay in touch with you throughout their college years and beyond. If nothing else, ask them to send you an e-mail at the end of the following term to identify the one thing they learned in your course that they have found useful since the course ended. Or invite them to tell you whenever they see a good example of one of the concepts they studied in your class. Hearing from your students on an ongoing basis is not only interesting in and of itself, but can inform your decisions about what to emphasize in future classes. It also serves as a constant reminder that the things you do in those classes continue to affect your students for many years to come.

Some Final Comments

No matter how diligently you follow our advice—and the advice of others—in developing your teaching style and planning your teaching methods, some classes will inevitably go better than others. As one observer put it, "you must quietly accept that failure is part of the process" (Walck, 1997, p. 476). Still, we hope that the advice contained in this chapter will help to maximize your good teaching days and minimize the not-so-good ones. And remember that no matter which teaching techniques you feel most comfortable with, you must vary your methods to some extent from class to class, and within classes, too, so as to keep things interesting for your students and yourself (Lang, 2008). The most effective teachers engage their students by using multiple approaches, including lectures, lecturettes, in-class discussions or debates, small-group work, demonstrations, and the like.

Whether we consider a class to be a good one or a bad one depends largely on our students' reactions to us and to our teaching efforts, which includes the quizzes, exams, papers, and other graded assignments we use to evaluate their performance in our courses. Deciding on which of these assignments to choose and how to create them is the topic of the next chapter.

5

Evaluating Student Learning

Why do we evaluate our students? Are we interested in assessing their learning or are we merely interested in ranking them or providing ratings of their performance for the purpose of assigning grades? The traditional question that teachers ask about assessment is: "What evaluation instruments do I need to develop to be able to give valid grades in this class?" It has been suggested, though, that the fundamental assessment questions should be: "What kind of intellectual and personal development do I want my students to enjoy in this class, and what evidence might I collect about the nature and progress of their development?" (Bain, 2004, p. 152).

●●●●●

Assessment versus Evaluation

The terms *assessment* and *evaluation* are often used interchangeably, even though they can have somewhat different meanings. Assessment in education refers to compiling information to help learners improve their performance (what some would call *formative* feedback); evaluation adds a layer of judgment about the quality of the performance (what some would call *summative* feedback). In other words, assessment is measurement *for* learning, while evaluation is measurement *of* learning (Butler & McMunn, 2006). Accordingly, evaluation and assessment are justified by their incentive value—that is, providing rewards for achievement and punishment for failure—and by their information value—that is, providing knowledge of results that tells students what they already know and what they have yet to learn (Astin & Antonio, 2012). One observer put it this way: "assessment is a broad and evolving conceptualization of a process that teachers and students use in collecting, evaluating, and using evidence of student learning for a variety of purposes, including diagnosing student strengths and weaknesses, monitoring student progress toward meeting desired levels of proficiency, [and] assigning grades" (McMillan, 2013, p. 3). We agree with this view, so we will use *assessment* to refer to both functions. [For more detailed information on assessment in higher education, see resources such as Astin & Antonio (2012); Baehr (2007); Halpern (2013); McMillan (2013); Parker et al. (2001); and Suskie (2009). Many of these resources can be accessed at North Carolina State University's Internet Resources for Higher Education Outcomes Assessment (www2.acs.ncsu.edu/UPA/archives/assmt/rsrc_new.htm).]

Linking Teaching, Learning, and Grading

If you accept the dual roles assessment plays in higher education, you will want to link your grading system to your course objectives and student learning goals (Astin & Antonio, 2012; Davis, 2009; Erickson, Peters, & Strommer, 2006; Suskie, 2009; Svinicki & McKeachie, 2014; Walvoord & Anderson, 2010; Zlokovich, 2004). Or as Walvoord and Anderson put it, "teach what you are grading" and "grade what you are teaching" (2010, pp. 61, 66). This does not mean that you should teach only what will be on your exams, but that you should evaluate students on the important content in the course and devote considerable time and effort to teaching that content. Assignments and tests should be developed to measure the students' achievement of the learning objectives of your course; indeed, why would you spend time grading student work that does not address your course goals (Walvoord & Anderson, 2010)?

Further, as already mentioned, students should learn from the assessment process. Tests and other evaluated assignments should be an integral part of the learning process, serving to deepen students' understanding and improve their skills, not merely as the bases for giving grades (Brookfield, 2006).

Some Guidelines for Assessing Student Learning

The American Association for Higher Education's Principles for Good Practice in Assessing Student Learning (Astin et al., 2003) have generated seven guidelines for evaluating college students (Suskie, 2000, 2009).

These guidelines can be useful in making decisions about how and when to evaluate the learning that occurs in your courses.

1. First, you should *clearly identify your learning goals or objectives and share them with your students*. Explain which learning goals are most important to you, and which skills you want the students to acquire. Tell students how achieving these goals and skills can promote their education and spell out why you will be assessing their learning in the ways that you do. This information helps students understand and accept the importance of classroom assessment (Davis, 2009; McKeachie, 2002; Svinicki & McKeachie, 2014; Walvoord & Anderson, 2010; Zlokovich, 2004).

2. Point out that *your evaluation methods will be linked to the goals and skills you emphasize*. So, if you tell students that you want to promote their critical thinking skills, explain that this is why you will be assigning "thought papers," analytical essay exams, or comprehension-oriented multiple choice tests rather than instruments that focus on the definition of key terms. If teaching definitions or vocabulary is a major goal for you, say that, and use it as an explanation for your use of key-term tests (Clegg, 1994; Davis, 2009; Erickson et al., 2006; Jacobs & Chase, 1992; Ory & Ryan, 1993; Svinicki & McKeachie, 2014; Walvoord & Anderson, 2010; Zlokovich, 2004). Matching assessment instruments to learning goals is not as easy as it sounds, partly because it takes a lot of time to develop those instruments, which can be particularly challenging when you try to do so while the course is in progress rather than in advance. And even when we are not under time pressure it can be difficult to create instruments that preserve the links between assessment and learning goals. One recent study found that the vast majority of questions that faculty thought would require their students to use complex cognitive skills actually required no more than the recall of names, terms, or other specific facts (Erickson & Strommer, 1991). In other words, teachers are not always the best judge of which skills their assessment instruments require of students (Astin & Antonio, 2012). Later in this chapter we describe some methods that can help you to overcome this problem.

3. *Use many measurements and many kinds of measures*. Overall, the more evaluative components that go into determining a final grade, and the more varied those components are, the more valid that final grade is likely to be (Davis, 2009; Erickson et al., 2006; Jacobs & Chase, 1992; Ory & Ryan, 1993; Svinicki & McKeachie, 2014; Walvoord & Anderson, 2010; Zlokovich, 2004). Teachers who assign final grades based on, say, a midterm and a final exam or a term paper and a final exam are probably not gathering enough evaluative information to

reliably assess student learning or to assign valid grades. Further, evaluations based entirely on multiple choice exams or entirely on writing assignments might not give all students a chance to demonstrate the full extent of their knowledge (Anderson, 2001; Clegg, 1994; Erickson et al., 2006; Zlokovich, 2004).

4. *Help students to do their best on evaluative tasks.* For example, when assigning group projects, specify the outcomes you expect (A short written summary? An in-class presentation?), and let students review previous projects that have received high (or low) grades. If you plan to give multiple choice tests, offer students tips on how to take them, show and discuss sample questions in class, and perhaps provide past quizzes and exams to help students practice their test-taking skills. In other words, do what you can to help students clearly understand your assessment devices.

5. *Express confidence in your students.* As in every other aspect of teaching, encouraging your students to try hard and expressing confidence in their ability to accomplish their learning goals can help motivate them to do so.

6. *Don't let evaluation discourage cooperation.* Competition for grades is inevitable, and can be motivating, but be sure that your evaluation system does not create such intense competition that it discourages students from helping each other or working together.

7. *Evaluate your evaluation system.* If a disproportionately large number of students did poorly on your quizzes, exams, and other assessment instruments, ask yourself why this happened. Did the problem lie in the assessment instrument itself, with its linkage to your learning goals, with the way you taught the material, or perhaps with the students? Addressing these questions can be extremely helpful as you develop your teaching style and your evaluation systems.

Grading and Your Relationship with Students

Many teachers do not look forward to the grading process, both because they fear it will change their classroom climate and because they dislike the role of "judge." Yet "To teach is to judge" (Brookfield, 2006, p. 176), and "assessment is inherently a process of professional judgment" (Brookhart, 2011, p. 5). Unless you teach at an institution that does not assign grades, you are going to have to accept this role and the fact "that you establish the criteria according to which students are graded, that you evaluate them against those criteria, and that you and you alone are responsible for the grades you dispense" (Lang, 2008, p. 128).

You have to accept, too, that grading can change the relationship that you are trying to build with your class. Even if you have tried to create a "democratic" classroom in which students have a voice, when the first graded assignment is returned, the power differential between you and your students is starkly emphasized (Brookfield, 2006; Lang, 2008) and establishes your status as the first among equals. Grades can affect student–faculty relationships not only because of their academic consequences, but because students may perceive disappointing marks as reflecting badly on their self-worth (Brookfield, 2006).

Awareness of these facts, coupled with uncertainty about how to conduct valid assessments and discomfort with the grader role, can make the whole evaluative process quite stressful for teachers, especially inexperienced ones (Eble, 1988; Lang, 2008). Yet evaluating learning via grades is part of what departmental executive officers, your colleagues, and your students expect you to do. So in the next few sections we consider some specific strategies for making your assessments more valid and reliable, and thus fairer, and making the assessment process less stressful and more useful for you and your students.

● ● ● ● ●

Tests and Quizzes

The most commonly employed option for evaluating student performance is the test and its briefer cousin, the quiz.

Tests

Tests can be constructed in many formats, but the most common ones in higher education are essay, short answer, and multiple choice. Students tend to study in different ways for different kinds of tests. For example, they are more likely to try to memorize specific terms and other factual information when studying for multiple choice tests. When preparing for essay tests, they are more likely to try to understand connections between key concepts (Erickson et al., 2006). To promote both kinds of study, some instructors create exams that include both multiple choice and essay questions (Erickson et al., 2006).

A final exam can be set up as nothing more than a test that covers material presented since the previous test, or it can contain items relating to the entire course. Cumulative exams are relatively rare in psychology courses, partly because students do not like exerting the extra effort required to prepare for them. This is a shame because there is mounting evidence that students—especially lower-achieving students—tend to retain course information longer when they have to take a cumulative final (Khanna et al., 2013; Lawrence, 2013; McDaniel & Wooldridge,

2012). With these data in mind, some instructors now give cumulative finals, and to help students get used to the idea of applying previously learned information to new concepts and ideas, they include cumulative items on all their tests and quizzes. We discuss this strategy further in the section of this chapter on applying cognitive psychology to teaching.

Quizzes

Giving short, graded or ungraded quizzes can also help students learn, partly because these instruments promote the kind of active information retrieval that is associated with long-term retention. Not surprisingly, quizzing often leads to higher scores on higher-stakes exams (Kouyoumdjian, 2013; Roediger et al., 2011). Quizzes also provide formative feedback, encourage students to keep up with reading assignments and to use self-quizzing as a learning tool, and may even reduce test anxiety (McDaniel & Wooldridge, 2012).

The mechanics of quizzing—for example, how often, in class versus online, open book versus closed book, announced versus unannounced—are often overlooked, but can be important. It appears that frequent quizzes, like other types of repeated assessments, are best for promoting learning (Astin & Antonio, 2012; Zlokovich, 2004), but beware of extremes. Daily quizzes can become burdensome, though there are ways to avoid this problem. For example, if you use student response devices ("clickers") instead of paper-and-pencil forms, you can present a few multiple choice items almost every day of the term. These are easy to take and easy to grade. You can also make quizzes part of collaborative learning by having students first take the quiz individually, then take it as a group. This format encourages peer interaction, promotes active learning, and provides immediate feedback (Kouyoumdjian, 2013).

This last point is important, because immediate feedback enhances learning. So if you give a multiple choice quiz in class, for example, it is worth taking time to immediately review the items and give students the opportunity to discuss the reasoning behind each correct answer. You might even turn this time into an active learning opportunity by asking students to discuss how each question could be revised so as to make each of the incorrect answers correct.

Online Considerations

Online quizzing is becoming a more popular way of allowing students to practice retrieval while providing low-stakes feedback on what they know and don't know. While online quizzing is the primary format in online courses, many teachers of blended or face-to-face courses also use online quizzing.

Allowing students to take quizzes online frees up class time and, depending on the quizzing software available, students may be given immediate feedback of results, information about why wrong answers were wrong, and even the chance to re-quiz themselves on the same content using alternative forms containing different items. More sophisticated adaptive quizzing software such as PrepU provides each student with quiz items based on their responses to previous questions. Such software even directs students to review specific textbook content at the end of each quiz, thus providing the corrective feedback often lacking in online quizzes. These systems are likely to become commonplace in the near future.

Essay and Short-Answer Tests

Essay and short-answer tests can be constructed relatively quickly, provide an assessment of students' writing ability, and can easily set tasks that require high-level analysis of course material, including problem-solving skills and complex thinking (Erickson et al., 2006; Jacobs & Chase, 1992). Essay test items can be written in the form of restricted response questions or extended response questions. Restricted response questions are especially useful for measuring students' ability to interpret and apply course information in a specific domain (Gronlund & Linn, 1990; Linn & Gronlund, 2000). An example might be: "Discuss three ways in which classical and operant conditioning differ, and give an example of each difference." Extended response questions are broader and provide students with fewer guidelines; for example, "Compare the personality theories of Freud, Jung, and Adler." Many psychology teachers prefer restricted response questions because their relatively limited scope makes it possible to include more of them in a particular exam. Posing several restricted response questions allows for a broader sampling of course content on each exam. Whatever you do, be sure to set aside enough time to grade essay and short-answer tests because, although they can be written quickly, they require a lot of time to grade with care. And make sure your essay questions will assess higher-order thinking, and are thus worth the time it takes to grade them (Erickson et al., 2006).

Writing Essay and Short-Answer Test Items

Here are some tips for writing good essay and short-answer test questions (Gronlund & Linn, 1990; Linn & Gronlund, 2000).

1. *Phrase each question to be as clear as possible.* For instance, "Describe at least two benefits and two disadvantages associated with punishment" is clearer than "Discuss the role of punishment."

2. *Write enough questions to assess learning goals in several topic areas, but not so many that students won't have enough time to write high-quality answers (remember that it will take students longer than it would take you* to write a good answer).

3. *Include information on the exam form about how much time students should devote to each question*, or at least list the number of points each question is worth (Jacobs & Chase, 1992; Ory & Ryan, 1993). This information helps students develop a plan for making the best use of their time.

4. If you want students to study the widest range of course content, *require them to answer all essay items on your test.* Allowing them to choose a subset of items means that students are taking different tests, making it more difficult to compare their performance (Jacobs & Chase, 1992; Ory & Ryan, 1993). Measurement experts argue that if you do let students choose a subset of essay items, make it a large subset—five out of six, for example (Jacobs & Chase, 1992; Ory & Ryan, 1993). Allowing too much choice (e.g., two out of six), might lead students to focus their reading and studying on just a few major concepts in each section of the course and ignore the rest. Teachers who want to reduce students' anxiety about essay tests or who want to discover only what students know (and how well they know it) allow them to answer only a small subset of questions or even let them write about the ideas or concepts that they found most intriguing (Erickson et al., 2006).

Table 5.1 provides some examples of the types of essay questions you can construct.

Table 5.1 Sample Essay Questions

1. Compare and contrast X and Y in regard to given qualities. Example: How would the James-Lang and Cannon-Bard theories of emotion explain the experience of fear?

2. Present arguments for and against an issue. Example: What are the advantages and disadvantages of bilingual education?

3. Illustrate how a principle explains facts. Example: How does arousal theory explain the fact that having an audience present can sometimes improve and sometimes disrupt a person's ability to perform a behavior?

4. Illustrate cause and effect. Example: Describe the evidence you would require to confirm that differing styles of parenting cause differences in children's personalities.

5. Describe an application of a rule or principle. Example: How would you take advantage of context-dependent memory to help you do your best on your next psychology exam?

6. Draw new inferences from data. Example: What potential weaknesses in the U.S. court system are suggested by research on the nature and limitations of human memory?

7. Describe how the elements comprising a situation, event, or mechanism are interrelated. Example: Describe an example of how genetic and environmental factors might combine to influence the development of a shy, fearful, or aggressive personality.

8. Analyze a situation, event, or mechanism into its component parts. Example: List at least four factors that might be responsible for the appearance of schizophrenia and how each of these factors might contribute to the disorder.

Note. These items illustrate some of the many formats you can use in writing essay exam items (Jacobs & Chase, 1992). Whatever formats you choose, be sure to have a colleague, and especially a nonexpert, read each item to be sure its meaning is clear.

Scoring Essay and Short-Answer Tests

Essay tests can be scored using analytical or holistic (global quality) methods (Erickson et al., 2006; Ory & Ryan, 1993). In the holistic scheme, you assign a score to each student based on either the overall quality of the answer relative to other students' answers or in relation to your own subjective set of criteria (Ory & Ryan, 1993). One way you can do this is to separate essays into piles as you read, for example, excellent, good, fair, weak, and unacceptable. Keep in mind, though, that you might have to reread essays and readjust your criteria as the answers get better or worse as you work your way through the essays. Another problem with this approach is that it is nearly impossible for you to precisely describe your grading criteria, thus making it difficult to justify your grades when students inquire or complain about them.

The analytical method results in grades that are usually easier to defend, because it requires that you use a rubric to determine an essay test grade. (Rubrics can also be used to determine and justify grades on any kind of written assignment, as noted later in the section of this chapter on writing assignments.)

One way to develop a rubric is to first write an "ideal answer" to each essay question, then identify the specific features of that answer that will have predetermined point values. So if you wrote an essay question that asks students to evaluate the validity of the DSM-5 for diagnosing mental disorders, you could compare each essay to your ideal answer and award points—up to some maximum score—based on which, or how many, expected elements appear (e.g., two points for each strength or weakness correctly named). The grade assigned to the test as a whole is based on the total number of points earned (Linn & Gronlund, 2000; Ory & Ryan, 1993). You can also develop a rubric using primary trait analysis, which means identifying the features of an answer that will garner points. For example, you might identify five concepts that should be included in a good response, and then rate each of them, if they appear, in terms of levels of quality (Erickson et al., 2006; Svinicki & McKeachie, 2014; Walvoord & Anderson, 2010). (You can find templates of primary trait rubrics at www4.wccnet.edu/departments/curriculum/includes/assessment_levelone/rubric_templates.pdf.)

Once you have your rubrics in hand you are not quite ready to start grading essays or short-answer tests because you first have to decide how you will deal with features of answers—such as errors in spelling or grammar—that might be irrelevant to the learning goals of your course but can affect students' ability to reach their long-term career goals. If you are going to subtract points for such errors, it is a good idea to include this decision in your rubric and to let students know about it in advance.

When the time comes to read a set of essay exams, find a quiet place to work that will be relatively free of distractions, and don't try to grade the entire set in one sitting. Know the limits of your ability to concentrate, and when you identify signs of fatigue, impatience, or "scanning" instead of reading, stop, take a break, or do something else for a while. Distributing the grading task over several sessions will minimize the chance that stress responses will have influenced your grading decisions. As you read, be sure to write comments in the margin that will help the student understand the basis for your scoring of each answer. Don't forget to jot a note of praise for particularly good answers. If your class is too large to allow you to write individual comments on short-answer tests, be sure to make a list of the most common errors and discuss them with your students in class (see Chapter 6).

When grading essay exams containing more than one item, score all students' answers to the first question before going on to the next one (Davis, 2009; Svinicki & McKeachie, 2014). This arrangement is especially important if you are using a holistic scoring method. Reading all responses to the same question makes it easier to compare students' performance and minimizes the development of halo effects in which your reaction to a student's answer to one item might affect your scoring of that student's later answers. To reduce the development of halo effects caused by reading students' responses in the same order time after time, shuffle the stack of exams every time you finish reading all the answers to a given item.

Finally, conceal the students' names on the cover sheet of the exam (or have students identify themselves by a code number). If you don't know whose responses you are reading, it is less likely that your scoring of those responses will be biased by positive or negative expectations or impressions of particular students (Davis, 2009; Malouff, Emmerton, & Schutte, 2013; Svinicki & McKeachie, 2014).

If you have no experience grading essay or short-answer tests, you will soon discover that reading them carefully and grading them systematically takes an enormous amount of time. Therefore, before deciding to use essay or short-answer tests in your course, estimate how much time it will take to grade each question, increase that estimate to be on the safe side, calculate the total amount of time required to grade each student's exam, and multiply the result by the number of students you expect to enroll in your class. Then multiply that figure by the number of essay or short-answer tests you plan to give, and decide whether the resulting time commitment is realistic in light of your other academic and personal responsibilities (Zlokovich, 2004).

Multiple Choice Tests

If the time required for grading essay or short-answer tests is likely to be unmanageable, consider using a multiple choice format for some or most of your student performance evaluations. Multiple choice tests can be quickly scored electronically and the results downloaded into your LMS gradebook. In addition, the difficulty level and other information about each multiple choice item's performance can be assessed by item analysis programs available through most exam scoring software.

Some teachers believe that multiple choice tests are capable of measuring only lower-level learning outcomes such as facts and definitions. But the poor reputation of multiple choice exams stems, we think, from the fact that the questions on many such exams are poorly written and/ or aim only at assessing students' abilities at rote memorization. However, a good multiple choice exam can assess a variety of learning objectives, assess a wide range of student understanding, and increase the validity and reliability of your evaluation process (Erickson et al., 2006). For example, multiple choice tests can be constructed so that they trigger recall (not recognition) of information—both information pertaining to the correct answer and information pertaining to the incorrect alternatives. So well-constructed multiple choice items might be even better than essay exams for promoting long-term retention (Little et al., 2012).

Although multiple choice tests can be graded quickly, they take a long time to write, and as described later, even more time to write well (Jacobs & Chase, 1992; Ory & Ryan, 1993). One way to spread out the workload is to write two or three multiple choice items immediately after each class period, when the material, and students' reactions to it, are fresh in your mind (Ebel, 1965; Erickson & Strommer, 1991; Jacobs & Chase, 1992; Ory & Ryan, 1993). This strategy helps ensure that all of the important material covered in class is also covered on the exam. It might also result in better-quality items that are more closely linked to your learning goals, because you will be concentrating more intensely on each item's wording, clarity, accuracy, and level than might be the case during a last-minute item-writing marathon. You can also use the printed, electronic, or online banks of multiple choice items that are available through the publisher of your textbook, but remember that the quality of these test item banks is often uneven. Many of them can be edited, though, so you can fix the items you don't like to make them fit your course, thus giving you more time to write fresh items to assess knowledge about material that you presented in class, but that might not be covered in the textbook.

Writing Multiple Choice Items

Because good multiple choice questions can assess *knowledge*—remembering key concepts or ideas; *understanding*—recognizing the concepts in specific contexts or forms; and *thinking*—applying the ideas in different situations (Erickson et al., 2006), there is no reason to use them to assess only recall of specific facts and definitions, unless that matches your learning objectives.

Here are some useful guidelines for writing multiple choice items (Davis, 2009; Erickson et al., 2006; Erickson & Strommer, 1991; Linn & Gronlund, 2000; Ory, 2003; Suskie, 2011; Svinicki & McKeachie, 2014):

1. *Each item should have one, and only one, correct or clearly best answer.* This simple rule is easy to state, but devilishly difficult to follow, mainly because it is so easy to miss double meanings and slight errors of phrasing that make two alternative answers plausible. In fact, it is often only when a student asks for clarification of an item or argues with its scoring that it dawns on you that the item is not as good as you thought it was. It is virtually impossible to avoid writing a few potentially ambiguous multiple choice items on every exam or quiz, but careful proofreading—by you and at least one other person—can go a long way toward catching and fixing these items before they reach your students. Incidentally, you can discourage arguments from students about which item option is correct by writing your exam instructions to say that students should pick the BEST answer. (See Chapter 6 for ideas about fair handling of students' complaints about "bad" exam items.)
2. *Keep items as concise as possible.* Write short, straightforward items, and avoid irrelevant information or excessive verbiage. Don't use vocabulary that is confusing or likely to be unfamiliar (Suskie, 2011). And don't include in the question information that is designed to teach new material. Thus, Example A would be a better item than Example B:

Example A

Harry believes that men and women CANNOT be "just friends." He asked nine people to rate "On a scale from 0 (not at all) to 10 (definitely) how strongly they believe that men and women can be friends." The ratings were: 1, 1, 1, 1, 7, 8, 9, 9, 10. Which measure of central tendency would best support Harry's claim that most people do NOT believe that men and women can be friends?
A. mode
B. mean
C. median
D. range

Example B

When Harry met Sally they had a debate about whether men and women can be friends. Harry decided to ask random people, "On a scale from 0 (not at all) to 10 (definitely), how strongly do you believe that men and women can be friends?" Their responses were as follows: 1, 1, 1, 1, 7, 8, 9, 9, 10. Harry really wants to convince Sally that most people do NOT believe that men and women can be friends. Therefore, he should use the _____ of the data.
A. mode
B. mean
C. median
D. range

3. *The item stem should be meaningful in itself; should contain as much of the item's content as possible; and should be free of irrelevant material.* Example A is better than Example B:

Example A

William James pioneered the _____ approach to psychology.
A. functionalist
B. psychodynamic
C. humanistic
D. ehavioral

Example B

William James
A. founded the functionalist school of psychology.
B. founded the psychodynamic school of psychology.
C. founded the humanistic school of psychology.
D. founded the behavioral school of psychology.

4. *Avoid using negatives in the item stem unless you feel they are necessary for assessing particular aspects of student learning.* Negative phrasing tends to make items seem more complicated and, especially under the stressful conditions of an exam, students can easily become confused about what the question is actually asking. If and when you do use negative wording, be sure to capitalize or italicize the negative word. Example A is better than Example B:

Example A

Robbie is an accountant who must deal with a massive influx of work every year for tax day on April 15th. Which of the following is NOT likely to mediate the stress in Robbie's work?

A. positive reappraisal
B. perception of control
C. the predictability of the stressor
D. planful problem solving

Example B

Robbie is an accountant who must deal with a massive influx of work every year for tax day on April 15th. To prepare for the increased work load he always hires temporary workers to help with the paperwork. Which of the following is not likely to mediate the stress in Robbie's work?
A. positive reappraisal
B. perception of control
C. the predictability of the stressor
D. planful problem solving

5. *All response alternatives should be plausible, but different enough from the correct alternative to demonstrate students' learning of concepts, principles, applications, and the like.* Therefore, if the correct response to an item is "negative reinforcement," good alternatives might be "punishment," "positive reinforcement," and "differential reinforcement." In other words, the incorrect responses should come from the same pool of knowledge as the correct response, but unless you are trying to create an extremely difficult item or to pose a "trick" question (which we do not recommend), be sure that the incorrect choices are not so similar to the correct one that even your best students might miss the distinction. Although it is tempting to include implausible, funny, or ridiculous alternatives just to break the tension of the exam, remember that using too many of these or using them too often can make the exam results less meaningful.

6. *All response alternatives should be grammatically consistent with the item stem so as not to eliminate some of them from consideration or give away the correct answer.* Example A is better than Example B, which disqualifies two response alternatives on grammatical grounds alone:

Example A

Cameron has learned to need a certain drug in order to feel confident. He is _____ this drug.
A. tolerant of
B. addicted to
C. psychologically dependent on
D. physically dependent on

Example B

Cameron has learned to need a certain drug in order to feel confident. He is _____ on this drug.
A. tolerant
B. addicted
C. psychologically dependent
D. physically dependent

7. *Avoid using terms in the correct response alternative that match or contrast sharply with words in the stem and thus give away the answer.* Example A is better than Example B:

Example A

Denise has learned that her ex-boyfriend frequents their former favorite coffee shop in the late evenings and she now does NOT go to the coffee shop after dinner. Denise is demonstrating
A. avoidance conditioning.
B. escape conditioning.
C. spontaneous recovery.
D. extinction.

Example B

Denise has learned that her ex-boyfriend frequents their former favorite coffee shop in the late evenings and she now avoids going to the coffee shop after dinner. Denise is demonstrating
A. avoidance conditioning.
B. escape conditioning.
C. spontaneous recovery.
D. extinction.

8. *All response alternatives should be about the same length so as not to give away the correct choice.* This can be trickier than it sounds because it is often necessary to include qualifying phrases in the correct answer to distinguish it from the incorrect alternatives. Write the correct answer first, then all the others. Example A is better than Example B:

Example A

Aggression is defined by psychologists as
A. any social interaction in which people do not cooperate with each other.
B. any social interaction in which one person threatens another.
C. an act that involves the expression of anger or hostility.
D. an act that is intended to cause harm or damage to another person.

Example B

Aggression is defined by psychologists as
A. fighting.
B. threats.
C. anger.
D. an act that is intended to cause harm or damage to another person.

9. *Unless there is a compelling reason not to do so, the correct answer should be randomly placed in each of the alternative positions (e.g., A, B, C, or D), then adjusted if necessary to ensure that correct answers appear in each position about equally often.* Avoid the common tendency to place the correct answer in the third position, where test-wise students know it is likely to be.

10. *Minimize the use of special alternatives such as "any of the above," "all of the above," or "B or C, but not A."* These items can be challenging and useful for assessing particular learning goals, but overusing them can make an exam more difficult than you want it to be or—if the special alternatives are never the correct ones—easier than you want it to be.

11. *Watch for "interlocking" items when you review the exam as a whole.* In other words, make sure that students will not be able to discern the correct answer to one question from the information contained in another (Suskie, 2011).

12. *Remove all barriers that will keep a knowledgeable student from answering an item correctly* (Suskie, 2011). For example, don't use gender-specific or culture-specific examples that would unfairly penalize students who happen to lack a particular background. This can be a challenge. For example, we once wrote an item for our final exam in introductory psychology that made reference to "Rudolph the Red-Nosed Reindeer." While many students found the item funny, the international students in our class were confused, even though they didn't have to know who "Rudolph" was to answer the question. Other examples might include items on probability that require familiarity with the game of poker or items on statistics that require knowledge of the length of a football field (Erickson et al., 2006; Ory, 1993).

We hope the following checklist will be helpful to you in preparing your tests and avoiding many of the problems typically encountered when administering them (Clegg, 1994).

Checklist 5.1 Things to Remember When Writing and Administering Tests

1. *Don't wait until the last minute to start writing tests,* especially multiple choice tests. Write a question or two after each class session.

2. *Use a table of specifications to match your test items to your testing goals and the level of skill to be assessed.* Match items to learning objectives.
3. *Spell-check your tests and ask others—including someone who can take a nonexpert student perspective—to read them for errors, inconsistencies, or confusing content.*
4. *Write tests using language that is respectful and inclusive of all your students.* As described in Chapter 6, items should include ethnically diverse names and situations and should not perpetuate stereotypes.
5. *Place similar types of items together*—multiple choice items should be in one part of the test, short-answer items in another part, and essays in another part.
6. *Provide explicit and clearly written directions for taking the test,* including the maximum number of points possible on each item, and in the case of essay items, the recommended amount of time the student should allocate to each.
7. *Allow a reasonable amount of time to answer all the items you have written.* One minute per multiple choice item, 2 minutes for each short-answer item, 10 to 15 minutes for each restricted response essay item, and about 30 minutes for an extended response essay item is about right (Brothen, 2012; Svinicki & McKeachie, 2014).
8. *Be sure that the test is printed clearly, and in a minimum of 12-point font,* so that it is easy to read, and make sure that no item is interrupted by a page break. If you have created alternative forms of the test for use in large classes or in crowded classrooms, use different-colored paper for each, but be sure the type is readable on both forms.
9. *Create and double-check the accuracy of answer keys* before administering multiple choice tests. Do the same with rubrics for scoring essay and short-answer tests. Doing so will help you spot imbalances in the position—A, B, C, or D—of correct response alternatives and possible problems in how you will grade items.
10. Once tests have been copied for distribution, *count the pages to be sure they are all there, and check to see that they have been collated in the correct order.* Make a few more copies than you think you will need, in case some copies are incomplete or illegible.
11. During the class session prior to each test, *remind students about bringing pencils, erasers, calculators, or other materials they will need for the test.* (Most experienced teachers bring a small supply of eraser-equipped pencils with them to avoid disruptions caused when students try to borrow them from other students.)
12. In large classes, *develop a time-saving procedure for efficiently distributing test forms and answer sheets.* We allow students to pick up answer sheets as they enter the room, and then have proctors distribute alternate test forms from collated piles along each row such that students seated next to each other always have different forms.

13. *Administer each test yourself,* even if you have proctors available to help, and stay active and engaged in the testing situation. Surfing the Web on your iPad during an exam tells your students that you don't care much about the test or the testing process.

14. *Decide and tell your students whether you will answer questions during the test.* However, if a student discovers a significant misspelling, a missing item, or other important problem with the test, announce the correction to the entire class immediately.

15. *Minimize the stress of the testing situation by arriving early, being friendly, and staying calm.* In addition to the pencils already mentioned, bring tissues for students whose sniffling colds are disturbing others and hand sanitizer for students using the tissues—and for yourself and your proctors when accepting exams from obviously ill students.

16. *Establish your plans for dealing with cheating on tests* (see Chapter 6).

Tables of Specifications

Whether you decide to use essay, short-answer, multiple choice, or other test items, and regardless of the format you choose, we suggest that you analyze each test and quiz by creating a table of specifications (Jacobs & Chase, 1992; Ory & Ryan, 1993). As you can see in Table 5.2, each row of this table should represent one concept, phenomenon, principle, theory, or other content element to be tested. Each column should represent a cognitive skill to be demonstrated, such as defining terms, comparing concepts, applying principles, analyzing information, and the like. Each of the table's cells thus represents the intersection of a particular bit of course content and the level of skill being tested. You can use this table to plan the content and level of the items you are about to write, or those you choose from a test item bank. If you have already written or chosen a set of items, you can enter a digit representing each item into the cell that best represents its content and level. Looking at the resulting pattern of entries will tell you how well the test or quiz covers the lectures and assigned readings and at what level.

Alternative Testing Formats

By tradition, most psychology faculty administer their tests in a classroom, where it is expected that each student will work alone and without reference material. Some instructors, however, use open-book or take-home formats instead of or in addition to this traditional format. And, of course, online classes necessitate the use of out-of-classroom exams (see our "Online Considerations" section later in this chapter and our discussion in Chapter 7).

Table 5.2 Sample Table of Specifications

Content	Knowledge	Cognitive Skills	
		Comprehension	Application
Classical Conditioning	1	1	2
Shaping			1
Reinforcement	1	1	
Observational Learning		1	
Latent Learning			1
Cognitive processes	1		

Note: This small table of specifications was created to plan a 10-item quiz on learning principles in an introductory psychology course. Tests and quizzes need not assess every possible concept at every possible cognitive level. Notice that, here, three items test basic knowledge (definitions), three more test deeper understanding, and four test students' ability to apply what they know about the concepts tested. Such tables can be created for any course using Bloom's taxonomy of cognitive skills (revised): (Anderson & Krathwohl, 2001; Bloom et al., 1956; Jacobs & Chase, 1992).

Open-Book and Take-Home Exams

Open-book exams are often given in classes, such as statistics courses, where the instructor's goal is for students to be able to solve problems or analyze data using formulas, information, and procedures that students cannot, need not, or should not be expected to memorize. In such courses, the textbook provides the formulas, tools, or other information students need to correctly deal with the problems or issues set forth in the exam. Davis noted that "open-book exams simulate the workplace, where people routinely use reference books and other resources to solve problems, prepare reports, or write memos" (2009, p. 367). Open-book exams also reduce student anxiety, but they do not necessarily improve performance, possibly because students study less for such tests or spend too much time looking for answers (Davis, 2009).

Take-home exams—a subtype of open-book exams—are popular in psychology courses in which students are asked to respond to essay test items at a length and depth of analysis that could not occur given the time constraints of a classroom test session. Some psychology teachers prefer to give take-home essay exams in lieu of in-class essay exams because doing so affords students more time in which to research their facts, organize their thoughts, and create more considered—and more neatly presented—responses. Items on take-home final exams, for example, might ask students to integrate material learned throughout the academic term. This type of exam could be especially appropriate for a senior capstone course. One teacher (Paul Travis) argued for take-home exams by saying, "I want my students to prepare them-selves intellectually, to concentrate on what they understand and how they reason with what they comprehend. I don't want them to spend time trying to outguess me about what fact I might ask them to recall. If they understand, they know which information is worth remembering" (Bain, 2004, p. 160).

Other teachers, though, don't give take-home exams because of con-cerns that students might get help from other people, not just from their textbook or other approved sources. This threat to test validity does exist, of course, even when students sign pledges to work alone, so you will have to decide whether the benefits of a take-home exam outweigh its poten-tial disadvantages. If you do give a take-home exam, don't be surprised if not all of your students are pleased. With no time limits to guide them, some students worry that they have not spent enough time—or as much time as other students—answering the questions. As a result, some might allow a take-home exam—especially a take-home final exam—to con-sume so much of their time that they neglect studying for exams in other courses. Setting a page limit on the students' responses can help with this problem. Another way of dealing with both the time-management and test-security problems is to use a "hybrid approach" (Jacobs & Chase, 1992) in which you give students a week or so to think about, study for, and even draft answers to all the essay questions that might appear on the upcoming exam. The students will thus be better prepared to give thoughtful answers to the questions you actually include on the in-class exam.

Collaborative or Group Testing

Collaborative learning methods suggest yet another approach to testing (Davis, 2009; Lusk & Conklin, 2002; Mitchell & Melton, 2003) in which students are allowed to take exams in groups and each group member earns the same grade. In a related option, students take part of an exam individually, then collaborate on another part. Some instructors offer students the option of taking an exam individually or as part of a group. If you decide to use any version of collaborative testing, be sure that you have thought through exactly what grading procedures you will use, and of course, announce them ahead of time. When used with care, collabora-tive testing can provide an excellent way of encouraging student–student interactions in your course and may promote deeper understanding of the material while relieving some of the stress associated with exams (Davis, 2009).

Online Considerations

Our discussion of the development of good classroom quizzes and tests is also relevant to the online environment, but the administration of online quizzes and exams is a more complex enterprise. Many online instructors regard quizzes as homework (thus assigning minimal points for them), because there is no easy way to guarantee that the students actually took the quiz (instead of a friend), or took it without help from a friend or the textbook (Svinicki & McKeachie, 2014). One hopes that most students do take the online quizzes appropriately, but even if they don't, the practice they receive by thinking about the course content should help them learn the material. Closed-book online exams are a different story.

For one thing, many online instructors use prepackaged test banks to provide questions for quizzes, so that students might face different items each time they retake a quiz. However, many instructors prefer to write their own exams, meaning that the students will be taking exams that contain exactly the same questions. This makes the exam setting important. Most LMSs have an exam feature, but you need to understand what each setting you choose actually means. For example, the first time one of the authors administered an online exam, she used the default settings, not realizing that students were able to keep guessing until they chose the correct answer! Luckily, there was documentation of each student's attempts, so we were able to go back and "fix" this, but this entailed looking at every response of every student—a painstaking process. So, if you don't understand what all the options mean, be sure to have your campus instructional technology group explain them. Double-check that the parameters of the exam are set correctly—for example, the exact date (double-check year if you are teaching this course several times), the exact time that the exam opens and closes, and exactly how much time each student has to take the exam. Be sure, too, that students can save their work as they move through the exam. In many online exam formats, students only save their answers at the end of the exam and this means that a power glitch or student error could result in losing all of the student's work.

Second is the problem of where students take the exam. In one of the author's online course, we offer students three options for taking the exam. All exams are administered via the computer, to make the exam experience as similar for all students as possible. Option One is to take the exam at a computer lab on campus (several of our students live either on campus or a short drive away) at a specific time and which we proctor. Option Two is to take the exam at an approved testing site off campus (who provide proctors)—most of which are on other college campuses. The National College Testing Association (www.ncta-testing.org/cctc/find.php) provides testing locations throughout the United States. Option Three is to use ProctorU, which is often the only option available for international students. The ProctorU Web site describes its service as follows:

ProctorU is a live online proctoring service that allows students to take exams online while ensuring the integrity of the exam for the institution. The service uses proctors who monitor exam takers in three ways. ProctorU proctors:

1. Authenticate the test taker's identity to ensure that the person being monitored is the correct student.

2. Observe the test taker via a webcam. The student is connected to a real person who guides him/her through the process.

3. Watch the test taker's screen in real time and see everything the student is doing both at the location and on screen.

(www.ao.uiuc.edu/support/source/student_
services/proctoru_tech.html)

Both Proctor U and approved testing sites charge students a fee for each exam based on the amount of time it is scheduled to last, so you might want to take cost into consideration when deciding on the number of exams for your course. Be sure to let students know about these costs before they sign up for the course, because only the more experienced online students may be already be aware of them.

Be aware, too, that many of the strategies that teachers recommend for use on paper-and-pencil tests are not feasible for use online. For example, students can't underline important information, and they may not be able to skip a question and come back to it later. Nevertheless, there is evidence that students perform about the same on online tests as they do on paper-and-pencil tests (Davis, 2009; Frein, 2011). Further, students' reactions to online or computer-based testing seems to be based mainly on their experience with this format. One study, for example, found that those who have had experience with computer-based testing were more likely to want to take future exams the same way (Frein, 2011).

* * * * *

Written Assignments

Writing assignments will help your students to improve their writing skills and will help you to better evaluate their knowledge of course material. In addition, as described later in this book, most writing assignments can be configured to serve as active learning and critical thinking exercises. To make the most out of your writing assignments, think about them developmentally—that is, in terms of the academic level of your students and your course materials. In an introductory course, brief writing assignments might be best, while at an advanced level a longer paper requiring higher-order thinking might be a more appropriate choice (Soysa et al., 2013). As always, the assignment should be tied to your learning objectives, and as already noted, it is essential that you develop grading rubrics for every assignment (for in-depth discussion of and templates for rubrics, see Stevens & Levi, 2005; for a review of rubric use in higher education, see Reddy & Andrade, 2010).

Many instructors avoid assigning papers because of the work involved in grading them. This is a legitimate concern, but there are ways to make grading more efficient. These include the use of rubrics, allowing students to write in teams, the use of peer reviewers, and electronic submissions.

Having students write a paper in pairs not only reduces the number of papers you will have to read, but usually increases their quality (Sturtridge, 2012). One of the authors sets aside two class sessions in her honors seminar each term in which student groups write papers. Each group member is to have read a different resource on the same topic and the group is given time to discuss the information. Then they spend the rest of the class period writing a three-to-five-page paper answering the questions that are posed in the assignment. This has resulted in rich and focused group discussions leading up to the writing, as well as evidence that students are integrating information from different sources.

Peer review is another option that highlights an important aspect of the writing process. This option consists of having each student read one to three other students' papers and provide feedback. Both the author and the reviewer can benefit from this review process, but only if you are explicit about what is expected of peer reviewers. Explain that, in addition to making general comments about the draft, reviewers should address a set of more specific questions—such as the strengths and weaknesses of the paper, whether there are sections that are unclear, and what additional problems need attention. Nilson proposed a more extensive list of items to which peer reviewers should respond, including the following (2003, p. 36):

1. What one or two adjectives (aside from short, long, good, or bad) would you choose to describe the title of the paper?
2. In one or two sentences only, state in your own words what you think the writer's position is.
3. Use a highlight pen to mark any passages that you had to read more than once to understand what the writer was saying.
4. Bracket any sentences that you find particularly strong or effective.

You might even ask peer reviewers to "grade" rough drafts using the same set of criteria—the same grading rubric—that you yourself will use when reading the final drafts. This strategy will not only clarify the reviewers' task, but will give them a preview of how their own paper measures up to your expectations.

Finally, electronic submission can streamline your grading of student papers because you do not have to take class time to collect them, and providing feedback is becoming easier as more LMSs include an inline grading component that allows you to make comments on the electronic papers much as you would on paper copies (see Blackboard, for example). In addition, you can cut and paste often-used forms of feedback so that you don't have to repeatedly type the same comments and suggestions. Electronic submission also makes it easy to document who actually turned in the assignment and when it was turned in.

Types of Assignments

Typical writing assignments in psychology courses include term papers, term projects, one-minute papers, mini-papers, journals, 3–2-1 assignments, and student portfolios and self-assessments, among others.

Term Papers or Term Projects

Traditional writing assignments in smaller classes have involved term papers or a term project, and though the trend has been away from such assignments in recent years, many instructors still find such assignments consistent with their learning objectives and class level. If you use such assignments, be sure to explain—in detail and in writing—what you expect from the paper or project and when it is due. Be sure to set up a series of deadlines for completing various stages of the assignment—for example, topic, annotated bibliography, outline, rough draft (Angelo & Cross, 1993; Davis, 2009). If nothing else, give your students a deadline by which to submit for your approval a short description of the topic they plan to write about or study. This simple step will save you a lot of time and effort later, because many students initially choose a topic or research question that is too broad or vague to be addressed effectively within your page limit or time limit. By helping students refine their original question at an early stage, you will help them to avoid false starts and academic disasters while increasing the chances of eventually reading a high-quality paper. In other words, intervene with early feedback rather than criticizing the final product after it is too late to be changed. To put it more succinctly, replace "autopsy" with "coaching" (Walvoord & Anderson, 2010). Be sure also to specify exactly the kinds of project resources that are acceptable and unacceptable. In the days before the Internet, applying this caveat mainly involved warning students against citing sources such as *Cosmopolitan* magazine or other less than scholarly sources, but today it requires us to warn students about Web sites that, although easily accessible, may be utterly unreliable. Indeed, class discussion of what makes a particular Web site reliable is a good critical thinking exercise. If you are in a computer-facilitated classroom, you can show students examples of more and less reliable kinds of Web sites and help them distinguish between .edu, .net, .org, .gov, and .com sites. And, as we discuss in Chapter 7, many academic libraries provide online guidelines for assessing the credibility of Web sites.

One-Minute Papers

At the opposite end of the writing assignment spectrum is the Classroom Assessment Technique (CAT) known as the one-minute paper (Angelo & Cross, 1993). Often assigned to clear up "muddy points" from previous class sessions, they can be used in other contexts as well. The papers are short and focused. Many instructors use the information that students provide about unclear concepts as a guide to developing the next class presentation, rather than as a graded writing component. One instructor goes so far as to e-mail her students individually about their one-minute papers, providing corrective feedback and thus enhancing the teacher–student contact—the first principle of good practice in undergraduate education (Lucas, 2010). Microthemes are even shorter writing assignments that involve asking students to write a summary of the class presentation, answer a question about the material that the teacher has posed, or write a response to a particular theme (e.g., provide one example of how operant conditioning affects your own life). They are often written on five-by-eight cards, forcing students to be succinct (Smit, 2010).

Mini-Papers

Mini-papers lie somewhere between term papers and one-minute papers. You can assign several of them in a given semester to cover a broad spectrum of course material. For example, one of us assigns 10 mini-papers that require introductory psychology students to consult information from 10 of the 18 chapters in the textbook. These assignments include summarizing the culture-specific motivational messages contained in a children's book, describing subtle gender stereotypes in birth congratulation cards, writing a new item for an IQ test, and reporting on the results of an exercise in violating a social norm. Other short assignments can be used to assess students' content knowledge, such as by asking them to design an experiment on some topic or to describe the sensory structures involved in blindness or deafness.

Journals

As an alternative to mini-papers, consider asking students to keep and periodically submit a course-related journal. Such journals can contain several types of entries (Bronstein & Quina, 1988), including responses to specific instructor questions (e.g., "If you had to give up one of your senses, which would it be, and why?"), reactions to a particular lecture or reading assignment, records of daily observations (e.g., dreams, moods, or stressors), questions about course material, and thoughts about how course topics are linked. In short, journals can provide a bridge between course content and student experiences and between instructor and student (Bolin, Khramtsova, & Saarnio, 2005; Connor-Greene, 2000; Fisher, 1996). Journals that require students to write many times a week—summarizing what they have learned and discussing what they don't understand—are also good learning experiences for students (Smit, 2010).

Writing brief comments about what students have written in their journals is yet another way to apply the first principle for good practice in teaching—encouraging student–faculty contact. This contact can be especially important in large classes, where many students might not have the chance or the inclination to participate in class discussions. These students might welcome the opportunity to share their ideas with you in a written format, where they can better organize their thoughts, and can have greater control over what they say and how much they choose to say (Fisher, 1996). Sensitive instructor responses to journal entries can also help build trust between the instructor and student, and reflect the seventh principle of good undergraduate education, namely respecting students' diverse talents and ways of learning. Many instructors report that journal writing increases student learning, and there is at least one study showing that grades in a class requiring journal entries were higher than in a comparable class that did not require journal entries (Connor-Greene, 2000). Further, in end-of-term evaluations students have reported that journal assignments deepened their understanding of course material (Bolin et al., 2005; Connor-Greene, 2000; Fisher, 1996; Hettich, 1990; Stevenson, 1989).

Typically, instructors rate journal entries on criteria such as whether an entry is accurate, whether the examples are appropriate, the depth of thinking exhibited, the quality of writing, or the number of entries (Connor-Greene, 2000; Fisher, 1996; Hettich, 1990). However, some instructors use "effort-based" grading and simply scan entries for errors or good examples, rather than grading the overall content (Bolin et al., 2005).

3-2-1 Assignments

A 3-2-1 assignment integrates a little bit of writing that is related to students' understanding of reading assignments. First, the students read the assignment, describe its three most important concepts, and provide justification for their choices. Next, they identify two concepts or ideas in the reading that they did not understand. Finally, they formulate one question they would like to ask of the textbook's author. Ideally, this question should reflect curiosity about a topic in the reading (Van Gyn, 2013). This third aspect of the assignment is given only for those sections of the book where the reading is more difficult, and if the questions are submitted electronically just prior to the students' next class (as part of just-in-time teaching), the instructor can use them to focus on those aspects of the reading that were most confusing and/or interesting.

Student Portfolios

The student portfolio offers students a chance to reflect on their efforts, progress, and learning in your course (Jacobs & Chase, 1992; King, 2002b; Svinicki & McKeachie, 2014). Like the teaching portfolios discussed in Chapter 8, student portfolios that are created for the purpose of assessment contain a collection of a student's work over some period of time, including previous writing assignments, graded exams, course projects, and other materials. Portfolios are usually in electronic rather than printed form because digital artifacts will help students compile later portfolios, perhaps for a job application (Scott, 2012). An assessment e-portfolio, then, can be a "purposeful collection of student work designed to showcase a student's progress toward, and achievement of, course-specific learning objectives" (Lorenzo & Ittelson, 2005, p. 1).

Portfolios are usually submitted for formative feedback at mid-semester and again at the end of the term, when they are evaluated by the instructor. They can be graded using a pass-fail criterion or a letter grade, and, as with all writing assignments, the criteria for evaluation should be outlined when the portfolio assignment is made. One instructor provides a portfolio assignment as an option to writing a term paper, and specifies that it can include a collection of "news and magazine clippings illustrating psychological concepts, articles and archival sources and data, photographic essays, animations, Internet sites and presentations, student produced videos and CDs, student constructed models, interviews and visits with specialists and experts, among other possibilities" (King,

2002b, p. 4). Each item in the portfolio is to be accompanied by a written reflection about what the student learned about it and how it was connected to the course's content. It has even been suggested that at least one piece of the portfolio include students' reflections on an "instructive failure" (Svinicki & McKeachie, 2014). Portfolios might also contain critiques of journal articles, reflections on videos shown in class, summaries of presentations by guest speakers, and the like (Sanders, 2001).

Student portfolios do take a lot of time to read and grade, and, unfortunately, some students spend too much time collecting items and not enough time reflecting on them (King, 2002b). However, many teachers feel that the disadvantages of assigning portfolios are outweighed by their advantages—including helping students to apply the theories and concepts they learn in psychology, encouraging students to engage course material more deeply, to display creativity, and to communicate their knowledge and understanding through a channel that goes beyond traditional exams and papers (King, 2002b).

Student Self-Assessment

Though teaching does involve ranking students in terms of knowledge retained, teachers also have the opportunity to help students develop self-assessment techniques by encouraging them to reflect on the processes involved in taking tests, completing writing assignments, and participating in group projects (Erickson et al., 2006; Svinicki & McKeachie, 2014). This aspect of teaching can involve no more than asking students to evaluate their contributions to a group's work, using criteria the teacher has established, or can go so far as to ask them to develop the criteria on which their work will be evaluated. You can also promote students' reflection on their writing efforts by asking them to describe what they did well on a paper and to provide examples, and to list what they think were weaknesses in the paper. Asking for this kind of information at the time students submit an assignment will give students a chance to self-assess before they receive potentially biasing feedback from you (Svinicki & McKeachie, 2014).

One instructor we know asks students to use the grading rubric supplied with the assignment to grade their own papers before they submit them. Another instructor allows his students the option of sitting with him as he grades their papers. This instructor believes that these "grading conferences" allow for greater clarity, both in what the student meant when writing the paper and in what the instructor meant in his comments. He also believes that the grading conference allows him to provide better quality feedback to the student, including specific suggestions for improvement (Latham, 2011).

Another approach to student self-assessment is to ask students to reflect on their goals for the course at the beginning of the term and then, at the end of the course, describe what they feel they actually learned (Weimer, 2012c).

Other Writing Assignments

There are many other kinds of writing assignments to consider for your course. For example, you can ask students to write letters addressed to friends or relatives in which they explain course material, or you can ask them to summarize what they found during a course-related search of the Internet (Davis, 2009; Erickson et al., 2006; Svinicki & McKeachie, 2014). You can ask them to write book reviews, letters to the editor, critiques of research studies, and even journal articles in APA style (Davis, 2009). In other words, in making writing assignments, consider options that go beyond the format of the standard term paper. Asking students to write for several different audiences and in several different genres can help them to increase their understanding of the material (Smit, 2010). Nontraditional assignments are likely to be especially interesting and challenging for your students to write and especially interesting for you to read and grade (Davis, 2009).

Online Considerations

Grading typically takes a lot of time and effort in any teaching situation, but even more so in an online course. For example, when grading papers or exams from a face-to-face class, you can point out common mistakes and misconceptions and address them in class. Not only does this save you time, but even students who did not miss the item in question or who did not make that particular mistake in their paper may learn something from in-class feedback. This communal feedback is difficult to achieve online. True, you can post announcements on the course discussion board about the most commonly missed items and explain why certain responses were incorrect, but the richness of a class discussion is lost. Further, because online students "see" you only in an electronic format, you have to exert more effort to promote individual student–instructor interaction. This means that you will have to provide more detailed grading information than might be necessary in a face-to-face course. In addition, the mechanics of grading online may not be ideal. Most LMSs link multiple choice exams and quizzes to the gradebook. Some even include an inline grading system that allows you to grade electronic papers much as you would paper ones—for example, writing comments in appropriate places, and so forth. Unfortunately, other LMSs do not have these helpful features, meaning that there may be more steps than usual in transferring grades into the gradebook in an online environment. Some of these same LMS problems do appear in face-to-face classrooms, too, but with face-to-face, paper-and-pencil assessment items, you can gather and grade them anywhere—an option not available in a totally online course.

● ● ● ● ●

Applying the Psychology of Learning to Student Evaluation

In the persona of Father Guido Sarducci, comedian Don Novello touted the advantages of the "Five Minute University," where students could spend five minutes learning all the information they would have remembered five years after completing a college degree. This hilarious notion is based on the not-so-funny fact that, no matter how you evaluate your students, the results all too often reflect their ability to store information until it is no longer needed for the purpose of earning a good grade. The fact that most students forget most of what they hear or read in a course within a few weeks or months is consistent with the results of laboratory research on human learning and memory in general. Students' performance on tests does not necessarily reflect long-term retention, which is what most teachers think of as learning (Halpern & Hakel, 2002). While there is probably no way to ensure that students will forever remember everything in our courses, research in cognitive psychology suggests that certain evaluation procedures might help students to retain course information longer and in a more useable format (see also Ambrose et al., 2010 for an in-depth discussion of how students learn).

Massed versus Distributed Practice: The Spacing Effect

One of the most robust research findings is that long-term retention is improved when students engage in numerous study sessions (distributed practice) rather than when they "cram" during a single session on the night before a quiz or exam (massed practice) (Bjork, 1979, 2013; Cepada et al., 2006; Dunlosky et al., 2013; Graesser, 2011; Rohrer & Pashler, 2010). With this in mind, consider giving enough exams and quizzes that students will be reading and studying more or less continuously. You can also promote distributed practice by including a few unannounced "pop" quizzes (Ruscio, 2001; Willyard, 2010). Some instructors avoid giving pop quizzes for fear of creating a stressful classroom atmosphere, but this strategy allows students to reap the benefits of the steady reading and studying and regular class attendance that pop quizzes encourage.

Retrieval Practice: The Testing Effect

There is overwhelming evidence that the more students practice retrieving information, especially in different settings, the more they will learn (Dunlosky et al., 2013; Karpicke & Blunt, 2011; Roediger & Karpicke, 2006a, 2006b; Rohrer & Pashler, 2010). This testing effect occurs even when students receive no feedback on the results of the test and even when they are more confident in their ability after studying rather than after taking a test (Roediger & Karpicke, 2006a). In other words, "testing, although typically used merely as an assessment device, directly potentiates learning and does so more effectively than any other modes of study" (Rohrer & Pashler, 2010, p. 1).

Not everyone is convinced about the virtues of frequent classroom testing, though. Some instructors believe, for example, that the focus of class time should be on active learning and creative activities. There is also concern that students will balk at being required to take daily or frequent tests. Fortunately, both approaches can coexist. Frequent testing can help students to better understand and retain the material they need to successfully engage in active learning and other class activities, and when teachers present and explain the rationale for frequent testing in an authoritative fashion, student will understand the need for frequent testing (see Roediger & Karpicke, 2006b, pp. 205–206 for examples).

So, the "take-home message" seems to be that instructors should plan their testing program to promote learning as well as to assess it—and be sure to explain this rationale to their students.

Desirable Difficulties

Robert Bjork (1979, 1999, 2013a, 2013b) coined the term *desirable difficulties* to describe training conditions that are difficult for the student and appear to impede performance during training, but later result in long-term retention. Desirable difficulties "include spacing rather than massing study opportunities; interleaving rather than blocking practice on separate topics; varying how to-be-learned material is presented; providing intermittent, rather than continuous, feedback; and using tests, rather than presentations, as learning events" (Bjork, 2013b Graesser, 2011; Nelson et al., 2013). He argues that to be most effective in the long run, we need to "slow down" learning and we can do this by interleaving concepts to be learned rather than teaching concepts "in blocks." For example, we can address important concepts frequently and in different contexts rather than covering them only once during a course. In other words, if material is important, it should not just be "covered" and then dropped; it should presented throughout the course and interwoven with other concepts.

Like spacing and frequent testing, the creation of desirable difficulties can improve students' long-term retention of course material. You can take advantage of desirable difficulties by giving cumulative exams and quizzes that require students to retrieve information about past as well as current course material. Similarly, you can teach your content as an integrated whole, rather than in separate units. So, talk about neurotransmission, for example, not only in relation to the biological chapter of an introductory psychology textbook, but also when presenting topics such as learning, drug effects, stress and coping, and mental disorders.

Bjork reminds us that creating desirable difficulties requires that we do things that are "unintuitive and unappealing," but that these things promote our goal of promoting long-term retention, not just short-term performance on tests. And as in the case of frequent testing, students will accept and even appreciate your research-based methods if you present them with confidence and in the context of a broader authoritative teaching approach (see Chapter 4).

Feedback

Learning is also enhanced when students receive prompt and constructive feedback that helps them to identify and correct mistakes (Chickering & Gamson, 1987; Desrochers & Zell, 2013; Dinham, 1996; Ory, 2003). If many days, or even weeks, pass between taking a test and receiving feedback on it, an important learning opportunity will have been missed. In fact, there is evidence that even when students fail a test, the experience can enhance learning as long as the feedback is immediate (Hays, Kornell, & Bjork, 2012). Yet many instructors pay too little attention to this vital aspect of teaching. They may delay returning exams for many days, or even weeks, or return them without discussing them because they don't want to listen to complaints or because they believe that the discussion would take up too much class time.

We believe, however, that at the very least you should describe and discuss in class the most frequently missed items. Fortunately, some instructors go beyond this minimum to provide an opportunity for students to work individually or in groups, in class or outside of class, to find the correct answers and/or fix their mistakes. This process can maximize learning from the exam they just took (Weimer, 2013b) and may improve their scores if they are tested on the same material in the future.

The feedback we provide our student should be informative rather than punitive. Rather than merely writing something like "vague" or "No!" on an essay exam, take time to explain why the student did not receive full credit for an answer (Desrochers & Zell, 2013). Be sure to point out what they did well and provide information on how they can improve (Desrochers & Zell, 2013; Smit, 2010). Constructive, helpful feedback "provides clear directions for the future and instills in the learner the desire to engage in further inquiry. It is written understandably and invites the learner to discuss with the teacher anything that strikes her as unfair, unclear, or unjustified" (Brookfield, 2006, p. 178). The characteristics of helpful feedback include:

- *Clarity*—students know what criteria are being used to judge, for example, rubrics;

- *Immediacy*—feedback comes soon enough to provide immediate knowledge of results;

- *Regularity*—students' work is commented on regularly, not just once or twice during the semester;

- *Accessibility*—students can understand the language and examples in the feedback;

- *Individualized*—"the more individualized the feedback the student receives the more she feels it is important to learn the abilities or skills the teacher is trying to develop. Giving detailed, clearly individualized attention to learners' efforts makes it clear that you consider it important that they learn the desired content and also shows that you respect the effort they have made" (Brookfield, 2006, p. 186);

- *Affirming*—always acknowledge the students' efforts and achievements before making critical comments;

- *Future Oriented*—provide clear suggestions for specific actions students should make to make progress;

- *Justifiable*—describe how your comments will be in the students' best long-term interests and that they come from a concern for their learning; and

- *Educative*—"Keep asking yourself 'What can this person learn from my comments?'" (Brookfield, 2006, 185–187).

Contrary to what you might hear from some of your more cynical colleagues, many students do pay heed to the feedback that teachers take the time to provide. They are particularly responsive to feedback that is specific, detailed, and individualized (Jonsson, 2012), that is based on previously presented rubrics, and that combines positive and supportive comments with critical ones (Smith, 2008). This last point is important because negative comments can be particularly painful for some students, especially those who, as mentioned earlier, may have difficulty separating criticism of their writing from criticism of themselves as human beings.

Of course, some students do ignore feedback, and though it may be because they are not interested in learning, it may also be for other reasons, including a lack of understanding of the academic jargon or terminology or lack of knowledge about how to use feedback (Jonsson, 2012). To maximize the likelihood that students will take in and act on feedback, teachers should present it in ways that focus on task compliance (to what extent did the student do what the assignment requested) and quality (how did the student's work compare to previously described examples of excellence), and should help the student to understand abstract criteria such as "coherence" (Sadler, 2010). Unfortunately, teachers often give feedback that is so focused on justifying the grade they gave (e.g., why it was a B and not an A-), that they forget to suggest how students might use the feedback to develop a specific action plan for doing better on the next assignment (Weimer, 2012b).

Further, feedback is also easy to ignore when, as is usually the case, it takes the form of one-way communication from teacher to student. As mentioned already, one way to overcome this problem is to provide ongoing feedback on and discussion of various stages of an assignment rather than just grading the final product (Nicol, 2010). Keep in mind, too, that students can provide feedback to each other by sharing and critiquing written assignments, and that classroom assessment techniques (CATS) can help students gain quick feedback on their own learning (Svinicki & McKeachie, 2014). Finally, remember that to be most valuable, feedback in all its forms should be more or less continuous throughout the term, not concentrated at the end of the course (Astin & Antonio, 2012).

Online Considerations

Most of the assessment-for-learning techniques we have discussed here will work very well in an online environment. Frequent testing or quizzing is actually easier to do electronically and without taking "class time." Creating desirable difficulties will work in some situations, too, but online teachers tend to have less control over how material is learned. For example, some online classes open all of the content to students at the beginning of the course, and students can go through the material at their own pace. Although most online courses are structured on a weekly basis, students can work ahead and thus might be engaged with different material than the student who is "on track." In addition, it is difficult if not impossible to talk through with students the frustration created by desirable difficulties. And because most online courses allow students to access the material whenever they desire, they can concentrate their work even when they would be better off distributing it.

While feedback to students is important in any type of class, it is especially crucial for students in online courses because, for example, misconceptions cannot be cleared up in class. And because students are working with class material alone, it is easy for them to feel isolated; individualized feedback can help them to feel that they are a part of the class. We recommend that you look at your LMS carefully if you are at the stage of being able to choose. Some LMSs make it relatively easy to provide frequent feedback; others do not.

With the advent of inline grading in some LMSs, providing detailed, personal feedback on written assignments for student in an online class or in a face-to-face class requiring online submission is actually as easy, or easier, than writing comments on paper. In one study, students and faculty felt that e-feedback procedures "increase clarity of feedback compared to handwriting, save paper and ink resources, and result in faster and also better, more detailed feedback." And while most faculty did not think e-feedback saved them time, they did feel that such feedback enhanced student learning (McCabe, Doerflinger, & Fox, 2011).

⬤ ⬤ ⬤ ⬤ ⬤

Some Final Comments

Like other aspects of your teaching, the perceived quality and fairness of the quizzes, exams, papers, and other graded assignments you give can have a significant impact on your students' reactions to you and your courses. Their reactions to being evaluated, and your reactions to their reactions, will either support or undermine the teacher–student relationship that we see as the touchstone for success in teaching psychology. We examine that relationship and its complexities in the next chapter.

6

●●●●●

Faculty–Student Relationships

The Ethical Use of Teacher Power
Managing the Classroom Climate
Recognizing Student Demographics
Enhancing Students' Motivation to Learn
Dealing with Students' Excuses and Complaints
Classroom Incivilities
Addressing the Problems of Problem Students
Academic Dishonesty
Providing Academic Help
Writing Letters of Recommendation
Some Final Comments

Interacting with students is the most exciting, and sometimes the most difficult, aspect of teaching. Most students will enter your courses with positive expectations about you and with high hopes of enjoying themselves and doing well. These expectations provide the foundation for a good learning experience and a good teaching experience. The suggestions we have made in previous chapters should help you build on that foundation by offering a well-organized course in a fair and consistent manner that conveys your concern for teaching effectively. In this chapter, we offer additional suggestions that are focused specifically on forging productive, mutually respectful relationships with your students and on preventing and dealing with the relationship problems that can arise.

●●●●●
The Ethical Use of Teacher Power

Teaching in an ethical fashion is the cornerstone of teacher–student interactions, but the ethics of teaching are not emphasized to graduate students as much as those governing research, testing, and therapy (Komarraju & Handelsman, 2012). Although the APA's Ethical Principles for Psychologists (2010) regarding competence, confidentiality, and avoiding harm (e.g., sexual harassment and multiple relationships) are certainly applicable to educational settings, teaching is rarely mentioned. (For a discussion of APA ethics and education, see Clay, 2013.) The main exception is Standard 7.03, Accuracy in Teaching, which states: "Psychologists take reasonable steps to ensure that course syllabi are accurate regarding the subject matter to be covered, bases for evaluating progress and the nature of course experiences. . . . When engaged in teaching or training, psychologists present psychological information accurately."

Fortunately there are other sources of ethical guidance. Patricia Keith-Spiegel and her colleagues organized their casebook, *The Ethics of Teaching,* around eight general, ethical principles in teaching: respect for the autonomy of others (students); doing no harm; benefit to others (enhancing student welfare); fairness and equity; fidelity and honesty; dignity; caring; and doing one's best (Keith-Spiegel et al., 2002, pp. xvii–xix). G. William Hill and Dorothy Zinsmeister (2012) provided additional guidelines, pointing out that ethical teachers have disciplinary competence; teach effectively through effective pedagogy; provide balanced content and free inquiry; respect students; foster academic integrity; use objective and fair assessments; protect students' privacy; and maintain professionally appropriate relationships with students. Let's consider these characteristics in more detail.

Disciplinary Competence

It goes without saying that you should know what you are talking about when you teach (Komarraju & Handelsman, 2012). Meeting this standard is not always easy because, due to staffing cutbacks and other administrative problems, many teachers find themselves assigned to teach courses that are outside their areas of expertise or specialization. Still, ethical teachers do all they can to become as knowledgeable as possible about course content (Huston, 2009). It is unethical to teach a course in which one has no background or is unable to prepare enough to meet a minimum level of competence.

Effective Teaching through Effective Pedagogy

Ethical teachers make it a practice to stay as up to date as possible on research-based teaching methods (Pusateri, 2012). It is important to read journals on the teaching of psychology and/or on teaching in higher education generally, as is attending teaching conferences and online teaching events when possible. Most of all it is vital that teachers use the information they gain, including from psychological research on learning (e.g., Bjork, 2013; Dweck, 2008) in designing their courses and planning their pedagogy.

Balanced Content and Free Inquiry

As already mentioned, APA's Standard 7.03 states that ethical teachers present course materials and assign readings that fairly represent the state of the science in the areas of psychology covered by their courses (APA, 2010). So even though you might not be a great fan of certain psychological theories, methods, or points of view, ethical practice requires that you at least make your students aware of that material and of the research findings related to it (Komarraju & Handelsman, 2012). In addition to providing fair and balanced coverage of course content, you also have an ethical obligation to ensure that the content is as current as possible. Presenting out-of-date or discredited information in a psychology course is not only misleading, it is unethical. In addition, you should ensure that your students feel free to question your assertions in an appropriate fashion and to assert competing ideas for discussion without fear of punishment or penalty.

Respect for Students

Most students are respectful of their teachers, and teachers can maintain that respect by returning it in kind. This means applying rules fairly and consistently to all students in all situations, following a consistent grading policy throughout the term, and displaying no bias in favor of or against specific individuals or groups (Komarraju & Handelsman, 2012). And indeed, most instructors know that it would be unethical to behave in ways that reflect derogatory beliefs or attitudes toward students on the basis of disabilities or sexual orientation or racial or ethnic background (Hill & Zinsmeister, 2012; Komarraju & Handelsman, 2012), but some faculty may be less concerned about respecting nonprotected classes such as older adults, members of Greek organizations, and athletes. They may see students in these groups as "fair game" for teasing (Jolly, 2008; Simons et al., 2007). One student athlete reported a professor in a 400-student lecture class said, "It's an easy test. Even athletes can pass" (Simons et al., 2007, p. 251). We are sure the class laughed, but derogatory comments aimed at nonprotected groups have no place in any classroom.

Fostering Academic Integrity

Ethical instructors design their courses so as to foster academic integrity. They not only reward students for following rules, but go out of their way to increase students' awareness of behaviors that are considered dishonest in an academic setting (see our discussion of academic integrity later in this chapter).

Objective and Fair Assessments

Ethical instructors employ the kind of assessment instruments described in Chapter 5. These assessments are effective, tied to course objectives, and fair to all of the students in the class (Komarraju & Handelsman, 2012; Pusateri, 2012). Similarly, our advice in Chapters 2 and 3 about clearly announcing and strictly adhering to one's grading system is in accord with APA ethical standards. These standards state that students should know how they will be evaluated and that evaluation be based solely on announced criteria. The standards also state that teachers should provide students with an accurate description of the course, including information in the syllabus about grading procedures (APA, 2010; Saville, 2012). Ethical considerations also underlie our discussion in Chapter 2 regarding the importance of writing a syllabus that is thought out in advance so that the teacher need not deviate from it.

The same can be said about the importance of returning quizzes, tests, and other graded assignments as soon as possible. Doing so is consistent not only with effective teaching principles, but with APA Standard 7.06, which requires psychology faculty to provide timely and specific feedback to students (it is also consistent with Teaching Principle 4: Good Practice Gives Prompt Feedback).

Protecting Students' Privacy

The obligation to protect your students' right to privacy is outlined in the APA's (2010) Standard 7.04, as well as in the Family Educational Rights and Privacy Act of 1974 (FERPA). As outlined in FERPA, students' privacy rights extend to all educational records, including grades, and the procedures used for posting grades and returning graded assignments.

Many instructors are surprised to find, for example, that it is illegal to post quiz, exam, or final grades on an office door or on an electronic bulletin board using the last five digits of university ID numbers to identify students. Fortunately, today's LMSs eliminate the need to do so because the LMS gradebook allows students to get the results of an exam or quiz almost immediately. Most LMS gradebooks also allow students to see the mean, standard deviation, and frequency distribution of their class's scores, without seeing other students' scores or grades. FERPA also bars teachers from returning physical papers, quizzes, exams, or other graded assignments in a manner that might allow students to see any score or grade other than their own. Accordingly, it is neither legal nor ethical to allow students to look for their results by searching in a pile of graded material in the classroom or, say, in a box outside your office.

You can get further information about FERPA at www.ed.gov/policy/gen/guid/fpco/ferpa/index.html, and view a tutorial about its key features at www.registrar.illinois.edu/staff/ferpa_tutorial/.

Professionally Appropriate Relationships with Students

Even if you have never taught before, your students will (correctly) perceive you as having power and authority, if for no other reason than you will be assigning their grades. For example, unless you tell them otherwise, students will probably address you as "Professor" or "Doctor," and they will look to you to establish the rules and the style of interaction that will prevail in the course. This power differential needs to be acknowledged and taken into account in all aspects of the faculty–student relationship (Wilson, Smalley, & Yancey, 2012).

For example, APA Standard 7.07 warns psychology teachers not to engage in sexual relationships with students or anyone else over whom they have or are likely to have evaluative authority. In our view, there are no exceptions to this rule, and those who violate it are likely to be guilty of sexual harassment. Most instructors know that having, expressing, or acting on sexual or romantic feelings toward students is unethical (APA, 2010; Hill & Zinsmeister, 2012; Keith-Spiegel et al., 2002; Komarraju & Handelsman, 2012; Wilson et al., 2012). Even when initiated with the best of intentions on both sides, such relationships contain inherently coercive elements that can be psychologically harmful to the student involved. Further, once the relationship becomes public (as it eventually will), it will undermine the teacher's relationship with the rest of the class by raising doubts about his or her character and the fairness of the course grading system.

Ethical teaching also requires that instructors not accept gifts from students, and while most teachers recognize the inappropriateness of receiving cash or jewelry, many do not realize that "gifts" can also include small favors or even party invitations from students in their classes (Komarraju & Handelsman, 2012). Further, many instructors are surprised to discover that "placing personal considerations ahead of obligations to students" could also be considered unethical (Komarraju & Handelsman, 2012). For example, it might be fun to go to the movies after a long day at school, but an ethical teacher will give up that pleasure if it means being able to finish grading exams in time to return them on the promised date. It would be unethical, too, to provide extra credit to students who engage in behaviors, such as donating blood, that are unrelated to the course, but of personal significance to their teacher (Hill & Zinsmeister, 2012).

Similarly, ethical teachers do not impose their personal political, moral, or religious beliefs on students. It is all too easy to err in this regard, because the views you express in a lecture or discussion about psychology, or anything else, will carry the weight of authority, and if you push those views too hard, students could feel coerced to accept them or even adopt them—on papers and exams, at least. Remember, too, that casual remarks that appear to condone excessive drinking, illegal drug use, or the like can legitimize these activities in students' minds, even though you might have meant them as a joke or to show that you are "cool."

Online Considerations

Several ethical dilemmas are accentuated in an online course. For example, teacher competency includes not only knowledge of course content and pedagogy, but also enough technical expertise to teach the course effectively. Gaining this competency may require you to take courses that have been developed to train online teachers (e.g., Sloan Consortium or the University of Illinois Online Network Program).

The use of media and print resources in an online course can also be a much bigger problem than it is in a traditional classroom (Elison-Bowers & Snelson, 2012). "Fair use" often covers instructors in face-to-face courses who use clips from YouTube or videos from textbook Web sites, but a much stricter standard applies if these same resources are to be used online. So, although there are efforts under way to ease these standards for online courses, ethical online instructors today must be diligent in ensuring that they do not infringe on copyrights.

Online instructors also have the added burden of maintaining student privacy in a totally digital format (Elison-Bowers & Snelson, 2012). This is because in online courses, as with most LMSs, students' activities are tracked every time they log on. This includes the amount of time they take to complete quizzes or other assignments, and depending on how teachers set up the system, exactly how students responded to or changed answers on individual questions. In other words, online teachers have much more information about their students' behavior than they do in face-to-face classes, and thus have an increased obligation to make sure that this information remains confidential and secure (Elison-Bowers & Snelson, 2012).

• • • • •

Managing the Classroom Climate

Upholding the highest ethical standards is just one element of the social and psychological climate you create in the classroom. The nature of that climate will have a strong influence on your students' classroom attendance and their academic progress in your course (Erickson, Peters, & Strommer, 2006; Leamnson, 1999; Lescher, 2013; Wilson & Ryan, 2012; Wilson et al., 2012). All else being equal, students tend to stick with and learn more from classes in which they feel comfortable and valued as individuals (Sleigh & Ritzer, 2001; Sleigh, Ritzer, & Casey, 2002). These perceptions are especially important among first-year students, who might enter the college classroom with the greatest trepidation and the strongest need for support.

Establishing Rapport

Students are more likely to feel comfortable and valued if you go out of your way to establish rapport with them. In the context of teaching, *rapport* refers to the process of creating emotional connections between teacher and student (Buskist & Saville, 2001; Wilson & Ryan, 2012; Wilson et al., 2012).

Establishing rapport is not a magical process. Student surveys suggest that rapport is built mainly by following the principles of good teaching practice that we outlined in Chapter 1 and illustrated in other chapters. In one such survey, the teacher behaviors that contributed most to the development of rapport were, in order of importance: displaying a sense of humor; being available to students before, after, or outside of class; encouraging class discussion; showing interest in students; knowing students' names; sharing personal insights and experiences with the class; relating course material using everyday terms and examples; and understanding that students sometimes have problems that hinder their progress (Buskist & Saville, 2001). Other studies suggest that rapport is also enhanced by an appropriate degree of personal disclosure by the teacher (Lescher, 2013; Wilson et al., 2012).

Rapport is facilitated, too, when teachers display a cluster of nonverbal behaviors that includes eye contact, smiles, an expressive speaking style, establishing physical proximity during interactions, using appropriate movements and gestures, appearing relaxed, and spending time with students (Andersen, 1986). These behaviors are referred to as *immediacy* because they create the impression that the teacher is psychologically engaged with the students and the class, not an aloof figure who is merely going through the motions of teaching. Verbal behaviors that reinforce the sense of immediacy include asking students about their work, soliciting students' views on course-related matters, and offering praise for good work. As you might expect, students tend to like teachers who display immediacy, and tend to work hard in those teachers' courses (Anderson, 1999; Sanders & Wiseman, 1994). One study found that students taking difficult courses performed better and had more confidence in their abilities if they also had a positive relationship with their professor (Micari & Pazos, 2012). A concept similar to rapport, called *pedagogical caring,* refers to five related aspects of teacher behavior: preparation and enthusiasm; encouragement and providing a safe environment; recognition of diversity of students' learning approaches; checking on comprehension; and providing constructive feedback (Bandura & Lyons, 2012).

The Professor-Student Rapport Scale might be useful in assessing rapport in your own classes (Ryan, Wilson, & Pugh, 2011; Wilson & Ryan, 2013; Wilson, 2012). You can go a long way toward establishing rapport simply by being friendly with students, but don't try to be their friend (Buskist, 2013c; Clement & Whatley, 2012). Ethical and pedagogical considerations require that you maintain a certain degree of professional distance. As one instructor put it, "When dealing with students, your goal as a professor should always be to adopt a tone that is friendly, not familiar" (Buller, 2010, p. 190).

Ensuring Inclusiveness

Remember that all classrooms are diverse, even if the diversity is not obvious. Some of your students will have learning disabilities, military experience, histories of abuse, international backgrounds, and the like (Plank & Rohdieck, 2013). To create a classroom climate in which all students feel comfortable and valued, you have to put yourself in the shoes of students who differ from you—or from the majority of their fellow students—in terms of ethnicity, religion, gender, age, sexual orientation, physical or sensory capacity, and the like.

So, for example, don't ask minority group students to represent their ethnic or cultural group's views of, say, putting children in day care, gay marriage, the value of achievement motivation, or other course-related topics. Singling out students in this way can easily make them feel uncomfortable, not only because it's impossible for them to summarize the views of the group they represent, but also because asking them to do so suggests the existence of a stereotype that applies to everyone in that group. It is fine to ask students to speak for themselves, but asking them to speak for a whole category of people—at the same time highlighting their membership in that category—is not a good way to make them feel included (Lieberg, 2008). In other words, treat students as individuals, not as representatives of specific groups.

Students' sense of inclusion is enhanced when their teacher makes an effort to pronounce their names correctly (Davis, 2009). Doing so is sometimes difficult, especially in relation to international students or those from minority cultures, but it is important. We ask these students to provide us with a phonetic spelling of their names, or we create our own spellings next to their names on our class roster. Greeting students by name as they arrive for class gives you a chance to practice pronouncing difficult names and to confirm the accuracy of your efforts. Those efforts help promote the broader goal of developing multicultural competence as a teacher (Phelps, 2012; Rodriguez & Bates, 2012; see also APA's Multicultural Guidelines, 2002, 2008).

So, when developing your course, make sure that students will be exposed to diverse perspectives on the major themes of the course (Pittenger, 2006). Try to choose readings that are gender neutral and do not perpetuate stereotypes (Davis, 2009), and consider inviting guest speakers or using media resources (such as TED talks) that provide diverse perspectives. In lectures and discussions, use references and examples that are diverse enough to let your students know that you don't presume they are all Americans, heterosexuals, Christians, males, whites, blacks, females, or representatives of any other particular group. Mixing male and female pronouns and using gender-neutral pronouns are the most obvious ways to convey awareness and acceptance of student diversity, but there are many others, too. If you are discussing research on religiosity, for example, use the more inclusive phrase "house of worship" rather than specifics such as churches, synagogues, or mosques (Davis, 2009). In lecturing about interpersonal attraction, remember that attraction can be heterosexual, homosexual, or bisexual. Because in some places marriage is not an option for your homosexual students, they are more likely to feel included if you refer to "marriage or partnerships" and to "couples" rather than just "married couples." Similarly, avoid repeated comments or references that presume everyone in the class is a sports fan, an avid hunter, a devotee of current TV shows, or has any other characteristics that give special access to the meaning of your lectures. And it should go without saying that it is inappropriate to make sarcastic or joking comments about any condition or any group of people. Consider how you would feel if your teacher made light of obesity or dementia or some other mental or physical condition or disorder that was a problem for you or a loved one. It is easier to avoid making such mistakes if you keep in mind that every aspect of behavior and behavior disorder will be represented among your students or in someone they know.

In setting up teams for class discussions or cooperative learning, assign students to their groups. If you let students form groups on their own, their choices might maintain preexisting cliques or exclude certain individuals based on gender, ethnicity, or other demographic characteristics. Creating diversity in such groups benefits all students by ensuring that they interact with peers who differ from themselves, peers with whom they might otherwise never have exchanged ideas or gotten to know (Davis, 2009).

When writing quiz and exam questions, use ethnically diverse names for hypothetical people and make sure that the examples and terms used will be familiar to all your students. Like fish unaware of the water they swim in, we can all be unaware of the cultural waters in which we are immersed, so whenever possible ask one or more colleagues (ideally someone representing the other gender and perhaps another culture) to review your exam items and give you feedback about those that might contain gender-specific or culture-bound content.

Finally, remember to include the entire class with your eyes. As suggested in Chapter 4, scan the entire classroom as you speak, making eye contact with everyone, not just your favorite students or the ones who are most responsive and interested. Doing so not only ensures that you can see all students who raise a hand or show a puzzled expression, but also lets all students know that they are part of the class—even those in the last row or in the far corners, those who usually don't participate in discussions, and anyone else you might otherwise be tempted to pass over for some reason (Svinicki & McKeachie, 2014).

Dealing with Sensitive or Controversial Topics

Many psychology courses cover sensitive or controversial topics that students do not normally address and about which they hold strong, emotionally charged views. It can be challenging to maintain a comfortable classroom climate when lecturing about or leading discussions on such topics (Miller & Flores, 2012; Seward, 2002). We don't pretend to know how to handle these situations to perfection, but there are some things you can do to turn these discussions into opportunities for teaching and learning rather than just a free-for-all expression of divergent points of view (Miller & Flores, 2012).

For example, be sure to have empirical data available to enlighten students about the facts surrounding the topic under discussion. Encourage students to recognize the difference between what they believe, what they feel, and what they know. Another way to keep the level of discussions on a high plane is to assign groups of students to study each of several different viewpoints on a sensitive or controversial topic, and then to summarize that viewpoint in a classroom presentation. This approach allows the class to consider differing perspectives on the topic that are based on each group's research, not on the casual and possibly ill-advised comments of one individual. The result might be a more moderate and balanced discussion from which everyone can learn (Allen, 2000; Heuberger, Gerber, & Anderson, 1999). This process has been described as "disagreeing in an agreeable manner" (Desrochers, 2000). This same goal can also be achieved by assigning students to read articles or essays that represent varying points of view on the topic to be discussed in class (Heuberger et al., 1999). Before discussing the role of sociocultural variables on, say, achievement motivation or prejudice, you could make students aware of other perspectives by asking them to read a magazine or newsletter that was written for members of a particular ethnic group, gender, religious group, or sexual orientation (Seward, 2002). You might even ask students to write a page in which they speculate about how their behavior and thinking and motivation and outlook on life might have been different if they were of a different race, gender, or sexual orientation (Seward, 2002).

Some more specific guidelines that have served us well over our years of teaching are predicated on the assumption that you have established an atmosphere of openness and mutual respect early in the course (Anderson, 1999). The first of these is to be prepared (Allen, 2000; Seward, 2002). Part of that preparation involves recognizing your own strongly held views on certain topics, and, in accordance with ethical standards, resolving not to let those views turn your classroom into a setting for persuasion or proselytizing. Further, think about how you want the class discussion to proceed, and give your students time to prepare and think about each planned discussion, possibly by inviting them to submit (perhaps anonymously) written questions or comments about each topic on the day before it is covered in class (Brooke, 1999). You can use these questions and comments to tailor your lectures and to frame discussions. Simply reminding students about an upcoming controversial topic may be enough to motivate them to do the reading associated with that topic, and perhaps to begin considering what they think about it and what they want to know about it.

Second, present sensitive material in a mature and straightforward way. Model a serious academic approach that your students can emulate. If the topic includes mention of masturbation or oral sex, for example, use the terms themselves, not vague references to "self-abuse" or "sodomy." Similarly, use these terms in a natural way. If you seem hesitant to use certain words or to address certain topics, your students probably will be, too, when the time comes to ask questions or engage in a discussion. If you are not entirely comfortable describing or discussing certain topics in class, practice discussing the material in private to help yourself get used to dealing with it.

Third, acknowledge that people might have strong feelings and differing views on topics such as evolutionary theories of mate selection or racial differences in cognitive skills. If you have developed (and, ideally, published in your syllabus) ground rules for class discussion, remind students about them before the discussion begins. Make it clear at the outset that although concern over political correctness need not stifle the expression of opinions or the posing of questions, everyone must consider the rights and feelings of others and should expect others to do the same. If you encounter comments that are extreme or intemperate, point out that although everyone has the right to hold and express personal views, discussion in an academic classroom must occur in an atmosphere of mutual respect (Allen, 2000; Marin, 2000). If inappropriate or harmful comments continue, don't ignore them, but handle them with care. As mentioned in relation to classroom discussions in Chapter 4, there is not much point in castigating students who make inappropriate comments because doing so is unlikely to alter—and might even solidify—those students' views. An overly harsh response will probably also lead those students to refrain from further discussions on any topic, and worst of all, will stop the current discussion in its tracks. Instead, as also described in Chapter 4, you can use such comments to create "teachable moments" that serve not only to enlighten the speaker and the class, but also to move the discussion forward (Anderson, 1999). Above all, use humility, humor, and goodwill to defuse hostility and suspicion and to promote openness and collegiality, and let students know that you are available if they want to talk individually about their concerns regarding sensitive or controversial topics.

Online Considerations

Creating a good classroom environment is especially difficult in an online class. First, most of the attributes of immediacy, for example, eye contact and smiling, do not apply to an online environment. Thus, creating a bond between yourself and your students takes much more effort and requires different skills. Rapport in an online course primarily revolves around how your course is structured and how available and approachable you are. Your course must contain aspects that involve teacher feedback and opportunities for informal student–teacher interaction. As already noted, rapid feedback is essential in an online course, so giving some early, low-stakes assignments for which you provide quick and personal feed-back can enhance teacher–student rapport. Of course, setting up a discussion board where students can ask questions is important, but so, too, is your monitoring of that discussion board and providing quick responses to clarify confusion and answer questions. If there is a synchronous aspect to your course, use video as well as audio so that students can see you as you interact with them, thus allowing you to express some of the immediacy characteristics we described earlier. Just as in a face-to-face course, if you really care about your online students you will have to find ways to demonstrate that caring. Anything you can do to make yourself more human, approachable, and "authentic" will aid in the development of rapport in your online course.

Discussing controversial topics online is fraught with special difficulties. This is partly because, as is well known, most people are more apt to make impolite and incendiary comments online than in face-to-face conversation. Thus it becomes even more important than usual to set ground rules for civility at the beginning of your online course and it is even more critical to closely monitor online discussions. And don't forget to monitor yourself. That self-disclosing or marginally inappropriate "off-the-cuff" comment that popped out of you in a face-to-face class might be quickly forgotten, but it will be preserved forever online, so just as when communicating in daily e-mails, present yourself as if you were communicating to a worldwide audience.

Recognizing Student Demographics

As we said in Chapter 1, if you have taught in higher education for a considerable period of time, you have probably noticed that the demographics of the students in your classroom have changed. For example, the general increase in enrollment in institutions of higher education is primarily due to an influx of older students (i.e., those over 25), female students, minority students, and first-generation students (Hoover, 2013; NCES, 2012; U.S. Census Bureau, 2012). So the student population in higher education is more diverse than ever. For example, up to 75% of undergraduates can be classified as "nontraditional," meaning that they may be older than usual, employed full time, financially independent, have dependents other than a spouse, are single parents, and even lack a high school diploma (Hanson et al., 2011). This diversity can lead to more intellectually stimulating classrooms and also to a wider range of approaches to learning and to academics in general.

Generation Y

Many teachers feel that today's students lack motivation, hold disrespectful attitudes, are irresponsible about completing assignments on time (or at all), are too dependent on their instructors, cheat on tests or plagiarize papers, and feel entitled to good grades and special treatment simply because they come to class (Kopp et al., 2010; Lippmann, Bulanda, & Wagenaar, 2009; Nilson, 2010; Singelton-Jackson, Jackson, & Reinhardt, 2010; Twenge, 2009, 2013). Research on student entitlement has even resulted in a set of *Academic Entitlement Scales* to measure it (Kopp et al., 2010). There is debate about whether hyper-entitled, unmotivated, dependent, irresponsible, and dishonest students are more numerous now than in the past (e.g., Arnett, 2010; Eckersley, 2010; Greenberger et al., 2008; Roosevelt, 2009; Trzesniewski & Donnellan, 2010; Twenge, 2009, 2013; Twenge & Campbell, 2001), but there is no doubt that some students do expect to get a B in their courses just for showing up and that they make more demands on our time and energy, just as we perceive them as putting less effort into their academic work (Kopp et al., 2010; Lippmann et al., 2009; Nilson, 2010; Singelton-Jackson et al., 2010; Twenge, 2009, 2013).

These students make a teacher's job more difficult, but they also challenge us to become better teachers (Hanson et al., 2011; Nevid, 2011; Twenge, 2013). For example, they often ask why they are being asked to do particular readings or are expected to complete difficult assignments. By explaining the reasoning behind our assignments, we can give students access to our thinking about the course and can make connections across topics and concepts that students might not have seen on their own (Twenge, 2013). Some specific strategies for teaching Generation Y students are discussed in Chapters 4 and 7 (Berk, 2009, 2010; Eisner, 2004).

Students with Disabilities

As noted in Chapter 1, the past decade has seen a doubling in the number of undergraduates who have been designated as Learning Disabled (LD), or as having Attention Deficit Disorder (ADD) or Attention Deficit Hyperactivity Disorder (ADHD) (Vickers, 2010). Some instructors worry that these diagnoses are too prevalent and give an unfair advantage to students who receive them, especially after the U.S. Congress amended the Americans with Disabilities Act (ADA) to broaden the definition of "disability" and its protection under law. Others have advocated even further reforms, including a "universal design" in college courses (Carroll, 2012; Darby, 2013; Scott, McGuire, & Foley, 2003; Scott, McGuire, & Shaw, 2003;

Vickers, 2010). "The concept of universal design is that products and environments should be designed for everyone, including people with disabilities" (Carroll, 2012, p. 130). The idea is that by applying the principles of universal design, higher education courses would be accessible to all and few, if any, students with disabilities would have to ask for special accommodations (Scott et al., 2003). For example, because students tend to perform better on exams when time pressure is not intense, teachers could write exams that can be completed in less than the allotted time. By giving this extra time, the exams become better measures of knowledge for all students, including those whose learning disabilities or other problems might have led them to ask for accommodation. (For a more detailed description of universal design applied to higher education, see Carroll, 2012; Burgstahler & Cory, 2008; Scott, McGuire, & Foley, 2003).

Universal design has not been widely adopted, so on most campuses students with physical or cognitive disabilities are responsible for letting you know about their situation and requesting special accommodations in your course. In our experience, the most common accommodation requests are for extra time to complete exams or for a distraction-free exam location. Less commonly, visually impaired students ask that exams and quizzes be made available in Braille or that the items be read to them under supervision in a special testing center. Many students, especially first-year students, are unaware of the steps they need to take to request accommodations, so invite such requests on the first day of class by asking special needs students to contact you immediately. Put this invitation in your syllabus, too. This is important because special needs accommodations cannot usually be made retroactively. That is because it might well be considered capricious—and certainly unfair to other students—if a teacher were to allow a student who did poorly on an exam to retake it under different circumstances after suddenly claiming special needs status (Curzan & Damour, 2000). So invite special needs students to meet with you in private and follow their lead on the terminology they use in discussing their disability (Davis, 2009). Ask them to explain why they need the accommodation and how the accommodation will help them. If you feel that the requested accommodation is unreasonable, delay your decision for a day or two so that you can contact the campus office that can advise you about the options available to you under campus policies, the amended ADA, and other relevant statutes.

Our own policy has been to provide requested accommodations whenever possible, not only as required by the rules, but also in the context of fairness to all of our students. For example, although we routinely provide a quiet, supervised seminar room in which students with certain learning disabilities can take exams, these students must take the exam on the same day, and at the same time, as all other students. We think that deciding what is fair and reasonable accommodation goes beyond the formal requirements of the ADA. Suppose that, on the basis of a cognitive disability, a student asks to be given essay exams instead of the multiple choice exams you normally write. Would accommodating this request give you the same assessment information that you get from other students? If not, should you—and would you have time to—give essay exams for all students? Would it be fair to let international students use a dictionary during multiple choice exams to look up the meaning of unfamiliar words? Answering such questions requires you to decide which accommodations you can and cannot offer in the context of preserving the academic integrity of your course. Making those decisions is easier once you have reflected on your course goals and what methods of instruction you feel are necessary in reaching them, what outcomes are required of all students (and why), what methods of assessing student outcomes are necessary (and why), and what levels of student performance on these measures are acceptable to you (Scott, 1997). Or as one instructor described it, "Is this learning disorder a condition that prevents the student from mastering the material at all or from demonstrating mastery in one manner but not in every manner? . . . The key issue must always be to distinguish essential abilities from desirable abilities" (Buller, 2010, p. 192). (For additional resources on providing reasonable accommodations to special needs students, visit www.disability resources.org/, a Web site that lists disability resources by topic and U.S. state; also see the Association on Higher Education and Disability's Supporting Accommodation Requests, 2012.)

Online Considerations

Are the students virtually "sitting" in your online course the same as the students who are actually sitting in your face-to-face class? There is little evidence that student demographics vary between the two formats (Artino, 2010; Colorado & Eberle, 2010; Harrell & Bower, 2011; Picciano, Seaman, & Allen, 2010). Does a student enrolled in your online course have the same chance of academic success as a student enrolled in your face-to-face class? Possibly not. There is considerable evidence that attrition rates are higher in online courses than in face-to-face courses, regardless of the level of the institution, and older students have a higher attrition rate than those in the traditional student age range (Patterson & McFadden, 2009). Ironically, community college students are at an increased risk of failing, despite the fact that online education has flourished at community colleges (Jaggars & Bailey, 2010; Xu & Jaggars, 2011).

Students tend to enroll in online courses for two main reasons. First, some students have heavy time commitments and they perceive (usually correctly) that an online course can provide the flexibility they need (Picciano et al., 2010). Second, students often believe (incorrectly) that an online course will be easier than its face-to-face counterpart (Driscoll et al., 2012). Teachers should keep these factors in mind when developing online courses. They should also recognize that many online students will need more structure, more interactions with the instructor, and more corrective feedback than will the majority of students in face-to-face classes.

As for students with disabilities, many campuses offer faculty workshops specifically focused on techniques for establishing equal access to online courses, most often in terms of universal design. So if you are developing an online course or currently teaching one, be sure to take advantage of these and other opportunities to ensure that your course is accessible to all students (Davis, 2009).

⬤ ⬤ ⬤ ⬤ ⬤

Enhancing Students' Motivation to Learn

Consider the following assessments of college students' motivation to learn:

"The general level of intellectual interest among undergraduates is low. Their collective life is not characterized by intellectual curiosity and intelligent discussion."

"With the general obscuring of college's original purpose and function, it has unfortunately become a kind of glorified playground. It has become the paradise of the young."

These sentiments might have been expressed last week at a psychology faculty meeting, but they were actually written more than 80 years ago (Angell, 1928; Gauss, 1933). Obviously, concern over students' apparent lack of motivation to learn what we want to teach them has a long history, and remains a topic of lively discussion and complaint at every teaching conference we have ever attended.

Intrinsic and Extrinsic Motivation

Some instructors feel responsible for motivating students to succeed in their courses and to invest the amount of time and work necessary to do so (Brophy, 2010; Ciaccio, 2004; Lombardi, 2011; Pink, 2009). The ideal student, they claim, is one who is driven by intrinsic motivation, especially by a love of learning and a desire to acquire knowledge for its own sake (McKinney, 1999). These instructors tend to be disappointed and scornful when they realize that the behavior of even their best students is motivated to a considerable extent by extrinsic factors, particularly grades and the points that determine those grades. This grade orientation should come as no surprise. After all, achieving good grades is a main gateway to the occupational and financial success that students in Western cultures are taught to want.

Nevertheless, teaching is enjoyable when students care about what they are learning, not just about the grades they will earn for learning it. So if you want to increase students' intrinsic motivation, you will also want to increase the intrinsic value of your course. You can do this in a variety of ways.

First, be sure at the outset that your students understand the structure and goals of the course. If students see the course as an organized whole, they tend to be more motivated to succeed in it than if they perceive it as an obstacle course made up of seemingly pointless and unrelated tasks (Beard & Senior, 1980).

Second, do all you can to make your course content and your presentations as varied and interesting as possible. As described in Chapter 4, this can include the use of demonstrations, active learning strategies, critical thinking exercises, and the like. Challenging your students to engage the material, rather than just read about it, can make it more likely that they will actually begin to want to learn more (Zepke & Leach, 2010). Don't forget to describe and illustrate the importance of each new topic, and how it relates to aspects of everyday life that are important to your students (Forsyth & McMillan, 1991; Sleigh, McCann, & Kadah-Ammeter, 2012). For example, if you are presenting information on color vision, let students test themselves for color blindness; in covering memory, include demonstrations of how students can improve performance on a mock quiz by using mnemonics and other memory enhancement tools.

Third, remember that students are more motivated to learn when they are given a measure of control over what they are learning (Forsyth & McMillan, 1991). You can take advantage of this fact when making writing assignments, for example. Rather than assigning all students the same topic, offer them the choice of several topics or several variations on a main topic.

Finally, let students experience your enthusiasm for the course content and for learning itself. Tell them about some of the psychology books you are reading, about new information you discovered at a recent conference, or about current events that are related to your course (McKinney,

1999). In other words, make the assumption that, once students begin to discover the intrinsically interesting aspects of your course, they will become just as enthusiastic about it as you are; some of them actually will (Mester & Tauber, 2000)!

Attendance

When psychology teachers fail to display the caring, enthusiasm, immediacy, and other elements of effective teaching that we have described in this book, students are likely to see class attendance as a necessary evil or a tedious chore (Sleigh et al., 2002). One survey found that more than two-thirds of students would miss class more often than they already do if they could get a copy of the professor's lecture notes (Sleigh & Ritzer, 2001). Another survey found that the most important factor influencing student attendance was the amount of classroom material they thought would appear on exams (Sleigh et al., 2002).

Yet students who attend classes on a regular basis tend to perform better on exams and papers than students who attend infrequently (Moore, 2003; Shimoff & Catania, 2001). In fact, one meta-analysis of the literature found that class attendance was "a better predictor of college grades than any other known predictor of academic performance, including scores on standardized admission tests, such as the SAT, high school GPA, study habits and study skills" (Crede, Roch & Kieszczynka, 2010, p. 272). If you agree that it is important for students to attend your classes, it becomes that much more critical to enhance students' intrinsic motivation to do so.

You can also seek to increase their extrinsic motivation. For example, let students know that you will be testing them on material that will be presented only in class. The mere process of taking attendance can also dramatically increase your head count, even if attendance is not factored into final grades (Shimoff & Catania, 2001). Just knowing that their name will be called in class, or that it will not appear on a daily sign-in sheet or student response ("clicker") system roll call, can be enough to bring some students to class. Giving unannounced quizzes or extra credit test items at the end of class on randomly selected days can also motivate students to attend more regularly. You can of course make attendance mandatory or penalize students for missing classes. These policies may have a small positive effect on student grades (Crede et al., 2010), but we don't favor them. Forcing students to come to class might expose them to more course material, but it does not guarantee improved performance and because most people don't like to be forced to do things, mandatory attendance policies can create resentment, hostility, and disengagement—even among students who would have come to class voluntarily.

Although we agree that attendance should not be mandatory, we long ago agreed to disagree with each other on how much to emphasize attendance. One of us never mentions attendance. He sees himself offering a product and a service in which adult consumers have expressed at least a nominal interest, and he allows them to decide how much of that product and service they wish to consume. At the same time, he sees it as his job to make the product (psychology) and the service (the teaching of psychology) as interesting and beneficial as possible. To him, patterns of voluntary attendance serve as a barometer of how interesting his classes are, at least in terms of motivating students to show up. If classroom attendance is relatively high regardless of the topic being covered (or when the next quiz or exam is scheduled), he can be fairly sure that his teaching style is sufficiently engaging to make students want to hear what he has to say (Friedman, Rodriguez, & McComb, 2001). If attendance is consistently lower than normal for certain scheduled topics, he tries to find ways to make those topics more interesting, while maintaining his standards for course quality. (He could probably fill every seat at every class by doing a comedy routine or showing provocative videos, but this is not what we have in mind.)

Your other author feels that many students, especially first-year students, do not recognize the potential value of coming to class. She feels that it is only when most students attend consistently that a good classroom environment can be established. Accordingly, she stresses the importance of attendance, offers regular reminders of the material to be covered during the next class session, and lets her students know that she hopes they will show up. Her syllabus states that:

> Attendance is very important in this class. You miss important information and the class misses your input every time you are not in class. I will take attendance every day, not to penalize you if you are absent, but to match names and faces. If you must miss class, be sure to talk to a classmate who was in attendance to get the day's notes and assignments.

This information can be especially influential in large classes, where many students feel that they won't be missed and that they won't miss anything if they skip class (Moore, 2003). Whatever attendance policy you choose for your own courses, stick to it. Make it explicit in your syllabus, and explain your rationale for it in person.

Students' Goals and Attributional Processes

As mentioned in Chapter 1, research by Carol Dweck and her colleagues suggests that students vary in their academic goals and attributional tendencies, each of which can strongly influence their response to you, your course requirements, your assignments, your grading system, and your efforts to motivate diligent study habits (Dweck, 2008, 2010; Rattan, Good, & Dweck, 2012; Yeager & Dweck, 2012).

This research suggests that some students approach your course with a "growth mindset" whereas others tend to have a "fixed mindset." Those with a growth mindset believe that they can develop their intelligence and attributes over time. Thus, they are more interested in acquiring skills and learning course content than in how their performance will be evaluated. These students are motivated to increase their competence, to seek challenges that foster learning, and to persist in the face of difficulty (Dweck, 2008, 2010; Mayer & Sutton, 1996). They believe that effort is a positive attribute (Dweck, 2007). When they seek help, students with a growth mindset are likely to ask for explanations, hints, and other forms of task-related information, not for quick, easy answers that remove the challenge from the situation. They experience satisfaction in learning for its own sake. Because students with a growth mindset tend to view intelligence as fluid, not fixed, they do not become too upset by obstacles or failures because they do not see these as indicating a general lack of ability (Dweck, 2008, 2010; Dweck & Leggett, 1988; Svinicki, 1998). And because they view adversity and setbacks as "challenges," they tend to be more resilient and to show higher achievement (Yeager & Dweck, 2012).

In contrast, students with a fixed mindset tend to be more interested in appearing "smart" than in the process and benefits of learning itself. Dweck describes these students as motivated to attain positive evaluations and to avoid negative ones, which leads them to avoid challenges when possible and to be less persistent at difficult tasks before asking for help (Dweck, 2008, 2010). They usually just want the right answer, not tips on how to find it themselves. Students with a fixed mindset tend to view their successes as personal achievements that make them "smart" relative to others (Dweck, 2008, 2010; Svinicki, 1998). Because they view intelligence as a fixed characteristic, they are likely to be upset by failure at an academic task because it indicates a general lack of ability (Dweck, 2008, 2010; Dweck & Leggett, 1988; Svinicki, 1998). These students may shy away from academic challenges because they believe that making mistakes or exerting too much effort both reflect low ability (Dweck, 2008, 2010; Eppler & Harju, 1997). They become "afraid of effort because effort makes them feel dumb" (Dweck, 2007, p. 35) and, as a result, they not only exert less effort to learn, but may consider cheating when they hit a setback (Dweck, 2007).

Notice that a key difference between these two motivational mindsets lies in how students interpret failure. From the growth mindset perspective, mistakes are seen as signals to try harder or to alter learning strategies whereas students with a fixed mindset see mistakes as a sign of inability that makes it pointless to keep trying. So when these latter students encounter difficult material or do poorly on an early exam, they tend to experience learned helplessness.

These mindsets tend to be relatively stable within individuals, but they can shift somewhat in response to experience and situational factors. For example, a student who is competent in, say, mathematics might display a growth mindset in a new math course, but a lack of confidence in musical ability might lead the same student to adopt a fixed mindset in a music class (Svinicki, 1998). Keep this in mind when you meet with students to discuss the problems they might be having in your course. It might be useful to help them identify the role that their goals and attributional tendencies play in creating those problems. This is particularly true when dealing with "grade-grubbers"—students whose intense focus on grades and tenacity in arguing over every item on every quiz or exam can drive teachers to distraction. You might be able to help these students see that their preoccupation with grades rather than with actually learning course content makes it all too easy to become discouraged about a low quiz score, especially if they see failure as indictment of their mental ability. Point out, too, that if they let a failure experience make them feel stupid, they might start devoting less time to your course and more time to courses that make them feel "smart." The end result could be an unnecessarily poor grade in your course. Encourage these students to view low scores as a wake-up call, not a threat to their sense of self-worth, and work with them to develop a specific plan for spending more, not less, time studying material for your next quiz.

What else can you do to encourage a growth mindset? You might think that praising students' "smarts" would help, but this can actually reinforce a fixed mindset. Praising effort and its beneficial results (e.g., "I can see that you worked really hard on that paper") is more likely to lead to a growth mindset and a realization that hard work can yield academic accomplishments (Dweck, 2007). Dweck and her colleagues offer other related suggestions: praise the learning process and the student's persistence rather than just the product; emphasize that learning takes effort; teach specifically about the existence of the two mindsets; emphasize challenges not threats to success; point out progress; and when students fail, remind them that though they are "not yet" there, they can still get there (Dweck, 2010). Dweck recently summarized her results as follows: "We have found that what students need the most is not self-esteem boosting or trait labeling; instead, they need mindsets that represent challenges as things that they can take on and overcome over time with effort, new strategies, learning, help from others, and patience. When we emphasize people's potential to change, we prepare our students to face life's challenges resiliently" (Yeager & Dweck, 2012, p. 312). It also helps if you have a growth mindset yourself. One study found that teachers with a fixed mindset were more likely to counsel low-performing students out of the course, rather than provide feedback designed to produce improvement (Rattan et al., 2012).

Online Considerations

Motivating students to learn in an online course requires more creativity than in a face-to-face class. Aside from any synchronous components, attendance is irrelevant, but it is important that students are motivated to complete the work in a timely manner. You can help students to do so by setting up a weekly schedule that varies little. That way, students will know, for instance, that their journal entries are due on Thursday, replies are due by Sunday, quizzes must be completed by Friday, and so forth. This structure encourages students to engage with your course in a predictable pattern, thus increasing the likelihood that they will finish their work on time.

Students' motivation to learn online will also be enhanced if you provide feedback that is frequent and detailed, and conveys enthusiasm for the course and confidence that the student is capable of doing well in it. We have found it effective to send individual e-mails that praise effort and results when students complete a project or journal entry in a particularly good manner.

As we have emphasized repeatedly, the most important aspect of a good online experience is the faculty–student relationship. So, in addition to providing timely and substantive feedback, get to know your students; be accessible and respond to them in a timely manner; post a brief weekly announcement; and try to make your online classroom fun (Jones, 2013b).

Finally, from the first day of the course (and we open our course a week before the term officially begins to give students experience with the Web site) online students need to be disabused of the idea that the course is going to be easy. At the same time, we have also found that students can be overwhelmed if the entire course is available from the first day. To avoid this problem, we open up the first half of our course at the beginning of the term and open up the second half a week before the midterm.

• • • • •

Dealing with Students' Excuses and Complaints

At some point in every academic term, some of your students will ask you for help or accommodation in relation to their special needs, requests, excuses, and problems. Your response to these students will significantly shape your relationship with them, and with the rest of your students, too. Remember, first, that you do not have to accommodate every request or accept every excuse to preserve good relationships with students. If your students perceive that you make your decisions carefully, fairly, and reasonably, even an unwelcome outcome need not permanently harm faculty–student rapport. In fact, dealing with students in a firm but fair fashion can go a long way toward reinforcing students' perceptions of you as a caring teacher.

Student Excuses

Your efforts to nurture good faculty–student relationships will be frequently challenged by the need to deal with students' excuses for missing (or delaying) a quiz or exam, or the deadline for a term paper or other assignment. As you probably know, these excuses can range from the tragic to the ludicrous, and everything in between. Any of them can be genuine and any of them can be phony, so your tricky task is to discriminate one from the other without becoming too cynical or too gullible (Abernethy & Padgett, 2010; Caron, Whitbourne, & Halgin, 1992). In one study, 72% of undergraduate students reported having used a false excuse at least once, and less than 25% of their instructors asked for documentation of the phony excuse (Roig & Caso, 2005). Failing to detect phony excuses can give a few dishonest students an unfair advantage over the rest of the class, in terms of extra study or preparation time, and possibly information about exam content. Ironically this advantage does not necessarily translate into better grades. In fact, the correlation between course grades and frequency of excuse making appears to be significantly negative (Roig & Caso, 2005; Schwartz, 1986).

The way you handle excuses conveys a message to your students about your teaching philosophy, and most particularly about whether you view students as partners or adversaries, the degree to which you trust them, and how much you care about them. Your excuse policies and procedures will also influence the number and nature of the excuses you will receive in the future. We recommend taking a firm, consistent, rational, and caring approach to excuses that incorporates a "trust, but verify" policy. Treat every excuse as genuine but, in fairness to the entire class, require that it be verified by supporting documentation (see Figure 6.1). We have found that this authoritative approach is widely accepted by students, and it gives us sufficient time to consider (and investigate, if necessary) the validity of each excuse instead of making snap decisions or ad hoc changes in course policy (Bernstein, 1993).

**APPLICATION FOR A PSYCHOLOGY 100 MAKE-UP EXAMINATION
FALL SEMESTER, 2014**
Dr. Sandra Goss Lucas

After completing the information requested below and obtaining the necessary signature, please return this form to me. Once I have verified the accuracy of the information you have provided, and confirmed that your reason for requesting a make-up exam is acceptable, an alternate exam date, time, and place will be arranged. All make-up exams will take place after the regular exam.

Important note: Unless you are requesting a make-up exam because of a last-minute illness or emergency, this form must be turned in at least five days before the date of the regularly scheduled exam. If you miss this deadline you will not be eligible for a make-up exam.

Please provide the following information:

I, _____ certify that I am unable to take the Psychology 100 exam scheduled for _____, 2014 because (please be clear and specific when describing your reason and be sure to obtain a confirming signature):

Your name:_____   Your signature: _____

Your ID# _____   Your phone number: _____

Your e-mail address:_____

Confirmed by (please print name): _____

Signature: _____

Position or relationship to student:_____

Telephone number:_____

E-mail address:_____

Fig. 6.1 Excuse Documentation Form. We have used this form to help students establish the legitimacy of their excuse for missing an exam. We suggest that you provide about half a page of space for students to describe the reason for their request. You can create versions of this form for dealing with excuses relating to any academic situation.

Complaints about Test Items and Grades

One of the greatest threats to the quality of the faculty–student relationship stems from students' perceptions that course grading is unfair, or that a teacher is callous and uncaring in the face of student requests to review and reconsider grading decisions. These perceptions might be inaccurate, but can be easily formed nonetheless if you fail to clarify the grading system in your syllabus, especially if you don't offer a clear and accessible procedure through which students can respond to the grading of every quiz and exam item.

The first step in establishing a fair and open grading review process is, as mentioned in Chapter 4, to develop an efficient plan for returning quizzes and exams in class. With that plan in place, there will be enough class time to review the scoring of some or all of the test items. It is just as important to have a plan for handling the complaints that students will inevitably make about some items.

We recommend that you set up and explain an organized test return system well before you begin to return the first graded assignment. Then follow that system to the letter when returning your first quiz or exam and in every instance thereafter. Your students will soon understand that your rules and procedures are designed to give them a fair forum for making comments and complaints, and that discussion of test items in class should focus on learning from mistakes, not fishing for points.

The system we use works well in classes large and small, and is especially useful in relation to multiple choice tests, but it can also be adapted for use with short-answer items, essay tests, and even term papers, assuming that you have used a clear grading rubric (see Chapter 5).

Let's consider multiple choice tests first. After grading a quiz or exam, we create a frequency distribution that ranks all the items from most to least missed. Next, before distributing the students' test results in class, we explain that our goal is to help everyone better understand the course material associated with the items they missed. We explain, too, that to satisfy the curiosity of the largest number of students as quickly as possible, we will review the test items in the order of difficulty, beginning with the one that was most often missed.

Like many other psychology faculty, we give students their test results, but not a copy of the test, so we show the test items on PowerPoint slides. We describe the correct answer for each, explain why it is correct, and explain why various frequently chosen options are incorrect. We often invite students who have responded correctly to the item to explain why their answer is correct. If you use this system to review short quizzes, you should have time to cover all the items. In the case of longer exams, reviewing the 10 to 20 most difficult items—or as many as time allows—should satisfy the questions and concerns of the vast majority of your students. If you don't have time to cover all the items, be sure to invite students to come to your office hours or send you an e-mail to discuss their questions about any remaining items.

As you review test items in class, invite students to ask questions, but don't get bogged down in long discussions. If students raise questions or suggest item interpretations that create uncertainty in your own mind about how items should be graded, don't feel compelled to make a decision on the spot. Later reflection might lead you to regret that decision. We suggest that, instead, you invite students to fill out a form on which

REQUEST TO REVIEW GRADING OF AN EXAM ITEM

Item #_____   TestForm_____

I believe that answer _____ should also be considered correct because:

I found supporting evidence on page(s) _____in the textbook.

Name_____   Student ID #_____

Fig. 6.2 Test Item Review Form. Allowing students to submit forms like this one not only eases students' (and teachers') tension and emotional distress in class, but lets students know that you will seriously consider their questions, comments, and alternative interpretations about test item grading. We suggest that you provide about a page of space for students' rationale for an alternative answer.

they can present their argument in written form (see Figure 6.2). On the days you are discussing graded assignments, place these forms on a chair or table where students can easily pick them up as they leave or have the form posted on your LMS for students to fill out and return either in class or electronically. Set a short deadline for submitting the forms, and explain that you will carefully review them before announcing your final decisions in class or via a group e-mail message. In our experience, only students with well thought out complaints take the time to complete these forms. If you decide that a complaint is valid, announce that you will give credit to everyone whose response deserves it. If you reject an appeal, announce that, too, and jot a brief response on all review request forms before returning them to the students.

A different version of the same system can be used to handle complaints about grades on essay exams or other written assignments. Here, too, it is important to give your students time to reflect on their grade and your reasons for assigning it before they raise objections (Svinicki, 1998). Accordingly, we ask students to carefully reread their own work and our comments about it, and then—if they still feel we have been unfair or misguided—to resubmit the work along with a detailed statement indicating why we should reconsider our grading decision. We do not allow students to submit a writing assignment for possible re-grading on the day it was returned to them. Requiring students to carefully evaluate both their writing and our response tends to abort many complaints by students who become aware of the mistakes or misstatements that led to the grade they received. At the same time, reading the reasons that other students offer when requesting an improved grade gives us the opportunity to thoughtfully reconsider our earlier judgment and to correct any mistakes we might have made.

When students do come to discuss test items or grades during your office hours, remember that your demeanor during these conferences can solidify or undermine the student–faculty relationship. The meetings might be only a minor part of your day, but your students will consider them important, even vital. They might want to understand material that has eluded them, or they might hope you will find it possible to raise their grade enough that they can retain a scholarship or avoid academic probation. Whatever the case, they are probably not there simply to challenge your authority (Svinicki, 1998; Zlokovich, 2001). Keeping this in mind can help you avoid becoming defensive and turning the conference into an adversarial situation. It can also help you to listen more carefully to what students are actually saying and what they are actually requesting. In many cases, for example, when students come to your office to complain about a grade, they don't really expect you to change it; they might simply want to tell you how they feel about your grading system, or about the course. If you are unapologetically firm about your course policies, but also sympathetic and ready to listen, these sessions could well become fruitful discussions of the demands of college life, of students' motivation and study habits, and of how they can best prepare for future quizzes and exams. Or not. Inevitably, a few students wish only to cajole you into giving them some kind of special consideration. They might not react well when you explain that it would be a violation of capricious grading rules to grant their request. Try to stay calm in such circumstances. It is far better for students to go away angry and feel apologetic later than for you—in your position of power in the relationship—to lose your cool and then feel the need to apologize to your student.

⦾ ⦾ ⦾ ⦾ ⦾

Classroom Incivilities

Having raised the topic of unpleasant interactions with students, let's consider them in more detail. Happily, the worst of these interactions are rare and will probably involve only a tiny minority of students during your teaching career. Nevertheless, it is important to understand what can happen and to be prepared to handle untoward teaching-related events, in the classroom and beyond. Here again, remember that the way you deal with one student can affect your relationship with the rest of your class.

The fact is that most students are nice people who are fun to teach and are in class to learn. Still, some of them do occasionally behave in ways that create problems for their teachers. The most common student behavior problems, known as *classroom incivilities* (CIs), have been defined as "any action that interferes with a harmonious and cooperative learning atmosphere in the classroom" (Feldman, 2001, p. 137). Research suggests that faculty and students agree that the following are all examples of classroom incivility: continuing to talk after being asked to stop, coming to class drunk or high, exhibiting nonverbal disrespect for others, talking loudly with others, making disparaging remarks, swearing, cell phone ringing, texting, sleeping, coming to class late or leaving early, and using technology for nonclass activities (Bjorklund & Rehling, 2010; Rehling & Bjorklund, 2010). The same research also revealed that, perhaps because they are in a better position to see some of these behaviors, students perceive CIs as occurring more frequently than do faculty. Another study found that students want and expect faculty to respond firmly to control or eliminate classroom incivilities, including by directly addressing the offender(s) (Boysen, 2012).

As discussed later, the number and nature of the classroom incivilities you will encounter are influenced partly by your teaching style. In fact, it has been suggested that incivilities displayed by *faculty* can engender student incivilities (Black, Wygonik, & Frey, 2011; Braxton & Bayer, 1999; Knepp, 2012). Students describe two kinds of faculty incivilities, those involving incompetence and lack of interest in teaching and those involving lack of respect for students (Stork & Hartley, 2009). These perceptions were echoed in a large-scale study of the behavior of faculty in higher education. That study identified seven categories of professorial behavior that were seen to violate the norms of teaching and to merit punitive action (Braxton & Bayer, 1999): condescending negativism, inattentive planning, moral turpitude, particularistic grading, personal disregard, uncommunicated course details, and uncooperative cynicism. Specific examples included chronic lateness to class, unannounced absenteeism from class, gross profanity, and making demeaning or humiliating comments to students during class (Twale & DeLuca, 2008).

Handling Classroom Incivilities

Trust us, not all student incivilities arise in response to bad teaching. Even the most organized, experienced, and caring teacher has to deal with them from time to time. Teachers who are female, young, nonwhite, and of low academic rank (e.g., graduate student instructor, adjunct) are at elevated risk for experiencing CIs (Alberts, Hazen, & Theobald, 2010; Knepp, 2012). Accordingly, we think it is especially important for these at-risk faculty to dress professionally. While this might seem to be an unimportant detail, there is evidence that dressing professionally does help to differentiate you from your students and to promote a more respectful response from them (Clement & Whatley, 2012). No matter how you dress, the key to handling classroom incivility is not to take it as a personal affront. If you can remain calm and objective, it will be easier to think rationally about the behavior and what to do about it.

By far, the most common form of classroom incivility takes the form of minor classroom disruptions, particularly when students talk to each other or text during class presentations. These type of disruptions require your attention because they can interfere with other students' ability to follow the class presentation, and may even derail your own train of thought. Again, try not to take this behavior personally. True, it is impolite, and it also sends a message that the talking or texting students are not interested in your presentation. However, remember that, especially in larger classes, many students have the mistaken idea that you cannot see them, let alone hear them. In short, they might well be trying to entertain themselves, not offend you.

We suggest that you deal with inappropriate behaviors as soon as you detect them and that your first steps be firm but not extreme (Knepp, 2012). In the case of inappropriate talking, the simplest tactic is to stroll over to where the talkers are seated; this will usually put a stop to their talking. If the problem continues, you can pause, look at the offending students, and ask if they have a question about the lecture. This tactic has several advantages. First, it stops the talking. Second, by making the assumption that the students were talking about course material, you give them the opportunity to save face by actually asking a question. Third, this tactic lets the students know that you can see and hear them, and that their talking is disruptive (it sends the same message to other students who might otherwise have started their own conversations). Fourth, you have let everyone know that you care enough about your students to make sure they can hear you. Fifth, you have asserted your right to authority and control in the classroom without appearing to be too harsh.

If the same students' talking has been a problem before, ask to see them after class or in your office for a discussion (Tiberius & Flak, 1999). It is crucial that this discussion takes place in private. No matter how much you think the students deserve to be embarrassed in public, or how satisfying you think it might be to you and others in the class, this is usually a no-win strategy. It not only engenders strong negative feelings in the embarrassed students, it can make you seem petty, abusive, and out of control in front of your class. Instead, sit down with the offending students and remind them that their behavior is inappropriate, that it is disrupting the concentration of other students, and that it is interfering with your job as a teacher. Ask them to either refrain from talking to each other or to agree not to sit near each other in the future. We suggest that you follow the same general strategy of increasingly strong interventions in relation to other kinds of classroom incivilities, too.

Remember that whether the inappropriate classroom behavior involves students kissing each other, sending or receiving text messages, or surfing the Internet, the way you deal with one person's incivility can have a ripple effect on the other students' perceptions of you (Kounin, 1977; Kuhlenschmidt & Layne, 1999; Silvestri & Buskist, 2012). If your response style is reasonable and measured, it will solidify your standing as an authoritative, but fair, teacher. If it is excessive, capricious, or abusive, you run the risk of alienating the entire class. It might take some time, and some mistakes, before you learn to strike just the right note in such situations, but with experience and a caring attitude, you will do it.

Preventing Classroom Incivilities

Ultimately, the best way to deal with classroom incivilities is to prevent them. As described in Chapter 3, you can start the prevention process on the first day of class by summarizing the rules for classroom behavior you have included in your syllabus (Black et al., 2011; Boice, 1998a; Carbone, 1999; Davis, 2009; Gonzalez & Lopez, 2001; Landrum, 2011; Silvestri & Buskist, 2012). Your students will come from diverse backgrounds and will have had diverse experiences with classroom etiquette, so don't assume that all students will already know what behaviors you consider acceptable and unacceptable (Appleby, 2001; Astin, 1993; Knepp, 2012). For example, many students do not perceive the classroom use of their personal Internet connected devices as uncivil or rude (Schuldt et al., 2012). About 92% of students admit using their phones to text during class and 10% acknowledge that they have texted during an exam (Tindell & Bohlander, 2012). For them, this is just normal. Indeed, the average college student uses Internet devices in the classroom to text, surf the Internet, and access social media (e.g., for nonclass activities) about 11 times a day. This despite the fact that more than 80% of these students admit that these activities cause them to pay less attention in class and to miss course information (McCoy, 2013). Adding to the irony and contradictions, these same students feel that instructors should develop course policies to discourage nonacademic Internet usage, but not strictly enforce them.

So be sure to describe and discuss the reasons for your rules about cell phone use, arriving late, leaving early, talking during class presentations, and the like. Some instructors even ask students to sign a statement affirming that they have read and understood the classroom rules (Carbone, 1999; Silvestri & Buskist, 2012).

Many classroom incivilities are the by-product of students' normal pattern of "multitasking," not an attempt to undermine their teacher's authority. As a case in point, consider the high number of students who send and receive texts during class. As noted earlier, this is an activity that many students do not regard as the least bit inappropriate, let alone offensive. When one of the authors recently asked a student to meet in private to discuss why he was constantly texting while working in the classroom with other students on a group project, he was truly shocked that his texting could be considered disrespectful to her and his group. He immediately promised to stop texting, and he kept his promise.

You may be able to decrease multitasking-related classroom incivilities by presenting research showing how inefficient multitasking actually is, including research showing that it is negatively correlated with course grades (Burak, 2012; Clayson & Haley, 2013; Ellis, Daniels, & Jauregui, 2010). You might use a demonstration to show that even on simple tasks, multitasking increases cognitive load and errors (Strayer, Watson, & Drews, 2011). First, ask your students to count out loud from 1 to 10; then ask them to recite the alphabet from A through J. They will perform both tasks quickly and easily. But if you then ask them to perform both tasks at once—so that they have to say 1 A, 2 B, 3 C, and so on, they will have far more trouble doing so, and it will take far more time.

Whether classroom incivilities remain the small problem they normally are or become a bigger problem depends largely on you—not only on how you handle problem students' uncivil behavior, but on whether your teaching style encourages or discourages such behavior. Teachers who habitually read their lecture notes in a monotone or who respond to students' questions with sarcasm or hostility can expect a higher incidence of student incivility than those who use active learning methods and who make it clear through the quality of their preparation and presentations that they care about teaching and about their students (Knepp, 2012; Stork & Hartley, 2009). For example, instructors who, during their first few class sessions, displayed the behaviors described earlier as "immediacy" are likely to encounter far fewer and far milder instances of classroom incivility than other instructors. The most important elements of immediacy in this regard are: (a) arriving in class early enough for informal chats with students; (b) a moderate amount of movement around the classroom during lectures; (c) maintaining eye contact with students; (d) use of active learning methods; (e) marking one's class notes with reminders to slow down, pause for questions, and check for student understanding; and (f) listening patiently to student questions (Boice, 1998a). Other ways to reduce the likelihood of student incivility have also been identified. These include being "transparent" in your teaching (e.g., explain why you are making the assignments you make); allow student to provide input through informal early feedback and discussion about the course and your teaching style; make yourself available to students (e.g., always show up for your office hours and encourage students to attend); model the behaviors you desire of your students (e.g., take out your cell phone at the beginning of class, turn it off, and put it away); use humor, not sarcasm; and praise often and punish sparingly (Black et al., 2011). As one observer put it, "the opportunity for disruption in the college classroom is directly related to students' perception of their treatment by the instructor and other students, their sense of security, their perception of the classroom as a comfort zone, and the quality of the interpersonal rapport that exists" (Anderson, 1999, p. 71). This assertion is especially accurate in relation to large classrooms, where a sense of anonymity and isolation from the instructor can foster the highest rates of uncivil behavior (Carbone, 1999). No wonder, then, that, in classes of any size, reducing students' perceived anonymity and isolation by learning students' names and employing lots of active learning techniques has been found to decrease classroom incivilities (Boice, 1998a; Carbone, 1999).

Addressing the Problems of Problem Students

The behavior that earns problem students their title may go well beyond the scope of classroom incivilities. Problem students' actions can run the gamut from pathetic to annoying to disruptive to unbalanced. Some of these people are very bright; some are less so. Some are highly motivated but scattered; others don't seem to care about much of anything. Some are a problem mainly in your class; others create problems for the entire campus. Problem students have been described as falling into eight categories, including the compliant, the anxious-dependent, the discouraged, the independent, the hero, the "sniper," the attention seeker, and the silent (Mann et al., 1970). Most experienced teachers recognize—and can probably attach a name and face to—each of these categories. When it comes to giving advice about how to actually deal with the problems of problem students, though, we prefer our own somewhat less extensive taxonomy. The tips listed in the following sections are based to some extent on classroom management research, and to a large extent on our own experiences (Goss, 1995).

The "Everything-Always-Happens-to-Me" Student

These students have the best of intentions, but some external force always seems to interfere with their plans to meet their academic responsibilities. They show up an hour late for the exam because they overslept when their alarm didn't go off (even if the exam was at 7 P.M.). They can't submit their term paper on time because the printer jammed just as they were trying to print it out 15 minutes before class. In other words, these are friendly students who seem utterly bewildered by all the "bad luck" that interferes with their best efforts to do the right things at the right times. Dealing with this type of problem student is relatively simple. Be sympathetic, but apply your rules, even if it means that the student gets a penalty—or even a zero—on an exam or a paper. In addition, advise the student to take advantage of any time-management or organizational skills workshops that might be offered on your campus. Many instructors are hesitant to take this "tough love" approach because they feel sorry for the student. However, in being lenient they fail to consider three things. First, the student's apparent misfortunes might be part of a long-standing pattern of irresponsibility, poor planning, and last-minute activity that has been excused and supported in the past by family, friends, and other teachers. Second, the basic principles of learning suggest that giving the student special consideration is likely to perpetuate this problematic pattern. Third, making ad hoc decisions to bend the rules for certain "unfortunate" students can be unfair to other students, and can even be construed as a violation of capricious grading regulations. In short, don't feel guilty about enforcing the course rules you set down in your syllabus at the beginning of the term. You must be accountable for your behavior as a teacher, and you can do your students a service by helping them learn to be responsible for theirs.

The "I-Disagree-with-Everything-You-Say" Student

Most teachers want to nurture students' critical thinking skills, including the tendency to question what they are told by authority figures. So we should be pleased and supportive when students challenge what we say in class, especially when they ask for more evidence or present conflicting evidence of their own. Occasionally, however, you might encounter a problem student who disagrees with virtually everything you say simply as a way of challenging your credibility, attracting attention, or both. Research in classroom management suggests that these problem students fall into one of two subtypes: the low-achieving student whose challenges take the form of long, marginally relevant discourses or emotional arguments against your presentation, and the high-achieving student whose challenges are logical, but essentially mischievous attempts to disrupt and discredit your presentation.

The key to dealing with both subtypes of students is to first figure out what is going on, and not jump to conclusions. Are these students creating a problem because they enjoy causing trouble or because they are simply unskilled at the rules of academic controversy? You can find out by assuming the latter, especially in the first few class sessions when the classroom climate has not yet been fully established. Accept the student's critical comments at face value, and reply objectively. A harsh early response to a student comment—even if you suspect it was a bit hostile—can discourage other students from asking or answering questions later on. If the student's subsequent questions and comments appear to have little or no intellectual purpose or content, the pattern will become clear to you, and your diagnosis will be confirmed by the rest of the class. Irritated by the problem student's attempts to sabotage the class with disruptive comments and picky questions, your students will react strongly whenever the problem student raises a hand or begins to speak. If you see them roll their eyes, shift in their seats, tap their pens and pencils, and look away, and you hear sighs, giggles, or whispered comments, it is time to take action to solve the problem (Fritschner, 2000).

We suggest that your first intervention be a "soft reprimand," which consists of scheduling a private chat. Tell the problem student that his or her classroom questions and comments are creating a problem for you and for the rest of the class. Explain what the problems are and ask if the student was aware of them. If, as sometimes happens, the student seems genuinely unaware that he or she has been creating problems, the solution is relatively easy. Let the student know that you are happy to discuss any aspect of course content and to listen to the student's views, but that in the interests of time it would be better to raise complex questions and challenging comments outside of class, in office hours, or by e-mail. A soft reprimand is usually enough to take care of the chronic disagreement problem. For one of us, a private chat with one such problem student ultimately led to a research project and a jointly authored journal article.

If a soft reprimand doesn't work, you will have to take further steps. The first of these is to avoid calling on the problem student in class, or to do so only rarely. Let the student know of your plans ahead of time, and provide a reminder during class, too, by saying something like, "I see your hand, Jack, but let's give someone else a chance to talk." Another method for dealing with the situation was suggested by a colleague who uses a system modeled after radio call-in contests. He tells the class that he will not always call on the first person to raise a hand, but will sometimes choose the third or fourth volunteer. This tactic not only allows him to call on a problem student only at his discretion, but it also encourages other students to participate more actively. Whatever method you choose, your students will love you for it!

If the problem student ignores such tactics by interrupting you without permission, have another conference in which you offer the options of behaving properly or dropping your course. In such cases, which you might never encounter, you should discuss the situation with your department executive officer to determine what campus security or student discipline proceedings might be necessary to remove the student from class.

The "Quick-to-Anger" Student

The label says it all. A quick-to-anger student has a hot temper and might become highly irritated and even verbally abusive about a low exam or quiz score, about your refusal to adjust a grade, or about your negative response to his or her request for, say, a deadline extension. Fortunately, these students are relatively few in number, and their outbursts are even more rare—mainly because of the power differential that exists between teacher and student. Still, here are a few tips for defusing what can be a very disconcerting situation.

If the student's anger is expressed during a class session, explain that this is not the time or the place to deal with it. Offer the student the opportunity to discuss the situation after class and in private; say something like "OK, I can see you're unhappy about this, so let's meet in my office right after class and we can talk it over." No matter how disrespectful the student's behavior might be, try not to take it personally, and don't get into a shouting match or an exchange of criticism in front of your class. Your students will have more respect for you if your response is firm but calm in the face of inappropriate anger.

If the angry outburst occurs in private, give the student a chance to speak without interruption. This can be exceedingly difficult, especially if the student is swearing, being disrespectful, or saying things that you believe are untrue. However, interrupting a tirade will accomplish nothing because the student will be unable to rationally process what you are trying to say; in fact, the interruption might make the student even angrier. At this stage, just listen, nod in understanding, and maintain steady eye contact and the most composed facial expression you can muster. As the student eventually runs out of steam, the emotional level of the situation will drop. You can usually be sure that the student has finished talking when the anger becomes tinged with sheepishness. The student might even apologize for having been so upset. At this point, you should acknowledge the student's anger, summarize your understanding of the problem or complaint, and offer whatever coherent, nonemotional, nonthreatening response you think is appropriate. For example, you might say something like, "Look, Jill, I realize how angry and disappointed you are about your midterm exam score, because it is obvious from what you have said that you studied long hours to get ready for it. We still have eight weeks to go in this course; why don't we talk about exactly how you are preparing for exams in general, and how you should be getting ready for the next one in my course."

The "Unbalanced" Student

In some cases, a student's anger, hostility, criticism, disruptiveness, or other inappropriate classroom behavior reflects a more general psychological problem that might be severe enough to qualify as a form of mental disorder. In these cases it is vital to remember that, even if you are a clinical or counseling psychologist, your responsibility as a teacher does not extend to providing psychological help. In fact, your responsibility is to treat troubled students just like other students. You can refer them to appropriate sources of help, or confirm that they are already getting such help, but trying to establish a therapeutic relationship with these students would be unethical (see the APA's Ethical Standard 3.05). The resulting dual role would create a conflict of interest that could easily lead to favoritism and capricious grading (APA Ethical Standard 7.06).

If you suspect—or your student tells you—that the problem you are trying to deal with privately involves a serious behavior disorder, be ready to make the appropriate referral if the student is not already getting help. This is not the time to be looking up phone numbers or searching for Web sites, so before you begin teaching on a new campus, prepare a list of contact details for the departmental or campus counseling service, local public and private mental health centers, inpatient psychiatric units and hospitals, domestic violence shelters, crisis services, and the like. It is also a good idea to become familiar with the services, clientele, and admissions criteria associated with each facility. Armed with this information, you will be better able to assist your student to seek help from the most appropriate source. Be sure to have access to this information in your office, at home, and in class, because you might be asked for a referral when you least expect it.

In rare cases, a student's psychological problems might be so severe or potentially dangerous that you will have no choice but to discuss the situation with your department executive officer or with campus mental health professionals. They will advise you about how such cases should be handled, and can, if necessary, arrange to remove the student from your class and perhaps from the campus.

The "I'm-Not-Here" Student

At the opposite end of the problem student spectrum is the person who avoids attracting your attention, never volunteers a question or an answer in class, never comes to your office hours, and accepts without complaint whatever grades you assign, no matter how poor those grades might be. Some teachers don't see these students as "problems," and in terms of actively causing trouble, perhaps these teachers are right. Students do have the right to structure their college experience in their own way. If they prefer to listen passively, do their reading, take their exams, and move on to the next course, so be it. In fact, many students consider "class participation" to involve nothing more than showing up regularly, remaining attentive during class, completing all assignments, and being prepared for class. This view probably accounts for why so relatively few students, especially in introductory psychology classes, participate in the active way that many instructors hope to see (Fritschner, 2000; Leamnson, 1999).

However, if quiet students are quiet because of shyness, fear, intimidation, or perhaps a culturally based reticence to attract attention, they might not be getting as much from your course as they could. We think that part of a psychology teacher's job is to reach out to these students and let them know that their active participation in class is not only desirable, but welcome (Bailey, 2003).

Perhaps the simplest way to do this is to greet quiet students by name when they come to class. Don't single them out at every class session, but if your initial greeting does not seem to make them uncomfortable, ask how they are doing, or if they had a nice weekend. If you require every student to come to an office hour early in the term (see Chapter 2), you can use this opportunity to learn more about these students and help them be more comfortable with you. This is also a good time to assess their expectations about the course and how they prefer to learn.

You can also start a dialogue with reticent students simply by writing personal comments on the exams, quizzes, or other written assignments you return to them. For example, you might note that the student did a good job on the assignment, or seems to be doing better on quizzes now. These comments let the student know that you care, and this message can be reinforced by offering to discuss some aspect of the course content, or lending the student a book that might be of interest. Remind these students that they can contact you for a chat over e-mail as well as in person. Small-group discussions and other cooperative learning activities can also sometimes help reticent students become more active members of the class. Your efforts might not turn reticent students into feisty fireballs, but you might make it easier for these students to talk to you one on one and, as a result, get the help and advice they might need.

Some students will inevitably present specific problems that we have not listed here. However, we hope that the advice we have offered (and summarized in Checklist 6.1) will help you to deal effectively with whatever problematic student behavior you might encounter.

Checklist 6.1 A Checklist for Dealing with Problem Students

Here are some important things to remember when dealing with various kinds of problem students.

1. **Be prepared.** As far as possible, establish your plans, rules, and procedures for dealing with the most common types of problem students before you encounter them.

2. **Be proactive.** Try to prevent classroom incivilities and other problematic student behavior by developing your course and your teaching style to be as engaging and caring as possible. In addition, be sure your syllabus lists your rules relating to attendance, classroom conduct, missed deadlines, and other potential sources of misunderstanding and faculty–student conflict.

3. **Be firm and consistent.** Say what you mean, and mean what you say. Apply your rules and procedures in the same way with all students. Don't make rules that you can't (or won't) enforce and don't make ad hoc exceptions beyond those you previously stated.

4. **Remain calm and mature.** Display an adult, professional demeanor at all times. Listen to students' points of view, even when they are angry, and try not to take their problematic behavior as a personal affront.

5. *Ask for help when necessary.* Don't be afraid to involve your colleagues or department or campus administrators if you are not sure how to deal with a problem student. Experienced colleagues in psychology and in other departments are a particularly good source of advice about what strategies and tactics have and have not worked well in the past, and about the written and unwritten rules that might apply in dealing with problem students.

●●●●●

Academic Dishonesty

You might have noticed that we did not include "the dishonest student" in our taxonomy of problem students. This isn't because we don't see academic dishonesty as a problem. On the contrary, we think it is such an enduring, widespread, culturally supported, and harmful problem that it deserves more detailed attention. Estimates of the prevalence of academic dishonesty vary widely, depending on sampling techniques, the type of dishonesty studied, and whether data come from experiments or surveys, but the problem has been recognized for decades (e.g., Bowers, 1964; Davis et al., 1992; Davis & Ludvigson, 1995; Maramark & Maline, 1993; McCabe & Trevino, 1993) and remains a major problem in higher education (e.g., McCabe, 2012; McCabe, Trevino, & Butterfield, 2001; Novotney, 2011). One study found that more than half of the teenagers surveyed admitted to cheating on a test in the past year and one-third said they had done so more than once (Novotney, 2011). At one small private college, 89% of students reported that they had been dishonest at least once (Graham, Monday, & O'Brien, 1994) and about 80% of college alumni surveyed reported having engaged in some form of academic dishonesty as undergraduates (Novotney, 2011; Yardley et al., 2009). Overall, the percentage of students admitting to academic dishonesty appears to be in the 50–75% range, so you are going to encounter some form of it in virtually all of your courses.

Categories of Academic Dishonesty

The code of student conduct published by the university where we have spent most of our teaching careers (University of Illinois, Student Code, 2013–2014, www.admin.illinois.edu/policy/code/article1_part4_1–402. html) contains a section that, in our view, does a good job of defining various forms of academic dishonesty. Accordingly, we will use the structure of this code as a framework for organizing our discussion of academic dishonesty and how to deal with it. We will address academic dishonesty that takes the form of cheating; fabrication; facilitating infractions of academic integrity; plagiarism; bribes, favors, and threats; and academic interference. These categories, and the definitions quoted later in this chapter, might or might not exactly match those prevailing at your institution, but we hope that they will help you recognize the scope of dishonest behaviors and the need to educate yourself and your students about what constitutes dishonest behavior and how it is dealt with in your department and on your campus.

Cheating

Cheating is defined as "using or attempting to use in any academic exercise materials, information, study aids, or electronic data that the student knows or should know is unauthorized. During examinations, students should assume that external assistance (e.g., books, notes, calculators, and communication with others) is prohibited unless specifically authorized by the instructor."

It is also cheating if students allow others to conduct research or prepare any work for them without your prior authorization. This aspect of the cheating concept includes, but is not limited to, the services of commercial term paper companies. In addition, "substantial portions of the same academic work may not be submitted for credit more than once without authorization." This aspect of cheating is often misunderstood by college students, many of whom believe that once they create a piece of work, they can use it as they see fit.

Plagiarism

Plagiarism is defined as "representing the words or ideas of another as one's own in any academic endeavor." This includes "submitting the work of another as one's own," not properly citing direct quotes, not acknowledging paraphrases of another source, and not acknowledging information obtained in one's reading or research that is not common knowledge. Aside from cheating, plagiarism is probably the most common type of academic dishonesty that you will encounter.

Spotting plagiarism is often not too difficult. Look for papers that are only marginally related to the assignment; those with a tone or style that varies from the student's previous writing; that contain statistics and references not readily accessible to the student; that contain unexpectedly few grammatical errors; and, of course, papers that are extremely similar to one another (Curzan & Damour, 2000). There is also software such as TurnItIn, iThenticate, and Viper that can help you detect plagiarism. (See http://mashable.com/2012/08/29/plagiarism-online-services/ for a list of the top 10 plagiarism detection software programs.)

Fabrication

Fabrication is defined as "unauthorized falsification or invention of any information or citation in an academic endeavor. 'Invented' information may not be used in any laboratory experiment or other academic endeavor without notice to and authorization from the instructor or examiner." Fabrication also includes "altering the answers given for an exam after the examination has been graded" and "providing false or misleading information for the purpose of gaining an academic advantage, e.g. submitting false documents for the purpose of being excused from a scheduled examination or other academic assignment."

This form of dishonesty is usually reasonably easy to detect by checking the source of suspect written material, but do take special care when allowing students to review their exam answer sheets, especially if they are multiple choice forms. One of our students altered his answer sheet during the few minutes in which we allowed him to check its accuracy against our answer key. He then claimed that the optical scanner had erred in scoring his test and asked us to change his grade. Given that a scanner error is virtually impossible on a properly marked test form, we confronted the student with our suspicions and he admitted his deceit.

Facilitating Infractions of Academic Integrity

Facilitating infractions of academic integrity is defined as "helping or attempting to help another to commit an infraction of academic integrity, where one knows or should know that through one's acts or omissions such an infraction may be facilitated." This includes "allowing a student to copy one's work, taking an exam by proxy for someone else, and removing an exam from a classroom or other facility without authorization." Both the person who facilitates the infraction and the one who benefits from it are guilty of academic dishonesty.

The most common example of this form of dishonesty occurs when students allow other students to see and copy from their work during an examination. Another example of facilitating an infraction is impersonating another student for the purpose of taking an exam for that student. This scam is especially likely to occur in large classes in which the teacher and/or exam proctors do not know all students by sight.

Bribes, Favors, Threats

As their names imply, these forms of academic dishonesty are defined as "attempting to bribe, promising favors to, or making threats against any person with the intention of affecting a record of a grade or evaluation of academic performance." Although infractions in this category are rare, and might never happen to you, you should be aware that it is unacceptable for a student to offer you money, or anything else of value (including, say, free meals at a relative's restaurant or discounts at a friend's store), or to propose washing your car or painting your house or the like in exchange for a better grade or other academic consideration. Threatening your health or safety, too, is a wholly unacceptable way to try to improve one's grade. In the only such case that either of us has experienced, a large, angry student threatened to "mess up" his instructor if the student did not get the extra points he felt he deserved. Remaining calm (outwardly at least), the instructor picked up his office phone and called the campus police to report the situation. The startled student realized he had made a serious mistake and was abjectly apologizing by the time officers arrived. You might decide to handle such a situation in a different way, but we recommend that you never ignore threatening behavior; the very few students who engage in it must immediately discover that it will get them nowhere.

Academic Interference

Academic interference is defined as "tampering with, altering, circumventing, or destroying any educational material or resources in a manner which deprives any student fair access or reasonable use of that material or resource." These offenses tend to occur when a scarce resource, such as an article or book on reserve in the library, is stolen or damaged by one of the numerous students who are supposed to be sharing it.

Origins of Academic Dishonesty

Understanding who cheats and why can help you to develop plans for dealing with academic dishonesty. Some studies have found academic dishonesty associated mainly with male students, low grade point averages, and membership in Greek organizations (McCabe & Bowers, 2009; McCabe et al., 2001; Storch & Storch, 2002), but other associations have appeared as well (Lambert, Hogan, & Barton, 2003; McCabe et al., 2001; Novotney, 2011; Yardley et al., 2009). For example, the motivation to cheat appears to be greater among students who successfully cheated in high school, who believe they have to cheat in order to graduate, who believe that cheating will help a friend, or who have run out of time to study (Lambert et al., 2003; Yardley et al., 2009). However, the three most important influences on the prevalence of cheating in higher education relate to the culture of integrity on campus, peer influences, and the likelihood of reward versus punishment (McCabe et al., 2012).

Specifically, the best predictors of cheating are the degree to which students observe others cheating and the degree to which faculty are perceived as indifferent to academic dishonesty (McCabe et al., 2001; Prohaska, 2012; Rettinger & Kramer, 2009 Svinicki & McKeachie, 2014). When students perceive that "everyone does it," that dishonest students are unlikely to be caught and, if caught, unlikely to receive severe punishment, academic dishonesty is supported by campus culture (Davis et al., 1992; Jendrek, 1992; Lambert et al., 2003; McCabe et al., 2012). At the same time, more than 90% of college students say that academic dishonesty is wrong and that their teachers should not ignore the problem. Many faculty members do ignore it, though (Davis & Ludvigson, 1995; McCabe et al., 2012; Prohaska, 2012). As few as 20% of teachers in higher education report dishonest students to their department head or other academic official; some don't even confront the offending students, perhaps because they prefer to avoid the interpersonal and administrative hassles that would ensue and/or because they expect that their efforts to punish dishonest students will not be supported by the campus administration (Diekhoff et al., 1996; Jendrek, 1989; McCabe, 1993; McCabe et al., 2012).

Dealing with Academic Dishonesty

When faculty do decide to confront dishonest students, many do so in an informal, one-on-one private meeting. This approach may be ill advised, for several reasons (McCabe et al., 2012). First, it might violate the rules and policies set out by the psychology department or the campus for dealing with cases of suspected academic dishonesty. Second, it creates a situation in which the teacher assumes the roles of judge, jury, and executioner. Without an impartial hearing conducted in accordance with campus rules, the accused student is not only denied due process, but might be in a position to bring a formal complaint against the teacher, even though that teacher was only trying to be "nice." Finally, the outcome of an informal meeting will likely remain private. Yet if your suspicions about a student's academic dishonesty were to be upheld by a formal hearing, this fact would be noted in the student's file where it can serve to inform those who might have to deal with a subsequent offense. In other words, if you don't report dishonest students, they might be able to cheat their way to a degree (Jendrek, 1989; McCabe et al., 2012). With these points in mind, we always adhere to campus procedures relating to incidents of suspected academic dishonesty, beginning with a letter or e-mail to the student (see Figure 6.3), followed by a meeting with the student and others involved in the situation, followed by a letter or e-mail to inform the student of our decision and his/her options for responding to that decision (Figure 6.4).

In short, academic dishonesty can best be addressed at the institutional level (McCabe et al., 2001). It is the institution's responsibility to create a climate of academic integrity, and institutions that require reporting of violations of academic integrity or that have honor codes in place tend to experience less academic dishonesty (McCabe et al., 2001; Novotney, 2011; Prohaska, 2012; Schwartz, Tatum, & Wells, 2012; Shu, 2011). As one observer has put it, "students seem . . . to rise (or fall) to the ethical levels set by institutions and instructors" (Prohaska, 2012, p. 80). Perhaps the most important question to ask when contemplating the problem of academic dishonesty is how can we create an environment in which academic dishonesty is socially unacceptable (McCabe & Trevino, 1993).

Discouraging Academic Dishonesty

You can do a number of things to discourage various forms of academic dishonesty. Whenever you are giving an exam, always have at least one proctor working with you so that if you are answering a student's question or collecting exams, someone else is watching the rest of the class. Also arrange for students to sit as far apart as possible from each other. We request larger rooms to administer our exams so we can put students in every other seat. Tell students ahead of time that they will have to keep cell phones and other electronic devices turned off and in their backpacks. Tell them, too, that they will not be allowed to leave the room during the exam without permission and without an escort (Prohaska, 2012). If your exam is in multiple choice format, create several versions, each with a different sequence of items and each printed on differently colored paper. To discourage an imposter from taking a test for one of your students, require all students to show a photo identification card before entering the exam room. Once the test begins, you and your proctor(s) should remain active, moving constantly around the room during the entire exam period. If you suspect that a student is looking at another student's answer sheet or giving help to other students nearby, quietly

Student Name [sent **ALSO** via e-mail]
Student Address Student ID:
City, State, Zip Code

Dear (Student Name):

I am writing to inform you of my suspicion of a possible violation of academic integrity by you in (course and number) as defined by the *Student Code*, Article 1. Part 4. Academic Integrity. Please see http://admin.illinois.edu/policy/code/article1_part4_1–401.html for additional information about university policy and procedures.

Specifically, I believe that you may be guilty of (plagiarism, cheating, etc.) on your (paper, midterm, final examination, computer program, etc.) submitted on (date). The following information suggests a violation of our Student Code:

(Provide narrative that refers to such details as sections of paper underlined in attached copy that are identical to an Internet source, citing the source; behaviors observed by you or by exam proctors that led to suspicion of cheating on the examination; amount of correspondence on work submitted by two students or groups, etc.)

Under Section 1- of the Student Code, I must first notify you of your possible violation of academic integrity. This letter is that notification.

The *Student Code* permits you eight working days to respond to this allegation. Once that period has expired, I will review any response you have made to the charge described above, I will make a final determination regarding your innocence or guilt and, as necessary, will determine an appropriate penalty. You will receive notification of this outcome in writing.

If you have any questions about these policies and procedures, you can contact me at (phone or e-mail) [or course supervisor, if there is one other than you], and/or the Associate Head for Undergraduate Studies in the Psychology Department (Dr. _____). You can also read sections 1–402 through 1–404 of the Student Code that are available on the Web.

Sincerely,
(faculty full name)
(faculty title)

cc: Head, Department of Psychology

Fig. 6.3 Letter Outlining the Academic Dishonesty Charge.

Student Name   [sent **ALSO** via e-mail]
Student address   Student ID**:**
City-State-Zip

Dear (Student Name):

On (date), I charged you with a possible violation of academic integrity in (course and number). You responded to this charge on (date). Based on my review of the information available to me at this time, I find you in violation of the *Student Code*, Article 1. 402—(choose specific option from among the options listed in the Code).

I find that you (restate information from narrative of charge letter and the facts found).

Based on this finding that you are guilty of a violation, I have assigned the sanction of (code number in 1–403(c)) and will (describe the sanction assigned and its implications for the course).

This decision may be appealed to the head of the Psychology Department, Dr. _____, by (Date; 15 working days later than the date of this letter) by contacting Dr. _____ (insert contact details). Procedures for appeal are noted in the *Student Code* at http://admin.illinois.edu/policy/code/article1_part4_1–405.html. Questions concerning appeals within the department should also be addressed to Dr. _____. If you have specific questions regarding the sanction, please contact me at (phone).

Sincerely,
(faculty name)
(faculty title)

cc: Head, Department of Psychology

Fig. 6.4 Example of the Follow-Up Academic Dishonesty Letter.

move the suspected cheater(s) to a different seat, make a mark on the student's answer sheet to identify the point at which you intervened, and allow the student(s) to complete the test. The same goes for the discovery of a "cheat sheet" or other unauthorized material, which should be confiscated before allowing the student to continue. When the test is handed in, let the student know that they will be receiving a letter or e-mail from you (see Figure 6.3). We suggest that you allow cheating suspects to finish their tests because, in the event that the student has a satisfactory explanation for the apparent cheating, you will not have to re-administer the test or create a new one. (For information on what to look for while proctoring an exam, visit "How to cheat on a test" at www.wikihow.com/

Cheat-On-A-Test. Many of your students will have already done so, and the site can give you some ideas for how to prevent cheating.)

A good way to discourage plagiarism is to make sure that your students understand what it is, so include its official campus definition in your syllabus and/or in your description of all writing assignments. It is helpful, too, to design those assignments to be so specific that it will be difficult or impossible to find existing prototypes. For example, it might be easy for students to find a paper on "Application of human factors technology in equipment design," but probably not one focused specifically on the design of, say, hospital beds or barbeque grill controls. If you allow students to choose their own term paper topics, insist on seeing an outline of the proposed papers by some early deadline and then require students to turn in first drafts; this not only makes it more likely that students will do their own work, but it helps them get a better grade on the final draft. To discourage students from submitting for your course some version of a paper they have already submitted elsewhere, be explicit when assigning a book report or paper topic that you want students to read a book they have never read before or address a topic they have not written about in the past. You can also discourage the use of "term paper" mills simply by mentioning your awareness of them when making a writing assignment. You might also mention that many of these services can cost hundreds of dollars and often provide papers that are basically gibberish, and certainly do not follow the APA guidelines that most psychology faculty require (Ariely, 2012). One teacher purchased a paper from a "mill" and assigned students to write a critique of it (Davis, 2009). Steps like these may greatly diminish the chances that your students will use such "services."

To minimize the chance that someone will destroy or steal shared academic resources, put multiple copies of those resources on library reserve, or better yet, post them on your course's Web site. (As always, be sure that electronic posting does not violate any copyright laws. Indeed, a whole variety of computer-related academic infractions defined by applicable laws, contracts, or campus policies—such as unauthorized use of computer licenses, copyrighted materials, and intellectual property—apply to you to the same extent that they do to your students.)

There are other, more general, steps you can take to discourage various forms of academic dishonesty (Svinicki & McKeachie, 2014). First, consider providing multiple opportunities for students to earn course points, so that no one exam or paper has a massive influence on a student's grade. Second, be sure to discuss the topic of academic integrity in the syllabus so that all students are aware of what constitutes academic dishonesty and the procedures you will take if and when it occurs. Third, make reasonable demands of your students and make every effort to write valid exams. Some students cheat on exams because they see them as trivia contests and not as accurate assessments of what they know. Fourth, try to develop a group norm of academic integrity. One instructor (Svinicki & McKeachie, 2014) asks her students to vote on whether they will take their exams on the honor system. One dissenting vote does away with this choice, but asking for the vote demonstrates to students that the teacher is interested in academic integrity and believes that the students are, too. Fifth, stop and talk to the class if most students are not doing well on your exams. Try to find out why that is happening. By trying to help those who are not doing well in the course, you may well reduce their motivation to cheat. Finally, try to develop individual relationships with students when possible. As mentioned earlier, students are less likely to cheat when they feel that the instructor cares about them (Svinicki & McKeachie, 2014).

Online Considerations

Ensuring academic integrity is difficult in an online course. How do you know if a student taking a quiz is referring to a textbook or getting help from a friend? Though many instructors assume that online students are more likely to cheat, there is some evidence that online students may actually be less likely to cheat (Dietz-Uhler & Hurn, 2011; Stuber-McEwen, Wisely, & Hoggatt, 2009). Self-report surveys suggest that, when it does occur, online academic dishonesty is less common among students in education and the social sciences, when compared to students in engineering and the physical sciences (Sendağ et al., 2012). Further, first-year students report more online academic dishonesty, possibly because they are less likely to be aware of what constitutes academic integrity and the university policies surrounding it (Sendağ et al., 2012).

Most observers agree that when students perceive great psychological distance between themselves and their teacher, whether in online or face-to-face classes, they are more likely to feel disengaged and more likely to cheat (Dietz-Uhler & Hurn, 2011; Price, 2010; Stuber-McEwen et al., 2009). This suggests that academic dishonesty in online courses will be reduced when online teachers reduce the perceived distance between themselves and their students by being an active presence in the course.

In general, the academic integrity of online courses can be enhanced by clearly defining academic dishonesty, stating how you handle incidents of dishonesty, and decreasing the perceived distance between you and your students. And of course you should also consider using preventive measures as discussed in Chapter 5, such as requiring students to take exams through ProctorU—a service that identifies each student and monitors their eye movements and other behavior while they are taking their online examination. (For more information about this service, visit www.proctoru.com/.)

• • • • •

Providing Academic Help

Students arrive in your classroom with widely varying amounts of ability, motivation, and academic preparation. Some are especially likely to benefit from assistance from their teachers in order to succeed. Although it may be impossible to deal with each of those students individually, there are some simple things you can do to help all students do their best in your courses.

For example, you can include in your syllabus a section on "How to Do Well in This Course," which offers a detailed list of what it takes to succeed in the course (Pastorino, 1999). In our own syllabi, we stress the importance of keeping up with the readings, we encourage students to study for the quizzes and exams by using the practice quizzes and exams that appear on the textbook's Web site, and we even provide statistical summaries from previous classes showing how students' efforts in completing various assignments are related to final grades. You can also recommend that students read books about the behaviors that researchers have shown to be associated with academic success in higher education (e.g., Cuseo, Fecas, & Thompson, 2010; Schreiner, Louis, & Nelson, 2012).

In the following sections we offer specific suggestions for helping your students more effectively organize and think about the material to be learned, develop their study skills, and keep up with their reading assignments.

Providing Advance Organizers

Advance organizers serve to help students fit new course information into the framework of previously learned material (Ausubel, 1968, 2000; Ausubel, Novak, & Hanesian, 1978). This idea stems from research in cognitive psychology showing that it is easier to learn and remember new information if it can be related to information already in memory (Hilton, 1986; Palmisano & Herrmann, 1991). One way to provide an advance organizer in class is to put an outline of each day's lecture in a corner of a blackboard or in a section of each PowerPoint slide. If you are continuing a topic from a previous class session, include the earlier topics, too. This way, students can not only see how today's session will be organized and how the topics are related to one another, but how new topics are related to what was covered earlier.

You can also include advance organizers in your class presentations. For example, if you have already presented information about attachment theories in the developmental section of your introductory psychology course, you can refer back to that information (perhaps spending five minutes on it as a refresher) when covering object relations theories of personality and psychopathology later in the course. By reintroducing the concept of attachment, you are providing an advance organizer that can make it easier for your students to learn and remember information about object relations theory. We think that advance organizers are especially important in an introductory course, where the pace of presentation tends to be rapid and where it is easy for students to lose track of how seemingly unrelated topics are in fact linked to one another.

Telling a story that includes concepts that you are about to cover can act as another type of advanced organizer. For example, when introducing the concepts of sensation and perception, you could tell the story of Virgil, a blind man who regained his sight (sensations) in adulthood, but did not develop normal visual perception (Sacks, 1993). Students are intrigued to learn about the sensory versus perceptual aspects of vision illustrated in this story, and it provides them with a framework for thinking about the differences between sensation and perception that you describe later.

Advance organizers can also be provided through graphics (Knowledge Network for Innovations in Learning and Teaching, 2013). Concept maps and Venn diagrams often allow students to see connections and the "big picture" more easily than through text.

Finally, draw your students' attention to the advance organizers that might appear in their textbook. These organizers usually take the form of chapter outlines, preview questions, or features that highlight linkages between new material and material covered in previous chapters.

Promoting Effective Study Skills

Students who come to college with marginal study skills will face an uphill battle in many of their psychology courses. They might already be aware that they are at a disadvantage, but some students who did well in high school might suddenly discover that they lack the study skills required for success in psychology. We recommend that struggling students take the Study Behavior Checklist (SBC) to help them improve the efficacy of their study time (Gurung, Weidert, & Jeske, 2010). The SBC assesses "students' organizational behaviors (e.g., writing down when exams, assignments, and quizzes are due, setting up a study schedule); application behaviors (e.g., creating questions about the material); elaboration behaviors (e.g., paraphrasing the material, explaining it to another person); metacognitive behaviors (e.g., using practice exams to study); and resource use behaviors (e.g., asking a fellow classmate to explain the material) (Gurung et al., 2010, p. 30). While metacognitive skills are important, research indicates that no one single best set of study skills will work equally well for all students (Gurung et al., 2010).

Be aware, too, that study skills encompass more than general cognitive strategies and that sometimes students benefit from specific tips on how to study for specific courses. For example, one of our colleagues distributes a handout only to students who failed his first exam (Hendersen, 2002b). Entitled "Responding to Failure: A Survival Guide," the handout encourages these students to meet with the instructor, but also provides detailed information about developing effective study strategies, including questions to ask oneself while reading the textbook, how to best use lecture notes, how to use the textbook, the value of study groups, the pitfalls of rote memorization, the importance of a proper study environment, and the need to devote adequate time to studying.

It is also important to let students know what research has shown about study techniques that do and do not work. A recent meta-analysis of research on 10 learning techniques found that many of them were both ineffective and inefficient. These included summarizing concepts, highlighting/underlining text, using keyword mnemonics, using imagery while reading the textbook, and rereading the textbook (Dunlosky et al., 2013). These techniques *seem* useful, though, so it can be difficult to convince students not to highlight text and to practice retrieval instead of rereading text (See Einstein, Mullet, & Harrison, 2012 for a classroom demonstration showing that testing works better than rereading.)

With this in mind, we think that some discussion of techniques that *do* increase student learning should be a part of every course in psychology. (See Gurung & McCann, 2011, for a summary of how teachers can help their students study—including what *not* to do.) It is equally important to disabuse students of the notion that they have a particular learning style and that they would be more successful if only the teacher would teach in a manner that matched that personal style. Research on learning styles is clear: there is no evidence that learning styles actually exist, let alone should influence teaching methods (Pashler et al., 2008; Riener & Willingham, 2010).

Improving Note Taking

A clear and organized set of class notes is an important resource for effective studying, but many students are not as skilled at note taking as they should be. If you want proof of this assertion, try this: At the end of a class session, ask a few of your students to show you the notes they took that day. The results of this exercise can be disconcerting because although you might have made a first-rate class presentation full of well-organized content, vivid examples, and clever mechanisms for showing how all the topics are related to each other, some of the information might have been distorted in translation into students' notes, and its essential elements might never have reached students' notebooks at all. One small study of student note taking found that in general student note taking was poor, but that the quality of in-class notes was a significant predictor of academic performance (Chen, 2013).

There are several ways to help students improve their note-taking skills. First, give them information on the importance of good note taking, and how to do it more effectively (e.g., Pauk, 2001). Second, be sure that key terms and main concepts appear on your slides or on the blackboard as you talk about them. Students are more likely to take notes on information that arrives through more than one sensory channel. One study found that almost all students took notes on all information that was presented both orally and in writing, but that only about 27% did so when important information was only presented orally. Further, it was the academically marginal students who benefited most from the instructor's use of visual displays (Baker & Lombardi, 1985). A third way to encourage good note taking is to plan activities that require students to use their notes for purposes other than studying for a quiz or exam. If students have to rely on their notes to do well during the next class, they will be more likely to review, clarify, and reorganize those notes soon after they take them. This process, in itself, helps students to process course material more deeply and remember it longer (Ashcroft & Foreman-Peck, 1994). For example, the day after giving a lecture on the brain, we describe the symptoms of various neurological disorders, one patient at a time, and then ask our introductory psychology students to work in groups to decide which brain areas are impaired in each case. To guide them in this activity, the students are allowed to use only the notes they took during the previous class and while reading the textbook. This experience helps them realize how valuable note taking can be—especially if the notes are complete and well organized. Groups with the best notes tend to come up with good answers quickly. Students who come to class without notes are placed in a "no notes" group and have to come up with answers from memory. These students tend not to do as well on the activity, and soon recognize that there is no substitute for good notes.

To further emphasize the importance of this point, you might consider giving quizzes, or even exams, during which students can refer to the notes they have taken from lectures and the textbook. A variant on this idea is to allow students to bring one page of notes into a quiz or exam (specify a minimum font size). This option virtually guarantees that students will not only study for the exam, but will more actively process course material, if only to decide what information is important enough to include on their one precious page of notes.

One of the most enduring controversies relating to note taking is whether to give students copies of your PowerPoint slides. Some psychology teachers argue that when students have the slide content in front of them, they can listen to the lecture and not be distracted by trying to jot down the important ideas. Others argue that it is the very process of taking notes that solidifies the information in students' minds. They also argue that making the PowerPoint slides available encourages students to skip class and that it creates the false impression that they have all the most important information in hand and thus that they know more than they really do. Our own view is that providing students with only a bare-bones outline of the important points contained on slides allows them to concentrate on the oral presentation and also encourages them to take the more detailed notes needed to fill in the gaps (Ashcroft & Foreman-Peck, 1994). We think that students who do so, and thus summarize class information in their own words, will process that information more deeply and remember it longer.

Encouraging Students to Read

One of the most frustrating experiences we have encountered in teaching psychology is to develop an interactive class presentation designed to promote active learning, only to find out that many or most of the students did not read the assigned material and do not have the background to participate. We are not alone, and this common experience is especially troublesome in courses incorporating interteaching and in the flipped classroom. Many students fail to keep up with reading assignments even though they intended to do so and realize that it can help them get a good grade. The problem may reflect poor time management, the demands of work, family, and other courses, or even some form of reading disability (e.g., Berry et al., 2011). When talking to students who experience these problems, suggest that they seek help through whatever time-management, study skill, or rehabilitative programs your campus has to offer. Be aware, though, that students who initially kept up with the readings may stop doing so simply because they see no obvious connection between what is going on in class and what they are being asked to read (Satterlee & Lau, 2003; Svinicki & McKeachie, 2014). So when you assign reading, make sure that it does connect to in-class material and, as we mentioned in Chapter 3, take time on the first day of class to highlight its importance in terms of your course goals (Eble, 1988). Make sure, too, that students feel rewarded for advance reading by referring to textbook content during lectures whenever it is appropriate. And as the course proceeds, remind students of each week's reading assignment, why it is important, and how it will help them to understand the course content (Boyd, 2003).

Without taking special steps to encourage students to complete their reading assignments on time, you can safely assume that many and perhaps most, of them will not have done so. If you are not concerned that this situation will affect the quality of in-class activities and discussions, you can let the academic chips fall where they may, but if you want to improve those in-class experiences, you may have to become active in promoting advance reading. Some teachers have assessed the reading situation by handing out three-by-five cards on which students can anonymously say whether they are keeping up with the reading, and if not, why not (Satterlee & Lau, 2003). Reading these comments provides a starting point for deciding what to do next, whether it be to consult with colleagues, changing textbooks next terms, or perhaps setting up (or altering) a reading encouragement and reward system.

One of the authors, who teaches primarily first-year students, presents students with a reading schedule of 10–15 pages per day. While this originally seemed overly doting (couldn't they have done this on their own?), the reading calendar is consistently mentioned in students' course evaluations as being very helpful. She also gives daily low-stakes quizzes that cover the day's readings, which tends to help students follow that reading schedule.

Offering students ideas for reading strategies can help, too (Erickson et al., 2006; Nilson, 2013). For example, point out that students can get the most out of their textbook by using the book's pedagogical features (Boyd, 2003), including boldface terms, highlighted text, critical thinking exercises, self-tests, and chapter summaries to focus on the most important content. Many students tend to skip such pedagogical features—especially advance organizers and "boxed" information that is set apart from the regular text, so show them how valuable this information can be. Another way to reward students for reading is to assign short take-home exams that require students to read the text and critically analyze the material (Boyd, 2003). Finally, to reinforce the idea that you expect students to be reading their assignments, you could hand out three-by-five cards on random days and ask students to tell you, anonymously, what parts of that day's reading assignment they found clearest or most interesting, and what parts they found most confusing (Angelo & Cross, 1993; Satterlee & Lau, 2003).

Remember, though, that there is a limit on what you can and should do to help your students to do assigned readings. Trying endlessly to save them from themselves could be counterproductive, especially in the case of individuals who choose not to put in the time or effort necessary to succeed (Coffman, 2003). In such cases, the consequences of students' past choices might ultimately be more influential in shaping future choices than anything that you can do. In other words, we urge you to do all you can to provide help and resources for students who are motivated to succeed but who lack certain skills and information. However, we don't think you are obligated to assume full responsibility for your students' learning.

Online Considerations

As we have mentioned repeatedly, study skills, a sense of time management, and self-discipline are key attributes of successful students in online courses. Because there often is not a synchronous portion to an online course, we recommend that you present information about the importance of these success skills early in the course. You can post a message about these skills and/or assign students to watch Stephen Chew's videos on being successful in college (see Chapter 3). In addition, encourage students to read research-based information on strategies for academic success (e.g., Cuseo et al., 2010; Schreiner et al., 2012).

Unfortunately, online courses provide relatively few ways of assessing students' general academic skills. For example, it would be difficult, if not impossible, to give a daily quiz to assess reading, and one can't easily collect online students' notes. This means that online teachers may not become aware of their students' skill deficits until those students have fallen far behind their peers. So as we have mentioned before, it becomes incumbent on the online instructor to more diligently follow individual student progress and to begin a dialogue with students who are seen to be at risk of failing.

In some ways, online teachers can operate like face-to-face teachers in providing help to students. They can point out the importance of advance organizers and other pedagogical devices just as well in online courses as in face-to-face ones (Chen & Hirumi, 2009). Suggestions for how to read the textbook and other hints for doing well can also be offered in an online course.

●●●●●

Writing Letters of Recommendation

One of the most common, but often least anticipated, aspects of the faculty–student relationship comes in the form of requests from students to write letters of recommendation in support of their efforts to obtain employment, financial aid, study abroad, admission to graduate or professional school programs, or other opportunities. Many teachers find these requests a burden because they can require considerable time and effort—especially when the student is an unknown quantity or when the student's characteristics are well known but not particularly commendable.

Our advice is to be honest with every student who requests a letter of recommendation. If you know the student well and feel comfortable writing a strong letter, say so, and perhaps ask for further information, such as the student's résumé, a grade transcript, and a summary of the job or scholarship or program for which the student is applying. Having this information will allow you to write a personalized and appropriately targeted letter. Be sure to include in that letter as many details as truthfully possible about the student's excellent performance in your class. Employers, graduate schools, and scholarship committees are often looking for evidence of a well-rounded personality, so mention the student's extracurricular activities, communication skills, class participation and presentations, written work, and ability to interact with you and with fellow students. Go into as much detail as possible, describing, for example, the nature of the course requirements, the group work done in your class, and the student's role in it. End your letter by comparing the student with the other students you have taught and provide a short reprise of the student's strengths (Curzan & Damour, 2000; Davis, 2009).

If you don't feel that you can truthfully write a strong letter, tell the student. If the problem is simply that you do not know the student well enough (a common situation in larger classes), advise him or her to seek a letter from an instructor who does. If these unfamiliar students tell you that none of their other instructors know them well, either, or that they have two good letter writers lined up, but need a third letter to meet the requirements of an application package, you can offer to write what is essentially a form letter. Be sure to explain that this letter will contain only a statement that the student was a member of your class and earned a particular grade. Mention that you might also add a note about the grade distribution, and your general impression (if any) about the student's motivation and demeanor in the class. If you can't write a strong letter because you have little or nothing good to say about the student, and in fact, have some rather negative things to say, we suggest that you lay your cards on the table. In such cases, we say something like this: "Look, because of_____, _____, and_____, I am really not the best person to write a letter for you. In fact, my letter might hurt rather than help your chances." Most students who hear this will immediately go elsewhere.

Limit your letter to one or two pages and proofread it carefully. Be sure to indicate how you have known the student and in what capacity (e.g., student in your class, assistant in your lab). Avoid commenting on students' personal attributes, such as ethnicity or marital status, and be sure to end your letter with an overall evaluation of the student's suitability for the position or program in question and indicate that you would be happy to provide more information if needed. And don't forget to ask students to let you know if their application was successful (Davis, 2009).

The first few letters of recommendation you write will probably be the most difficult and will take the most time, simply because you will not yet have a template to follow. To make the task easier, ask colleagues for examples of letters they have written (they will first have to remove identifying information), and look at sample letters or templates in other sources (e.g., Curzan & Damour, 2000; Davis, 2009). Then ask one or more colleagues to read and comment on your first draft (again, identifying information should be removed). Figure 6.5 illustrates two different kinds of letters of recommendation.

Some students will give you printed recommendation forms on which you can write your letter or will direct you to a Web site where you can upload your letter. Many recommendation forms have a place where students can waive their right to see the letter you write. Some students fail to waive this right, but we recommend that they do so because the letter will have greater impact on the recipient if it is clear that the letter writer's comments were not influenced by concern over the student's reaction to them. This advice is especially appropriate, in our view, when you have been honest with the student about the kind of letter you can write.

Dear_____:

Mr. Tyrone _____ has asked me to write in support of his application for _____ . I am happy to do so. Tyrone was a student in my introductory psychology course at the University of Illinois, Urbana-Champaign during the fall semester of 2014. In a class of 110, Tyrone stood out as an excellent student. He earned one of the highest grades in the course and demonstrated a wide variety of academic skills. For one thing, he was very responsible and involved in his education. My class met at 8:30 in the morning and he had a perfect attendance record. He was also an active participant in the class, and all of his assigned work was turned in on time and complete.

I require extensive writing and different types of writing in my course. In addition to short-answer and essay questions on quizzes and exams, I make 12 "mini-assignments" (1–2 pages each) that require students to either apply a concept that they have recently learned or to be creative in developing new material. I also assign a major paper (10–15 pages) that requires students to watch a film with psychological content and then critically analyze how that film presented the psychological concept. The students are also required to read a journal article related to the film's psychological content and tie that article, the information presented in class, and their textbook information to a critical analysis of the film's portrayal of the psychological issue. I also require students to select a popular cartoon that relates to some topic in psychology and to tie the cartoon back to the textbook and classroom presentations. Tyrone received full credit on all of these writing assignments—an outstanding accomplishment.

Tyrone is not one to just follow the crowd. In class discussions he was articulate and thoughtful. And he was not afraid to present a viewpoint that was opposite to that of most students in the class. He was very attentive during class, making appropriate comments, asking and answering questions, and helping other students solve problems in some small-group exercises I assign in class. Finally, Tyrone is a genuinely nice person. He is enthusiastic about learning, open to new

Fig. 6.5 Examples of Letters of Recommendation.

experiences, optimistic, and gets along well with others. I very much enjoyed having him in my class. He is definitely in the top 10% of all undergraduate students that I have worked with in my 25 years of teaching.

If I can answer any further questions or provide any additional information, please do not hesitate to contact me. My office phone number is _____ and my e-mail address is _____.

Sincerely,

Dear_____:

Ms. Tasha _____ has asked that I write in support of her application for admission to _____. Tasha was a student in my introductory psychology class at the University of South Florida during the fall semester of 2014. She earned only a C in the course, but I found Tasha to be a very enthusiastic student, one who is more interested in learning course material than in what grade she will receive at the end. She not only displayed this interest in class discussions, but went beyond normal course requirements in pursuit of current psychological information. Tasha was also faithful in attending class and turned in all her assignments on time. She was also one of the few students in the class who took advantage of the opportunity to have me read a first draft of her term paper. In summary, I believe that Tasha is a fine person and an eager student.

While not outstanding academically in my course, she was a pleasure to have in class. I hope you will give her your most serious consideration. If I can be of further help, please do not hesitate to contact me.

Sincerely,

⬤ ⬤ ⬤ ⬤ ⬤

Some Final Comments

We think that the best part of teaching psychology is the opportunity to work with and build productive relationships with students. We think that the worst part of teaching psychology is dealing with students whose characteristics and behavior make it hard to remember the best part. We hope that the guidelines and suggestions that we have provided will help you minimize the number of negative interactions you have with your students and maximize the positive ones (see Checklist 6.2).

Checklist 6.2 A checklist of items related to establishing and maintaining productive faculty–student relationships.

1. Use your authority and power as a teacher in an ethical manner. Be aware of, and follow, the APA's ethical guidelines related to teaching.

2. Establish rapport with your students by being positive, keeping a sense of humor, being available to students, and showing interest in them.

3. Display immediacy behaviors such as appearing relaxed, smiling, making eye contact with students, using an expressive speech style, and using appropriate movement and gestures.

4. Be inclusive of all students—learn to pronounce their names, use diverse references and examples, create mixed student groups, make eye contact with all students, and write inclusive questions for your quizzes and exams.

5. Invite students with special needs to contact you early in the semester. Evaluate these students' requests for accommodations in light of the integrity of your course and its goals.

6. Establish policies at the beginning of the term for dealing with late papers, missed exams, complaints about test items, grades, and other academic work issues; adhere to those policies in relation to all students.

7. Minimize the likelihood of classroom incivilities by developing rules for classroom conduct, letting students know about those rules, and then enforcing them.

8. If you have to deal with a problem student, maintain a composed and professional demeanor while allowing the student to vent views and feelings without interruption. Then discuss the problem in a rational manner to help the student learn what helpful steps or resources might be available.

9. Before each new semester, create or update a list of campus resources for helping students who are upset, troubled, or otherwise in need of assistance that are beyond the scope of your role as a teacher.

10. Become familiar with campus and departmental policies and procedures regarding academic dishonesty. Follow these guidelines carefully when you act on suspected cases of academic dishonesty in your classes.

11. Try to make your course intrinsically interesting by relating its content to students' lives, incorporating relevant new material, and presenting it in the most compelling manner possible.

12. Develop your attendance policy in light of your course goals; be sure your students know and understand your policy.

13. Become familiar with FERPA and your institution's guidelines concerning students' privacy rights. Always adhere to these guidelines in planning and teaching your courses.

7

●●●●●

Teaching with Technology

We offer this chapter with some trepidation because by the time a book or even a journal article on teaching technology is published, what was "cutting edge" has become mainstream practice, has not borne out initial expectations, or has been superseded by the next big thing. In fact, educational technology has developed so quickly that even educational researchers have been unable to keep up with it (Njenga & Fourie, 2010). So in this chapter we concentrate on some of the mainstream teaching technology that has been shown to enhance both the physical and the virtual classroom.

As you read, keep in mind that *innovation* and *technology* are not synonymous terms (Light, Cox, Calkins, 2009) and that adding technology in the classroom does not necessarily increase student learning (Howard, 2012; Njenga & Fourie, 2010). In fact it is the teacher, not the teacher's technology, that has the greatest impact on student learning. In one study, for example, some instructors in a multisection course used presentation software and some did not. When student attitudes and learning were analyzed, the software was irrelevant—neither aiding nor hindering student learning. It was the main effect of the instructor that was most significant (Hardin, 2007). So "technology decisions are essentially teaching and learning decisions" (Svinicki & McKeachie, 2014, p. 261), because technology is a tool that can enhance good teaching, not something that can replace good teaching (Nevid,

2011). Remember, too, that if it is to be of real value, technology must be applied in the service of achieving your course goals. Some teachers, for example, use technology to create the flipped classroom that we mentioned in other chapters. They make background course material available outside of class, thus freeing class time for discussions, demonstrations, and active learning and critical thinking exercises (Bowen, 2006, 2012).

Regardless of what use you make of teaching technology, it is generally best to integrate it slowly and carefully. This is sometimes difficult to do on campuses where information technology (IT) staff encourage faculty members to adopt new technology simply because it is available, but without adequately analyzing whether and how the technology will help those particular faculty members. Even administrators at some schools push faculty to use technology because they believe it is what the students want, thus "putting the technological cart in front of the pedagogical horse" (Howard, 2012, p. 164). To avoid being swept along willy-nilly by the technological tide, take the time to attend campus workshops or presentations hosted by the technology vendors, and ask for individual support from your IT people. Be aware, though, that the quality of these events can vary. One department chair found his campus's technology workshops to be "Tupperware parties" focused on convenience and not education (Jaschik, 2010). For additional ideas, visit Sue Franz's Web site Technologies for Academics: Finding New Technologies so You Don't Have To (http://suefrantz.com).

In other words, try to go beyond learning what technology is available and what it is designed to do. Ask yourself what are its advantages and limitations for your teaching. How likely is it to help your students learn in your course and, just as important, how likely is it to make your life easier or more complicated? And what are the potential disadvantages: How difficult will it be for you and your students to master? Is it so inflexible that you will be forced to change the way you teach or grade? You should only decide to adopt new technology after really learning about it, analyzing its plusses and minuses, and carefully thinking about where, when, and how it can enhance your course. And don't forget to get feedback from colleagues on your campus and elsewhere who have already adopted it. Even after you do decide to try new technology, start small if possible, perhaps by using it in a limited way or with just one section of students. If you overhaul an entire course in order to incorporate new technology, and then discover significant problems you had not anticipated, you will be in for a long and difficult term. You can always expand the use and scope of your new technology once you have had some experience with it. Keep the following guidelines in mind when making decisions about the use of teaching technology (Bush, Pantoja, & Roen, 2003; McNeely, 2013):

1. Choose technology that enhances your learning goals and objectives.
2. Be prepared for the technology to fail—have a work-around or back-up plan.
3. Learn how to troubleshoot the technology.
4. Make use of technical, pedagogical, and administrative support—don't be afraid to ask for help.
5. Learn the technology by doing the technology—for example, explore and experiment with the technology you are adopting.
6. Remember that learning and teaching is a process; don't expect things to go perfectly the first time.
7. Students expect technology in their classes, but they also crave interaction—whether it comes via technology or face-to-face exchanges.
8. The technology you choose must be available to all students; they must all be able to use it, and they will expect their instructor, not IT staff, to explain it to them.
9. The technology should promote interaction with course material and the instructor (simply using PowerPoint slides during a lecture does not do that).
10. The technology should have practical applications to course work (e.g., learning to use Google Docs to create a portfolio for a final project).

Tools of Technology

There are many ways to categorize academic technologies. Michelle Pacansky-Brock, for example, describes *emerging technologies* as "cloud-based applications, that are easily stored online and accessible from anywhere with an internet connection; Web 2.0 tools, that make the creation and sharing of multimedia content simple; social media, technologies that transform communications into a highly interactive experience; and mobile apps, applications that are designed to operate on mobile devices (smartphones or tablets)" (2013, p. 1). (If you are interested in exploring these technologies in more depth, we highly recommend her book, *Best Practices for Teaching with Emerging Technologies*.) However, we are going to organize this section around Svinicki & McKeachie's (2014) classification of the technology tools that are currently in use in many technology-enhanced classrooms. These fall into four categories: Communication Tools; Presentation Tools; Information Searching and

Resource Management Tools; and Learning (Course) Management Systems (LMSs).

● ● ● ● ●

Communication Tools

E-mail and Text

Most instructors use e-mail to communicate with students (even though when communicating with each other, students prefer to text). E-mail is a quick and inexpensive way to set up meetings, discuss misconceptions about the course content, and even submit assignments. But, as we discussed in Chapter 2, faculty do need to be proactive in setting up student expectations about the appropriateness of e-mail content and the speed of response, and course syllabi should include this information. The fact that e-mail is asynchronous, depersonalized, and immediate sometimes leads students to send emotional messages that are not well thought out (Wilson & Florell, 2012). (For tips on responding to critical student e-mail, see Peck, 2013.)

Texting provides an alternative to e-mail communication between faculty and students. A system such as Cel.ly allows you to text all of your students at once by having them sign up and thus no phone numbers need to be exchanged.

Virtual Office Hours

Office hours, whether face to face or virtual, are also discussed in Chapter 2. Students often do not take advantage of face-to-face office hours, but you can encourage students to do so through a program called YouCanBookMe (https://youcanbook.me/howitworks.jsp), which links with your Google Calendar. It displays a calendar showing when you are available and allows students to sign up online for a face-to-face meeting.

Virtual office hours are a necessity if you are teaching online, but they are a nice addition to face-to-face courses, too. Web-conferencing programs such as Skype and Collaborate (previously Wimba and Elluminate) give students the option of contacting you from anywhere and give you the option of holding office hours anywhere. There is a variety of Web-conferencing software; for a good comparative review, see Wikipedia (http://en.wikipedia.org/wiki/Comparison_of_web_conferencing_software). Remember, though, whatever program you choose, you will want to be the one to show students how to use it.

Student/Classroom/Individual Response Systems

Though the official term for these devices is *student* or *classroom* or *individual response system*, most people just call them "clickers." Whatever term you prefer, these devices allow even the largest classes to be interactive. Most clickers require a receiver to be plugged into a classroom computer. As technology has become more sophisticated, the transmission range has increased, so that these systems can operate even in very large lecture halls, and, because of automatic frequency switching features, they will not interfere with or suffer interference from systems operating in nearby classrooms. Most clickers also allow the input of text, not just A, B, C, D, E choices, and some systems allow input from smartphones or tablet computers (see Anderson & Serra, 2011).

The pedagogical value of clickers in the classroom continues to be investigated. There are some obvious advantages to using them. They allow everyone to contribute in class, regardless of class size or student characteristics (e.g., shy students who would never raise their hands to speak will respond anonymously to even the most sensitive survey questions). Clickers also allow teachers to have instantaneous and candid feedback about everything from the quality of that day's lectures, to ratings of students' classroom presentations, to the number of students who have understood a particular concept (Goldstein, 2013; Lantz, 2010; Rhem, 2009). Clickers can also be used to administer frequent, even daily, quizzes to take advantage of the testing effect in promoting long-term retention of course material. And, because clicker technology can easily be linked to a teacher's LMS, the scores on those quizzes can go directly into a gradebook with just a few computer strokes.

Clickers can also be used to ask questions that go far beyond recall of facts and definitions, requiring students to engage in deeper, more critical thinking about course material (Bruff, 2011). For example, teachers can ask students to choose the one *best* answer from among several partially correct alternatives in a way that requires them to weigh evidence for and against each. Items can also be created to gain insight into students' misconceptions about course topics by analyzing the frequency with which various incorrect alternatives are chosen. Finally, there is little doubt that clickers can be used to increase classroom attendance (Case & Hentges, 2010). Indeed, some instructors, especially those who teach large enrollment classes, use clickers primarily to take attendance. If they also award points for classroom participation and the opportunity to earn those points comes at the end of class, students tend not to leave early.

Do clickers actually help to increase student learning? We wish we could be more encouraging, but although most students report that they like to use clickers, and thus may be more motivated to attend classes that use them (Landrum, 2013), there is little evidence that the use of clickers actually increases student performance (Anthis, 2011; Ellicker & McConnell, 2011). Further, students are smart, so the unmotivated ones have been quick to circumvent the attendance-taking and quizzing function of clickers by skipping class but sending their clicker with a friend who plans to attend. We spotted one student in a large lecture hall who had no fewer than four clickers on his desk and was carefully responding to each instructor question on each clicker.

Aside from fraud, are there other disadvantages to clickers? In the eyes of some, yes. For one thing, if you are set up to ask graded quiz questions in class, it may not be easy to switch quickly to anonymous mode so that students will feel comfortable honestly answering sensitive questions (Lantz, 2010). Further, clicker systems can carry a financial cost if students are required to buy a response device. One critic noted that "the idea of wasting money on a device no more sophisticated pedagogically than raising your hand drives me nuts, whether it is students' money or the university's" (Bugeja, 2008). Indeed, smartphones and tablets are likely to become the future standard choice for student response systems because most students already own one.

Web 2.0

"The term Web 2.0 was coined in 2004 to refer to Web sites and applications that foster collaboration, user participation, interactivity, and content sharing. Web 2.0 includes blogs, microblogs, wikis, social networks, tagging and bookmarking, online discussion boards, multimedia and file sharing, syndication, podcasts, and multi-user virtual environments" (Davis, 2009, p. 181). The characteristics of Web 2.0 have been described as follows:

- facilitating individual creation and manipulation of digital information and artifacts;
- offering strong support for, and low barriers to, sharing individual creations;
- harnessing the "power of the crowd," the collective intelligence of large groups of people in problem solving, forecasting, and other activities in which the independent judgments of participants are aggregated;
- maximizing the architecture of participation, whereby the precision or value of an application or service improves over time as usage increases; and
- affirming openness in source software and content distribution that allows users to access, reuse, and recombine (mashup) digital materials.

(Davis, 2009, p. 181)

Web 2.0 tools can support a range of pedagogical approaches. "They have the potential to provide new forms of immersion through, for example, 3D-environments . . . they offer a range of new ways in which knowledge can be represented, discussed and shared . . . they offer a range of ways in which collaborative learning activities can be supported . . . they support reflective practice and mechanisms for peer critiquing" (Conole & Alevizou, 2010, p. 41). "Effective use of new technologies requires a radical rethink of the core learning and teaching design process; a shift from design as an internalized, implicit and individual crafted process to one that is externalized, explicit and shareable with others" (Conole & Alevizou, 2010, p. 43). While there are many different tools under the umbrella of Web 2.0, a report by the Higher Education Academy (HEA) emphasized media sharing, media manipulation and mash-ups, instant messaging, chat and conversational arenas, online games and virtual worlds, social networking, blogging, social bookmarking, recommender systems, wikis and collaborative editing tools, and syndication (Conole & Alevizou, 2010, pp. 47–53). All of these tools are used today in higher education; here we briefly consider the four that we see most often, namely discussion boards, blogs, social media, and wikis.

Discussion Boards/Chat and Conversational Arenas

Most LMSs have a discussion board/forum capability. *Discussion boards* are easily set up and enable discussion of topics or questions posted by either students or the instructor. A *threaded discussion* focuses around a topic or question, often posed by the instructor. There are also "course" discussion boards where students may post questions about the course that are often answered by fellow students. Some discussion forums are used to merely supplement the syllabus or clarify course content, for example, by answering questions about course structure, or clearing up misconceptions about course concepts. However, participation in discussion boards can also be a graded component of the course. One of the authors requires students to post five "applied concept journals" during the semester. The students are to choose two concepts from the current chapters being discussed, define the concepts in their own words, and provide personal examples of how the concepts appear in or apply to their own lives. After posting their own concepts, students are required to respond to at least one post by another student. They can either verify that the examples and definitions are correct, and offer their own, or they can point out that the other student has either incorrectly defined the terms or provided examples that don't fit the concepts. Such assignments can increase student-to-student communication in classes; even in small classes students are likely to report that they feel that they know their classmates better in classes using discussion boards than in their other classes.

Chat rooms enable groups of students to work on projects or study together. They are essential in online courses that require group work, but can also be of value in face-to-face classes where students are busy and may be commuters, because chat rooms enable students to work together regardless of where they are.

There are also more sophisticated chat programs available, some of which use avatars and game-like environments, including video and audio communication (Conole & Alevizou, 2010; Quinn, 2012).

Blogs and Microblogging

The word "blog" is a contraction of "Web-based log," which is a chronological online journal in which the writer posts entries (Bridges, Harnish, & Sillman, 2012). Some universities support their own blog sites, but there are also "hosted blog sites" such as Blogger or Tumbler (tumblr) (Bridges et al., 2012). Blogs can be personal reflective journals, conduits for disseminating information and/or for interacting about themed concerns. In psychology classes, blogs can be graded assignments—as students post reflections or comments about classroom material or current events related to psychology, or identify psychological content in movies or books. Other students in the class can follow these postings to create a dialogue. These interactions can be valuable and informative, but teachers who require students to post to a blog have to remember that it will take considerable time to grade them all (Bridges et al., 2012). Instructors must also keep privacy concerns in mind; if they use blogs as a vehicle for promoting personal reflection, it might be a good idea to give students the option of letting only the teacher view the reflections.

Although there are several *microblogging* programs, the most popular is Twitter. Twitter allows only 140 characters per message but can still be used for educational purposes. For example, by assigning each class a hashtag #, students can see what aspects of the course their fellow students are discussing (Zax, 2009). One professor pauses part way through a class session and asks students to log onto the class Twitter account and pose a question about the material she has presented. She then sifts through the "tweets" to find common ambiguities and addresses them before the class ends (Zax, 2009). Many professors who use Twitter feel that it reduces the psychological distance between themselves and students, especially in large classes. Some research supports this impression. In one study, both students and the instructor were found to be more engaged in the learning process in Twitter versus non-Twitter sections of a course and, in addition, the "Twitter" students outperformed the "non-Twitter" students (Junco, Elavsky, & Heiberger, 2012; Junco, Heiberger, & Loken, 2011).

Social Networking/Social Media

There are two types of academic social interactions; between instructor and learners and between learners and other learners. While social media technology has facilitated the interactions between instructors and students, its main value has been in enhancing student–student interactions (Quinn, 2012). These days, students can communicate with each other though text messaging, e-mail, and social networks. Research suggests that, in particular, using the social networking site Facebook for class discussions not only increases student engagement in their courses but also cultivates a sense of community among students (Hurt et al., 2012). In fact, some institutions are developing social media guidelines to encourage faculty to create a Facebook page for each class and then require students to join that page (Pingree & Zakrajsek, 2013). Facebook pages are also an integral part of some of the Mass Open Online Courses (MOOCs) that we discuss later (Witte & Mock, 2013). Instructors who use Facebook in their courses argue that students are more likely to share resources and encourage each other and less likely to compete. Others claim that Facebook communication allows students to connect psychological concepts to their own lives and to events happening in the world, even when they are not in class (Chamberlin, 2013). In one multisection class, students who used the Facebook discussion in their section demonstrated a deeper understanding of the material and achieved higher grades than did students in a "non-Facebook" section (Chamberlin, 2013). One instructor who uses Facebook as a discussion forum gave this advice to those who are considering a Facebook site for their classes: promote it by talking about it in class and in the syllabus; set up a separate personal account; post in moderation; repeat information in class if you have made Facebook optional; fact check the information that students post; and welcome the criticism that comes as students exchange information regarding content that is confusing them (Chamberlin, 2013). Proponents of using social media as a form of teaching technology see such sites as more interactive than other alternatives. One observer put it this way: "Posting an announcement on Blackboard (LMS) is the equivalent of asking them to come to office hours in your building. Posting on Facebook is more like showing up in the dorms for dinner" (Bowen, 2006, p. 2).

Students sometimes use Facebook as a platform for working on group projects, even if they are given in-class time or space on the course Web site to do so. Indeed, some instructors have developed assignments that utilize Facebook and other social networks simply because they realize that many students spend an inordinate amount of time there anyway. One instructor of abnormal psychology developed an optional assignment in which students were to create and manage a Facebook profile of a major psychologist within a private classroom network (McBride, 2013).

The use of social networking in higher education has not been without controversy. Some instructors and some students believe that it is inappropriate for faculty to have accounts on social networking sites such as Facebook or MySpace (Malesky & Peters, 2012). Yet a 2011 special report by *Faculty Focus* (a research-based e-mail newsletter for instructors in higher education from Magna Publications) found that almost 85% of faculty already have Facebook accounts, about 50% have Twitter accounts, and about 66% use LinkedIn. "It has been said that Facebook is a backyard barbecue, Twitter is a cocktail hour and LinkedIn is a business luncheon" (Bart, 2011, p. 9). So, it is not surprising that faculty use LinkedIn rather than Facebook or Twitter for professional purposes; only about one-third of faculty befriend undergraduate or graduate students prior to the students' graduation (Bart, 2011).

More information about social media and their use in psychology courses is available in a variety of sources (e.g., Freberg & Freberg, 2012; Heiberger & Junco, 2011).

Wikis

Wikis involve the co-construction of content and centralized documents on a shared Web server (e.g., Google Docs) so that students can edit those documents rather than retain individual copies. They are collections of Web pages with information that can be edited by anyone. "As with Wikipedia, the most famous wiki of all, users can add content to existing pages, restructure the information on existing pages, create new pages, and create links between existing and new pages" (Karasavvidis, 2010, p. 221).

Wikis can be an excellent tool for facilitating group projects. Students are able to log on to the wiki site wherever they are and create and edit the working document. One of the authors used wikis in her online introductory psychology course and found that this not only encouraged student interaction—because finding a time for groups to meet either online or face to face is difficult—but also made the group projects easier to grade. Most LMSs will allow you to track the development of the wiki by reading the text that individual students have entered or edited. Having this information makes it much easier to identify the "social loafers" and reward those who did most of the work, something not possible in nondigital group projects.

Instructors can use wikis as part of their professional development. For example, all of the instructors in the introductory psychology course at the University of Illinois, Urbana-Champaign have access to an introductory psychology wiki where they can post assignments, give suggestions for media examples of concepts, post potential exam questions for feedback, and update and fact check other posts. In this way, all instructors have access to teaching materials for the course and those materials can be updated and edited by the instructors and the course director.

Presentation Tools

When you say "presentation software" everyone assumes you mean PowerPoint, because this Microsoft product is used almost universally. But believe it or not there are options, such as Prezi or Cmap, that allow you to map concepts and easily move them around on the screen (Svinicki & McKeachie, 2014). You can also use lecture capture software (such as Adobe Captivate, Camtasia, or Jing) to record live lectures that can be put online for a face-to-face course, a hybrid or blended course, a flipped classroom, or a totally online course. (See http://en.wikipedia.org/wiki/Comparison_of_screencasting_software for a comparison of software and Educause's guidelines for using lecture capture http://net.educause.edu/ir/library/pdf/eli7044.pdf.)

Whether it involves PowerPoint or not, presentation software has become almost ubiquitous in the higher education classroom. It can be an excellent tool, but like all the others discussed in this chapter, its value depends on how it is used. While undergraduates expect and enjoy PowerPoint presentations in their classrooms and some instructors find PowerPoint pedagogically useful, it can also be distracting, and thus interfere with learning, if the slides encourage students to mindlessly copy the information presented. After all, it is difficult for students to absorb what their teacher is saying while they are simultaneously attempting to read and write (Orlando, 2013a). Furthermore, classrooms centered around presentation software may discourage student questions and participation (Hill et al., 2012) simply because the environment emphasizes the slides (which may be the brightest stimulus in a darkened room) rather than the teacher (who in many technology-enhanced classrooms is relegated to a darkened corner behind a podium (Daniel, 2005, 2010, 2013). Critics also point out that presentation slides are often created to focus on format rather than content, using bullet points that can obscure relationships between concepts; using misleading or inaccurate slide titles; and using so many slides that what could have been an interesting lecture becomes just "one damn slide after another" (Tufte, 2003a, p. 4).

With these criticisms in mind, let's consider some "best practices" when using presentation software. Some of these items are based on common sense, but even teachers who have been using presentation software for a long time may find it helpful to remind themselves of some Do's and Don'ts. (If you don't want to bother reading them, you can find funny and informative presentations on what to avoid when using PowerPoint at www.youtube.com/watch?v=KbSPPFYxx3o and www.slideshare.net/jessedee/you-suck-at-powerpoint-2.)

1. Do not use presentation software in every class, and don't use it for the full session (Burke, Ahmadi, & James, 2009; Davis, 2009). Use the "mute" function or click "b" in PowerPoint to black out the slides and change the focus to you as the instructor or to a class activity (Berk, 2012a). Be sure to blend lecture with active and interactive classroom events (Svinicki & McKeachie, 2014).
2. Limit the number of slides you use (Davis, 2009). This is especially difficult if you have been adding information to your PowerPoint presentation every time you teach, but often, less is more when it comes to slides.
3. Make sure your slides are readable. Choose a simple template and/or a background that will not detract from the words or images. Avoid logos and irrelevant graphics (Berk, 2012a). Use a minimum of 30-point font for text and larger font for titles (Berk, 2012a). Stand in the back of your classroom and make sure you can easily read every word. Choose colors carefully (Davis, 2009; Svinicki & McKeachie, 2014). "Graphic designers recommend picking high-contrast colors with a *cool background* (blues or greens), which recede from your eyeballs, and *warm font*, to which your eyes are drawn and which commands attention; the combination should be easy to read" (Berk, 2012a, p. 4). This will be particularly welcomed by students with visual disabilities.
4. To increase students' understanding of what the slide is about, use short full-sentence headings (Berk, 2012a).
5. Use minimal amounts of text and bullet points—preferably not more than three per slide (Berk, 2012a; Davis, 2009; Svinicki & McKeachie, 2014). Indeed, some designers argue that there should be only one main point per slide. Others believe that you should avoid bullet points altogether (Orlando, 2013a).
6. Some argue that presentation software should only be used for visuals—pictures and diagrams that would take too long to draw on a blackboard or whiteboard (assuming you even have one) and that illustrate the concepts that you are discussing (Klemm, 2007; Orlando, 2013a). It is acceptable to create slides just to store the URLs for videos or other media that you plan to use in the classroom.
7. Avoid "gimmicks" that distract from the main purpose of the slide, including things like flying text, pointless sounds, gratuitous clip art, silly animations, and the like (Berk, 2012a; Davis, 2009).

8. Don't read your slides (if you have visually impaired students in your classroom give them your slides ahead of time). The slides should accompany and guide your presentation; they should not *be* your presentation (Svinicki & McKeachie, 2014).

9. Always face your class, not the screen, as you present. If you don't you might find a lot of students gone when you turn around.

10. Practice with your classroom equipment and double-check before-hand that the software you plan to use actually works on the computer you will be using in class. And as with all teaching technology, be sure to have a backup plan in case the Internet is down or there are other technical glitches when you get to class (Davis, 2009; McKeachie & Svinicki, 2014).

Audio and Visual Information

Audiovisual material in the classroom can be a welcome accompaniment to a good classroom presentation, but research has shown that illustrations, photos, animations, and videos can overwhelm students' attentional capacity, and so such material should be used with care, and primarily to underscore the major points the instructor is trying to make. So rather than showing a 40-minute video to explain or illustrate a concept, consider showing relevant clips from that video, assuming it is appropriate to break the information into segments. Similarly, if students are working through material online, set up your videos or animated illustrations so that they arrive in relatively short clips specific to each aspect of the material you are teaching and that allow students to click an icon when they are ready to proceed (Novotney, 2012).

Also, if you are using your PowerPoints in an online course, consider adding your own narration to the slides; many students will find it easier to listen to your voice as they look at the PowerPoint than to read the content of the slide before or after reading whatever text goes along with it. If you do add a narrative, speak in a conversational rather than formal way (Novotney, 2012).

Podcasts

Podcasts involve the distribution of digital audio and/or video files (McGarr, 2009). Many podcasts consist of audio-only files that students download from a Web site and listen to on MP3 players. These files are differentiated from other audio media in that they are often edited and indexed (Scutter et al., 2010). Some are discipline specific while others are course specific (see Azar 2012 for examples of psychology-related podcasts).

Course-specific podcasts may consist of recordings of a teacher's previous lectures and are made available so that students can review them for clarification or exam preparation (Scutter et al., 2010). Some podcasts are linked to PowerPoint slides on a course Web site that students can look at as they listen. Other podcasts provide supplemental course material that offers additional information and more detailed explanations of course concepts and perhaps suggestions for further reading (Scutter et al., 2010). Students, too, may be asked to create podcasts about course material, either for their own use or as graded assignments (McGarr, 2009). There is some evidence that students who become involved in the creation of podcasts tend to better understand course material and receive higher grades than other students (Lazzari, 2009), though such differences may also be attributable to differential motivation to learn.

Though podcasts have great potential value, if they consist of nothing more than reruns of course lectures, they may suppress class attendance, thus depriving students who merely listen to them of the active learning experiences that take place during class. For this reason, you might want to create podcasts that offer further explanations of difficult concepts, not just a replay of your lectures (Scutter et al., 2010). Yet another problem is that, despite one's best efforts to make high-value podcasts, some students may not bother to listen, especially once the novelty of doing so has worn off (Robinson & Kazlauskas, 2010). So if you do decide on podcasts, be sure that listening to them will meet a specific student need, and/or fulfill a graded assignment.

Videos

Clips from feature-length films can be used in class or online (via YouTube, for example) to dramatically illustrate course material, such as examples of psychological disorders or treatment methods (Sherer & Shea, 2011). When choosing these clips, be sure that they accurately portray the concept you wish to illustrate. Otherwise, if something in the clip contradicts the text or your lectures, students may misremember the film as being correct and give incorrect answers on a test or quiz. If there are small inaccuracies in an otherwise valuable clip, be sure to warn students about them beforehand (Butler et al., 2009).

Beyond the world of feature films is a vast array of educational videos or video clips. You can narrow your search for academically appropriate online videos by using Web sites specifically designed for academia (Sherer & Shea, 2011). Two prominent sites are TeacherTube (www.teachertube.com/staticPage.php?pg=about) and Academic Earth (http://academicearth.org/about).

Also available are complete videotaped lectures (see MIT Open Courseware), explanations of difficult concepts (see Khan Academy: www.khanacademy.org), and talks by prominent psychologists (e.g., TED talks: www.ted.com/talks).

● ● ● ● ●

Information Searching and Resource Management Tools

In pursuing the goal of promoting critical thinking, it is vital to help students learn to evaluate the validity of the information they encounter, especially online. This includes helping them restrict their search for information to legitimate and scientifically respectable sources. Despite psychology instructors' best efforts to enlighten students about the importance of doing so, many students still have difficulty distinguishing between Web sites that provide authoritative information and those that may be merely a personal blog or a commercial enterprise. Most university library Web sites offer guidelines about how to judge the validity of a Web site. (See, for example, the University of Illinois library guidelines at www.library.illinois.edu/ugl/howdoi/webeval.html.) In addition, faculty need to re-educate students about plagiarism, helping them distinguish and define what is "common knowledge" given the prevalence of digital information (Svinicki & McKeachie, 2014).

Faculty also need to help students navigate databases and use search engines effectively (Svinicki & McKeachie, 2014). For example, most students know how to use Google, but few know how to use Google Scholar or PsycInfo to find research and scientific papers. Learning to become critical consumers of information found online is a valuable asset that will serve students well throughout their lives.

● ● ● ● ●

Learning Management Systems

In Chapter 1 we introduced the concept of Learning Management Systems (LMS), or course management systems as they are sometimes called. "LMS technology features personal communication via email; group communication via chatting and forums; posting content including syllabus, papers, presentations and lesson summaries; performance evaluation via question and answer repositories, self-assessment tests, assignments, quizzes and exams; instruction management via messaging, grade posting and surveys; and more" (Naveh, Tubin, & Pliskin, 2010, 127–128). LMSs provide an easy way to distribute resources (e.g., post articles, assignments, etc.), communicate with students—often through the use of discussion boards, give quizzes and exams without using class time, manage student grades (and give students secure access to them), and give access to collaboration and reflection tools such as wikis, podcasts, and blogs (Svinicki & McKeachie, 2014).

Currently available LMSs can be categorized as proprietary (for profit) or open source (free). "Blackboard" is becoming the biggest proprietary LMS as it has now absorbed WebCT and several other former LMSs. Moodle is a prominent open-source LMS. There are pros and cons associated with both types of LMSs. Web designers and technologically sophisticated faculty tend to like open-source software because they can customize it to fit their institutions and courses. Many less tech-savvy faculty prefer the less flexible, but perhaps less challenging proprietary LMSs. In any case, these days, most faculty in psychology are using some kind of LMS in their face-to-face and hybrid or blended courses, and they are a virtual must in online courses. Research on LMSs suggests that for students to be satisfied with them, the course Web site must be easy to navigate and must complement and enhance course content. First-year students, especially, tend to find LMSs, particularly their forum feature, to be of value (Naveh et al., 2010).

Teaching Online

We have included sections about teaching online throughout this book, so in this chapter we just make some general comments about it. If you are planning an online course, or are already teaching one, we recommend, first, that you take a look at the resources of the Multimedia Educational Resource for Learning and Online Teaching (MERLOT) organization (www.merlot.org/). This open source of information is international and provides a repository of materials that can be used for a multitude of online courses.

Second, we urge you to be aware of some of the special ethical challenges associated with teaching online by reading discussions about them (e.g., Elison-Bowers & Snelson, 2012).

Finally, we want to point out the distinction between "traditional" online courses and Massive Open Online Courses (MOOCs). Although they share some characteristics, they offer different types of learning experiences for students. Let's consider both now.

MOOCs

As of 2013, only 2.6% of institutions of higher education offered Massive Open Online Courses (MOOCs), though another 9.4% had MOOCs in the planning stage. Indeed, MOOCs are growing in number and are slowly gaining acceptance, especially at research-oriented institutions (Allen & Seaman, 2013). Only about one-third of higher education institutions had no plans to offer MOOCs. The MOOC movement has now gained enough momentum that Google has released an online MOOC-building tool.

The stage was set for the MOOC explosion in 2001, when MIT's OpenCourseWare offered free online access to some of its undergraduate and graduate courses. Since then, for-profit companies such as Coursera and Udacity have partnered with about 100 universities, including such prestigious ones as UC Berkeley, Stanford, the University of Michigan, the University of Pennsylvania, Duke University, and the University of Illinois at Urbana-Champaign, to offer a wide variety of MOOCs. Nonprofit organizations, such as Mitx and Harvard and MIT's EdX and Stanfords's Class2Go, are also developing MOOCs on their campuses. While many MOOCs are focused in STEM areas such as math, engineering, and computer science, they are also being developed in social sciences and the humanities.

MOOCs differ from traditional classes in almost every way. They are typically free of charge and do not offer academic credit (although some offer a certificate of completion or a "statement of accomplishment"). To be considered a student, you only need to log on to the course Web site once. MOOCs are based primarily on lectures, typically presented as a series of videos usually lasting less than 10 minutes each (research shows that students pay attention for six to nine minutes and then attention wanes; Witte & Mock, 2013), and often posing a couple of quiz questions aimed at helping students assess their understanding of the material. Students can also give feedback, complete homework, and may take a final exam. Grading written assignments is impossible, so some instructors "crowd source" the grading (Svinicki, 2013). For example, one instructor is working on a system in which each student's paper is graded by five classmates and each student, in turn, grades the papers of five fellow students. He and fellow MOOC designers are even working on a system that can identify students who are assigning obviously inaccurate grades (Pappano, 2012).

MOOCs usually have no registration limit, so thousands or even tens of thousands of people anywhere in the world can enroll in them; all they need is an Internet connection (Pappano, 2012).

This open format greatly expands access to higher education experiences for those who might otherwise be shut out of such experiences, but although MOOC students may be interested in the course, many are not really prepared for postsecondary level classes, or may have little or no background in the discipline being addressed (Svinicki, 2013). It is no wonder, then, that the percentage of enrollees who actually complete MOOCs is extremely low (Pappano, 2012; Witte & Mock, 2013).

This high dropout rate is just an amplified form of the dropout problem that plagues "traditional" online courses, especially in community colleges (Xu & Jaggers, 2011). MOOC promoters argue that "success" in an MOOC is not necessarily measured by course completion. When MOOC students are surveyed about their satisfaction with the course, most are highly satisfied, even if they just watched a few videos on the course Web site (Witte & Mock, 2013). However, as we have noted elsewhere, instructor "presence" is one of the keys to a successful online course and some MOOCs utilize a "just push play" format (Witte & Mock, 2013). But even in a course with instructor presence, how does it work with thousands of students? In addition, there is also less opportunity in an MOOC to create a "community of learners" (Svinicki, 2013).

Among the other challenges facing the MOOC movement are figuring out how to generate a revenue stream adequate to support the enterprise (or make a profit) and how to certify students who have completed the courses. Coursera has a "verification of identity" option (using video and keystroke patterns, for example), for which they currently charge $39, that verifies that the student was the actual person engaging in the learning activities (Witte & Mock, 2013). With this verification process, Coursera is exploring offering Coursera courses to allow teachers to fulfill the K-12 continuing education teacher requirement.

Legal issues including copyright are of concern, especially because some software cannot be sent to some countries (Witte & Mock, 2013). In addition, there are concerns about the intellectual property rights that MOOC faculty might exercise over the content they develop as well as about the fact that, almost of necessity, MOOCs perpetuate passive rather than active learning (Rivard, 2013). So although these mass courses have the potential to radically change the way that higher education is delivered (Paldy, 2013), many thorny problems will have to be addressed before MOOCs join the mainstream in higher education (Snyder, 2012). (For a discussion of issues in developing an MOOC, see the University of Illinois *Guide to Massive Open Online Courses (MOOCs), 2013* at http://mooc.illinois.edu/docs/moocs-at-illinois-guide.pdf.)

⬤ ⬤ ⬤ ⬤ ⬤

"Traditional" Online/Distance Learning

One of the biggest problems facing the expansion of online courses is the issue of quality. Those instructors who developed the first online courses were obviously eager to do so and also willing to learn the technology they needed for the task. But it is unreasonable to assume that all faculty members have the pedagogical and instructional design knowledge to develop a good online course. As a result, many faculty members who want (or have been assigned) to teach online may need to be paired with an instructional designer and perhaps other consultants, too. In other words, good course design for an online course is likely to involve a group. That is because, while many online courses once consisted of little more than narrated PowerPoint slides, faculty are now "challenged to move beyond the notion of a course covering content to the idea of a course as . . . a series of learning environments and activities" (Oblinger & Hawkins, 2006, p. 14).

This challenge is important because when asked about how much they liked online, face-to-face, and blended teaching formats, students in one survey ranked face-to-face courses first, hybrid/blended courses next, and online courses last (Castle & McGuire, 2010). But format alone does not tell the whole story. The most important factor related to student learning and satisfaction in this survey was course content, followed by the instructor's ability to connect with and motivate students. Course delivery format was rated as least important (Castle & McGuire, 2010), meaning that, even online, instructors have the opportunity to promote student learning and satisfaction. Another study found that the best predictors of student satisfaction with online courses were learner-content interactions, learner–instructor interaction, and Internet self-efficacy, in that order (Kuo, Walker, Belland & Schroder, 2013). In other words, the strongest predictor of student satisfaction was a well-designed online course.

Unfortunately, the development of standards for high-quality online course design has been slow to emerge and difficult to assess. It is beyond the scope of this book to provide instructions on the development of online courses, but we think that the guidelines used by the University of Illinois at Urbana-Champaign in helping faculty think about developing online courses are worth repeating here (University of Illinois Campus Resources for Faculty, 2013):

- "Let the content lead" (e.g., what are your learning objectives, how can you present your material better?).
- "Keep it Simple."
- Remember that you are "teaching to a global audience" (e.g., think about captions and realize that analogies made with students in your culture will not work with students accessing the course in another culture).
- Video is an opportunity (e.g., video can be a legitimate publishing form, so be aware of the integrity of your teaching methods and the research you discuss).

■ Make use of teamwork and resources (don't reinvent the wheel).

In addition, we recommend several excellent guides to the development of online courses (e.g., Brawner, 2011; see Ko & Rossen, 2010; Palloff & Pratt, 2013; Thormann & Zimmerman, 2012).

To end this section, let's consider 10 "best practices for teaching online" (Boettcher & Conrad, 2010).

1. *Be present at the course site.* Students expect you to be online when they are, so set up expectations as to when you will and will not be available. It is best if you can be present daily and it is important to let students know if you are going to be offline for more than two days. Remember that instructor presence is vital, especially when you express willingness to help students who fall behind (Novotney, 2012). You can make your presence known through a welcome letter and course orientation (especially on video), posting frequent announcements, encouraging student interactions through discussion boards, posting a blog, setting up virtual office hours, and providing detailed digital feedback on assignments. A consistent instructor presence demonstrates caring, creates a comfortable learning environment, helps to create a sense of community, and even improves student performance (Kennette & Redd, 2013; Lehman & Conceicao, 2010). But don't make students feel that you are *always* present, because that can stunt discussion among students, and don't overwhelm students with too many e-mails or posts.

2. *Create a supportive online course community.* Encourage learner-to-learner communication by asking (or requiring) students to introduce themselves and post a picture. Set up an open student forum, one that is for the type of social exchange that occurs naturally in a face-to-face class. Set up groups of four to six students and encourage them to "meet" virtually to discuss course content and study for exams. Develop group projects that require them to work together. As a result of arrangements like this, two musicians in one of the author's online classes discovered each other's interests and now play in a group together.

3. *Develop a set of explicit expectations for the students, and yourself, with respect to how you will communicate and how much time students should be working on the course each week.* This figure will vary by course, institution, and instructor (are you willing to be available on weekends?) One study found that students who were on the online course Web site for 11–15 hours per week were the most self-regulated and satisfied with the course (Kuo et al., 2013).

4. *Set up a variety of large group, small group, and individual work experiences.* Just as in a face-to-face class, variety holds attention. Also,

remember that while some students thrive in group situations, others prefer working alone, so by developing all types of assignments and activities you will be more likely to satisfy most students.

5. *Create synchronous and asynchronous activities.* While most online courses are asynchronous, try to provide opportunities for synchronous conversations, for example, through virtual office hours, Skyping, or even talking on the phone.

6. *Ask for informal feedback early in the term.* This feedback is important in all types of courses, but it is essential in online courses. The third week of the course is a good time to ask for feedback on what seems to be working, how things can be improved, and what students need help with.

7. *Discussion boards are the "heart and soul" of an online course community,* so prepare discussion posts that invite responses, questions, interaction, and reflection. To promote the most in-depth discussions, be sure to use open-ended questions.

8. *Search out and use content resources that are available in digital format.* While many students prefer printed textbooks, e-texts are becoming more sophisticated and interactive. If possible, make your textbook available to students in multiple formats. And as noted previously, make use of good Internet resources, such as Khan Academy and TED talks.

9. *Combine core concept learning with customized and personalized learning.* This means identifying core concepts, perhaps in the form of learning objectives and then expressing willingness to guide students through the more complex material.

10. *Plan a memorable closing and wrap-up activity for the course.* As we discussed in Chapter 3, many teachers give a lot of thought and planning to the beginning of the course, but let the course just "run out" at the end. Especially in an online course, try to tie things together at the end. Asking students to create a "Top 10 list of things I learned that I will use in my own life" is not a bad way to bring things to a close.

●●●●●

Some Final Comments

Technology is a ubiquitous teaching tool and like all tools has the potential for positive or negative outcomes, depending on how it is used. When technology supplements and enhances student learning, it can be a true asset to teaching. Even back in the late 1990s, it was clear that educational technology could enhance Chickering and Ehrmann's (1996) *Seven Principles for Good Practice in Undergraduate Education,* and we expect that more recent technological advances can do the same. For example, when technology allows more access to college courses it can be a boon to higher education, but when it is used only to demonstrate your proficiency with a jazzy new toy, or because your administration thinks students expect it, it may be a waste of time and effort. So if you are considering the adoption of a particular technology, be sure to read Educause's "7 Things You Should Know about . . . ", which provides a quick summary of essential information about any particular technology (www.educause.edu/research-and-publications/7-things-you-should-know-about).

We tend to agree with Jose Bowen (2012), who in his book called *Teaching Naked* supports the idea of flipping the classroom by putting lecture material online and otherwise keeping technology out of sight during class. Doing so, he argues, can help face-to-face classes become truly interactive learning experiences that can motivate and enhance intellectual curiosity; deepen student perspective by working on problems; allow students to receive feedback on their writing and improve their communication skills and reflective abilities; and allow for high-level cognitive processing by having discussions that challenge beliefs and highlight linkages among course concepts (Bowen, 2012). Whether you decide to "flip" your classroom, and indeed whether you decide to use educational technology, we hope that this brief overview of the current technological scene will help make your decision a more informed one.

8

Assessing and Improving Your Teaching

Sources of Evaluative Feedback on Teaching
Student Evaluations
Evaluations by Colleagues
Self-Evaluation
Faculty Development Activities
Some Final Comments

The previous chapters have focused on helping you to carefully plan, thoroughly prepare, and effectively teach your courses. Now it is time to consider how you can evaluate the outcome of your teaching efforts, identify areas of weakness, and develop a plan for making improvements in those areas. These considerations are important not only because they can affect your prospects for salary increases, retention, promotion, and tenure, but also because teaching is more satisfying and enjoyable—for you and your students—when you have found ways to do it to the best of your ability.

We first identify several sources and varieties of evaluative information about your teaching, and then look at some of the ways you can most profitably use that information to become a better teacher. As you read, remember that the process of regularly gathering, carefully considering, and constantly adjusting to teaching evaluations is not just for new teachers. No matter how experienced we are, all teachers can always find ways to do better in one area or another. In our view, only those who have stopped caring about the quality of their teaching have stopped seeking or attending to feedback about their performance.

Sources of Evaluative Feedback on Teaching

You can get evaluative feedback on your performance as a teacher from four main sources; students, colleagues in your department and in other psychology departments, faculty development activities, and yourself.

The timing of the feedback determines whether it is formative or summative. *Summative* feedback comes at the end of the course and serves to "grade" your teaching and suggest improvements. This kind of feedback is often used to make decisions about tenure, promotion, and salary. *Formative* feedback, in contrast, is gathered during a course and serves to tell you about what you are doing well and not so well while there is still time to make adjustments.

Although policies and traditions vary at different institutions, most teaching evaluations tend to be summative and tend to come in the form of end-of-course evaluations provided by students. In fact, the collection of summative feedback is usually mandatory, especially for faculty who are not tenured or at the highest academic rank. So while most of your attention (and concern) might be focused on the summative evaluations that affect administrators' decisions about you, don't forget to gather formative evaluations, too. Formative evaluations can alert you to problems or to the need for changes in your teaching style or methods that will ultimately affect summative evaluations.

⸙ ⸙ ⸙ ⸙ ⸙

Student Evaluations

Student evaluation of teaching (SET) is a controversial matter, especially when it plays a role in faculty salaries, tenure, promotion, and retention. The main criticisms of SET can be summarized as follows (Feldman, 2007; Hativa, 2013a, 2013b; Lang, 2013):

1. Because of their immaturity, lack of experience, and capriciousness, students cannot make reliable or valid judgments about their instructor and the quality of instruction immediately after taking a course.
2. Only colleagues with excellent publication records and expertise are qualified to teach and to evaluate their peers' instruction.
3. Good instruction and good research are so closely allied that it is unnecessary to evaluate them separately.
4. Most student rating systems are little more than popularity contests that award the highest ratings to instructors who are warm, friendly, humorous, assign little homework, and are "easy graders."
5. Student ratings are affected by the time and day the course is offered.
6. Student ratings are not useful for improving instruction.
7. Teaching is an art whose quality cannot be quantified.

Yet these familiar criticisms have themselves been criticized as mythical because they have no basis in empirical research (Marsh, 2007; Theall &

Feldman, 2007). Advocates of SET point out that empirical research actually supports dramatically different conclusions (e.g., Marsh, 1984, 2001, 2007; Marsh & Roche, 1997, 2000; Patrick, 2011). For one thing, the interrater reliability of students' evaluations of their teachers has been found to range from 0.74 in classes of 10 to 25 students to 0.95 in classes of 50 students or more (Marsh & Roche, 1997). Further, high student evaluations are strongly associated with desirable teacher characteristics such as enthusiasm, energy, and interest in teaching the course, and somewhat associated with personality dimensions related to these characteristics (e.g., extraversion, openness, agreeableness, and conscientiousness; Patrick, 2011). Student ratings are not significantly associated with teachers' gender, age, ethnicity, teaching experience, or research productivity (Cashin, 1995; Hativa, 2013b; Theall, 2010). Nor are those ratings significantly related to potentially confounding factors such as the level or type of course taught, the time of day classes meet, class size, or students' age, gender, year in school, grade point average, most personality traits, and prior interest in the course subject matter (Cashin, 1995; Hativa, 2013b; Marsh, 2007; Marsh & Roche, 1997). Teachers who are learning centered (i.e., emphasize active learning and student participation) tend to get higher evaluations than those who are subject/ teacher centered (i.e., emphasize information transmission to passive learners) (Richardson, 2005). Student ratings are indeed related to the amount of work assigned and to the leniency of the grading system, but the direction of the correlation is opposite to what critics of student ratings claim. Teachers who employ more stringent grading standards and assign heavier (but still reasonable) student workloads tend to receive higher student evaluations than those who are more lenient and less demanding (Cashin, 1988; Centra, 1993; Hativa, 2013b; Marsh, 2007; Marsh & Roche, 1997, 2000; Watkins, 1994). Even the famous "Dr. Fox" studies (see Ware & Williams, 1975 for the original study) have limited applicability. These studies appeared to show that entertaining lecturers who present no course content receive higher student ratings than those who present substantial course content, but in a boring manner. In reality, though, the "Dr. Fox effect" appears only on the "instructor enthusiasm" dimension. On other dimensions, such as knowledge of material, "Dr. Fox's" ratings were no higher than the boring instructor's. In other words, although students enjoy an entertaining instructor, they can easily discriminate between style and content, and they recognize that style alone is not enough to justify high overall ratings (Hativa, 2013b). In fact, students appear to value a course more, and to be more satisfied with it, when teachers require them to work hard to learn challenging material (Hativa, 2013a, 2013b; Marsh & Roche, 2000; McKeachie, 1997a; Richardson, 2005).

Finally, student evaluations are positively correlated with a variety of commonly agreed-on indicators of good teaching, including the amount of material students learn in the course (Lowman, 1998; Marsh, 2007; Marsh & Roche, 1997). The validity of student ratings is also suggested by the fact that these ratings tend to improve after teachers engage in structured efforts to improve their teaching (Marsh & Roche, 1997).

Herbert Marsh summarized the research on SETs as follows:

> [they] are multidimensional; reliable and stable; primarily a function of the instructor who teaches a course rather than the course that is taught; relatively valid against a variety of indicators of effective teaching; relatively unaffected by a variety of variables hypothesized as potential biases; and seen to be useful by faculty as feedback about their teaching, by students for use in course selection, and by administrators for use in personnel decisions.
>
> (2007, p. 319)

Given what we have said in other chapters about the basic principles of good teaching, the value of creating an inclusive classroom atmosphere, and the importance of establishing productive relationships with students, it should come as no surprise that teachers who try their best to teach well, and who care about their teaching, tend to get the best evaluative feedback from their students (Bain, 2004; Cashin, 1995; Junn, 1994; Lowman, 1995, 1998; Marsh & Roche, 1997; McKeachie, 1997a, 1997b; Murray, 1997; Pepe & Wang, 2012; Seldin, 1999a). When students in one study were asked to describe the best college courses they had taken, they reported a comfortable classroom atmosphere and interesting course content as the most important components (Levy & Peters, 2002). They also said that instructors in those courses "had a sense of humor and were entertaining; were excited about the material . . . (had) a caring attitude toward students, and . . . were approachable" (Levy & Peters, 2002, p. 47). These teachers were lauded for blending lecturing with a variety of other more active teaching techniques.

By contrast, in two retrospective surveys, former students portrayed their worst teachers as having shown no enthusiasm for their subject matter, having been detached and aloof, and having provided students little encouragement, support, or help (Carson, 1999; McKinney, 2001). These teachers were described as arbitrary, unfair, contradictory, and autocratic, not only in their grading systems, but in relation to individual students. They were said to have belittled and embarrassed some students, sometimes by making sexist or racist comments, while showing favoritism toward others. They were remembered, too, as showing scant concern for how they presented material, and especially for disorganized, confusing lectures that were delivered in a monotone and came straight from the textbook. Also included among the "worst" teachers were those who were entertaining and lenient, but who were perceived as holding their students and themselves to a low standard. These teachers were described as giving "Mickey Mouse" assignments and as offering "light and painless" classes in which lectures were aimed at the least able students and from which little was learned (Carson, 1999). Respondents in both surveys said that their worst teachers made them feel some combination of fear, anger, and frustration; caused them to lose interest in the course content; and taught them little or nothing (Carson, 1999; McKinney, 2001). Perhaps the best summary of the attributes of these "worst" teachers came in the form of Kenneth Eble's (1983) seven deadly sins of teaching:

1. ***Arrogance:*** Presenting yourself as superior in status and knowledge, always presuming oneself to be right, and failing to consider other viewpoints.
2. ***Dullness:*** Boring your students with tedious, unrelenting lectures or other unchanging routines of teaching; offering no opportunities for active learning.
3. ***Rigidity:*** Teaching so as to convey the authoritarian idea that you know what is best for those over whom you have power.
4. ***Insensitivity:*** Saying things that show you do not empathize with your students and/or failing to respond to students' signals of interest, confusion, or concern.
5. ***Vanity:*** Engaging in self-promotion or self-congratulation in class, including overemphasizing one's own work or point of view.
6. ***Self-indulgence:*** Allowing oneself to meet only minimum standards as a teacher; exhibiting laziness, lack of effort, and disinterest in the course and the students.
7. ***Hypocrisy:*** This one appears in many forms, but one of the most common is seen in teachers who decry their students' lack of motivation to learn, while themselves displaying a lack of motivation to teach.

Formative Student Evaluations

You can expect to receive higher student ratings not only by letting students know you care about them, but also by staying in close touch with them throughout the course. This communication process includes giving students plenty of opportunities to let you know what they think of you, your teaching style, the course organization, and the like. You might not be able to address some of their criticisms (e.g., "This class meets too early in the morning"), but others might be easy to fix (e.g., "You move through the slides too quickly."). Whatever the case, you can be sure that your students will appreciate the chance to provide you with formative evaluations, and to hear more about why you have chosen to teach the course as you have. In fact, asking for formative evaluations can impress students enough to elevate your summative evaluations, even if it was impossible or inappropriate to make all the changes they requested! Collecting formative evaluations can even affect students' impressions of faculty in general by countering the prevailing view that teachers ignore the evaluations they are forced to collect at the end of the term (Lang, 2008; Sojka, Gupta, & Deiter-Schmelz, 2002).

What's the best way to gather formative evaluations from students? During the Middle Ages, university faculty in Europe could simply count their cash. At the end of each class session, they would remove their trademark mortarboard cap and stand, literally "hat in hand," at the back of the lecture hall. As the students filed out, they would place money on the mortarboard. The more they gave, the more they thought the lecture was worth (Weimer, 1988). Trust us: your students will not do this, even if you wear a mortarboard, so you will have to find other ways of collecting their formative evaluations.

One-Minute Papers

We suggest that you start gathering formative evaluation early, but that you start small. For example, to get feedback about the clarity of your class presentations you can pause after completing a section on, say, Kohlberg's model of moral development and ask students to write for a minute or so about anything they did not understand, or, at the end of class, about "What was the most important thing you learned today?" (Angelo & Cross, 1993; Lang, 2013). Reading these papers after class can tell you what to clarify during the next class session, and can also provide more general guidance about the pace of your class presentations, the number of examples you give, and the like.

Another option is to begin a class session by asking students to write a one-minute paper about their reactions to the presentation, demonstration, or activity that took place during the previous session. This method allows students more time for reflection, and also provides you with an indication of how much they recall about the earlier class. We recommend that you ask for this kind of feedback whenever you feel that a particular classroom presentation or activity did not go as well as you had hoped. Your students might or might not feel the same, but your next effort will undoubtedly benefit from their comments, and they will feel good about having the chance to help you improve. Our advice to focus on less-than-stellar class sessions might run counter to some teachers' tendency to avoid dwelling on "failure," but remember that one (or even several) bad class session does not make a bad course (Curzan & Damour, 2000). It is only when you miss the opportunity to correct mistakes that you harm your chances to teach more effectively.

Student Focus Groups

Another way to gather information about your teaching is through feedback sessions in the classroom (while you are absent) conducted by a member of your institution's teaching center, or by another instructor who is not involved with the class. These sessions focus on a list of questions about your teaching strengths and weaknesses (Light, Cox, & Calkins, 2009) that you help to develop. The facilitator of the discussion summarizes for you the information gained. The advantage of this type of feedback is that it is the result of student discussion and reflection, but its source remains anonymous.

Interim Evaluation Forms

You can collect more general evaluations of your teaching style and your course by asking students to complete a structured evaluation form as the course proceeds. We think that the best time to gather this interim evaluation is after the first three or four weeks, when students have become familiar enough with you, your course, and your quizzes or exams to comment knowledgeably, but while it is still early enough for you to make any changes that you think might be appropriate. To assess the impact of those changes, you might want to repeat the interim evaluation a few weeks later.

An interim evaluation, often referred to as *informal early feedback* (IEF), need not be elaborate or time consuming (see Table 8.1). You can simply ask students to take out a sheet of paper and list three things they like about the class so far, three things they don't like, and three suggestions for change. This format can be especially useful to new teachers because it virtually guarantees getting positive feedback as well as constructive criticism (McKeachie, 1997b). As an alternative, you might want to distribute index cards every few weeks and ask students to note "Here is what's working for me," and/or "Here is where I am having trouble" (Adams, 2012). Another option is to create a short survey about aspects of the course that are of greatest interest to you. You might ask students to complete sentences such as: "The textbook _____ "; "The teacher's ability to explain concepts is _____ "; or "The organization of the course _____ ." You might also ask students to "describe something that the instructor did not do that you personally would have found helpful" (Cashin, 1999). Sample forms can be found in Table 8.1.

Table 8.1 Sample Forms for Use in Gathering Formative Student Evaluations

PSYCH 100 EARLY FEEDBACK EVALUATION Circle your response to each question below.

How would you rate the instructor's overall teaching effectiveness?

1	2	3	4	5
Poor				Excellent

How would you rate the overall quality of this course?

1	2	3	4	5
Poor				Excellent

Most of the time, I find this class interesting.

1	2	3	4	5
Strongly Disagree	Somewhat Disagree	Neutral	Somewhat Agree	Strongly Agree

How would you rate the pace at which material is covered in class?

1	2	3	4	5
Much too slow	A Little Too Slow	Just Right	A Little Too Fast	Much Too Fast

The main points are understandable

1	2	3	4	5
Never				Almost always

The level of student participation is

1	2	3	4	5
Not enough				Just right

The instructor's use of PowerPoint slides is

1	2	3	4	5
Confusing				Very helpful

Use the following scale to indicate how much you have learned/enjoyed each of the topics below.

1	2	3	4	5
Strongly Disliked	Disliked	Neutral	Liked	Strongly Liked

____Research Methods ____Development ____Biological Aspects ____Sensation & Perception

EARLY SEMESTER FEEDBACK

Early semester feedback will help me improve my instruction. I need feedback on how well you think I'm presenting the material, how well you feel you are learning the material, and how you feel about my evaluation of your work. This feedback is not meant to be a final evaluation; it is a way for you to help me adapt my teaching style to your learning so that my teaching can be more effective. Your overall evaluation of my teaching will occur at the end of the semester. Please answer in ways that will help me understand how I can change my methods for the better. The examples cited in the questions are not meant to limit your responses,

1. What things do you like about this course; how can these things be made even better?
2. What things don't you like about this course; how can these things be changed?
3. What problems are you having learning the material? (For example, your and my preparedness, myteaching style, your study skills.)

4. If you were I, what would you change? (For example, my style, grading procedures, my accessibility to you, course format, workload.)
5. What can I do to structure the course so you will feel more like participating?

INFORMAL EARLY FEEDBACK

It is easy to remain attentive during class sessions.

1	2	3	4	5
disagree strongly	disagree somewhat	neutral	agree somewhat	agree strongly

The instructor is friendly toward students.

1	2	3	4	5
disagree strongly	disagree somewhat	neutral	agree somewhat	agree strongly

The instructor is well prepared for class.

1	2	3	4	5
disagree strongly	disagree somewhat	neutral	agree somewhat	agree strongly

I find the instructor's use of PowerPoint slides helpful.

1	2	3	4	5
disagree strongly	disagree somewhat	neutral	agree somewhat	agree strongly

I find the course Web site useful.

1	2	3	4	5
disagree strongly	somewhat disagree	neutral	agree somewhat	agree strongly

INFORMAL EARLY FEEDBACK

1. Rate my overall teaching effectiveness.

1	2	3	4	5
Poor				Excellent

2. I appear to be enthusiastic about teaching the course.

1	2	3	4	5
Not enthused				Enthused

3. I make good use of examples and illustrations.

1	2	3	4	5
Seldom				Usually

4. How would you characterize my ability to explain?

1	2	3	4	5
Poor				Excellent

5. I am well prepared for each class.

1	2	3	4	5
Seldom				Always

6. I provide adequate instructions for proceeding with course work (e.g., mini-assignments, class discussions, etc.).

1	2	3	4	5
Seldom				Always

7. I communicate the objectives of course work.

1	2	3	4	5
Seldom				Always

(Continued)

Table 8.1 (Continued)

8. I am easily approachable when students have course-related questions.

1	2	3	4	5
Seldom				Always

9. I raise challenging questions in class.

1	2	3	4	5
Seldom				Always

10. Mini-assignments, quizzes, and thought papers are returned with explanations of errors and suggestions for improvement.

1	2	3	4	5
Seldom				Always

11. Are my supplementary handouts valuable as learning aids?

1	2	3	4	5
Seldom				Always

12. I promote an atmosphere conducive to work and learning.

1	2	3	4	5
Strongly disagree				Strongly agree

13. I make you afraid to make mistakes.

1	2	3	4	5
Strongly disagree				Strongly agree

14. I listen attentively to what class members have to say.

1	2	3	4	5
Seldom				Always

15. I give advice on how to study for the course.

1	2	3	4	5
Strongly disagree				Strongly agree

16. I use humor effectively.

1	2	3	4	5
Seldom				Always

17. I encourage you to take an active approach to learning.

1	2	3	4	5
Seldom				Always

STEPHEN BROOKFIELD'S CRITICAL INCIDENT QUESTIONNAIRE

1. At what moment in the class this week did you feel most engaged with what was happening?
2. At what moment in the class this week did you feel most distanced from what was happening?
3. What action that anyone (teacher or student) took in class this week did you find most affirming and helpful?
4. What action that anyone (teacher or student) took in class this week did you find most puzzling and confusing?
5. What about the class this week surprised you the most? (This could be something about your own reactions to what went on, or something that someone did, or anything else that occurs to you.)

Note: From Brookfield (1996). Brookfield's Questions. The National Teaching and Learning Forum, 5, 8. Reprinted with permission. (For other formative evaluation forms, see Trudeau & Barnes, 2002).

To increase the chances that you will get candid and thoughtful responses, let your students know that their comments should be made anonymously, and reinforce that message, if you wish, by appointing a student to collect the forms and place them in a large envelope that he or she seals and delivers to you. (Some psychology faculty we know distribute their interim evaluation forms near the end of a class session so that they can leave the room while the students complete them.) In addition, emphasize the fact that you are asking for interim evaluations because you want to use the feedback to improve this course as well as your teaching skills in general.

Reading student evaluations can be a bit depressing because even the best teachers of psychology leave some students dissatisfied, and because new teachers, especially, tend to take positive comments for granted and brood about the negative ones. To help yourself view formative comments in an objective and rational way, create a two-by-two table and label its four cells as: *Positive Comments, Negative Comments, Suggestions for Improvement,* and *Factors beyond My Control.* A student's comment that "lectures are interesting" would go in the *Positive Comments* cell. "The quizzes are difficult" could go in either the *Negative Comments* or *Positive Comments* column, depending on your goals. If you deliberately give difficult quizzes to better prepare students for your tests, this would be a positive comment, but it should prompt you to tell the class why the quiz questions are difficult. "I hate early morning classes" goes into *Factors beyond My Control,* but let the students know that you are aware of how they feel, and perhaps plan to include a few more active learning events to keep everyone involved. "Put an outline on the board" would go in the *Suggestions for Improvement* cell.

We also suggest that you use the consultants at your campus instructional development office to help you interpret student feedback. They have seen many IEFs and can help you put student comments into perspective.

As already mentioned, you won't want to, or might be unable to, follow every student recommendation and correct every perceived fault, but after you have read and analyzed your formative evaluations, take a few minutes in class to thank your students for their comments, discuss their feedback, and explain any changes you will (or won't) be making. Before deciding what to change, tally the number of students who made various comments and suggestions. If only one person claims the class pace is too slow, the problem probably lies with that student; so during your classroom discussion of feedback, you might offer to discuss the problem with the person who made that comment. Similarly, if a few students find your pace too fast, and a few others think it is too slow, you are probably teaching at about the right pace. Again, however, mention that you realize that not everyone is satisfied with your teaching tempo and be sure to offer individual help to those who are struggling. Of greater concern are comments suggesting that students are nearly unanimous in perceiving your class presentations as confusing, boring, or overwhelmingly detailed. Such feedback should be a signal for you to consider how to address the problem. When in doubt about how to respond to student feedback, discuss it with an experienced colleague or someone at your campus instructional development office. These consultations can be extremely helpful in guiding changes that significantly improve teaching effectiveness (Marsh, 1987, 2007; Marsh & Dunkin, 1997).

Summative Student Evaluations

As you might expect, the same set of teacher behaviors that shape students' evaluations during a course tend to affect their ratings when the course is over. Accordingly if you have gathered formative student evaluations throughout your course, you will probably not be surprised by the summative evaluations you receive at the end of it. Nevertheless, some psychology teachers misinterpret the meaning of summative student evaluations. In particular, and regardless of their academic rank or tenure status, many still believe that students give higher ratings to instructors who teach less demanding courses or grade more leniently (Hativa, 2013b; Sojka et al., 2002). Some of these faculty members appear to employ a self-serving cognitive bias, in that they treat the poor ratings they might receive as the misguided comments of the disgruntled or the ungrateful while dismissing their colleagues' more favorable ratings as the inevitable result of offering an easy course in an entertaining manner. We even know instructors whose view of student ratings as a popularity contest causes them to worry that their academic standards are slipping if student evaluations get "too high."

In short, whereas most students would like to see their summative evaluations given more weight in the salary, promotion, and tenure decisions that administrators make about their teachers, as noted earlier, many of those teachers see student ratings as having little or no value. In fact, some psychology faculty—including some renowned for scientific research on other topics—argue that it is impossible to accurately measure the quality of teaching because no criteria for "good teaching" have ever been or ever will be established (Hativa, 2013b).

We would not argue that student ratings alone define teaching effectiveness, but the body of research cited earlier does show that summative student evaluations can have value, not only in guiding administrative decisions, but in helping teachers to teach better. So, even if your institution or department doesn't require that you collect summative student ratings, we suggest that you do so. Like students who never see the teacher comments that earned them a particular grade on a paper, it is hard to know what you are doing right and what you are doing wrong as a teacher if you get no end-of-term feedback about your teaching and your course.

Remember, too, that even if you are required to collect summative evaluations, the standard feedback form might not have been created by a measurement expert. It might not give you the summative information you need to evaluate your teaching in enough detail to guide good decisions about what changes to make. For example, many summative feedback forms ask students to provide only global ratings of the instructor (from, say, "good" to "poor") on just a few dimensions, such as "quality of teaching" or "personality" (see Figure 8.1). These forms are quick and easy to complete, but are not particularly informative because they do not provide much detailed feedback, and they do not address enough of the many dimensions on which a teacher's performance can and should be evaluated (Marsh & Bailey, 1993; Marsh & Dunkin, 1997; Marsh & Roche, 1997, 2000; Seldin, 1999a). We prefer to use more elaborate forms that allow students to rate us on a wide variety of dimensions and that allow us to insert dimensions in which we have a particular interest (e.g., "value of classroom demonstrations"). There are many of these more elaborate forms available. Some of them provide space for students to summarize in their own words what they think of the teacher and the course (see Figure 8.2).

1. Rate the instructor's overall teaching effectiveness.

1	2	3	4	5
Exceptionally Low				Exceptionally High

2. Rate the overall quality of this course.

1	2	3	4	5
Exceptionally Low				Exceptionally High

Fig. 8.1 Example of a Global Summative Student Evaluation Form.

A. What are the major strengths and weaknesses of the instructor?
B. What aspects of this course were most beneficial to you?
C. What do you suggest to improve this course?
D. Comment on the grading procedures and exams.
E. What was the best day of class and why?
F. What was the worst day of class and why?

Fig. 8.2 Example of a Multidimensional Summative Student Evaluation Form.

Unlike some teachers, we love to read these open-ended comments because, contrary to myth, students' written comments have a central theme and most comments are not negative. Students write truthful comments and though they obviously vary, they are not wildly inconsistent. Especially in large classes, the comments are coherent and themes emerge. It is a shame, in our opinion, that instructors and administrators rarely review open-ended comments in any systematic way, and often ignore them altogether in favor of focusing solely on rated items (Hativa, 2013b). By doing so, they miss important information about their teaching behaviors.

Interestingly, research suggests that even items chosen on the basis of their validity and reliability are seldom revalidated once the evaluation form has been in use. This can be a problem because all items are not equally salient to students. For example, items related to fairness in grading and using class time to help students learn the course content have been found to have the most relevance to students, while the textbook choice or the ability to participate actively were not of major concern (Hills, Naegle, & Bartkus, 2009). Along the same lines, Carol Lauer (2012) looked at faculty and student definitions of terms commonly used in SETs (Weimer, 2012a). She found that while most faculty believe a "not organized" comment from a student means that the student believes they did not follow the syllabus, only 11% of students used "not organized" that way. The rest indicated that when they say a faculty member is "not organized" they mean the teacher was not prepared, or did not seem to have a plan for the day, or even that there were long delays in returning graded work. Similarly, when students say a teacher was "not fair," most faculty believe they are referring to the grading system. In fact, students meant that the teacher has favorites and does not treat all students the same. With this research in mind, it is important to use summative forms that ask for specific information about well-defined terms.

Reading statistical summaries of students' ratings, combined with the (often humbling) experience of reading students' written comments, gives you two useful categories of evaluative information. The first is an aggregated profile of your strengths and weaknesses, a profile that can be compared from one term to the next or from one course to the next to evaluate the effectiveness of your efforts to improve various aspects of your teaching. The second is a more immediate and personal portrait of students' reactions to you and your course, a portrait that often contains telling and useful elements.

As we suggested in relation to formative feedback, you can get the most out of written summative remarks by creating a two-by-two grid to analyze them. You can also categorize the written comments by course ratings, for example, what those who rated the course highly said versus those who rated the course poorly. Or sort them thematically, by comments that focus on organization or communication or efficacy or independent learning (Light et al., 2009). Then consult with experienced colleagues and/or your campus instructional development consultants about what changes you can or should make in your teaching style and methods in response to the quantitative and qualitative summative feedback you have received.

While almost all researchers would agree that student ratings are a necessary source of evidence of teaching effectiveness, they are certainly not the only one available. Other sources include peer ratings, self-evaluation, videos, student interviews, alumni ratings, employer ratings, administrator ratings, teaching scholarship, teaching awards, learning outcomes, and teaching portfolios (Berk, 2005). We examine the first two of these next.

Online Considerations

Online evaluation of teaching can be used in relation to both face-to-face and online classes.

Many faculty have serious concerns about online evaluation of face-to-face courses. Some worry that much like the "flaming" that sometimes happens in online communication, students will provide lower ratings and more negative comments online than on a paper form. Others feel that only students who came to class regularly, and thus would be most likely to be present when the paper evaluation forms are handed out in class, are qualified to honestly and knowledgably evaluate the course and the instructor. However, an extensive review of the literature (Office of the Registrar, University of Oregon, 2013) found that most of these concerns are unwarranted. For example, a study conducted in 29 colleges found that, in general, on-campus and online evaluations of overall and instructional quality were similar. When differences are found, they show higher ratings on online versus paper evaluations and even more positive and useful open-ended comments (Burton, Civitano, & Steiner-Grossman, 2012; Hativa, 2013b; Heath, Lawyer, & Rasmussen, 2007; Johnson, 2003; Office of the Registrar, University of Oregon, 2013). Further, one can argue that the online comments of students who stopped coming to class can be valuable in that knowing why a student either failed to become engaged in the class, or became disengaged, can suggest where improvements to the class might be made (Office of the Registrar University of Oregon, 2013).

Unfortunately, student response rates do tend to be lower for online versus paper evaluations. Some institutions try to solve this problem by providing some type of incentive for completing online evaluations, while others use a "stick" instead of a "carrot." For example, they may use evaluation software that will not release a student's course grade until the course evaluation is completed. Some faculty march their students to computer labs at the end of the course and require that they complete instructor and course evaluations. Still others impose a one-term "lockout" from the campus faculty evaluation database (which many students use to learn about professors' reputations) if they do not complete all their course evaluations. While these strategies may increase response rates to some extent, they may create resentment, too. Accordingly, some have suggested a combined approach that makes it quick and easy for students to access and use the rating forms, sends reminder e-mails, offers incentives, and allows early access to final grades to students who complete all course evaluations (Berk, 2012b). It has been suggested, too, that the best approach would involve taking action to demonstrate to students that their teachers and administrators take their course evaluations seriously (Adams, 2012; Berk, 2012b).

Indeed, when students believe their rating make a difference, they provide evaluations on their own. This assertion is supported by the existence of at least four popular teacher evaluation Web sites: Rate My Professor; Rate My Teacher (United Kingdom, Canada, and Australia); Professor Performance (United States and Canada); and MyEdu. Many faculty worry that these ratings lack reliability and validity, especially given that any student can rate any professor, whether or not the student actually took the professor's course. We know of one case, for example, in which a professor rallied students in his large introductory psychology classes to rate his physical appearance as "hot" on Rate My Professor. Despite the fact that this "hotness" rating did not, shall we say, fully correspond to reality, he became the "hottest" professor in the United States for two years in a row. Such shenanigans notwithstanding, there is some evidence for the validity of the student ratings that appear on Rate My Professor (Brown, 2012, Gregory, 2012, Otto, Sanford, & Ross, 2008). An analysis of both the positive and negative language used by students posting on Rate My Professor found that "students favor professors who are demanding, yet helpful and attentive, and a class that is rigorous, fair, and informative, and thereby perceive quality teaching/learning to comprise the same" (Gregory, 2012, p. 169). "Students prefer teachers who were challenging, knowledgeable, helpful, and invested in their teaching" (Gregory, 2012, p. 174). Another study found that Rate My Professor ratings were significant predictors of instructors' performance as measured by SET ratings (Brown, 2012). And still another study found that Rate My Professor ratings were associated with student learning. For example, instructors showing clarity and helpfulness were rated highly, much as they are in research on SETs (Otto et al., 2008). Some faculty prefer to ignore such Web sites, but the fact that so many students use them to offer their opinions and make course choices suggests that teachers should at least compare the comments that appear online with those they receive from campus sources (Otto et al., 2008).

As for the reliability and validity of online student ratings of their online instructors, everyone seems to agree that more research is needed. One big problem in this area is that virtually all the research available on SET is based on traditional classroom settings, but because teachers have different roles in distance education, the results of that research may not apply equally to online courses (Richardson, 2005; Theall & Feldman, 2007). For example, do faculty–student rapport and faculty presentation skills mean the same things in online versus face-to-face courses (Theall, 2010)? Even the definition of a "class" is becoming more complex as modes of instruction become more varied (Dziuban & Moskal, 2011).

The manner in which online versus face-to-face courses are evaluated differs, too. For one thing, formative evaluation is often missing in an online course. And while summative evaluations of face-to-face classes most often involve the use of validated evaluation forms, the validity of online evaluations developed by instructors or course administrators may be less well established (Harrington & Reasons, 2005). Other unique issues also arise in online courses, including the fact that these courses are often developed by a team of professionals including instructional designers, and technical specialists who work along with the faculty member who teaches the course (Harrington & Reasons, 2005). In such cases, what and who are students evaluating? Are they able to separate their reactions to problems with course technology from their evaluation of the course instructor? Can a typical student evaluation form provide the information that all interested parties need to guide efforts at improvement?

One research team found that the most complete online course evaluation forms include items related to six domains of interest: readings and assignments; technological tools; instructor feedback and communication; clarity of outcomes and assignments; content format; and perhaps most important, course organization (Rothman et al., 2011). (For a discussion of available rubrics to evaluate online courses and for sample student evaluation of online teaching forms, see Drouin, 2012 and Rothman et al., 2011.)

⬤ ⬤ ⬤ ⬤ ⬤

Evaluations by Colleagues

Like evaluations from students, feedback from experienced colleagues can be of enormous value in improving your teaching, especially in areas such as your selection and mastery of course content, the organization of your course, the appropriateness of course objectives, instructional materials, and student evaluation instruments, and the application of appropriate methodology for teaching specific content areas (Berk, 2005; Cohen & McKeachie, 1980). As already mentioned, colleagues can also help you to objectively interpret and respond to summative student evaluation forms.

In many psychology departments, administrators or members of a teaching evaluation committee conduct classroom observations and/or review summative student evaluations, along with copies of instructors' syllabi, exams, writing assignments, and other course materials to determine ratings that affect decisions about those instructors' salary, retention, tenure, and promotion. If you receive such summative ratings from colleagues and they are not as high as you had hoped for, we urge you to seek further information about the factors that shaped them. Ask what specific aspects of your teaching need improvement, and consider getting outside help in making those improvements. However, don't let low ratings or less than complimentary comments in one area blind you to the fact that you are doing well in other areas. Those areas of strength are the foundation on which you can build and extend your teaching skills.

There are probably sympathetic colleagues in your department who have repeatedly taught the course you are teaching or are about to teach and who will be happy to give you the benefit of their experience if you ask for it. Don't be afraid to ask. As described in Chapter 2, new teachers and even experienced teachers tackling a course for the first time can avoid a multitude of mistakes simply by getting informed advice on everything from writing a syllabus and choosing a grading system to planning class presentations and attendance policies (DeZure, 1999). We are not suggesting that you ask colleagues to plan your course for you; just ask them to review *your* plans (Weimer, 1996).

In addition, don't be afraid to ask for formative evaluations of your lecturing style, your classroom demonstrations and group activities, and other aspects of your teaching behavior. The simplest way to get these evaluations is to ask a colleague to visit a few of your classes each term. The ideal visitor is someone who can be both candid and supportive. These visits can provide many insights, especially if you schedule them on days when you are giving a particularly difficult presentation, administering or returning a quiz, performing a dramatic demonstration, or engaging in some other aspect of teaching about which you feel less than confident or would like to improve. Don't hesitate to ask the observer to make a structured observation—for example, to focus on specific teaching behaviors and simply record what they see without interpretation (Light et al., 2009). For example, if you feel that it is important to encourage student questions, ask the observer to keep track of how many occur. If this prospect sounds too intimidating, you might want to arrange for the first visit to take place on an "easy" teaching day, just to help you get used to being observed.

More colleges and universities are requiring such classroom visits as part of peer evaluation programs (DeZure, 1999). Some of them arrange for pairs of faculty—usually from different departments—to sit in on each other's classes. Others arrange for the department executive officer, a member of a teaching evaluation committee, or someone from the campus instructional development office to make the visits. A peer-review program at one large university, for example, included not only classroom visits, but written exchanges of information on course content and goals, reviews of exams, paper assignments, and other student evaluation instruments, and a two-week summer seminar on improving teaching (Bernstein, Jonson, & Smith, 2000). Some departments use "teaching squares" in which four teachers take turns observing and reflecting on one another's teaching sessions. Sometimes they simply do classroom observations, but they may also make digital recordings that allow their colleagues to later observe themselves during playback sessions that can evoke helpful discussions (Light et al., 2009).

Whether colleague visits to your classroom are required or you request them on your own, try to focus on what they can tell you about your teaching. To get the most from each visit, meet with the visitor beforehand to describe your goals for the class to be observed, outline and explain the methods you will be using, and identify the aspects of your teaching that you are most interested in improving. After the visit, meet to discuss the visitor's observations. Be open and willing to accept criticism as well as praise, and thank the visitor for helping you to strengthen your teaching skills. You might also want to ask the person to visit again later in the term to assess the results of your efforts to improve in areas of weakness. In fact, the true value of colleague visits lies in the formative feedback that comes during the detailed discussion that follows them. Unfortunately, some campuses that require colleague visits do not require this vital follow-up meeting. Feedback might thus come only in the form of quantitative peer ratings that are revealed much later as part of a summative evaluation. These peer ratings tend not to be terribly reliable, and not well correlated with either student ratings or other indicators of effective teaching (Marsh, 1987; Weimer, 1996).

In summary, keep in mind that colleagues can provide information that is unavailable from other sources, including helping you to decide on the content of your course, correcting flaws in exams and quizzes, and discussing many other course-related issues. Remember, too, that advice and feedback are available via e-mail from willing colleagues in other departments who teach in your subfield of psychology or who share your interest in teaching particular courses. There are also some especially valuable listservs for psychology teachers (see our list in Chapter 2).

Online Considerations

It may be difficult or impossible to set up direct peer observation of online teaching, but you can ask another distance educator to look at your materials and monitor discussion boards (assuming you grant them access to the course Web site). This kind of peer evaluation becomes primarily an evaluation of your materials and the extent to which you are using "best practices." There are several generic rubrics that instructors of online classes can use to assess their courses against "best practices" (see Drouin, 2012). Lack of direct observation of teacher–student interaction in online courses dilutes the nature of peer review and sometimes causes problems in setting promotion and tenure criteria that are equivalent to those used for faculty who teach face-to-face courses. As online education expands, we expect to see more in the literature about peer evaluation of online courses.

Self-Evaluation

There is no doubt that the process of collecting, reviewing, and analyzing feedback from others can be of enormous benefit in improving your teaching skills, but self-evaluation can be valuable, too (Richardson, 2005). The easiest way to evaluate your own teaching is to use a structured form that contains guiding questions about teaching objectives, instructor–student rapport, organization of the course, knowledge of the discipline, and the like (Berk, 2005). If you Google "faculty self-evaluation" you will find a multitude of forms that various colleges and universities use for this purpose. Unfortunately, some of them are set up to produce no more than an annual report (a.k.a. "brag sheet") that simply describes teaching, scholarship, and service activities (Berk, 2005). We advocate deeper and more useful forms of self-evaluation, including teaching portfolios and structured reflection.

Teaching Portfolios/Academic Portfolios

You can conduct a long-term self-evaluation of your teaching by creating a teaching portfolio, which is a dossier containing a statement of your teaching philosophy and reflections about your teaching, along with copies of syllabi, exams, quizzes, student evaluations, and other materials from all the courses you have taught. Teaching portfolios may appear as just one component of a more extensive academic portfolio, which is "a reflective, evidence-based collection of materials that documents teaching, research, and service performance" (Seldin & Miller, 2009, p. 2). Originally, portfolios were truly collections of paper in a folder, but of course today most of them are in electronic format. "One benefit of a portfolio approach to assessment is that it can provide both summative and formative data. With regard to summative assessment, portfolios allow for a more comprehensive and complex picture of teaching than a single end-of-term survey; with regard to formative assessment, the portfolio allows for continuous, systematic feedback to which the teacher can respond. Such portfolios are works in progress that allow the instructor to adjust teaching methods and redesign aspects of a course after examining results of both student and self-learning" (Schafer, Yost Hammer, & Bernsten, 2012, p. 71).

Detailed suggestions about how to create a teaching or academic portfolio are available in several books (e.g., Centra & Gaubatz, 2000; Davis, 2009; Knapper & Wright, 2001; Seldin, 1991; Seldin & Miller, 2009) and on the Web site of almost every major university's teaching centers (e.g., Brown University's Harriet W. Sheridan Center for Teaching and Learning offers a particularly impressive example). Although materials gathered for individual teaching portfolios will vary, they all begin with a statement of teaching philosophy. This is usually a one- to two-page description of how you see yourself as a teacher, and especially what you do and do not value in the teaching domain (Korn, 2012; Tracey, 2005). We recommend that you write your own statement before you read anyone else's. This will help you avoid "teaching jargon" or the latest "buzz words" and let your own thoughts come out. Remember to provide as many examples as possible of how you have (or plan to) put your philosophy into practice (Lang, 2013). If you are not sure how or where to start the process of examining your personal beliefs about teaching, you might consider asking yourself questions like these: "What would a metaphor for my view of teaching and learning be? How do I know when I have taught successfully? What outcomes do I want from my teaching?" (O'Neal, Meizlish, & Kaplan, 2007).

Another approach could be to:

- List up to five core values you possess, such as respect for others, strong work ethic, or sense of humor.

- Briefly describe the ways you display these values in your everyday life.
- List up to five qualities you admire in the teachers you've had.
- Describe the extent to which you possess these qualities and use them in the classroom (Hill & Buskist, 2005).

As noted in Chapter 2, having your teaching philosophy clearly in mind can ease decisions about course organization, planning, policies, and rules. For example, reviewing your teaching philosophy from time to time can remind you of why you decided on requiring (or not requiring) class attendance or why you use so few (or so many) definitional items on exams, and therefore whether it now makes sense to change those elements of your courses. James Korn (2012) summarizes this process in the following "flow" model: Philosophy → Objective → Methods → Learning → Evaluation → Reflection. Keep writing and revising your statement until you have a draft of your teaching philosophy that you are satisfied with, but in accordance with Korn's model, be aware that you will need to revisit and revise it periodically.

You should start collecting and saving portfolio-type materials as soon as possible, ideally during the first course that you teach—even if you are still a psychology graduate student. Starting early allows your teaching portfolio to grow more quickly as you acquire packets of material related to each course.

As your teaching portfolio expands in tandem with your teaching experience, begin to include material that goes beyond syllabi, exams, and the like. For example, include your written reflections about each course you teach, about specific teaching experiences, and about teaching in general (Rodriguez-Farrar, 2003; Schafer et al., 2012). Some argue that incorporating your personal reflections about teaching is one of the main benefits to be derived from a portfolio (Schafer et al., 2012).

In any case, your teaching portfolio should ultimately encompass all material related to your teaching, including (a) descriptions of the courses you teach and the way you teach them; (b) explanations and reflections about each course syllabus; (c) a summary evaluation of your teaching and the steps you have taken to improve; (d) a description of new courses you have developed and other curricular revisions in which you have participated; (e) copies of your writings or publications on teaching and learning (including research articles, talks, and workshops, and poster presentations at conferences); (f) statements from colleagues or consultants who have observed your teaching; (g) student and course evaluations; (h) any departmental statements about your teaching; (i) a list of the teaching honors, awards, or other recognition you have achieved; (j) statements from former students; (k) a video sample of your teaching style; (l) summaries of your students' scores on standardized tests;

(m) examples of graded student assignments and samples of especially creative work produced by your students; and (n) any other documentation that reflects your teaching (Davis, 2009; Lieberg, 2008; Perlman & McCann, 1996; Rodriguez-Farrar, 2003; Zubizarreta, 1999).

Organize these materials in a logical way and make sure that your portfolio has an easy to navigate menu. Clearly label each section, for example, Teaching Philosophy; Student Evaluations; and so forth. Ask others, including colleagues and your campus instructional development staff, to take a look at your portfolio and comment on it. You might even show it to some students to get their input, as well (Rodriguez-Farrar, 2003). Use this feedback to guide you in making whatever revisions to the portfolio that seem appropriate.

Feedback also comes naturally if you develop your portfolio as part of a group of teachers in your department or on your campus who are all doing the same and who meet regularly to present and discuss various portfolio components (Schafer et al., 2012). For the past several years, one of us has been involved in a campus certification program that, with staff from our Center for Innovation in Teaching and Learning, works with a select group of advanced graduate students to help them develop an academic portfolio for job applications. The students in this year-long program believe that their portfolio is better and richer because of the structured approach and the peer interaction and feedback.

Structured Reflection

Your teaching portfolio constitutes a formal body of material, but as already noted, the reflection component is essential. The overall quality of the portfolio will depend partly on your willingness to engage in some informal end-of-term reflection about what went right and what went wrong (Korn, 2003). Maryellen Weimer (2013d) suggests that you begin your reflection with two questions: "What am I doing that isn't promoting learning or very much learning?" "What am I doing that I've probably done the same way for too long?"

Weimer expands the concept of reflection when she talks about engaging in *structured, analytical* reflection or "coming to know ourselves as teachers" (2010, p. 23). In a similar vein, Parini (2005) talks about developing a teaching persona that he equates to finding a writing voice. He believes that your teaching persona depends on *why* you are teaching and your personality. And, he suggests, as you become more comfortable in the classroom, your teaching persona becomes less separate from yourself (Lang, 2008; Parini, 2005).

The first step in engaging in *structured* reflection is "develop(ing) a detailed understanding of what you do when you teach—how the mechanics of instruction are handled" (Weimer, 2010, p. 25). This involves reflecting on your teaching practices such as how you use and set up discussion, how well you listen to students, how you implement wait time, whom you call on, and so forth. Once you have an accurate picture of *how* you teach, then it is important to analyze *why* you choose to teach that way, for example, try to align your teaching beliefs with your teaching behaviors. Weimer calls this *critical reflection*. In this stage you ask yourself questions such as, "What are my assumptions that underlie my attendance policy or my policy on extra credit?" After engaging in reflection and critical reflection, you can begin to understand and possibly modify your "instructional identity."

Shadiow (2013) discusses multiple ways to engage in the reflective process but believes that being aware of "sticking points" or the tensions in your teaching is essential. When you examine critical incidents that occurred while you were teaching, you explore the incongruities between your teaching actions and assumptions. By looking at your moments of discomfort or disruption in your teaching you can develop insights into your teaching. Looking at the "stories" we tell ourselves about such moments or critical incidents help us reflectively grow as teachers.

Think, too, about which students or types of students you enjoyed teaching, which ones made you uncomfortable or seemed beyond your ability to influence, whether you were satisfied with class attendance, the distribution of final grades, and the nature and quality of your out-of-class contact with students (Chesler, 2003). Ask yourself whether these reflections reveal consistencies or inconsistencies between your teaching philosophy and teaching practice, and summarize your conclusions as you add to your teaching portfolio (Korn, 2003, 2012). Ask yourself these questions, too: If my next course were the last one I would ever teach, would I do anything differently, and if so, what? What is the one criticism that I am most fearful of receiving from a student? From a colleague? What has been my greatest accomplishment as a teacher in the last three years, and what has been my greatest failure? (Seldin, 1999b).

You will probably be surprised and pleased by the extent to which this kind of structured self-reflection can lead to beneficial changes in your teaching philosophy, improvements in your teaching methods, and a more informative teaching portfolio.

Online Considerations

Many of the components of a teaching portfolio are the same in a face-to-face classroom and an online classroom. You will have syllabi, student evaluations, assignments, and evidence of student learning. However, if you teach primarily online you will most likely want to include a discussion of your perception of online teaching in your teaching philosophy statement. It is crucial to incorporate the uniqueness of the online course environment into your teaching portfolio. For example, because discussion boards and "student lounges" involve written interactions, you might be able to use an excerpt showing how students worked on a group project you developed (always obtain written student permission to use their words and guarantee their anonymity). This is a bonus that is not available in a face-to-face class and it is even an easier process to incorporate materials from your online class into your portfolio.

Teaching an online course, especially when you are new at it, can provide a lot to ponder in your structured reflection. Questions about student–teacher interactions take on a different character online, but the gist of the questions you ask yourself in a structured reflection remain very much the same as those you ask yourself about face-to-face teaching.

Faculty Development Activities

A lot of valuable feedback about your teaching, and about how to improve it, will inevitably come from your students, from colleagues in your department, and from your self-evaluative efforts. However, the broader community of psychology teachers and faculty development experts can also offer a wealth of ideas about how to increase the effectiveness of your teaching.

Local Workshops and Seminars

Consider participating in local workshops and seminars for new teachers and graduate teaching assistants that might be offered by your campus's instructional development office, or by faculty development services on nearby campuses. Attending such events can help make you a better teacher, especially if they continue for several weeks and offer opportunities to practice and refine your skills and receive continuing feedback on your efforts (Weimer & Lenze, 1997). If these faculty development activities are not readily available, we recommend that you seek out, or even create, a teaching support group on your campus. The group might be made up of new teachers, or perhaps a mixture of new and experienced instructors from around campus or in the local area who are interested in improving and helping others improve their teaching. On one of the author's campuses, faculty and graduate students have "reading roundtables" where they read a book on teaching (e.g., Bain, 2004) and have regularly scheduled discussions on each of its chapters throughout the semester.

More than 20 years ago at the University of Illinois, Urbana-Champaign, a group of graduate students from various departments who had just completed a course on college teaching decided that there should be a campus-wide forum at which teaching problems and issues could be discussed. The result was the College Teaching Effectiveness Network (CTEN), an organization that continues to offer two or three evening programs, seminars, or workshops each semester. The graduate students who serve on the CTEN steering committee choose program topics and invite speakers from around the state. Over the years, these speakers have presented sessions on balancing time commitments, helping students read more effectively, teaching in a diverse classroom, the role of gender in the classroom, developing teaching portfolios, and the like. The audience is typically made up of graduate students from across the campus, but quite a number of young faculty members from many different departments also attend these sessions, which always include time for discussion and the opportunity to raise topics that might not have been on the formal program.

Consultants

The faculty development offices on most campuses offer individual consulting for teachers who wish to improve their teaching skills, and if this is true on your campus, take advantage of it. Faculty development consultants can offer a variety of services. For one thing, they will discuss with you the meaning and implications of your student and peer evaluations. As suggested earlier, those evaluations are more informative when they are systematically analyzed with the help of a consultant (Marincovich, 1999; Marsh, 1987; Theall, 2010; Weimer & Lenze, 1997). They also can conduct the student focus groups discussed previously.

To help you address your weaknesses and solidify your strengths, your faculty development consultant might arrange to make a digital recording of one or more of your regular classes to provide an even more representative sample of your teaching behavior for analysis. On these class days, be sure to tell your students what is going on, explain that the recording is being made to help you improve your teaching, and ask them to try to behave as if the camera were not there.

Discussion of these recordings usually takes place in private, and although watching them can be a bit stressful at first, it can also be very valuable—at least as valuable as reviewing evaluative comments from students, colleagues, administrators, or faculty development experts (Centra, 1993). For one thing, seeing yourself as your students see you provides a new perspective on your appearance, demeanor, teaching style, and teaching behaviors. After viewing yourself actually teaching, you will be better able to put yourself in your students' shoes and perhaps gain a better understanding of the basis for some of their evaluative comments. While watching the very first minute of his first teaching video, one of our teaching assistants exclaimed, "I will never wear those pants again!" You too might be less than happy with your classroom fashion statement, but more important, you might notice speech habits—such as repeatedly saying "uhm," or "well," or "OK?" or "you know?"—that detract from your presentation (Lowman, 1995). The video will also tell you if you are speaking loudly enough and slowly enough to be easily understood. It will be easy, too, to spot habits or rituals that might be annoying or distracting to your students. To help you focus more carefully on both visual and auditory aspects of your teaching, your consultant might suggest that you first play the recording as you normally would, then listen to the soundtrack alone, then watch the video without the sound. If you are speaking too quietly or too quickly, you will recognize this immediately while listening to the sound of the video without being distracted by its images (Lowman, 1995).

Your consultant will help you to address and alter these and other even more substantive teaching behaviors, and will remind you that the things you might wish to change are problems for other teachers, too. If you find yourself exclaiming, "I never realized I was so boring," your consultant will probably tell you that this is one of the most common self-criticisms that faculty express (Braskamp & Ory, 1994). It can be comforting to realize that you are not the only teacher who struggles with the problems you see in yourself, and knowing that others have overcome those problems can also provide additional motivation for change. Faculty are most likely to show improvement in areas of teaching weakness when their consultants offer concrete and specific suggestions for behavioral changes (e.g., "Stop and ask for questions at the end of every main heading in your class outline"), not vague suggestions, such as to "be more organized" (Weimer & Lenze, 1997). Don't be surprised to receive highly specific prescriptions for change, and if you are in doubt about what a consultant is suggesting, ask for examples and even behavior samples until you are sure about what you should be doing.

Teaching Conferences and Events

Excellent advice, helpful ideas, and invigorating support for your efforts to evaluate and improve your teaching are all available at conferences on the teaching of psychology. For example, the National Institute on the Teaching of Psychology (NITOP), which convenes in Florida in early January of each year, offers dozens of speakers, more than 100 poster presentations, and a wide variety of roundtable discussion sessions, all aimed at helping psychology faculty do a better job of teaching and at evaluating their teaching. You can find out more about this conference by visiting its Web site at www.nitop.org. Information about many other outstanding psychology teaching conferences is available from the STP Web site, http://teachpsych.org/conferences/conferences.php. Remember, too, that the conventions of many regional, national, and international psychology organizations offer preconvention institutes, workshops, or other programming dedicated to the teaching of psychology. For example, the Association for Psychological Science (APS) offers a Preconvention Institute on the Teaching of Psychology at its annual convention, and the annual convention of the APA always includes workshops and entire program tracks devoted to teaching psychology. The teaching events at both conventions are organized under the auspices of the STP. To find out more about what is being offered this year, visit the STP Web site or the Web sites of the APS and the APA (www.psychologicalscience.org and www.apa.org). If you are teaching psychology at the high school level, you should be aware of the psychology teaching programs, support, and other resources offered by an organization called Teaching of Psychology in the Secondary Schools (TOPSS), whose Web site can be found at www.apa.org/ed/precollege/topss.

Books and Journals

Ours is certainly not the only source of written material on the teaching of psychology, or about the teaching enterprise in general. Publishers such as APA Books and Jossey-Bass offer a wide variety of books and journals for teachers of psychology. Contact them to add your name to their mailing list, and you will be able to stay up to date on their latest publications. Other journals and newsletters, such as *College Teaching, The Teaching Professor,* and *The National Teaching and Learning Forum,* are not specific to the teaching of psychology, but can nevertheless be of considerable value, especially to new teachers.

You can also search for other books, journals, and journal articles on the teaching of psychology by visiting Questia at www.questia.com/searchglobal?q=keyword!teaching%20psychology!allwords#00000Book.

Online Considerations

In some respects, teaching is teaching, regardless of the venue in which you do it. Whether online or face-to-face, it still involves the transmission and exchange of ideas and the support of students in their learning. It still involves structuring the learning environment so that all students can comprehend the information. So to a great extent, it is just as helpful for online teachers to use teaching consultants, attend teaching conferences, and read about pedagogy in higher education. However, there are also books and articles that focus specifically on the unique challenges and opportunities of online teaching, so take advantage of them if you teach online. The books that we found especially useful are Ko and Rossen's *Teaching Online: A Practical Guide* (third edition); Pallof and Pratt's *Lessons from the Virtual Classroom: The Realities of Online Teaching* (second edition); and Thormann and Zimmerman's *The Complete Step-by-Step Guide to Designing and Teaching Online Courses*.

Some Final Comments

Most institutions and instructors use student ratings as a major source of teaching evaluation, and those ratings can indeed be reliable and valid for drawing conclusions about teaching quality. As is the case in measuring other complex concepts, however, the assessment of teaching should be approached using multiple sources of information, including observations and evaluations from faculty colleagues and expert consultants. No single source of data provides all the information you need to make a valid judgment about your overall teaching effectiveness (Ackerman, Gross, & Vigneron, 2009; Cashin, 1995). Accordingly, we have suggested that if you combine your own reflections about and analysis of your teaching skills with feedback from students, peers, and instructional specialists, you will not only have a more complete picture of your teaching as it is today, but you will be better able to improve your teaching effectiveness in the future. Investing the time and energy required to collect all this feedback will pay huge dividends, both in terms of your comfort in the classroom and in terms of the summative evaluations likely to be used in promotion and tenure decisions. Further, remember that the process of evaluating your teaching never ends. Even the most experienced instructors, including those who have received local, regional, and national teaching awards and other kudos from students and colleagues, are always striving to improve and fine-tune their teaching skills. We hope that you will do the same.

9

• • • • •

Integrating Teaching into Your Academic Life

Balancing Teaching, Research, and Service
Dealing with Teaching Anxiety
Strategies for Staying "Fresh" as a Teacher
Some Final Comments

Has reading this book left you wondering how you will find the time to deal with all that teaching entails, while still meeting the other obligations that you face as a member of the psychology department, let alone as a member of your family? If so, welcome to the club. The truth is that, no matter how much time you plan to devote to teaching responsibilities, it will be less than you need. Especially at the beginning of your teaching career, it always takes longer than you think to plan class sessions, meet with students (or answer their e-mail), grade exams or papers, set up and administer record-keeping systems, accommodate students with special needs, and the like. Don't despair. Your first term of teaching psychology will probably take more time than any subsequent one. This is because as you gain experience and build your arsenal of teaching materials, methods, and systems, the teaching process will become progressively easier and less time consuming—although it will never be effortless or quick. You will always have to find ways of balancing the effort to teach effectively with all your other academic efforts—such as writing; conducting research; going to departmental, college, and campus committee meetings; engaging in service activities; advising students; attending conferences; preparing grant proposals; and on and on (Buller, 2010; Colbeck, 2006; King, 2002a; Philipsen & Bostic, 2010).

We hope that some of the advice and ideas offered in this book will help you come to enjoy your teaching as much as we enjoy ours. In this final chapter, we offer some suggestions to help you better perform the academic balancing act your job might require and to minimize the stress of doing so.

● ● ● ● ●

Balancing Teaching, Research, and Service

A 2010–2011 Higher Education Research Institute survey asked full- and part-time faculty to identify the stressors in their lives. Their responses, listed from most to least stressful, were as follows: self-imposed high expectations; lack of personal time; working with underprepared students; managing household responsibilities; institutional budget cuts; institutional procedures and "red tape"; research or publishing demands; personal finances; teaching load; and committee work (Hurtado et al., 2012). In other words, a considerable amount of stress that higher education faculty experience comes from attempting to find balance in dealing with all of their expectations and responsibilities. The balance problem occurs partly because, compared to some other occupations, faculty do have a considerable amount of freedom in setting up their days, but that relative lack of structure allows them "the freedom to work themselves to death" (Colbeck, 2006, p. 47). Just as undergraduate women report more stress than undergraduate men, women faculty report higher levels of stress and more difficulty balancing expectations than do male faculty (Hurtado et al., 2012). Women in academia also worry more about gaining tenure, partly because women are indeed less likely than men are to do so (Colbeck, 2006).

In virtually every psychology department, faculty are expected to engage in at least two of three academic activities: teaching, research, and service. And while two-year institutions and four-year liberal arts colleges have traditionally emphasized the teaching and service functions, even they have begun to include research as part of the tenure evaluation process (Philipsen & Bostic, 2010). So today, almost no matter where you teach, you will be expected to conduct and publish research. The tension created by the simultaneous demands of teaching, research, and service is quite real, simply because—unless you have found a way to circumvent physical laws governing time and space—you can't be in two places at once. If you are in a committee meeting, you can't be working on your class presentations. If you are running an experiment in your lab, you can't be meeting with students in your office. Still, this does not mean that your interest in and pursuit of teaching, research, and service goals are incompatible or inherently conflicting (Loui, 2003).

The trick to finding balance lies in "working smart" (Prentice-Dunn, 2012). This means not only managing time so as to pursue all your goals, but also arranging things so that activities in each domain inform, support, and enhance each other (Loui, 2003). For example, if you are running a psychology research program, you can use the results of your work to illustrate class presentations in your research area. Examples from your lab can also illuminate your presentations in other courses that deal with principles of scientific research, experimental design, and research ethics. Conversely, preparing a class presentation based on your work or answering a question posed by a student in class might well trigger a train of thought that leads to an important development in your research. The skills you develop as a teacher are likely to improve your ability to make effective presentations at research conferences, and to serve the public by giving talks and interviews about the nature and significance of your research.

The mutually supportive elements of teaching, research, and service operate even in psychology departments where the clearest expectations and the most visible rewards are for conducting research and attracting research grants. As evidence for this assertion, consider the fact that many well-known researchers in psychology are also stellar teachers. These people use their own research, and their intimate knowledge of the research of others, to enliven their courses and offer their students an insider's glimpse of what is going on at the frontiers of progress in psychology. Even though some psychology professors at major research universities say that they would rather do research than teach, recent surveys show that about 97% of psychology faculty in general consider teaching an "essential" or "very important" part of their responsibilities (Berrett, 2012a; Hurtado et al., 2012).

Even if teaching is not a generally revered activity in your department, don't be fooled into thinking that no one cares about it or that it doesn't count at your institution as a whole (Kemp & O'Keefe, 2003). If you have a genuine interest in teaching and in becoming a better teacher, don't be afraid to pursue that interest. Many graduate students and young faculty members at research universities are reluctant to talk about their desire to teach psychology, and if you are in this category, keep your ears open, find out which of your colleagues are known for effective teaching, and ask them to help you along as you develop your courses and your teaching style. Find out, too, if your institution participates in the Preparing Future Faculty program. This program is sponsored by the Pew Trusts and the Association of Graduate Schools and offers graduate students and faculty opportunities to teach and to learn about teaching that they might not otherwise have (Kennedy, 1997). You can learn more about the Preparing Future Faculty program at www.preparing-faculty.org/.

Time-Saving Tips for More Efficient Teaching

Some of the most important advice your mentors are likely to give will involve basic rules for making efficient use of the time you have available for teaching-related activities. For example:

1. *Keep everything.* Even if you do not plan to create one of the teaching or course portfolios we discussed in Chapter 8, retain all your grade rosters, exams, quizzes, papers, student correspondence, student evaluations, or anything else related to each course for at least two years, and perhaps longer. Archive your semester on your LMS. Having these materials handy can save you a lot of time and trouble when a student asks to see a hand-scored paper from last term or claims that there was an arithmetical error on a final grade.

2. As noted in Chapter 4, *make notes about how each class session went,* not only in terms of what worked and what didn't, but also whether you were ahead of or behind the schedule listed in your syllabus. Spend a few minutes after each class marking up your notes to remind yourself of what to do and what not to do the next time you present that material, run that activity, or the like. These few minutes of reflection can help you to reshape your plans, avoid mistakes, fix problems, and thus save time when you start planning the next version of the course. To help in this regard, create a folder for each class session and use it to store the notes and other materials that you used or plan to use for that session. One of the authors keeps both an electronic and paper folder for each class session. The electronic folder contains her PowerPoint slides; outline for the class session; a reminder list of all the handouts, videos, books, demonstration equipment, and other things she will need for the session; resources for her LMS; and URLs for video clips and Web sites used during class or in preparing for the class. Her paper folder contains newspaper articles, notes on good examples or interesting applications of concepts, equipment necessary for class demonstrations and materials, student papers, written notes—all accumulated over the course of her teaching career. Both are of value in planning her future classes.

3. *Create your own versions of the teaching forms we described in Chapter 6* for dealing with student excuses, complaints about test items, and the like. Developing form-driven routines for handling these matters will not only save you time, but will also reduce the number of ad hoc decisions you will have to make each time you teach. Consider posting these forms on your LMS, so students will have access to them immediately and you will not have to remember to carry them with you.

4. *Build a directory of useful phone numbers, e-mail addresses, and Web sites* that will help you refer students to various kinds of help, to campus services and facilities, and to sources of additional course-related information. As noted in Chapter 6, having this material handy can make discussions and e-mail exchanges with students more efficient for you and more valuable for them.

5. Finally, *don't try to reinvent the wheel.* Whatever you encounter in your courses—whether it is students calling you at midnight or dogs mating in your classroom—has probably already happened to other teachers. So when you have found a mentor in your department or elsewhere, don't hesitate to consult with her or him on a regular basis—especially if it is your first year of teaching. Describe the teaching problems and challenges you are dealing with and ask for advice on what to do. And don't forget to look for resources at the STP Web site (www.teachpsych.org) and to consult with other colleagues who are teaching similar courses.

- - - - -

Dealing with Teaching Anxiety

"Teaching is public speaking, after all, and public speaking—no matter how many times you do it—requires preparation and energy, and for most of us it produces anxiety" (Lang, 2008, pp. 214–215). Indeed, fear of public speaking is quite a common affliction. For many psychology faculty, then, the stress of academic life stems not just from the constant effort needed to balance teaching, research, and service activities, but also from anxiety about teaching itself. In one small-scale survey, 87% of psychology faculty reported at least some anxiety associated with teaching, and 28% described their anxiety as very to extremely severe. These respondents' fear was related to standing in front of a class, to the prospect of being unable to answer students' questions, and to the possibility that students would make hostile comments (Gardner & Leak, 1994). Our long experience in helping graduate students prepare to teach psychology leads us to believe that the figures cited in this survey are probably accurate. If they are, it means that a lot of psychology faculty experience anxiety in the classroom that is severe enough to disrupt their performance as teachers, even after years of teaching.

Signs of Teaching Anxiety

Some signs of teaching anxiety, such as a quavering voice, are obviously fear related, but others appear as problematic teacher behaviors that are all too easily misinterpreted by students as evidence of incompetence, laziness, aggressiveness, or disinterest. These more subtle signs of disruptive anxiety in the classroom can appear as:

1. *Confused thinking,* especially when responding to students' questions. As anxiety interferes with access to the information they need

to answer a question, some teachers end up giving long, rambling, confused, and confusing answers. For others, anxiety might motivate hostile, sarcastic, or condescending responses that tend to discourage future questions.

2. *Avoidance tactics.* Some teachers who find dealing with students uncomfortable show it by being "too busy" to talk to students after class, failing to show up for scheduled office hours, or restricting student–faculty contact to e-mail exchanges. Those for whom present-ing in class is a frightening exercise might rely heavily on anything and everything they can think of to fill class time without having to make a presentation. This might include showing large numbers of videos, inviting lots of guest lecturers, and scheduling student presentations as often as possible.

3. *Poorly organized or overly organized lectures.* For some teachers, the mere thought of facing the next class is so threatening that they avoid planning their lectures until the last minute, if at all. This can result in class sessions that are uncomfortable for the teacher and excruciat-ingly boring for the students. Other teachers seek to deal with their anxiety by preparing meticulously for every class, including writing dense, detailed lecture notes that they end up reading, like a speech, to students who spend the class period doing little more than taking dictation.

4. *Development of overly rigid or overly lenient relationships with stu-dents.* Some teachers whose anxiety focuses on the possibility that students will be dissatisfied with their course or will pose challenges to their authority try either to intimidate students or to be so permis-sive as to remove any grounds for complaint. For those in the first category, the list of class rules and regulations they include in their syllabus (see Chapter 2) might be excessive. For example, we know of one psychology teacher who backed up his ban on the recording of his lectures with the threat of prosecution under provisions in his state's criminal code against privacy violations. At the other extreme are anxious teachers who will do anything to curry favor with stu-dents. Their exams are easy, their course requirements are flexible (they may allow students to vote on how many exams to have), they will raise a student's score or grade at the first sign of complaint (without regard for rules against capricious grading), and they might even reveal exam questions ahead of time in response to students' badgering.

5. *The appearance of "multiple personality."* Anxiety about teaching can cause a person who is normally calm, relaxed, and gracious in most situations to become defensive, hostile, and rigid in class. Part of this transformation might even include paranoid thinking; we have heard

normally levelheaded, rational professors express concerns that students are out to make them look foolish.

Ten Scary Myths about Teaching

If you have been experiencing anxiety about your own teaching, or in anticipation of teaching for the first time, we hope that the goal-setting exercises, course planning suggestions, classroom management tactics, and student–faculty relationship skills that we have discussed in previous chapters will make it easier for you to feel relaxed and confident as you teach. If you need some extra help to combat jittery feelings before and during classes, you might want to hone your relaxation skills by consulting one of several relaxation training resources (e.g., Bernstein, Borkovec, & Hazlett-Stevens, 2000; J. C. Smith, 2000). Remember, too, that what you tell yourself about teaching—and about yourself as a teacher—can also have a significant effect on your comfort level while teaching. Even if you are well prepared for class, you might still upset yourself with thoughts about not really being ready to teach, about not knowing enough psychology to be teaching it, about being a fraud or a phony, and the like. These irrational, self-defeating thoughts can interfere with effective teaching not only by distracting you during class, but also by raising your anxiety enough to disrupt your performance (Ellis & MacLaren, 2005).

We know how frightening these thoughts can be, because—like most other psychology teachers at the beginning of their careers—we suffered with these self-doubts ourselves. In fact, no one who cares about effective teaching can step in front of a psychology class for the first time without wondering how it can be that they are really the teacher! Fortunately, like your teaching skills, your self-confidence will grow with experience, especially if you can learn to think realistically and rationally about your role as a teacher. We think that the best way to keep yourself calm in the classroom, whether things are going well or not, is to recognize—and be ready to counter—10 myths about teaching that tend to make it far more stressful and anxiety provoking than it has to be. Here they are:

1. *I should always stay in the "teacher" role while I am teaching,* even if it means suppressing my spontaneous human responses. Trying to be emotionless, or unflappable, or detached, or to enact any other behavior that is not really yours, but that you feel goes with the "teacher" role can actually add an extra burden to your job in the classroom. Don't expect yourself to be superhuman. If something funny happens during class, such as a squirrel jumping through an open window into your classroom, don't try to ignore it. It is fine to be astonished and

amused along with your students. In short, combating the "teacher role" myth is as easy as letting your own personality come through to your students. Many teachers don't do this because of the myth described next.

2. *If I come out of the "teacher" role, I will lose the respect of my students.* This myth is a variant on the more widely held dysfunctional belief that if you let someone get to know you, they will discover how inadequate you are. It also carries the presumption that students are against you from the beginning and are constantly probing for weaknesses to attack. As noted in Chapter 6, the vast majority of your students want you to succeed and are ready to support you if you simply show basic human respect and make it clear that you care about them and about teaching. It will be easier to begin to reveal your real self in class if you deal with the next myth.

3. *As an all-knowing teacher, I should never allow myself to appear uncertain or uninformed, or to admit that I am wrong.* No one can ever know everything there is to know about psychology. Your students don't expect you to be omniscient, so why expect it of yourself? As described in Chapter 4, there is nothing wrong with letting your students know that, like them, you are a fallible human being. They won't mind your being imperfect, but they won't like it if you insist on posturing, "vagueing-it-up" when uncertain, or otherwise faking it in class.

4. *My students must respect me because I am their teacher.* Many teachers expect unwavering respect at all times from all of their students, and become very upset at any hint that their students are less than totally obsequious. In our view, these teachers' dismay, anger, and other negative reactions are a waste of emotional energy. Although we do believe that students should be respectful, we know from long experience that teachers don't always receive respect, at least not from every student. This fact of teaching life might not be desirable, but getting upset about it is not likely to help you to deal with the few problem students you might encounter. As described in Chapter 6, handling classroom incivilities is much easier and less stressful if you can remember not to take them personally. Stay calm, deal with the problem in class and perhaps in private after class, but don't jump to the conclusion that any disrespect from even one student is evidence of your lack of teaching ability.

5. *My students should always be interested in what I have to say.* It would be ideal if all our students were interested in everything we say and do in every class, but this is simply not always the case. We all have a tendency to let our attention drift during a colloquium or other presentation, so when you see a few students losing focus during class it

does not mean you are failing. Even if you see a lot of students losing focus during class, there is no need to panic. Use the information as a cue that it might be time to insert that demonstration or active learning exercise you had been planning, or to ask the class a question. It might also serve as a reminder to rework your plan for this section of this class session to make it more interesting the next time around. You might also encounter students who for some reason remain disengaged from your course material no matter how well you present it. If their bored expressions or other signs of disinterest bother you, discuss the situation with them outside of class (see Chapter 6). Perhaps they are required to take your class to fulfill an unwelcome requirement. In any case, remember that, sometimes, there is a mismatch between a student's goals and yours, and if this happens, there is no need to get upset about it or question your teaching ability.

6. *My students must learn everything I teach.* It would be great to see all your students achieve high test scores and to know that they will retain what they learned in your course for years to come. Unfortunately, not even the smartest and most motivated students will learn and remember everything you teach. And even if you were the best teacher in the world, some of your students will do better than others. Some will do poorly on tests and most will forget much, or even most, of your carefully presented course material within days of the final exam. In short, no matter how hard you work at organizing and presenting your courses, and no matter how reliable and valid your quizzes and exams, some of your students might not do as well as you and they had hoped, You don't have to be happy about such outcomes, but you should recognize they are inevitable in some cases, and that they do not always or entirely reflect on your teaching ability. Sometimes, and to some extent, poor student performance reflects lack of motivation or ability on the part of the student. If you have done all you can to teach well, to assist students who need help, and to evaluate their performance fairly, don't worry too much about the appearance of a bell-shaped curve on your grade distribution.

7. *Students are basically lazy, dull, unmotivated cheaters interested only in grades.* Teachers who behave in accordance with this myth—perhaps predicting on the first day of class that no one will do their reading on time or will all be downloading their term papers from the Internet— are likely to create an adversarial classroom atmosphere that makes teaching unnecessarily stressful for everyone concerned. You can eliminate this source of teaching stress by recognizing that most students do not fit this profile. Assume the best about your students and then deal with the problem cases as they identify themselves to you through their behavior.

8. *My class presentations should cover all the assigned readings in my course.* Unless they don't require much reading, teachers who are guided by this myth find themselves rushing through their material in a vain attempt to cover all of the topics included in the course's assigned readings. The result can be a hectic classroom experience that neither the teacher nor the students enjoy or benefit from. As described in Chapter 3, we believe that students can and should be expected to take some responsibility for independent learning, so don't feel guilty about not covering all the assigned material in class. Present a reasonable amount of material at a deliberate pace and in enough depth to stimulate students' interest in reading the textbook for themselves, and perhaps in taking additional psychology courses.

9. *This is my students' only class, or at least their only important class.* Many psychology faculty tend to overestimate the importance of their course in students' lives. Remember that some, or even most, of your students are not psychology majors and, in any case, must meet the reading and writing requirements of several other courses, too. So, even if your course is their most important course in some cosmic sense, your students still have to figure out how to meet your demands as well as those of other instructors. This fact is worth remembering when drawing up your required reading list, making writing assignments, and the like. If students' lack of class preparation, missed deadlines, or requests for extensions are a source of stress for you, perhaps a partial solution lies in a reexamination of how realistic your expectations are. We are not in favor of "dumbing down" courses or expecting the minimum from students, but we don't think there is any point in adding to the stress of teaching by trying to do too much. In our view, you can make your teaching less stressful, and ultimately more effective, if you adopt ambitious but realistic goals.

10. *I am in competition with my teaching colleagues.* This myth might ultimately be the most anxiety-provoking one of all. Taking a competitive approach to teaching, and worrying about where you are in terms of teaching excellence, is not likely to be very productive either in terms of improving your teaching skills or minimizing teaching anxiety. In fact, a competitive attitude perpetuates anxiety by isolating you from the help you might need to teach better and to make teaching more fun. If you can reject the competition myth, you will find it far easier to take advantage of the many sources of teaching assistance and advice we have outlined throughout this book.

In summary, teaching can be less stressful and more fun if you focus not only on what you put into your class presentations and how carefully you organize your courses, but also on being realistic about your teaching. Ease up on yourself and don't let yourself be governed by the self-defeating myths that can make teaching psychology seem a frightening prospect.

⦿⦿⦿⦿⦿
Strategies for Staying "Fresh" as a Teacher

How do you keep a positive outlook on teaching when time is at a premium and you know you are not being rewarded much by the administration for your teaching effectiveness? James Lang (2008) offers three suggestions for staying "fresh" as a teacher. He suggests, first, that you become a learner again—take a course or lessons in an area you know little about, but that you enjoy. This can remind you what it feels like to be a student, which is something we often forget when we have been experiencing only the teacher's perspective for a long time. Second, he suggests that you stay current on research on educational theory by reading the journal(s) in your discipline devoted to teaching research (e.g., *Teaching of Psychology*); reading about higher education teaching in general (e.g., *Chronicle of Higher Education*); subscribing to listservs devoted to teaching in higher education (e.g., *Tomorrow's Professor*); and reading one book on teaching per year. Finally, he suggests that you "be nosy," for example, that you check out what your colleagues are doing in their teaching, and/or consult with your campus center for teaching excellence.

Maryellen Weimer offers additional ideas to promote "inspired" college teaching throughout one's career, and we think it is fitting to end this book by listing her 10 principles for professional growth, many of which we have emphasized throughout (2010, pp. 1–23).

1. *Improvement is an opportunity.* She suggests that we build on our strengths rather than focusing on our weaknesses. She believes that this will indirectly address our weaknesses, but that a positive perspective leads to opportunities for new and different kinds of learning.
2. *Instructional growth isn't always easy.* She points out that content knowledge is not enough to be a good teacher, and that the other necessary skills (organization, clarity, enthusiasm, knowledge, and love of content) can be developed.
3. *Instructional growth involves risk.* Trying out new things, getting outside our comfort zone, leads to growth as a teacher. She put it this way: "Sometimes better teaching is about becoming a better person, and that's about as risky as a proposition gets" (p. 9).
4. *Focus efforts to improve on more and better learning for students.* Phrasing our instructional development around improving our students' learning rather than improving our teaching leads to more insightful changes.

5. *Improvement begins and ends with you.* We control the improvement process: we are in charge of our development as teachers.

6. *Student feedback can improve teaching and learning.* This is especially true of formative feedback, which can guide specific changes in our classroom behavior that can help our students learn.

7. *Colleagues can be valuable collaborators in the growth process.* We often have research colleagues with whom we can discuss and reflect on our research, but too few of us have teaching colleagues with whom to discuss and reflect on our teaching. Seek out teaching colleagues and perhaps exchange classroom observations with them.

8. *Teaching vitality depends on instructional health.* There are increasingly high expectations of teaching, research, and service—all three need to be done well, but teaching is undervalued at many institutions. Anything you can do to improve the "instructional health" of your institution will be an asset to your teaching.

9. *Set realistic expectations for success.* Setting expectations too high can lead to discouragement and abandonment of our professional growth activities.

10. *Teaching excellence is a quest; it's about the journey, not the destination.* "Teachers should not expect to finally get it right, to achieve that ultimate level of excellence. What motivates, inspires, and satisfies is not the teaching excellence, but the quest for it" (Weimer, 2010, p. 20).

●●●●●
Some Final Comments

In Chapter 1 we offered a list of basic principles for effective teaching. Like us, you probably found them all worthy, but in the crush of all else that impinges on your academic life, you might find it hard to keep them in mind when planning courses, developing course presentations, and dealing with students. So to remind yourself of how you want to conduct the teaching aspects of your academic career, why not post a copy of those principles in a prominent spot in your office, and perhaps even in your study at home? They can serve as useful guides when contemplating the many teaching decisions you will be making in the years to come.

We hope that this book will help you to make teaching one of the most rewarding aspects of your academic life. We hope, too, that you will continue to read and learn all you can about teaching, that you will try innovative techniques in your classrooms, and that you will do what you can to pass on what you have learned to those new teachers who, with sweaty palms and hopeful hearts, will follow in your footsteps. We wish you a successful journey.

Bibliography

Abernethy, A., & Padgett, D. (2010). Grandma never dies during finals: A study of make-up exams. *Marketing Education Review, 20*(2), 103–113.

Ackerman, D., Gross, B., & Vigneron, F. (2009). Peer observation reports and student evaluations of teaching: Who are the experts? *The Alberta Journal of Education Research, 55*(1), 18–39.

Adams, C. (2012). On-line measures of student evaluation of instruction. In M. E. Kite (Ed.), *Effective evaluation of teaching: A guide for faculty and administrators.* Retrieved from the Society for the Teaching of Psychology Web site: http://teachpsych.org/ebooks/evals2012/index.php.

Alberts, H., Hazen, H., & Theobald, R. (2010). Classroom incivilities: The challenge of interactions between college students and instructors in the US. *Journal of Geography in Higher Education, 34*(3), 439–462.

Allen, I., & Seaman, J. (2013). *Changing course: Ten years of tracking online education in the United States.* Retrieved from www.onlinelearningsurvey.com/reports/changingcourse.pdf.

Allen, M. (2000). Teaching non-traditional students. *APS Observer, 13*(7), 16–17, 21, 23.

Ambrose, S., Bridges, M., DiPietro, M., Lovett, M., & Norman, M. (2010). *How learning works: Seven research-based principles for smart teaching.* San Francisco: Jossey-Bass.

American Psychological Association. (2002). Ethical standards of psychologists and code of conduct. *American Psychologist, 57,* 1060–1073.

American Psychological Association. (2008). Report of the Task Force on the Implementation of the Multicultural Guidelines. Washington, DC: Author. Retrieved from www.apa.org/pi/.

American Psychological Association Ethical Principles for Psychologists and Code of Conduct, Including 2010 Amendments. (2010). Retrieved from www. apa.org/ethics/code/index.aspx?item=1.

American Psychological Association Guidelines on Multicultural Education, Training, Research, Practice, and Organizational Change for Psychologists. (2013). Retrieved from www.apa.org/pi/oema/resources/policy/multicultural-guidelines.aspx.

Andersen, J. (1986). Instructor nonverbal communication: Listening to our silent messages. In J. Civikly (Ed.), *Communicating in college classrooms: New directions for teaching and learning* (No. 26; pp. 41–69). San Francisco: Jossey-Bass.

Anderson, J. (1999). Faculty responsibility for promoting conflict-free college classrooms. *New Directions in Teaching and Learning, 77,* 69–76.

Anderson, J. (2001). Tailoring assessment to student learning styles: A model for diverse populations. *American Association for Higher Education Bulletin, 53,* 3–7.

Anderson, Lorin W., & Krathwohl, David R. (2001). *A taxonomy for learning, teaching and assessing: A revision of Bloom's taxonomy.* New York: Longman Publishing.

Anderson, M., & Serra, J. (2011). Mobile devices in the classroom—Are you getting it? *2011 ASCUE (Association of Small Computer Users in Education) Proceedings, 36*–40. Retrieved from www.ascue.org/files/proceedings/2011-final.pdf.

Angell, R. (1928). *The campus: A study of contemporary undergraduate life in the American university.* East Norwalk, CT: Appleton-Century-Crofts.

Angelo, T., & Cross, K. (1993). *Classroom assessment techniques: A handbook for college teachers* (2nd ed.). San Francisco: Jossey-Bass.

Anthis, K. (2011). Is it the clicker, or is it the question? Untangling the effects of student response system use. *Teaching of Psychology, 38*(3), 189–193.

Appleby, D. (2001). The covert curriculum. *Significant Difference: Newsletter of the Council of Teachers of Undergraduate Psychology, 10,* 1, 3.

Ariely, D. (2012, July 7). *Plagiarism and essay mills.* Retrieved from http://danariely.com/2012/07/17/plagiarism-and-essay-mills/.

Arnett, J. (2010). *Adolescence and emerging adulthood: A cultural approach* (4th ed.). Boston: Prentice Hall.

Aronson, E. (1978). *The jigsaw classroom.* Thousand Oaks, CA: Sage.

Artino, A. (2010). Online or face-to-face learning? Exploring the personal factors that predict students' choice of instructional format. *Internet and Higher Education, 13,* 272–276.

Artze-Vega, I. (2012, October 1). Active listening: Seven ways to help student listen, not just hear. *Faculty Focus.* Retrieved from www.facultyfocus.com/articles/teaching-and-learning/active-listening-seven-ways-to-improve-students-listening-skills/.

Ashcroft, K., & Foreman-Peck, L. (1994). *Managing teaching and learning in further and higher education.* London: Falmer.

Assessment and Evaluation—What is the Difference? (2007). Retrieved from www.icc.edu/innovation/PDFS/assessmentEvaluation/ASSESSMENTandEVALUATION2007.pdf.

Association on Higher Education and Disability (AHEAD). (2012, April). *Supporting accommodation requests: Guidance on documentation practices.* Retrieved from www.ahead.org/resources/documentation_guidance.

Astin, A. (1990). *The black undergraduate: Current status and trends in the characteristics of freshmen.* Los Angeles: Higher Education Research Institute, Graduate School of Education, University of California.

Astin, A. (1993). *What matters in college? Four critical years revisited.* San Francisco: Jossey-Bass.

Astin, A., & Antonio, A. (2012). *Assessment for excellence: The philosophy and practice of assessment and evaluation in higher education* (2nd ed.). Lanham, MD: Rowman & Littlefield with American Council on Education.

Astin, A., Banta, T., Cross, K., El-Khawas, E., Ewell, P., Hutchings, P. et al. (2003). *9 principles of good practice for assessing student learning.* Washington, DC: American Association for Higher Education. Retrieved from www.aahe.org/assessment/principl.htm.

Astin, A., Parrott, S., Korn, W., & Sax, L. (1997). *The American freshmen: Thirty year trend.* Los Angeles: Higher Education Research Institute, Graduate School of Education and Information Studies, University of California.

Ausubel, D. (1968). *Educational psychology: A cognitive view.* New York: Holt, Rinehart, & Winston.

Ausubel, D. (2000). *The acquisition and retention of knowledge.* London: Kluwer Academic.

Ausubel, D., Novak, J., & Hanesian, H. (1978). *Educational psychology: A cognitive view* (2nd ed.). New York: Holt, Rinehart, & Winston.

Azar, B. (2012). Psychology continues to expand its reach with podcasts that showcase the academic, the scientific and the clinical sides of the field. *Monitor on Psychology, 43*(1), 23.

Azer, S. (2011). Introducing a problem-based learning program: 12 tips for success. *Medical Teacher, 33,* 808–813.

Baehr, M. (2007). Distinctions between assessment and evaluation. In S. Beyerlein, C. Homes, & D. Apple (Eds.), *Faculty guidebook: A comprehensive tool for improving faculty performance* (4th ed.) (pp. 441–444). Plainfield, IL: Pacific Crest. Retrieved from www.pcrest2.com/institute_resources/PAI/4_1_2.pdf.

Bailey, J. (2002). Remembering 100 student names: Beginning an introductory psychology course with a demonstration of memory. *Association for University Regional Campuses of Ohio, 8,* 176–185.

Bailey, J. (2003, January). *The quiet student: Methods for ending the silence.* Presentation at the National Institute on the Teaching of Psychology. St. Petersburg Beach, FL.

Bain, K. (2004). *What the best college teachers do.* Boston: Harvard University Press.

Baker, L., & Lombardi, B. (1985). Students' lecture notes and their relation to test performance. *Teaching of Psychology, 12,* 28–32.

Bandura, R., & Lyons, P. (2012). Instructor care and consideration toward students—What accounting students report: A research note. *Accounting Education: An International Journal, 21*(5), 515–527.

Barnett, J., & Francis, A. (2012). Using higher order thinking questions to foster critical thinking: A classroom study. *Educational Psychology, 32*(2), 201–211.

Barrick, K. (1998, March). *Creating a syllabus.* Presentation to University of Illinois, Urbana-Champaign Faculty, Urbana.

Bart, M. (2011). (Ed.). *Faculty focus special report: Social media usage trends among higher education faculty.* Retrieved from www.facultyfocus.com/wp-content/uploads/images/2011-social-media-report.pdf.

Bean, J. (2011). *Engaging ideas: The professor's guide to integrating writing, critical thinking, and active learning in the classroom* (2nd ed.). Hoboken, NJ: Jossey Bass.

Beard, R., & Hartley, J. (1984). *Teaching and learning in higher education* (4th ed.). London: Harper and Row.

Beard, R., & Senior, I. (1980). *Motivating students.* London: Routledge & Kegan Paul.

Beers, M., Hill, J., & Thompson, C. (2012). *The STP guide to graduate training programs in the teaching of psychology* (2nd ed.). Retrieved from http://teachpsych.org/ebooks/gst2012/index.php.

Benjamin, L. (2002). Lecturing. In S. Davis & W. Buskist (Eds.), *The teaching of psychology: Essays in honor of Wilbert J. McKeachie and Charles L. Brewer* (pp. 57–67). Mahwah, NJ: Lawrence Erlbaum Associates.

Benjamin, L. (2013). *Goodbye Dr. Chips, or When will college professors be required to teach no courses?* Presentation at the National Institute on the Teaching of Psychology. St. Petersburg Beach, FL. January 3–6.

Benjamin, L., & Lowman, K. (Eds.). (1981). *Activities handbook for the teaching of psychology* (vol. 1). Washington, DC: American Psychological Association.

Benjamin, L., Nodine, B., Ernst, R., & Blair Broeker, C. (Eds.). (1999). *Activities handbook for the teaching of psychology* (vol. 4). Washington, DC: American Psychological Association.

Berk, R. (2005). Survey of 12 strategies to measure teaching effectiveness. *International Journal of Teaching and Learning in Higher Education, 17*(1), 48–62.

Berk, R. (2009). Teaching strategies for the net generation. *Transformative Dialogues: Teaching and Learning Journal, 3*(2), 1–24.

Berk, R. (2010). How do you leverage the latest technologies, including Web 2.0 tools, in your classroom? *International Journal of Technology in Teaching and Learning, 6*(1), 1–13.

Berk, R. (2012a). Top 10 evidence-based, best practices for PowerPoint in the classroom. *Transformative Dialogues, 5*(3), 1–7.

Berk, R. (2012b). Top 20 strategies to increase the online response rates of student rating scales. *International Journal of Technology in Teaching and Learning, 8*(2), 98–107.

Bernstein, D. A (1983). Dealing with teaching anxiety. *Journal of the National Association of Colleges and Teachers of Agriculture, 27*, 4–7.

Bernstein, D. A. (1993). Excuses, excuses. *APS Observer, 6*, 4.

Bernstein, D. A. (2014). *Essentials of psychology* (6th ed.) Belmont, CA: Cengage Learning.

Bernstein, D. A., Borkovec, T. D., & Hazlett-Stevens, H. (2000). *New directions in progressive relaxation training: A guidebook for helping professionals* (2nd ed.). New York: Praeger.

Bernstein, D. A., Penner, L., Clarke-Stewart, A., & Roy, E. (2012). *Psychology* (9th ed.). Boston: Houghton Mifflin.

Bernstein, D. J., Jonson, J., & Smith, K. L. (2000). An examination of the implementation of peer review of teaching. *New Directions for Teaching and Learning, 83*, 73–85.

Berrett, D. (2012a). Today's faculty: Stressed, focused on teaching, and undeterred by long odds. *The Chronicle of Higher Education.* Retrieved from http://chronicle.com/article/Todays-Faculty-Stressed-and/135276/.

Berrett, D. (2012b). How "flipping" the classroom can improve the traditional lecture. *The Chronicle of Higher Education,* February 19. Retrieved from http://chronicle.com/article/How-Flipping-the-Classroom/130857/.

Berry, T., Cook, L., Hill, N., & Stevens, K. (2011). An exploratory analysis of textbook usage and study habits: Misperceptions and barriers to success. *College Teaching, 59*, 31–39.

Bies-Hernandez, N. (2012). The effects of framing grades on student learning and preferences. *Teaching of Psychology, 39*(3), 176–180.

Billson, J., & Tiberius, R. (1998). Effective social arrangements for teaching and learning. In K. Feldman & M. Paulsen (Eds.), *Teaching and learning in the college classroom* (2nd ed., pp. 561–576). Boston: Pearson Custom Publishing.

Bjerklie, L., & Mastel, L. (2012). Ten things we wish we knew about leadership before stepping into the classroom. *The Teaching Professor, 26*(10), 3.

Bjork, R. (1979). An information-processing analysis of college teaching. *Educational Psychologist, 14*, 15–23.

Bjork, R. (1999). Assessing our competence: Heuristics and illusions. In D. Gopher & A. Koriat (Eds.), *Attention and performance XVII. Cognitive regulation of performance: Interaction of theory and application* (pp. 435–459). Cambridge, MA: MIT Press.

Bjork, R. (2013a). *Applying cognitive psychology to enhance educational practice.* Retrieved from http://bjorklab.psych.ucla.edu/research.html.

Bjork, R. (2013b). Desirable difficulties perspective on learning. In H. Pashler (Ed.), *Encyclopedia of the mind.* Thousand Oaks, CA: Sage Reference.

Bjorklund, W., & Rehling, D. (2010). Student perceptions of classroom incivility. *College Teaching, 58*(1), 15–18.

Black, L., Wygonik, M. & Frey, B. (2011). Faculty-preferred strategies to promote a positive classroom environment. *Journal on Excellence in College Teaching, 22*(2), 109–133.

Bleske-Rechek, A. (2001). Obedience, conformity, and social roles: Active learning in a large introductory psychology class. *Teaching of Psychology, 28*, 260–262.

Bloom, B., Englehart, M., Furst, E., Hill, W., & Krathwohl, D. (1956). *Taxonomy of educational objectives: The classification of educational goals. Handbook 1: Cognitive Domain.* New York: David McKay.

Boehrer, J., & Linsky, M. (1990). Teaching with cases: Learning to question. In M. Svinicki (Ed.), *The changing faces of college teaching: New directions for teaching and learning* (pp. 41–57). San Francisco: Jossey-Bass.

Boettcher, J., & Conrad, R. (2010). Ten best practices for teaching online. *Tomorrow's Professor Blog, TP#1091.* Retrieved from http://cgi.stanford.edu/~dept-ctl/tomprof/posting.php?ID = 1091.

Boice, R. (1996). *First-order principles for college teachers: Ten basic ways to improve the teaching process.* Boston: Anker.

Boice, R. (1998a). Classroom incivilities. In K. Feldman & M. Paulsen (Eds.), *Teaching and learning in the college classroom* (2nd ed., pp. 347–369). Boston: Pearson Custom Publishing.

Boice, R. (1998b). New faculty as teachers. In K. Feldman & M. Paulsen (Eds.), *Teaching and learning in the college classroom* (2nd ed., pp. 241–255). Boston: Pearson Custom Publishing.

Bolin, A., Khramtsova, I., & Saarnio, D. (2005). Using student journals to stimulate authentic learning: Balancing Bloom's cognitive and affective domains. *Teaching of Psychology, 32*(3), 154–159.

Bonwell, C., & Eison, J. (1991). *Active learning: Creating excitement in the classroom.* ASHE-ERIC Higher Education Report No. 1. Washington, DC: The George Washington University School of Education and Human Development.

Bowen, J. (2006). Teaching naked: Why removing technology from your classroom will improve student learning. *National Teaching & Learning Forum, 16*(1), 1–5.

Bowen, J. (2012). *Teaching naked: How moving technology out of your college classroom will improve student learning.* San Francisco: Jossey-Bass.

Bowers, W. (1964). *Student dishonesty and its control in college.* New York: Bureau of Applied Social Research, Columbia University.

Boyce, T., & Hineline, P. (2002). Interteaching: A strategy for enhancing the user-friendliness of behavior arrangements in the college classroom. *The Behavior Analyst, 25*, 215–226.

Boyd, D. (2003). Using textbooks effectively: Getting students to read them. *American Psychological Society Observer, 16*, 25–26, 32–33.

Boyer, E. L. (1990). *Scholarship reconsidered: Priorities of the professoriate.* Princeton, NJ: The Carnegie Foundation for the Advancement of Teaching.

Boysen, G. (2012). Teacher responses to classroom incivility: Student perceptions of effectiveness. *Teaching of Psychology, 39*(4), 276–279.

Braskamp, L., & Ory, J. (1994). *Assessing faculty work: Enhancing individual and institutional performance.* Boston: Jossey-Bass.

Brawner, L. (2011). Quality by design: Helping faculty develop and maintain quality online courses. *ASCUE Proceedings, 48–53.* Retrieved from https://ascue.org/files/proceedings/2011-final.pdf.

Braxton, J., & Bayer, A. (1999). *Faculty misconduct in collegiate teaching.* Baltimore, MD: Johns Hopkins Press.

Brelsford, J. (1993). Physics education in a virtual environment. *In Proceedings of the 37th Annual Meeting of the Human Factors and Ergonomics Society.* Santa Monica, CA: Human Factors.

Bridges, K., Harnish, R., & Sillman, D. (2012). *Blogs in undergraduate psychology: Applications and advantages.* Retrieved from www.teachpsych.org/resources/documents/ebooks/eit2012.pdf, 1–8.

Bringle, R., & Duffy, D. (1998). *With service in mind: Concepts and models for service-learning in psychology.* Washington, DC: AAHE.

Bronstein, P., & Quina, K. (1988). *Teaching a psychology of people: Resources for gender and sociocultural awareness.* Washington, DC: American Psychological Association.

Brooke, C. (1999). Feelings from the back row: Negotiating sensitive issues in large classes. *New Directions in Teaching and Learning, 77,* 23–33.

Brookfield, S. (1990). *The skillful teacher.* San Francisco: Jossey-Bass.

Brookfield, S. (1996). Brookfield's questions. *The National Teaching & Learning Forum, 5,* 8.

Brookfield, S. (2006). *The skillful teacher: On technique, trust, and responsiveness in the classroom* (2nd ed.). San Francisco: Jossey-Bass.

Brookfield, S., & Preskill, S. (1999). *Discussion as a way of teaching: Tools and techniques for democratic classrooms.* San Francisco: Jossey-Bass.

Brookhart, S. (2011). Educational assessment knowledge and skills for teachers. *Educational Measurement: Issues and Practice, 30*(1), 3–12.

Brooks, D., Nolan, D., & Gallagher, S. (2000). *Web-teaching* (2nd ed.). Retrieved from http://dwb.unl.edu/Book/Contentsw.html.

Brooks, J., & Smith, V. (2011). Civic engagement through service learning. In R. Miller, E. Amsel, B. Kowalewski, B. Beins, K. Keith, & B. Peden (Eds.), *Promoting student engagement: Volume 1: Programs, techniques and opportunities* (pp. 70–73), Society for the Teaching of Psychology e-book: http://teachpsych.org/ebooks/pse2011/vol1/index.php#.UcR0THdfzTo.

Brophy, J. (2010). *Motivating students to learn* (3rd ed.). New York: Routledge.

Brothen, T. (2012). Time limits on tests: Updating the 1-minute rule. *Teaching of Psychology, 39*(4), 288–292.

Brown, K. (2010). Don't waste the first day of class. *Faculty Focus.* Retrieved from www.facultyfocus.com/articles/effective-teaching-strategies/dont-waste-the-first-day-of-class/.

Brown, M. (2012). When profs get graded. *APS Observer, 25*(7), 23–25.

Brown, N. (2000). *Creating high performance classroom groups.* New York: Taylor & Francis.

Brown University, The Harriet W. Sheridan Center for Teaching and Learning (2013). *Teaching portfolios.* Retrieved from www.brown.edu/about/administration/sheridan-center/teaching-learning/documenting-teaching-effectiveness/teaching-portfolios.

Bruff, D. (2011). Multiple-choice questions you wouldn't put on a test: Promoting deep learning using clickers. *Tomorrow's Professor Blog, TP#1083.* Retrieved from http://derekbruff.org/blogs/tomprof/?s=1083&submit=Search.

Buffington, P. (1996). *Cheap psychological tricks: What to do when hard work, honesty, and perseverance fail*. Atlanta, GA: Peachtree.

Bugeja, M. (2008). Classroom clickers and the cost of technology. *The Chronicle of Higher Education, Commentary*, December 5. Retrieved from http://chronicle.com/article/Classroom-Clickersthe/6009.

Buller, J. (2010). *The essential college professor: A practical guide to an academic career*. San Francisco: Jossey-Bass.

Bunce, D., Flens, E., & Neiles, K. (2010). How long can students pay attention in class? A study of student attention decline using clickers. *Journal of Chemical Education, 87*, 1438–1443.

Burak, L. (2012). Multitasking in the university classroom. *International Journal for the Scholarship of Teaching and Learning, 6*(2). Retrieved from http://academics.georgiasouthern.edu/jsotl/v6n2.html.

Burgstahler, S., & Cory, R. (2008). *Universal design in higher education: From principles to practice*. Cambridge, MA: Harvard Education Press.

Burke, L., Ahmadi, M., & James, K. (2009). Effectiveness of PowerPoint-based lectures across different business disciplines: An investigation and implications. *Journal of Education for Business, 84*(4), 246–251.

Burton, W., Civitano, A., & Steiner-Grossman, P. (2012). Online versus paper evaluations: Differences in both quantitative and qualitative data. *Journal of Computing in Higher Education, 24*(1), 58–69.

Bush, L., Pantoja, V., & Roen, D. (2003). Six major assumptions to learn by in technology-enhanced classrooms. *The National Teaching and Learning Forum, 12*(4), 8.

Buskist, W. (2013a). Preparing the new psychology professoriate to teach: Past, present, and future. *Teaching of Psychology, 40*(4), 333–339.

Buskist, W. (2013b). *Striving for excellence in your teaching: Some data, some theory, and a lot of practical advice*. Presentation at the National Institute on the Teaching of Psychology. St. Petersburg, FL. January 4.

Buskist, W. (2013c). *Practical suggestions for recognizing and resolving classroom incivility*. Presentation at the National Institute on the Teaching of Psychology. St. Petersburg, FL. January 3.

Buskist, W., & Saville, B. (2001). Rapport-building: Creating positive emotional contexts for enhancing teaching and learning. *APS Observer, 14*, 12–13, 19.

Buskist, W., Tears, R., Davis, S. F., & Rodrigue, K. (2002). The teaching of psychology course: Prevalence and content. *Teaching of Psychology, 29*, 140–142.

Butler, A., Zaromb, F., Lyle, K., & Roediger, H. (2009). Using popular films to enhance classroom learning: The good, the bad, and the interesting. *Psychological Science, 20*(9), 1161–1168. Retrieved from https://louisville.edu/psychology/lyle/ButlerEtAl-2009.pdf.

Butler, S. & McMunn, N. (2006). *A teacher's guide to classroom assessment*. San Francisco: Jossey-Bass.

Campbell, W., & Twenge, J. (2013). Narcissism unleashed. *Association for Psychological Science Observer, 26*, 28–29.

Cannon, R., & Newble, D. (2000). *A handbook for teachers in universities and college: A guide to improving teaching methods*. Sterling, VA: Stylus.

Carbone, E. (1999). Students behaving badly in large classes. *New Directions in Teaching and Learning, 77*, 35–43.

Carnegie Mellon, Eberly Center. (2013). *The syllabus: Creative syllabi*. Retrieved from www.cmu.edu/teaching/designteach/design/syllabus/samples-creative/.

Caron, M., Whitbourne, S., & Halgin, R. (1992). Fraudulent excuse making among college students. *Teaching of Psychology, 19*, 90–93.

Carroll, D. (2012). Ethical consideration in providing accommodations for students with disabilities. In R. Landrum & M. McCarthy (Eds.), *Teaching ethically: Challenges and opportunities.* (pp. 125–135). (May also be found at http://psycnet.apa.org/bookcollections/13496/.)

Carson, B. (1999). Bad news in the service of good teaching: Students remember ineffective professors. *Journal on Excellence in College Teaching, 10,* 91–105.

Case, K., & Hentges, B. (2010). Motivating student engagement with MySpace, clickers, and web-enhanced research labs. In S. Meyer & J. Stowell (Eds.), *Essays from excellence in teaching, IX,* 17–20.

Cashin, W. (1988). *Student ratings of teaching: A summary of research* (Idea Paper No. 20). Manhattan: Kansas State University, Division of Continuing Education. (ERIC Document Reproduction Service No. ED 302 567).

Cashin, W. (1995). *Student ratings of teaching: The research revisited* (Idea Paper No. 32). Manhattan: Kansas State University, Center for Faculty Evaluation and Development.

Cashin, W. (1999). Student ratings of teaching: Uses and misuses. In P. Seldin (Ed.), *Changing practices in evaluating teaching: A practical guide to improved faculty performance and promotion/tenure decisions* (pp. 25–44). Bolton, MA: Anker.

Cashin, W., & McKnight, P. (1989). Improving discussion. In M. Weimer (Ed.), *Teaching large classes well: New directions for teaching and learning* (No. 32; pp. 27–49). San Francisco: Jossey-Bass.

Castle, S., & McGuire, C. (2010). An analysis of student self-assessment of online, blended, and face-to-face learning environments: Implications for sustainable education delivery. *International Education Studies, 3*(3), 36–40.

Centra, J. (1993). *Reflective faculty evaluation: Enhancing teaching and determining faculty effectiveness.* San Francisco: Jossey-Bass.

Centra, J., & Gaubatz, N. (2000). Is there gender bias in student evaluations of teaching? *Journal of Higher Education, 70*(1), 17–33.

Cepeda, N., Pashler, H., Vul, E., & Wixted, J. (2006). Distributed practice in verbal recall tasks: A review and quantitative synthesis. *Psychological Bulletin, 132*(3), 354–380.

Cerbin, W. (2001). The course portfolio. *American Psychological Society Observer, 14,* 16–17, 30–31.

Chamberlin, J. (2013). "Like" it, or not: Psychology professors are making their courses a feature of their students' Facebook feeds in an effort to enliven class and enhance learning. *Monitor on Psychology, 44*(1), 60–63.

Chen, B., & Hirumi, A. (2009). *Effects of advance organizers on learning for differentiated learners in a fully web-based course.* Retrieved from www.academia.edu/293026/Effects_of_advance_organizers_on_learning_for_differentiated_learners_in_a_fully_Web-based_course.

Chen, P. (2013). The effects of college students' in-class and after-class lecture note-taking on academic performance. *The Asia-Pacific Education Researcher, 22*(2), 173–180.

Cherney, I. (2011). Active learning. In R. Miller, E. Amsel, B. Kowalewski, B. Beins, K. Keith, & B. Peden (Eds.), *Promoting student engagement: Volume 1: Programs, techniques and opportunities* (pp. 150–155). Society for the Teaching of Psychology e-book: http://teachpsych.org/ebooks/pse2011/vol1/index.php#.UcR0THdfzTo.

Chesler, M. (2003, January). Teaching well in the diverse/multicultural classroom. *AAHE Bulletin.com.* Retrieved from http://aahebulletin.com/member/articlesfeociology.asp.

Chickering, A., & Ehrmann, S. (1996). *Implementing the seven principles: Technology as lever.* Retrieved from www.tltgroup.org/programs/seven.html.

Chickering, A., & Gamson, Z. (1987). Seven principles for good practice in undergraduate education. *AAHE Bulletin, 39*(7), 3–7.

Chickering, A., & Gamson, Z. (1991). Applying the seven principles for good practice in undergraduate education. *New Directions for Teaching and Learning, 47*, 1–69.

Chism, N., & Bickford, D. (Eds.). (2002). *The importance of physical space in creating supportive learning environments: New directions for teaching and learning* (No. 92; pp. 1–97). San Francisco: Jossey-Bass.

Chu, J. (1994). Active learning in epidemiology and biostatistics. *Teaching and Learning in Medicine, 6*, 191–193.

Ciaccio, J. (2004). *Totally positive teaching: A five-stage approach to energizing students and teachers.* Alexandria, VA: Association for Supervision and Curriculum Development, 2004.

Clay, R. (2013). 2013 Education Leadership Conference: Ethics and education. *Educator: Newsletter of the APA Education Directorate, 12*, 1, 5–14.

Clayson, D., & Haley, D. (2013). An introduction to multitasking and texting: Prevalence and impact on grades and GPA in marketing classes. *Journal of Marketing Education, 35*(1), 26–40.

Clegg, V. (1994). Tips for tests and test giving. In K. Pritchard & R. McLaran Sawyer (Eds.), *Handbook of college teaching* (pp. 423–437). Westport, CT: Greenwood.

Clement, M., & Whatley, K. (2012). Friendly but not their friend. *The Teaching Professor, 26*(5), 4–5.

Coffman, S. (2003). Ten strategies for getting students to take responsibility for their learning. *College Teaching, 51*, 2–4.

Cohen, P., & McKeachie, W. (1980). The role of colleagues in the evaluation of college teaching. *Improving College and University Teaching, 28*, 147–153.

Colbeck, C. (2006). How female and male faculty with families manage work and personal roles. In S. Bracken, J. Allen, & D. Dean (Eds.), *The balancing act: Gendered perspectives in faculty roles and work lives.* Sterling, VA: Stylus.

Collins, K. (2003, January). *Students with disabilities at UIUC.* Presentation to University of Illinois, Urbana-Champaign. EOL 490 class, Urbana.

Colorado, J., & Eberle, J. (2010). Student demographics and success in online learning environments. *Emporia State Research Studies, 46*(1), 4–10. Retrieved from http://academic.emporia.edu/esrs/vol46/colorado.pdf.

Commonwealth University (VCU) Center for Teaching Excellence. (2013). *Online teaching and learning resource guide: 7 principles of good practice in online teaching.* Retrieved from www.vcu.edu/cte/resources/OTLRG/03_05_7Principles.html.

Connor-Greene, P. (2000). Making connections: Evaluating the effectiveness of journal writing in enhancing student learning. *Teaching of Psychology, 27*, 44–46.

Conole, G., & Alevizou, P. (2010). *A literature review of the use of Web 2.0 tools in higher education: A report commissioned by the Higher Education Academy.*

Retrieved from www.heacademy.ac.uk/assets/EvidenceNEt/Conole_Alevizou_2010.pdf.

Cooper, J., Robinson, P., & McKinney, M. (1994). Cooperative learning in the classroom. In D. Halpern (Ed.), *Changing college classrooms: New teaching and learning strategies for an increasingly complex world* (pp. 74–92). San Francisco: Jossey-Bass.

Cooper, M. (2003). *The big dummy's guide to service-learning.* Florida International University. Retrieved from www.fiu.edu/~time4chg/Library/big dummy.html.

Cramer, R. (1999). Large classes, intimate possibilities. *The National Teaching and Learning Forum, 8,* 5–6.

Creasman, P. (2012). *Considerations in online course design. IDEA Paper #52.* Retrieved from www.theideacenter.org/research-and-papers/idea-papers/52-considerations-online-course-design.

Crede, M., Roch, S., & Kieszczynka, U. (2010). Class attendance in college: A meta-analytic review of the relationship of class attendance with grades and student characteristics. *Review of Educational Research, 80*(2), 272–295.

Cress, C., Collier, P., Reitenauer, V., & Associates. (2005). *Learning through serving.* Sterling, VA: Stylus.

Curzan, A., & Damour, L. (2000). *First day to final grade: A graduate student's guide to teaching.* Ann Arbor: University of Michigan Press.

Cuseo, J., Fecas, V., & Thompson, A. (2010). *Thriving in college & beyond: Research-based strategies for academic success & personal development.* Dubuque, IA: Kendall Hunt.

Daniel, D. (2005). How to ruin perfectly good lecture. In B. Perlman, L. McCann, & B. Buskist (Eds.), *Voices of NITOP: Favorite talks from the National Institute on the Teaching of Psychology.* Washington, DC: Association for Psychological Science.

Daniel, D. (2010). Practical PowerPoint. In D.S. Dunn, J.C. Wilson, J. Freeman, & J. Stowell (Eds.), *Getting connected: Best practices for technology-enhanced teaching and learning in higher education.* New York: Oxford University Press.

Daniel, D. (2013). The dark side of pedagogy: An ecological perspective on the study and use of pedagogy in the classroom. In J. Holmes, S. Baker, & J. Stowell (Eds.), *Essays from excellence in teaching* (vol. 12, pp. 6–11). Retrieved from the Society for the Teaching of Psychology Web site: http://teachpsych.org/resources/e-book/eit2012/index.php.

Daniel, D., & Broida, J. (in press). Using Web-based quizzing to improve exam performance: Lessons learned. *Teaching of Psychology.*

Darby, A. (2013). Understanding universal design. National Education Association. Retrieved from www.nea.org/home/34693.htm.

Davis, B. (2009). *Tools for Teaching* (2nd ed.). San Francisco: Jossey-Bass.

Davis, S., & Ludvigson, H. (1995). Additional data on academic dishonesty and a proposal for remediation. *Teaching of Psychology, 22,* 119–121.

Davis, S., Grover, C., Becker, A., & McGregor, L. (1992). Academic dishonesty: Prevalence, determinants, techniques, and punishments. *Teaching of Psychology, 19,* 16–20.

Delaney, K. (2009, September 21). Ten tips for dealing with nervousness on the first day of class. *Faculty Focus.* Retrieved from www.facultyfocus.com/articles/effective-teaching-strategies/ten-tips-for-dealing-with-nervousness-the-first-day-of-class/.

Desrochers, C. (2000). Establishing expectations for our students. *The National Teaching and Learning Forum, 10,* 4–6.

Desrochers, C., & Zell, D. (2013). Providing timely and frequent feedback. *Tomorrow's Professor Blog, TP#1288*. Retrieved from http://derekbruff.org/blogs/tomprof/2013/11/07/tomorrows-professor-enewsletter-1288-providing-timely-and-frequent-feedback/.

Dey, E., Astin, A., & Korn, W. (1991). *The American freshman: Twenty-five year trends, 1966–1990*. Los Angeles: Higher Education Research Institute, Graduate School of Education, University of California.

DeZure, D. (1999). Evaluating teaching through peer classroom observation. In P. Seldin (Ed.), *Changing practices in evaluating teaching: A practical guide to improved faculty performance and promotion/tenure decisions* (pp. 70–96). Bolton, MA: Anker.

Diekhoff, G., LaBeff, E., Clark, R., Williams, L., Francis, B., & Haines, V. (1996). College cheating: Ten years later. *Research in Higher Education, 37*, 487–502.

Dietz-Uhler, B. & Hurn, J. (2011). Academic dishonesty in online courses. *Proceedings of the Association of Small Computer Users in Education, 44*, 71–77. Retrieved from www.ascue.org/files/proceedings/2011/2011-final.pdf#page=72.

Dinham, S. (1996). What college teachers need to know. In R. Menges & M. Weimer (Eds.), *Teaching on solid ground* (pp. 297–313). San Francisco: Jossey-Bass.

Does diversity make a difference? Three research studies on diversity in college classrooms. Washington, DC: American Council on Education and American Association of University Professors, 2000. May be obtained from www.acenet.eduorwww.aaup.org/.

Driscoll, A., Jicha, K., Hungt, A., Tichavsky, L., & Thompson, G. (2012). Can online courses deliver in-class results? A comparison of student performance and satisfaction in an online versus a face-to-face introductory sociology course. *Teaching Sociology, 40*(4), 312–331.

Drouin, M. (2012). What's the story on evaluations of online teaching? In M. E. Kite (Ed.), *Effective evaluation of teaching: A guide for faculty and administrators*. Retrieved from the Society for the Teaching of Psychology Web site: http://teachpsych.org/ebooks/evals2012/index.php.

Dunlosky, J., Rawson, K., Marsh, E., Nathan, M., & Willingham, D. (2013). Improving students' learning with effective learning techniques: Promising directions from cognitive and educational psychology. *Psychological Science in the Public Interest, 14*(1), 4–58.

Dweck, C. (1986). Motivational processes affecting learning. *American Psychologist, 41*, 1040–1048.

Dweck, C. (2007). The perils and promises of praise. *Educational Leadership, 65*(2), 34–39.

Dweck, C. (2008). *Mindset: The new psychology of success*. New York: Ballantine Books.

Dweck, C. (2010). Even geniuses work hard. *Educational Leadership, 68*(1), 16–20.

Dweck, C., & Leggett, E. (1988). A social-cognitive approach to motivation and personality. *Psychological Review, 95*, 256–273.

Dziegielewski, S. (2013). *DSM-5™ in action* (3rd ed.). New York: John Wiley & Sons.

Dziuban, C., & Moskal, P. (2011). A course is a course is a course: Factor invariance in student evaluation of online, blended and face-to-face learning environments. *Internet and Higher Education, 14*, 236–241.

Dziuban, C., Moskal, P., & Brophy, J. (2007). Student satisfaction with asynchronous learning. *Journal of Asynchronous Learning Networks, 11*(1), 87–95.

Ebel, R. (1965). *Measuring educational achievement*. Englewood Cliffs, NJ: Prentice Hall.

Eble, K. (1983). *Aims of college teaching*. Boston: Jossey-Bass.

Eble, K. (1988). *The craft of teaching* (2nd ed.). San Francisco: Jossey-Bass.

Eckersley, R 2010. Commentary on Trzesniewski and Donnellan: A transdisciplinary perspective on young people's wellbeing. *Perspectives on Psychological Science, 5*(1), 76–80.

Eggleston, T., & Smith, G. (2001, January). *Creating community in the classroom: Ice breakers and creative closures*. Poster at the 23rd National Institute on the Teaching of Psychology, St. Petersburg Beach, FL.

Eggleston, T., & Smith, G. (2002). Parting ways: Ending your course. *APS Observer, 15*(3), 15–16, 29–30.

Einstein, G., Mullet, H., & Harrison, T. (2012). The testing effect: Illustrating a fundamental concept and changing study strategies. *Teaching of Psychology, 39*(3), 190–193.

Eisner, S. (2004). Teaching generation Y college students: Three initiatives. *Journal of College Teaching and Learning, 1*(9), 69–84.

Elison-Bowers, P., & Snelson, C. (2012). Ethical challenges of online teaching. In R. Landrum & M. McCarthy (Eds.), *Teaching ethically: Challenges and opportunities* (pp. 55–65). Washington, DC: American Psychological Association. May also be found at http://psycnet.apa.org/bookcollections/13496/.

Ellicker, J., & McConnell, N. (2011). Interactive learning in the classroom: Is student response method related to performance? *Teaching of Psychology, 38*(3), 147–150.

Ellis, A., & MacLaren, C. (2005). *Rational emotive behavior therapy* (2nd ed.). Manassas Park, VA: Impact Publishers.

Ellis, Y., Daniels, B., & Jauregui, A. (2010). The effect of multitasking on the grade performance of business students. *Research in Higher Education Journal, 8*. Retrieved from www.aabri.com/manuscripts/10498.pdf.

Emmer, E., Everston, C., & Anderson, T. (1979, April). *The first week of class . . . and the rest of the year*. Paper presented at the meeting of the American Educational Research Association, San Francisco. ERIC Document Reproduction Service No. ED 175 861.

Enos, S., & Troppe, M. (1996). Service-learning in the curriculum. In B. Jacoby (Ed.), *Service-learning in higher education: Concepts and practices* (pp. 156–181). San Francisco: Jossey-Bass.

Eppler, M., & Harju, B. (1997). Achievement motivation goals in relation to academic performance in traditional and nontraditional college students. *Research in Higher Education, 35*, 557–572.

Ericksen, S. (1974). *Motivation for learning*. Ann Arbor: University of Michigan Press.

Erickson, B., Peters, C., & Strommer, D. (2006). *Teaching first-year college students*. San Francisco: Jossey Bass.

Erickson, B., & Strommer, D. (1991). *Teaching college freshmen*. San Francisco: Jossey-Bass.

Ewen, W. (1989). Teaching using discussions. In R. Neff & M. Weimer (Eds.), *Classroom communication: Collected readings for effective discussion and questioning* (pp. 21–26). Madison, WI: Magna.

Feldman, K. (1998). Identifying exemplary teachers and teaching: Evidence from student ratings. In K. Feldman & M. Paulsen (Eds.), *Teaching and learning in the college classroom* (2nd ed., pp. 391–414). Boston: Pearson Custom Publishing.

Feldman, K. (2007). Identifying exemplary teachers and teaching: evidence from student ratings. In R. Perry & J. Smart (Ed.), *The scholarship of teaching and learning in higher education: An evidence-based perspective* (pp. 93–129). New York: Springer.

Feldman, L. (2001). Classroom civility is another of our instructor responsibilities. *College Teaching, 49*(4), 137–140.

Fisch, L, (2001). Discussions: Seven guiding principles. *National Teaching and Learning Forum, 11*(1), 12.

Fisher, B. (1996). Using journals in social psychology class: Helping students apply course concepts to life experiences. *Teaching Sociology, 24*, 157–165.

Fiske, E. B. (2001). *Learning in deed: The power of service-learning for American schools.* Battle Creek, MI: W. K. Kellogg Foundation.

Forsyth, D. (2003). *The professor's guide to teaching: Psychological principles and practices.* Washington, DC: American Psychological Association.

Forsyth, D., & McMillan, J. (1991). Practical proposals for motivating students. In R. Menges & M. Svinicki (Eds.), *New directions for teaching and learning* (No. 45; pp. 53–65). San Francisco: Jossey-Bass.

Franz, S. (2013). *Cel.ly: Text message your classes for free.* Retrieved from http://suefranz.com/2013/05/16/cel-ly-text-message-your-classes-for-free.

Freberg, L., & Freberg, K. (2012). Incorporating social media in teaching and in research. *Excellence in teaching.* Retrieved from http://teachpsych.org/Resources/Documents/ebooks/eit2012.pdf.

Frein, S. (2011). Comparing in-class and out-of-class computer-based tests to traditional paper-and-pencil tests in introductory psychology courses. *Teaching of Psychology, 38*(4), 282–287.

Friedman, P., Rodriguez, F., & McComb, J. (2001). Why students do and do not attend classes: Myths and realities. *Teaching of Psychology, 49*, 124–133.

Fritschner, L. (2000). Inside the undergraduate college classroom: Faculty and students differ on the meaning of student participation. *The Journal of Higher Education, 71*, 343–362.

Fuller, R. (2005). *The essential features of the Personalized System of Instruction (PSI) or the Keller Plan.* Personalized System of Instruction (PSI), or Keller Plan, Materials. Paper 1. Retrieved from http://digitalcommons.unl.edu/cgi/viewcontent.cgi?article=1000&context=physicspsikeller.

Fullilove, R., & Treisman, P. (1990). Mathematics achievement among African American undergraduates at the University of California, Berkeley: An evaluation of the mathematics workshop program. *Journal of Negro Education, 59*, 463–478.

Fulton, K. (2012). Upside down and inside out: Flip your classroom to improve student learning. *Learning and Teaching with Technology, 39*(8), 12–17.

Gardner, L. E., & Leak, G. K. (1994). Characteristics and correlates of teaching anxiety among college psychology teachers. *Teaching of Psychology, 21*(1), 28–32.

Gaultney, J., & Cann, A. (2001). Grade expectations. *Teaching of Psychology, 28*, 84–87.

Gauss, C. (1930). *Life in college.* New York: Scribner's.

Gibbs, G. (1992). Control and independence. In G. Gibbs & A. Jenkins (Eds.), *Teaching large classes in higher education: How to maintain quality with reduced resources* (pp. 37–62). London; Kogan Page.

Gibbs, G., & Jenkins, A. (Eds.). (1992). *Teaching large classes in higher education: How to maintain quality with reduced resources.* London: Kogan Page.

Golde, C., & Dore, T. (2001). *At cross purposes: What the experiences of today's doctoral students reveal about doctoral education.* Pew Charitable Trusts. Retrieved from www.phd-survey.org/report%20final.pdf.

Goldstein, D. (2013). What are they thinking? Best practices for classroom response systems ("clickers"). *Tomorrow's Professor Blog, TP #1270.* Retrieved from http://derekbruff.org/blogs/tomprof/2013/09/12/tp-msg-1270-what-are-they-thinking-best-practices-for-classroom-response-systems-clickers/.

Gonzalez, V., & Lopez, E. (2001). The age of incivility: Countering disruptive behavior in the classroom. *AAHE Bulletin, 53*(8), 3–6.

Good, T. (2010). Forty years of research on teaching 1968–2008: What do we know now that we didn't know then? In R. Marzano (Ed.), *On excellence in teaching* (pp. 30–62). Bloomington, IN: Solution Tree Press.

Goodwin, S., Sharp, G., Cloutier, E., Diamond, N., & Dalgaard, K. (1981). *Effective classroom questioning.* Urbana-Champaign: University of Illinois, Urbana-Champaign, Center for Teaching Excellence (formerly Office of Instructional Resources).

Gordon, M., & Fay, C. (2010). The effects of grading and teaching practices on students' perceptions of grading fairness. *College Teaching, 58,* 93–98.

Goss, S. (1983). Student perceptions and classroom management (Doctoral dissertation). *Dissertation Abstracts International, 46–01,* 105.

Goss, S. (1995). Dealing with problem students in the classroom. *APS Observer, 8,* 26–27, 29.

Graesser, A. (2011). Improving learning. *Monitor on Psychology, 42*(7), 58–64.

Graham, C., Cagiltay, K., Lim, B., Craner, J., & Duffy, T. (2001). Seven principles of effective teaching: A practical lens for evaluating online courses. *The Technology Source.* Retrieved from http://technologysource.org/article/seven_principles_of_effective_teaching/.

Graham, M., Monday, J., & O'Brien, K. (1994). Cheating at small colleges: An examination of student and faculty attitudes and behaviors. *Journal of College Student Development, 35,* 255–260.

Grant, H., & Dweck, C. (2003). Clarifying achievement goals and their impact. *Journal of Personality and Social Psychology, 85,* 541–553.

Gray Wilson, S. (2013). The flipped classroom: A method to address the challenges of an undergraduate statistics course. *Teaching of Psychology, 40*(3), 193–199.

Greenberger, E., Lessard, J., Chuansheng, Chen & Farruggia, S. (2008). Self-entitled college students: Contributions of personality, parenting, and motivational factors. *Journal of Youth and Adolescence, 37,* 1193–1204.

Gregory, K. (2012). How undergraduates perceive their professors: A corpus analysis of Rate my Professor. *Journal of Educational Technology Systems, 40*(2), 169–193.

Gronlund, N., & Linn, R. (1990). *Measurement and evaluation in teaching* (6th ed.). New York: Macmillan.

Gurung, R., & McCann, L. (2011). How should students study? Tips, advice, and pitfalls. *Association for Psychological Science, 24*(4), 33–35.

Gurung, R., Weidert, J., & Jeske, A. (2010). Focusing on how students study. *Journal of the Scholarship of Teaching and Learning, 10*(1), 28–35.

Habanek, D. (2005). An examination of the integrity of the syllabus. *College Teaching, 53*(2), 62–64.

Hake, R. (1998). Interactive-engagement vs. traditional methods: A six thousand student survey of mechanics test data for introductory physics courses. *American Journal of Physics, 66,* 64–74.

Halpern, D. (2000). *Sex differences in cognitive abilities* (3rd ed.). Mahwah, NJ: Lawrence Erlbaum Associates.

Halpern, D. (2002). Teaching for critical thinking: A four-part model to enhance thinking skills. In S. Davis & W. Buskist (Eds.), *The teaching of psychology: Essays in honor of Wilbert J. McKeachie and Charles L. Brewer* (pp. 91–105). Mahwah, NJ: Lawrence Erlbaum Associates.

Halpern, D. (2003). *Thought & knowledge: An introduction to critical thinking* (4th ed.). Mahwah, NJ: Lawrence Erlbaum Associates.

Halpern, D. (2013). A is for assessment: The other scarlet letter. *Teaching of Psychology, 40*(4), 358–362.

Halpern, D., & Hakel, M. (2002) (Eds.) Applying the science of learning to university teaching and beyond. *New Directions for Teaching and Learning, 89.*

Halpern, D., & Hakel, M. (2003, July–August). Applying the science of learning to the university and beyond: Teaching for long term retention and transfer. *Change,* 36–41.

Hamann, K., Pollock, P., & Wilson, B. (2012). Assessing student perceptions of the benefits of discussions in small-group, large-class, and online learning contexts. *College Teaching, 60,* 65–75.

Hansen, E. (1998). Essential demographics of today's college students. *AAHE Bulletin, 51,* 3–5.

Hansen, R. (2006). Benefits and problems with student teams: Suggestions for improving team projects. *Journal of Education for Business, 82*(1), September/October, 11–19.

Hanson, T., Drumheller, K., Mallard, J., McKee, C., & Schlegel, P. (2011). Cell phones, text messaging and Facebook: Competing time demands of today's college students. *College Teaching, 59,* 23–30.

Hardin, E. (2007). Presentation software in the college classroom: Don't forget the instructor. *Teaching of Psychology, 34*(1), 53–57.

Hardy, M. (2001, January). *Extra credit: Gifts for the gifted?* Paper presented at the 23rd National Institute on the Teaching of Psychology, St. Petersburg Beach, FL.

Hardy, M., & Schaen, E. (2000). Integrating the classroom and community service: Everyone benefits. *Teaching of Psychology, 27,* 47–49.

Harrell, I., & Bower, B. (2011). Student characteristics that predict persistence in community college online courses. *The American Journal of Distance Education, 25,* 178–191.

Harrington, C., & Reasons, S. (2005). Online student evaluation of teaching for distance education: A perfect match? *The Journal of Educators Online, 2*(1). Retrieved from www.thejeo.com/ReasonsFinal.pdf.

Hativa, N. (2013a). Can faculty misinterpretation and misuse of student ratings results lead to the "dumbing down" of college education? *Tomorrow's Professor, Tips Message #1258.* Retrieved from http://cgi.stanford.edu/~dept-ctl/tomprof/posting.php?ID=1258.

Hativa, N. (2013b). *Student ratings of instruction: Recognizing effective teaching.* United States: Oron Publications.

Hays, M., Kornell, N., & Bjork, R. (2012). When and why a failed test potentiates the effectiveness of subsequent study. *Journal of Experimental Psychology: Learning,*

Memory, and Cognition, advance online publication. doi:10.1037/a0028468. Retrieved from http://bjorklab.psych.ucla.edu/pubs/Hays_Kornell_RBjork_inpress.pdf.

Heath, N., Lawyer, S., & Rasmussen, E. (2007). Web-based versus paper-and-pencil course evaluations. *Teaching of Psychology, 34*(4), 1–3.

Heiberger, G., & Junco, R. (2011). Meet your students where they are: Social media. *NEA Higher Education Advocate,* 6–9. Retrieved from www.nea.org/assets/docs/HE/1109Advocate_pg06-09.pdf.

Hendersen, R. (2002a, June). *Introductory psychology forum: Case studies for increasing student engagement.* Presentation to 2nd annual Summer National Institute on the Teaching of Psychology, St. Petersburg Beach, FL.

Hendersen, R. (2002b, June). *Responding to failure: A survival guide.* Distributed at the 2nd annual Summer National Institute on the Teaching of Psychology, St. Petersburg Beach, FL.

Hendersen, R. (2003). Good examples make better cases: Enhancing interaction in large classes. In H. Klein (Ed.), *Interactive innovative teaching and training: Case method and other techniques* (pp. 241–248). Needham, MA: World Association for Case Method Research and Application.

Herreid, C., & Schiller, N. (2013). Case studies and the flipped classroom. *Journal of College Science Teaching, 42*(5), 62–66.

Hettich, P. (1990). Journal writing: Old fare or nouvelle cuisine? *Teaching of Psychology, 17,* 36–39.

Heuberger, B., Gerber, D., & Anderson, R. (1999). Strength through cultural diversity: Developing and teaching a diversity course. *College Teaching, 47*(3), 107–113.

Heward, W. L. (1997). Four validated instruction strategies. *Behavior and Social Issues, 7,* 43–51.

Hill, A., Arford, T., Lubitow, A., & Smollin, L. (2012). "I'm ambivalent about it": The dilemmas of PowerPoint. *Teaching Psychology, 40*(3), 242–256.

Hill, C. (2013). The benefits of flipping your classroom. *Faculty Focus,* August 26. Retrieved from www.facultyfocus.com/articles/instructional-design/the-benefits-of-flipping-your-classroom/.

Hill, G. & Buskist, W. (2005, January). *Connecting with students: Making your philosophy of teaching come alive in the classroom.* Presented at the National Institute on the Teaching of Psychology, St. Petersburg Beach, FL.

Hill, G., & Zinsmeister, S. (2012). Becoming an ethical teacher. In W. Buskist & V. Benassi (Eds.), *Effective college and university teaching: Strategies and tactics for the new professoriate.* (pp. 125–133). Los Angeles: Sage. May also be found at www.sagepub.com/upm-data/43586_14.pdf.

Hills, S., Naegle, N., & Bartkus, K. (2009). How important are items on a student evaluation? A study of item salience. *Journal of Education for Business, 84*(5), 297–303.

Hilton, H. (1986). *The executive memory guide.* New York: Simon & Schuster.

Hilton, J. (2003, January). *You can run but you cannot hide: What every teacher needs to know about copyright.* Presented at the National Institute on the Teaching of Psychology, St. Petersburg Beach, FL.

Holland, H. (1965). *The spiral after-effect.* Oxford, England: Pergamon.

Hoover, E. (2013). Demographic change doesn't mean the sky's falling. *The Chronicle of Higher Education.* Retrieved from http://chronicle.com/blogs/headcount/demographic-change-doesnt-mean-the-skys-falling/35223.

Howard, C. (2012). Technology in higher education. In W. Buskist & V. Benassi (Eds.), *Effective college and university teaching: Strategies and tactics for the new professoriate* (pp. 163–172). Los Angeles: Sage.

Howard, J. (2013). For many students, print is still king. *The Chronicle of Higher Education.* Retrieved from http://chronicle.com/article/For-Many-Students-Print-Is/136829/.

Hsiung, C. (2012). The effectiveness of cooperative learning. *Journal of Engineering Education, 101*(1), 119–137.

Hurt, N., Moss, G., Bradley, C., Larson, L., Lovelace, M., Prevost, L., Riley, N., Domizi, D., & Camus, M. (2012). The "Facebook" effect: College students' perceptions of online discussion in the age of social networking. *International Journal for the Scholarship of Teaching and Learning, 6*(2). Retrieved from http://digitalcommons.georgiasouthern.edu/cgi/viewcontent.cgi?article=1324&context=int_jtl.

Hurtado, S., Eagan, M. K., Pryor, J. H., Whang, H., & Tran, S. (2012). *Undergraduate teaching faculty: The 2010–2011 HERI Faculty Survey.* Los Angeles: Higher Education Research Institute, UCLA. Retrieved from http://heri.ucla.edu/monographs/HERI-FAC2011-Monograph.pdf.

Huston, T. (2009). *Teaching what you don't know.* Cambridge, MA: Harvard University Press.

Jacobs, L., & Chase, C. (1992). *Developing and using tests effectively.* San Francisco: Jossey-Bass.

Jaggars, S., & Bailey, T. (2010). *Effectiveness of fully online courses for college students: Response to a Department of Education meta-analysis.* Community College Research Center (CCRC). Retrieved from www.eric.ed.gov/PDFS/ED512274.pdf.

Jaschik, S. (2010). The lost arts of teaching. *Tomorrow's Professor Blog, TP# 1034.* Retrieved from http://ceit.uq.edu.au/content/tomorrows-professor-stanford-university-lost-arts-teaching.

Jendrek, M. (1989). Faculty reactions to academic dishonesty. *Journal of College Student Development, 30,* 401–406.

Jendrek, M. (1992). Students' reactions to academic dishonesty. *Journal of College Student Development, 33,* 260–273.

Jenkins, A. (1992). Active learning in structured lecture. In G. Gibbs & A. Jenkins (Eds.), *Teaching large classes in higher education: How to maintain quality with reduced resources* (pp. 63–77). London: Kogan Page.

Johnson, D., Johnson, R., & Smith, K. (1991). *Cooperative learning: Increasing college faculty instructional productivity* (ASHE-ERIC Higher Education Rep. No. 4). Washington, DC: The George Washington University, School of Education and Human Development.

Johnson, D., Johnson, R. & Smith, K. (1998a). Research on cooperative learning. In K. Feldman & M. Paulsen (Eds.), *Teaching and learning in college classrooms* (2nd ed., pp. 467–483). Boston: Pearson Custom Publishers.

Johnson, D., Johnson, R., & Smith, K. (1998b). Cooperative learning returns to college: What evidence is there that it works? *Change, 30,* 26–35.

Johnson, G. (1995). *First steps to excellence in college teaching* (3rd ed.). Madison, WI: Magna.

Johnson, T. (2003). Online student ratings: Will students respond? *New Directions in Teaching and Learning, 96,* 49–59.

Johnstone, A., & Percival, F. (1976). Attention breaks in lecture. *Education in Chemistry, 13*, 49–50.

Jolly, J. (2008). Raising the question #9: Is the student-athlete population unique? And why should we care? *Communication Education, 57*(1), 145–151.

Jones, J. (2011, August 26). Creative approaches to the syllabus. *The Chronicle of Higher Education, ProfHacker*. Retrieved from http://chronicle.com/blogs/profhacker/date/2011/08/page/2.

Jones, R. (2013a). Why demand originality from students in online discussion forums? *Faculty Focus*, December 16. Retrieved from www.facultyfocus.com/articles/asynchronous-learning-and-trends/why-demand-originality-from-students-in-online-discussion-forums/.

Jones, R. (2013b). Keeping students engaged in online classrooms. *Faculty Focus*, September 16. Retrieved from www.facultyfocus.com/articles/online-education/keeping-students-engaged-in-the-online-classroom/.

Jones-Wilson, T. (2005). Teaching problem-solving skills without sacrificing course content. *Journal of College Science Teaching, 35*(1), 42–46.

Jonsson, A. (2012). Facilitating productive use of feedback in higher education. *Active Learning in Higher Education, 14*(1), 63–76.

Junco, R., Elavsky, M., & Heiberger, G. (2012). Putting Twitter to the test: Assessing outcomes for student collaboration, engagement and success. *British Journal of Educational Technology*. Retrieved from http://onlinelibrary.wiley.com/doi/10.1111/j.1467-8535.2012.01284.x/pdf.

Junco, R., Heiberger, G., & Loken, E. (2011). The effect of Twitter on college student engagement and grades. *Journal of Computer Assisted Learning, 27*(2), 119–132.

Junn, E. (1994). Experiential approaches to enhancing cultural awareness. In D. Halpern (Ed.), *Changing college classrooms* (pp. 128–164). San Francisco: Jossey-Bass.

Kahu, E. (2013). Framing student engagement in higher education. *Studies in Higher Education, 38*(5), 758–773.

Karasavvidis, I. (2010). Wiki uses in higher education: Exploring barriers to successful implementation. *Interactive Learning Environments, 18*(3), 219–231.

Karpicke, J. & Blunt, J. (2011). Retrieval practice produces more learning than elaborative studying with concept mapping. *Science, 333*, 772–775.

Keith, K. (2011). The last word: Engaging students for life. In R. Miller, E. Amsel, B. Kowalewski, B. Beins, K. Keith, & B. Peden (Eds.), *Promoting student engagement: Volume 1: Programs, techniques and opportunities* (pp. 195–197). Society for the Teaching of Psychology e-book: http://teachpsych.org/ebooks/pse2011/vol1/index.php#.UcR0THdfzTo.

Keith-Spiegel, P., Whitley, B., Balogh, D., Perkins, D., & Wittig, A. (2002). *The ethics of teaching: A casebook* (2nd ed.).Mahwah, NJ: Lawrence Erlbaum Associates.

Keller, F., & Sherman, J. (1974). *The Keller plan handbook*, Menlo Park, CA: Benjamin.

Kellum, K., Carr, J., & Dozier, C. (2001). Response-card instruction and student learning in a college classroom. *Teaching of Psychology, 28*(2), 101–104.

Kelly, R. (2010). Making the most of the first day of class. *Faculty Focus*. Retrieved from www.facultyfocus.com/articles/effective-classroom-management/making-the-most-of-the-first-day-of-class/.

Kemp, P., & O'Keefe, R. (2003). Improving teaching effectiveness: Some examples from a program for the enhancement of teaching. *College Teaching, 51*, 111–114.

Kennedy, D. (1997). *Academic duty.* Cambridge, MA: Harvard University Press.

Kennette, L., & Redd, B. (2013). Creating a sense of instructor presence in online courses. *E-xcellence in Teaching Essays,* September 25. Posted to PSYTEACH. http://teachpsych.org/news/psychteacher.php.

Kerr, M., & Payne, S. (1994). Learning to use a spreadsheet by doing and by watching. *Interacting With Computers, 6,* 3–22.

Khan, S. (2012). Why long lectures are ineffective. *Time Ideas Education.* Retrieved from http://ideas.time.com/2012/10/02/why-lectures-are-ineffective/.

Khanna, M. (2011). Community service engagement: How our students benefit from this service and how to encourage them to pursue community service. In R. Miller, E. Amsel, B. Kowalewski, B. Beins, K. Keith, & B. Peden (Eds.), *Promoting student engagement: Volume 1: Programs, techniques and opportunities* (pp. 41–45). Society for the Teaching of Psychology e-book: http://teachpsych.org/ebooks/pse2011/vol1/index.php#.UcR0THdfzTo.

Khanna, M., Brack, A., & Finken, L. (2013). Short-and long-term effects of cumulative finals on student learning. *Teaching of Psychology, 40*(3), 175–182.

King, R. (2002a). Managing teaching loads: And finding time for reflection and renewal. *APS Observer, 15,* 13–14, 35–36.

King, R. (2002b, January). *Portfolio development: Using authentic learning assignments in psychology courses.* Poster presented at the Institute on the Teaching of Psychology, St. Petersburg Beach, FL.

Kirk, D. (2009). Ten tips for dealing with nervousness on the first day of class. *Faculty Focus.* Retrieved from www.facultyfocus.com/articles/effective-teaching-strategies/ten-tips-for-dealing-with-nervousness-the-first-day-of-class/.

Klemm, W. (2007). Computer slide shows: A trap for bad teaching. *College Teaching, 55*(3), 121–124.

Knapper, C., & Wright, W. (2001). Using portfolios to document good teaching: Premises, purposes, practices. *New Directions of Teaching and Learning, 88,* 19–29.

Knepp, K. (2012). Understanding student and faculty incivility in higher education. *The Journal of Effective Teaching, 12*(1), 32–45.

Knowledge Network for Innovations in Learning and Teaching. (2013). Retrieved from http://tccl.rit.albany.edu/knilt/index.php/Advance_Organizers.

Ko, S., & Rossen, S. (2010). *Teaching online: A practical guide* (3rd ed.). New York: Routledge.

Komarraju, M., & Handelsman, M. (2012). Preparing to teach: Becoming part of an ethical culture. In R. Landrum & M. McCarthy (Eds.), *Teaching ethically: Challenges and opportunities.* (pp. 191–201). May also be found at http://psycnet.apa.org/bookcollections/13496/.

Kopp, J., Zinn, T., Finney, S., & Jurich, D. (2010). *"I can't believe she gave me a C!": Measuring entitlement in higher education.* Retrieved from www.nera-education.org/NERA_BestPaperGradStudent2010.pdf.

Korn, J. (2003, July). Writing a philosophy of teaching. *Excellence in Teaching, 5,* Retrieved from www.PSYCHTEACHER@list.kennesaw.edu/.

Korn, J. (2012). Writing and developing your philosophy of teaching. In W. Buskist & V. Benassi (Eds.), *Effective college and university teaching: Strategies and tactics for the new professoriate* (pp. 71–79). Los Angeles: Sage.

Kounin, J. (1977). *Discipline and group management in classrooms.* Huntington, New York: Robert E. Krieger Publishing Company.

Kouyoumdjian, H. (2013). *The how, when, where and why of quizzing.* Presentation at the National Institute on the Teaching of Psychology. St. Petersburg Beach, FL. January 3–6.

Kuh, G., Cruce, T., Shoup, R., Kinzie, J., & Gonyea, R. (2008). Unmasking the effects of student engagement on first-year college grades and persistence. *The Journal of Higher Education, 79*, 540–563.

Kuhlenschmidt, S., & Layne, L (1999). Strategies for dealing with difficult behavior. *New Directions in Teaching and Learning, 77*, 45–57.

Kulik, C., Kulik, J., & Bangert-Drowns, R. (1990). Effectiveness of mastery learning programs: A meta-analysis. *Review of Educational Research, 60*, 265–299.

Kulik, J., Kulik, C., & Cohen, P. (1979). A meta-analysis of outcome studies of Keller's personalized system of instruction. *American Psychologist, 34*, 307–318.

Kuo, Y., Walker, A., Belland, B. & Schroder, K. (2013). A predictive study of student satisfaction in online education programs. *The International Review of Research in Open and Distance Learning, 14*(1), 16–38.

Kusto, A., Afful, S., & Mattingly, B. (2010). Students' perceptions of and preferences for professors. *The New School Psychology Bulletin, 8*(1), 47–55.

Lambert, E., Hogan, N., & Barton, S. (2003). Collegiate academic dishonesty revisited: What have they done, how often have they done it, who does it, and why did they do it? *Electronic Journal of Sociology.* Retrieved from www.sociology.org/content/vol7.4/lambert_etal.html.

Landrum, R. (2013). The ubiquitous clicker: SoTL applications for scientist-educators. *Teaching of Psychology, 40*(2), 98–103.

Landrum, R. (2011). Faculty perceptions concerning the frequency and appropriateness of student behaviors. *Teaching of Psychology, 38*(4), 269–272.

Lang, J. (2008). *On course: A week-by-week guide to your first semester of college teaching.* Boston: Harvard University Press.

Lang, J. (2013). 4 steps to a memorable teaching philosophy. *The Chronicle of Higher Education.* Retrieved from chronicle.com/article/4-Steps-to-a-Memorable/124199/.

Lantz, M. (2010). The use of "clickers" in the classroom: Teaching innovation or merely an amusing novelty? *Computers in Human Behavior, 26*, 556–561.

Latham, B. (2011). Teachable moments: The grading conference. *The Teaching Professor, 25*(7), 1.

Lauer, C. (2012). A comparison of faculty and student perspectives on course evaluation terminology. *To Improve the Academy, 31*, 195–211.

Lawrence, N. (2013). Cumulative exams in the introductory psychology course. *Teaching of Psychology, 40*(1), 15–19.

Lazzari, M. (2009). Creative use of podcasting in higher education and its effect on competitive agency. *Computers & Education, 52*(1). doi:10.016/j.compedu.2008.06.002. Retrieved from www.sciencedirect.com/science/article/pii/S0360131508000948.

Leamnson, R. (1999). *Thinking about teaching and learning: Developing habits of learning with first year college and university students.* Sterling, VA: Stylus.

Lehman, R., & Conceicao, S. (2010). *Creating a sense of presence in online teaching: How to "be there" for distance learners.* San Francisco: Jossey-Bass.

Leonard, J., Mitchell, K., Meyers, S., & Love, J. (2002). Using case studies in introductory psychology. *Teaching of Psychology, 29*, 142–144.

Lescher, T. (2013). *How can I build and maintain classroom rapport?* Retrieved from www.tlpd.ttu.edu/home//TLPDCTeachingResources/documents/Rapport%20White%20paper.pdf.

Levy, G., & Peters, W. (2002). Undergraduates' views of best college courses. *Teaching of Psychology, 29*, 46–48.

Lieberg, C. (2008). *Teaching your first college course: A practical guide for new faculty and graduate student instructors.* Sterling, VA: Stylus.

Lieberg, C. (2013). *Ten unspoken questions from new college students during the first days of class.* Retrieved from www.google.com/url?sa=t&rct=j&q=&esrc=s&source=web&cd=1&ved=0CCYQFjAA&url=http%3A%2F%2Fmctcctl.files.wordpress.com%2F2014%2F01%2Ften_unspoken_questions_from_new_college_students_during_the_first_days_of_class.doc&ei=ENB7U87sDo-eyATL-YCABw&usg=AFQjCNGoIc24RI6gv19WpiCRJI4LuAPqyw&bvm=bv.67229260,d.aWw.

Lieu, O. (2012). Student evaluation of instruction: In the new paradigm of distance education. *Research in Higher Education, 53,* 471–486.

Light, G., Cox, R. & Calkins, S. (2009). *Learning and Teaching in Higher Education: The Reflective Professional.* Thousand Oaks, CA: Sage.

Linn, R., & Gronlund, N. (2000). *Measurement and assessment in teaching* (8th ed.). Upper Saddle River, NJ: Merrill.

Lippmann, S., Bulanda, R., & Wagenaar, T. (2009). Student entitlement: Issues and strategies for confronting entitlement in the classroom and beyond. *College Teaching, 57*(4), 197–204.

Little, J., Bjork, E., Bjork, R., & Angello, G. (2012) Multiple-choice tests exonerated, at least some of the charges: Fostering test-induced learning and avoiding test-induced forgetting. *Psychological Science, 23*(11), 1337–1344.

Liu, O. (2012). Student evaluation of instruction: In the new paradigm of distance education. *Research in Higher Education, 53,* 471–486.

Loftus, M. (2013). Keep the lecture, Lose the lectern. *Tomorrow's Professor Blog, #1293.* Retrieved from http://cgi.stanford.edu/~dept-ctl/cgi-bin/tomprof/enewsletterWithSurvey.php?msgno=1293.

Lombardi, J. (2011). Got motivation? Six great resources for instructors at every level. *College Teaching, 59,* 150–153.

Lorenzo, G., & Ittelson, J. (2005). Demonstrating and assessing student learning with e-portfolios. *Educause Learning Initiative Paper #3.* Retrieved from http://net.educause.edu/ir/library/pdf/eli3003.pdf.

Loui, M. (2003, April). *What do professors do all day and why do they do it?* Presentation, University of Illinois, Urbana-Champaign.

Love, B. (2013). Finishing strong: End-of-class review to improve relationships, measurement, and learning outcomes. *College Teaching, 61,* 151–152.

Lowman, J. (1987). Giving students feedback. In M. Weimer (Ed.), *Teaching large classes well: New directions for teaching and learning* (No. 32; pp. 71–83). San Francisco: Jossey-Bass.

Lowman, J. (1995). *Mastering the techniques of teaching* (2nd ed.). San Francisco: Jossey-Bass.

Lowman, J. (1998). What constitutes masterful teaching. In K. Feldman & M. Paulsen (Eds.), *Teaching and learning in the college classroom* (2nd ed., pp. 503–513). Boston: Pearson Custom Publishing.

Lucas, G. (2010). Initiating student–teacher contact via personalized responses to one-minute papers. *College Teaching, 58*(2), 2010.

Lusk, M., & Conklin, L. (2002). Collaborative testing to promote learning. *Journal of Nursing Education, 42,* 121–124.

MacGregor, J. (1990). Collaborative learning: Shared inquiry as a process of reform. In M. Svinicki (Ed.), *Changing faces of college teaching: New directions for teaching and learning* (No. 42; pp. 19–30). San Francisco: Jossey-Bass.

MacGregor, J. (2000). Restructuring large classes to create communities of learners. In J. MacGregor, J. Cooper, K. Smith, & P. Robinson (Eds.), Strategies for energizing large classes: From small groups to learning communities. *New Directions for Teaching and Learning, 81*, 47–61.

Maier, M., & Panitz, T. (1996). End on a high note: Better endings for classes and courses. *College Teaching, 44*, 145–148.

Makosky, V., Sileo, C., Whittemore, L., Landry, C., & Skutley, M. (Eds.). (1990). *Activities handbook for the teaching of psychology* (vol. 3). Washington, DC: American Psychological Association.

Makosky, V., Whittemore, L., & Rogers, A. (1987). *Activities handbook for the teaching of psychology* (vol. 2). Washington, DC: American Psychological Association.

Malesky, L. & Peters, C. (2012). Defining appropriate professional behavior for faculty and university students on social networking websites. *Higher Education, 63*, 135–151.

Malouff, J., Emmerton, A., & Schutte, N. (2013). The risk of a halo bias as a reason to keep students anonymous during grading. *Teaching of Psychology, 40*(3), 233–237.

Mann, R., Arnold, S., Binder J., Cytrynbaum, S., Newman, B., Ringwald, B., & Rosenwein, R. (1970). *The college classroom: Conflict, change, and learning.* New York: John Wiley & Sons.

Maramark, S., & Maline, M. (1993). *Issues in education: Academic dishonesty among college students.* Washington, DC: U.S. Department of Education, Office of Research.

Marchese, T. (1997). Service-learning in the disciplines: An interview with monograph series editors Robert Bringle and Edward Zlotkowski. *AAHE Bulletin, 49*(7), 3–6.

Marin, P. (2000). The educational possibility of multi-racial/multi-ethnic college classrooms. In *Does diversity make a difference? Three research studies on diversity in college classrooms.* Washington, DC: American Council on Education and American Association of University Professors.

Marincovich, M. (1999). Using student feedback to improve teaching, In P. Seldin (Ed.), *Changing practices in evaluating teaching: A practical guide to improved faculty performance and promotion/tenure decisions* (pp. 45–69). Bolton, MA: Anker.

Marsh, H. (1984). Students' evaluations of university teaching: Dimensionality, reliability, validity, potential biases, and utility. *Journal of Educational Psychology, 76*, 707–754.

Marsh, H. (1987). Students' evaluations of university teaching: Research findings, methodological issues, and directions for future research. *International Journal of Educational Research, 11*, 253–388.

Marsh, H. (2001). Distinguishing between good (useful) and bad workload on students' evaluations of teaching. *American Educational Research Journal, 38*(1), 183–212.

Marsh, H. (2007). Students' evaluations of university teaching: A multidimensional perspective. In R. Perry & J. Smart (Eds.), *The scholarship of teaching and learning in higher education: An evidence-based perspective* (pp. 319–384). New York: Springer.

Marsh, H., & Bailey, M. (1993). Multidimensional students' evaluations of teaching effectiveness: A profile analysis. *Journal of Higher Education, 69*, 1–18.

Marsh, H., & Dunkin, M. (1997). Students' evaluations of university teaching: A multidimensional perspective. In R. Perry & J. Smart (Eds.), *Effective teaching in higher education: Research and practice* (pp. 241–320). New York: Agathon.

Marsh, H., & Roche, L. (1997). Making students' evaluations of teaching effectiveness effective. *American Psychologist, 52*, 1187–1197.

Marsh, H., & Roche, L. (2000). Effects of grading leniency and low workloads on students' evaluations of teaching: Popular myth, bias, validity or innocent bystanders? *Journal of Educational Psychology, 92*, 202–228.

Marshall, P., & Losonczy-Marshall, M. (2010). Classroom ecology: Relations between seating location, performance, and attendance. *Psychological Reports, 107*(2), 567–577.

Marzano, R. (2010). Developing expert teachers. In R. Marzano (Ed.), *On excellence in teaching* (pp. 212–245). Bloomington, IN: Solution Tree Press.

Mayer, S., & Sutton, K. (1996). *Personality: An integrative approach.* New York: Macmillan.

McBride, E. (2013). *Freud on Facebook: Teaching psychology with social media.* Poster presented at the National Institute on the Teaching of Psychology. St. Petersburg, FL. January 3–6.

McCabe, D. (1993). Faculty responses to academic dishonesty: The influence of student honor codes. *Research in Higher Education, 34*, 647–658.

McCabe, D., & Bowers, W. (1994). Academic dishonesty among males in college: A 30 year perspective. *Journal of College Student Development, 35*, 5–10.

McCabe, D., & Bowers, W. (2009). The relationship between student cheating and college fraternity or sorority membership. *National Association of Student Personnel Administrators Journal, 46*, 573–586.

McCabe, D., Butterfield, K., & Trevino, L. (2012). *Cheating in college: Why students do it and what educators can do about it.* Baltimore, MD: Johns Hopkins Press.

McCabe, D., & Trevino, L. (1993). Academic dishonesty. *Journal of Higher Education, 64*, 522–538.

McCabe, D., & Trevino, L. (1997). Individual and contextual influences on academic dishonesty: A multicampus investigation. *Research in Higher Education, 38*, 379–396.

McCabe, D., Trevino, L., & Butterfield, K. (2001). Cheating in academic institutions: A decade of research. *Ethics & Behavior, 11*(3), 219–232.

McCabe, J., Doerflinger, A., & Fox, R. (2011). Student and faculty perceptions of e-feedback. *Teaching of Psychology, 38*(3), 173–179.

McCoy, B. (2013). Digital distractions in the classroom: Student classroom use of digital devices for non-class related purposes. *The Journal of Media Education, 4*(4), 5–15.

McDaniel, M., & Wooldridge, C. (2012). The science of learning and its application. In W. Buskist & V. Benassi (Eds.), *Effective college and university teaching: Strategies and tactics for the new professoriate* (pp. 49–60). Los Angeles: Sage.

McGarr, O. (2009). A review of podcasting in higher education: Its influence on the traditional lecture. *Australasian Journal of Educational Technology, 25*(3), 309–321.

McGlynn, A. (2001). *Successful beginnings for college teaching: Engaging your students from the first day.* Madison, WI: Atwood.

McKeachie, W. (1997a). Good teaching makes a difference—And we know what it is. In R. P. Perry & J. C. Smart (Eds.), *Effective teaching in higher education: Research and practice* (pp. 396–411). New York: Agathon.

McKeachie, W. (1997b). Student ratings: The validity of use. *American Psychologist, 52*, 1218–1225.

McKeachie, W. (2001). *McKeachie's teaching tips: Strategies, research, and theory for college and university teachers* (11th ed.). Boston: Houghton Mifflin.

McKeachie, W. (2002). *Teaching tips: Strategies, research, and theory for college and university teachers* (12th ed.). Boston: Houghton Mifflin.

McKeage, K. (2001). Office hours as you like them: Integrating real-time chats into the course media mix. *College Teaching, 49*, 32–37.

McKinney, J., McKinney, K., Franiuk, R., & Schweitzer, J. (2006). The college classroom as a community: Impact on student attitudes and learning. *College Teaching, 54*(3), 281–284.

McKinney, K. (1999). Encouraging student motivation. *The Teaching Professor, 13*, 4.

McKinney, K. (2001). The teacher with the most negative impact on me. *The National Teaching and Learning Forum, 10*, 7–8.

McMillan, J. (2013). Why we need research on classroom assessment. In J. McMillan (Ed.), *SAGE handbook of research on classroom assessment: Classroom assessment in the context of learning theory and research* (pp. 1–28). Retrieved from http://knowledge.sagepub.com/view/hdbk_classroomassessment/SAGE.xml.

McNeely, B. (2013). *Using technology as a learning tool, not just the cool new thing.* Retrieved from Educause Web site: www.educause.edu/research-and-publications/books/educating-net-generation/using-technology-learning-tool-not-just-cool-new-thing.

McTighe, J. (2010). Understanding by design. In R. Marzaon (Ed.), *On excellence in teaching* (pp. 270–299). Bloomington, IN: Solution Tree Press.

Menges, R., & Weimer, M. (1996). *Teaching on solid ground: Using scholarship to improve practice.* San Francisco: Jossey-Bass.

Mervis, J. (2001). Student survey highlights mismatch of training, goals. *Science, 291*, 408–409.

Mester, C., & Tauber, R. (2000). Acting lessons for teachers: Using performance skills in the classroom. *APS Observer, 13*, 12–13, 25.

Meyer, R., & Weaver, C. (2013). *Case studies in abnormal behavior* (9th ed.). Boston: Pearson Education.

Meyers, C., & Jones, T. (1993). *Promoting active learning: Strategies for the college classroom.* San Francisco: Jossey-Bass.

Micari, M., & Pazos, P. (2012). Connecting to the professor: Impact of the student-faculty relationship in a highly challenging course. *College Teaching, 60*, 41–47.

Michaelson, L., Sweet, M., & Parmelee, D. (Eds.). (2008). Team-based learning: Small-group learning's next big step. *New Directions for Teaching and Learning, 116*.

Miller, H., & Flores, D. (2012). Teaching controversial issues, liberally. In W. Buskist & V. Benassi (Eds.), *Effective college and university teaching: Strategies and tactics for the new professoriate* (pp. 155–162). Los Angeles: Sage. May also be found at www.sagepub.com/upm-data/43586_14.pdf.

Miller, J., & Chamberlin, M. (2000), Women are teachers, men are professors: A study of student perceptions. *Teaching Sociology, 28*, 283–298.

Miller, R., Amsel, E., Kowalewski, B., Beins, B., Keith, K., & Peden, B. (Eds.). (2011). *Promoting student engagement: Volume 1: Programs, techniques and opportunities.* Society for the Teaching of Psychology e-book: http://teachpsych.org/ebooks/pse2011/vol1/index.php#.UcR0THdfzTo.

Millis, B., & Cottell, P. (1998). *Cooperative learning for higher education faculty.* Phoenix, AZ: Oryx Press.

Mitchell, N., & Melton, S. (2003). Collaborative testing: An innovative approach to test taking. *Nurse Educator, 28,* 95–97.

Moore, M., Moore, R., & McDonald, R. (2008). Student characteristics and expectations of university classes: A free elicitation approach. *College Student Journal, 42*(1), 82–89.

Moore, R. (2003). Attendance and performance: How important is it for students to attend class? *Journal of College Science Teaching, 32,* 367–371.

Moran, D. (2000, June). *Is active learning for me?* Poster presented at APS Preconvention Teaching Institute, Denver, CO.

Mulryan-Kyne, C. (2010). Teaching large classes at college and university level: challenges and opportunities. *Teaching in Higher Education, 15*(2), 175–185.

Multhaup, K. (2008, Spring). Using class discussions to improve oral communication skills. *Teaching Tips (APA Division 20—Adult Development and Aging),* pp. 8, 18. Retrieved from www.apadivisions.org/division-20/publications/newsletters/adult-development/2008/04-issue.pdf.

Murray, B. (2000). Learning from real life. *APA Monitor, 31,* 71–72.

Murray, H. (1997). Effective teaching behaviors in the college classroom. In R. Perry & J. Smart (Eds.), *Effective teaching in higher education: Research and practice* (pp. 171–204). New York: Agathon.

The National Center for Case Study Teaching in Science Case Collection: Psychology (2013). Retrieved from http://sciencecases.lib.buffalo.edu/cs/collection/results.asp?search=psychology&subject_headings=&educational_level=&type_methods=&topical_areas=&x=0&y=0.

National Center for Education Statistics (NCES). (2012). Retrieved from http://nces.ed.gov/fastfacts/display.asp?id=98.

National Center for Education Statistics. (1999, August). Statistical Analysis Report. *An institutional perspective on students with disabilities in postsecondary education.* Washington, DC: United States Department of Education, Office of Educational Research and Improvement. NCES 1999–046.

National Center for Education Statistics. (2001). *Digest of Education Statistics, 2000.* Washington, DC: United States Department of Education, Office of Educational Research and Improvement. NCES 2001–034.

National Center for Educational Statistics. (2013a). Retrieved from http://nces.ed.gov/programs/digest/d12/tables/dt12_443.asp.

National Center for Educational Statistics. (2013b). Retrieved from http://nces.ed.gov/programs/coe/indicator_csb.asp.

National Center for Educational Statistics. (2013c). Retrieved from http://nces.ed.gov/programs/coe/indicator_cea.asp.

National Center for Educational Statistics. (2013d). Retrieved from http://nces.ed.gov/programs/digest/d12/tables/dt12_376.asp.

National Endowment for the Arts. (2007). *To read or not to read: A question with national consequences.* Retrieved from www.nea.gov/research/toread.pdf.

National Service-Learning Clearinghouse. (2003). *What is service-learning?* Retrieved from www.servicelearning.org/article/archive/35/.

Naveh, G., Tubin, D., & Pliskin, N. (2010). Student LMS use and satisfaction in academic institutions: The organizational perspective. *Internet and Higher Education, 13,* 127–133.

Neff, R., & Weimer, M. (1989). *Classroom communication: Collected readings for effective discussion and questioning.* Madison, WI: Magna.

Nelson, S., Arnold, K., Gilmore, A., & McDermott, K. (2013). Neural signatures of test-potentiated learning in parietal cortex. *The Journal of Neuroscience, 33*(29), 11754–11762.

Nevid, J. (2011). Teaching the millennials. *APS Observer, 24*(5), 53–56.

Nicol, D. (2010). From monologue to dialogue: Improving written feedback processes in mass higher education. *Assessment & Evaluation in Higher Education, 35*(5), 501–517.

Nilson, L. (2003). Improving student peer feedback. *College Teaching, 51*(1), 34–38.

Nilson, L. (2010). Teaching the millennial generation. *Tomorrow's Professor Newsletter, #1047*. Retrieved from http://cgi.stanford.edu/~dept-ctl/tomprof/posting.php?ID=1047.

Nilson, L. (2013). *Getting students to do the readings*. Retrieved from www.nea.org/home/34689.htm.

Nilson, L. (2014). Self-regulated learning from live lectures. *Tomorrow's Professor Blog, #1297*. Retrieved from http://derekbruff.org/blogs/tomprof/2014/01/13/tomorrows-professor-enewsletter-1297-self-regulated-learning-from-live-lectures/.

Njenga, J., & Fourie, L. (2010). The myths about e-learning in higher education. *British Journal of Educational Technology, 41*(2), 199–212.

Norcross, J., & Dooley, H. (1993). Faculty use and justification of extra credit: No middle ground? *Teaching of Psychology, 20*, 240–242.

Novak, G., & Patterson, E. (2010). An introduction to just-in-time-teaching. In S. Simkins & M. Maier (Eds.), *Just-in-time-teaching: Across the disciplines, across the academy* (pp. 3–23). Sterling, VA: Stylus.

Novotney, A. (2011). Beat the cheat. *Monitor on Psychology, 42*, 54–57.

Novotney, A. (2012). Making e-learning work: Boost your students' success with these tips for teaching online. *Monitor on Psychology, 43*(1), 60–62.

O'Brien, J., Millis, B., & Cohen, M. (2008). *The course syllabus: A learning-centered approach* (2nd ed.). San Francisco: Jossey Bass.

O'Neal, C., Meizlish, D., & Kaplan, M. (2007). Writing a statement of teaching philosophy for the academic job search. *Center for Research on Learning and Teaching Occasional Papers, No. 23*. Retrieved from www.crlt.umich.edu/sites/default/files/resource_files/CRLT_no23.pdf.

Oblinger, D., & Hawkins, B. (2006). The myth about online course development: "A faculty member can individually develop and deliver an effective online course." *Educause Review, 41*(1), 14–15.

Office of the Registrar, University of Oregon (2013). *Response rates and accuracy of online course evaluations*. Retrieved from http://registar.uoregon.edu/course_evaluations/accuracy_and_validity.

Oltmanns, T., Neale, J., & Davison, G. (2012). *Case studies in abnormal psychology* (9th ed.). New York: John Wiley & Sons.

Onwuegbuzie, A., Witcher, A., Collins, K., Filer, J., Wiedmaier, C., & Moore, C. (2007). Students' perceptions of characteristics of effective college teachers: A validity study of a teaching evaluation form using a mixed-methods analysis. *American Educational Research Journal, 44*(1), 113–169.

Orlando, J. (2013a). Improve your PowerPoint design with one simple rule. *Faculty Focus*, November 11. Retrieved from www.facultyfocus.com/articles/teaching-with-technology-articles/improve-your-powerpoint-design-with-one-simple-rule/.

Orlando, M. (2013b). Nine characteristics of a great teacher. *Faculty Focus,* January 14. Retrieved from www.facultyfocus.com/articles/philosophy-of-teaching/nine-characteristics-of-a-great-teacher/.

Ory, J. (2003). The final exam. *American Psychological Society Observer, 16,* 23–24, 34–35.

Ory, J., & Ryan, K. (1993). *Tips for improving testing and grading.* Newbury Park, CA: Sage.

Otto, J., Sanford, D., & Ross, D. (2008). Does ratemyprofessor.com really rate my professor? *Assessment & Education in Higher Education, 33*(4), 355–368.

Pacansky-Brock, M. (2013). *Best practices for teaching with emerging technologies.* New York: Routledge.

Paldy, L. (2013). MOOCs in your future. *Journal of College Science Teaching, 42*(2), 6–7.

Palloff, R., & Pratt, K. (2013). *Lessons from the virtual classroom: The realities of online teaching* (2nd ed.). Jossey-Bass: San Francisco.

Palmisano, M., & Herrmann, D. (1991). The facilitation of memory performance. *Bulletin of the Psychonomic Society, 29,* 557–559.

Pappano, L. (2012). The year of the MOOC. *New York Times,* November 2. Retrieved from www.nytimes.com/2012/11/04/education/edlife/massive-open-online-courses-are-multiplying-at-a-rapid-pace.html?_r=0.

Parini, J. (2005). *The art of teaching.* New York: Oxford Press.

Parker, P., Fleming, P., Beyerlein, S., Apple, D., & Krumsieg, K. (2001). *Differentiating assessment from evaluation as continuous improvement tools.* 31st ASEE/IEEE Frontiers in Education Conference, October 10–13, Reno, NV.

Parkes, J., & Harris, M. (2002). The purposes of a syllabus. *College Teaching, 5,* 55–61.

Parry, M. (2010). *Tomorrow's college.* Retrieved from http://chronicle.com/article/Tomorrows-College/125120.

Pascarella, E., Salisbury, M., & Blaich, C. (2011). Exposure to effective instruction and college student persistence: A multi-institutional replication and extension. *Journal of College Student Development, 52*(1), 4–19.

Pascarella, E., & Terenzini, P. (2005). *How college affects students. Volume 2: A third decade of research.* San Francisco: Jossey-Bass.

Pashler, H., McDaniel, M., Rohrer, D., & Bjork, R. (2008). Learning styles: Concepts and evidence. *Psychological Science in the Public Interest, 9*(3), 106–119.

Pastorino, E. (1999). Students with academic difficulty: Prevention and assistance. *APS Observer, 12,* 10–11, 26.

Patrick, C. (2011). Student evaluations of teaching: Effects of the Big Five personality traits, grades and the validity hypothesis. *Assessment & Education in Higher Education, 36*(2), 239–249.

Patterson, B., & McFadden, C. (2009). Attrition in online and campus degree programs. *Online Journal of Distance Education Administration, 12*(2). Retrieved from www.westga.edu/~distance/ojdla/summer122/patterson112.html.

Pauk, W. (2001). *How to study in college* (7th ed.). Boston: Houghton-Mifflin.

Paul, R., & Elder, L. (2001). *The miniature guide to critical thinking: Concepts and tools.* The Foundation for Critical Thinking. www.criticalthinking.org.

Peck, A. (2013). OMG RU really going to send that? E-mail communication with students. *E-xcellence in Teaching Essays,* June 12. Retrieved from *PSYTEACHER* http://teachpsych.org/news/psychteacher.php.

Penny, L., & Murphy, E. (2009). Rubrics for designing and evaluating online asynchronous discussions. *British Journal of Educational Technology, 40*(5), 804–820.

Pepe, J., & Wang, M. (2012). What instructor qualities do students reward? *College Student Journal, 46*(3), 603–614.

Perkins, D., & Tagler, M. (2011). Jigsaw classroom. In R. Miller, E. Amsel, B. Kowalewski, B. Beins, K. Keith, & B. Peden (Eds.), *Promoting student engagement: Volume 1: Programs, techniques and opportunities* (pp. 195–197). *Society for the Teaching of Psychology e-book:* http://teachpsych.org/ebooks/pse2011/vol1/index.php#.UcR0THdfzTo.

Perlman, B., & McCann, L. (1996), *Recruiting good college faculty: Practical advice for a successful search.* Bolton, MA: Anker.

Phelps, R. (2012). Diversity and diversity issues in teaching. In W. Buskist & V. Benassi (Eds.), *Effective college and university teaching: Strategies and tactics for the new professoriate* (pp. 145–154). Los Angeles: Sage. May also be found at www.sagepub.com/upm-data/43586_14.pdf.

Philipsen, M., & Bostic, T. (2010). *Helping faculty find work-life balance: The path toward family-friendly institutions.* San Francisco: Jossey-Bass.

Picciano, A., Seaman, J., & Allen, J. (2010). Educational transformation through online learning: To be or not to be. *Journal of Asynchronous Learning Networks, 14*(4), 17–35.

Pingree, A., & Zakrajsek, T. (2013). Encouraging student-faculty interactions outside of class. *Tomorrow's Professor Blog, TP#1238.* Retrieved from http://derekbruff.org/blogs/tomprof/2013/03/18/tp-msg-1238-encouraging-student-faculty-interaction-outside-of-class-2/.

Pink, D. (2009). *Drive: The surprising truth about what motivates us.* New York, NY: Penguin Group.

Pittenger, D. (2006). Teaching psychology when everyone is an expert. In W. Buskist & S. Davis (Eds.), *Handbook of the teaching of psychology.* Malden, MA: Blackwell.

Plank, K., & Rohdieck, (2013). *The assumption we make about diversity.* Retrieved from www.nea.org/home/34691.htm.

Prentice-Dunn, S. (2012). Teaching in the context of professional development and work-private life balance. In W. Buskist & V. Benassi (Eds.), *Effective college and university teaching: Strategies and tactics for the new professoriate* (pp. 39–47). Los Angeles: Sage. May also be found at http://bama.ua.edu/~sprentic/Prentice-Dunn%20%282012%29.pdf.

Price, C. (2010). Incivility, inattention, and multitasking! Oh My! *Essays from E-xcellence in Teaching: 2010 Volume 10,* 10–14. Retrieved from http://teachpsych.org/ebooks/eit2010/index.php#.UgFBs23XvTo.

Prieto, L., & Meyers, S. (2001). *The teaching assistant training handbook: How to prepare TAs for their responsibilities.* Stillwater, OK: New Forums Press.

ProctorU. www.ao.uiuc.edu/support/source/student_services/proctoru_tech.html.

Prohaska, V. (2012). Strategies for encouraging ethical student behavior. In R. Landrum & M. McCarthy (Eds.), *Teaching ethically: Challenges and opportunities* (pp. 79–88). May also be found at http://psycnet.apa.org/bookcollections/13496/.

Pryor, J., Eagan, K., Blake, L., Hurtado, S., Berdan, J., & Case, M. (2013). Higher Education Research Institute (2013). *American Freshman National Norms Fall 2012.* Brief report retrieved from www.heri.ucla.edu/briefs/TheAmericanFreshman2012-Brief.pdf; full report retrieved from www.heri.ucla.edu/monographs/TheAmericanFreshman2012-Expanded.pdf.

Pusateri, T. (2012). Teaching ethically: Ongoing improvement, collaboration, and academic freedom. In R. Landrum & M. McCarthy (Eds.), *Teaching ethically: Challenges and opportunities* (pp. 9–19). May also be found at http://psycnet.apa.org/bookcollections/13496/.

Quinn, C. (2012). Going social with mobile learning. *Tomorrow's Professor Blog, TP #1205*. Retrieved from http://cgi.stanford.edu/~dept-ctl/tomprof/posting.php?ID=1205.

Rattan, A., Good, C., & Dweck, C. (2012). "It's OK—Not everyone can be good at math": Instructors with entity theory comfort and demotivate students. *Journal of Experimental Social Psychology, 48*, 731–737.

Rattan, A., Naidu, N., Savani, K. & Dweck, C. (2012). Can everyone become highly intelligent? Cultural differences in and societal consequences of beliefs about the universal potential for intelligence. *Journal of Personality and Social Psychology, 103*(5), 787–803.

Reddy, Y., & Andrade, H. (2010). A review of rubric use in higher education. *Assessment & Evaluation in Higher Education, 35*(4), 435–448.

Rehling, R., & Bjorklund, W. (2010). A comparison of faculty and student perceptions of incivility in the classroom. *Journal on Excellence in College Teaching, 21*, 73–93.

Renner, E. (2013). The difference between practice and theory. *Faculty Focus*, November 18. Retrieved from www.facultyfocus.com/articles/teaching-with-technology-articles/the-difference-between-practice-and-theory/.

Rettinger, D., & Kramer, Y. (2009). Situational and personal causes of student cheating. *Research in Higher Education, 50*, 293–313.

Rhem, J. (2009). Clickers. *The National Teaching & Learning Forum, 18*(3), 1–4.

Richards, H., Brown, A., & Forde, T. (2006). Addressing diversity in schools: Culturally responsive pedagogy. National Center for Culturally Responsive Educational Systems (NCCRESt). Retrieved from www.nccrest.org/Briefs/Diversity_Brief.pdf.

Richardson, J. (2005). Instruments for obtaining student feedback: A review of the literature. *Assessment & Evaluation in Higher Education, 30*(4), 387–415.

Riener, C., & Willingham, D. (2010). The myth of learning styles. *Change Magazine*, September/October, 33–35.

Rivard, R. (2013). Beyond MOOC hype. *Tomorrow's Professor Blog, TP#1269*. Retrieved from http://derekbruff.org/blogs/tomprof/2013/09/09/tp-msg-1269-beyond-mooc-hype/.

Robinson, K., & Kazlauskas, A. (2010). Have podcasts lived up to expectations? *Proceedings of ASCILITE Sydney 2010*. Retrieved from www.ascilite.org.au/conferences/sydney10/procs/Robinson-poster.pdf.

Rodriguez, M., & Bates, S. (2012). Aspiring to ethical treatment of diverse student populations. In R. Landrum & M. McCarthy (Eds.), *Teaching ethically: Challenges and opportunities* (pp. 101–111).

Rodriguez-Farrar, H. (2003). *The teaching portfolio*. The Harriet W. Sheridan Center for Teaching and Learning at Brown University. Retrieved from www.brown.edu/Administration/Sheridan_Center/publications/teacport.html.

Roediger, H., & Karpicke, J. (2006a). Test-enhanced learning: Taking memory tests improves long-term retention. *Psychological Science, 17*, 249–255.

Roediger, H., & Karpicke, J. (2006b). The power of testing memory: Basic research and implications for educational practice. *Perspectives on Psychological Science, 1*, 181–210.

Roediger, H., Pooja, A., McDaniel, M., & McDermott, K. (2011). Test-enhanced learning in the classroom: Long-term improvements from quizzing. *Journal of Experimental Psychology: Applied, 17,* (4), 382–395.

Rohrer, D., & Pashler, H. (2010). Recent research on human learning challenges conventional instructional strategies. *Educational Researcher, 39,* 406–412.

Roig, M., & Caso, M. (2005). Lying and cheating: Fraudulent excuse making, cheating, and plagiarism. *The Journal of Psychology, 139*(6), 485–494.

Roosevelt, M. (2009). Student expectations seen as causing grade disputes. *New York Times.* Retrieved from www.nytimes.com/2009/02/18/education/18college.html?_r=0.

Rosenthal, D. (2002). The case method—A joint venture in learning: A message from the editor. *Journal on Excellence in College Teaching, 13,* 1–141.

Rothman, T., Romeo, L., Brennan, M., & Mitchell, D. (2011). Criteria for assessing student satisfaction with online courses. *International Journal for e-Learning Security, 1*(1/2), 27–32.

Ruhl, K., Hughes, C., & Schloss, P. (1987). Using the pause procedure to enhance lecture recall. *Teacher Education and Special Education, 10,* 4–18.

Ruscio, J. (2001). Administering quizzes at random to increase students' reading. *Teaching of Psychology, 28*(3), 204–206.

Ruskin, R. (1974). *The personalized system of instruction: An educational alternative* (ERIC/Higher Education Research Rep. No. 5). Washington, DC: American Association for Higher Education.

Ryan, R., Wilson, J., & Pugh, J. (2011). Psychometric characteristics of the professor-student rapport scale. *Teaching of Psychology, 38*(3), 135–141.

Sacks, O. (1970). *The man who mistook his wife for a hat and other clinical tales.* New York: Harper & Row.

Sacks, O. (1993). A neurologist's notebook: To see and not see. *New Yorker,* May 10. Retrieved from www.willamette.edu/~mstewart/whatdoesitmean2see.pdf.

Sacks, O. (1996). *An anthropologist on Mars: Seven paradoxical tales.* New York: Vintage Books.

Sadler, D. (2010). Beyond feedback: Developing student capability in complex appraisal. *Assessment & Evaluation in Higher Education, 35*(5), 535–550.

Sanders, J., & Wiseman, R. (1994). The effects of verbal and nonverbal teacher immediacy on perceived cognitive, affective, and behavioral learning in the multicultural classroom. In K. Feldman & M. Paulsen (Eds.), *Teaching and learning in the college classroom* (2nd ed., pp. 623–636). Boston: Pearson Custom Publishing.

Sanders, L. (2001). Improving assessment in university classrooms. *College Teaching, 49,* 62–645.

Satterlee, J., & Lau, P. (2003, March). *Heading for meaning: Techniques for encouraging active reading.* Presentation at CTEN Teaching Workshop Series, University of Illinois, Champaign, IL.

Saville, B. (2011). Interteaching: A behavior-analytic approach to promoting student engagement. In R. Miller, E. Amsel, B. Kowalewski, B. Beins, K. Keith, & B. Peden (Eds.), *Promoting student engagement: Volume 1: Programs, techniques and opportunities* (pp. 128–133), Society for the Teaching of Psychology e-book: http://teachpsych.org/ebooks/pse2011/vol1/index.php#.UcR0THdfzTo.

Saville, B. (2012). The ethics of grading. In R. Landrum & M. McCarthy (Eds.), *Teaching ethically: Challenges and opportunities* (pp. 31–42). Washington, DC: American Psychological Association. May also be found at http://psycnet.apa.org/bookcollections/13496/.

Saville, B. (2013). Interteaching: Ten tips for effective implementation. *APS Observer, 26*(6), Retrieved from www.psychologicalscience.org/index.php/publications/observer/2013/february-13/interteaching-ten-tips-for-effective-implementation.html.

Saville, B., Lambert, T., & Robertson, S. (2011). Interteaching: Bringing behavioral education into the 21st century. *The Psychological Record, 61,* 153–166.

Saville, B., Zinn, T., Brown, A., & Marchuk, K. (2010). Syllabus detail and students' perceptions of teacher effectiveness. *Teaching of Psychology, 37,* 186–189.

Saville, B., Zinn, T., & Jacobsen, K. (2012). Leading discussions. In W. Buskist & V. Benassi (Eds.), *Effective college and university teaching: Strategies and tactics for the new professoriate* (pp. 107–114). Los Angeles: Sage.

Sawyer, R., Prichard, K., & Hostetler, K. (2001). *The art and politics of college teaching: A practical guide for the beginning professor* (2nd ed.). New York: Peter Lang Publishing.

Sax, L., Astin, A., Korn, W., & Mahoney, K. (1999). *The American freshman: National norms for fall 1999.* Los Angeles: Higher Education Research Institute, Graduate School of Education and Information Studies, University of California.

Sax, L., Astin, A., Korn, W., & Mahoney, K. (2000). *The American freshman: National Norms for Fall 2000.* Los Angeles: Higher Education Research Institute, Graduate School of Education and Information Studies, University of California.

Sax, L., Bryant, A., & Gilmartin, S. (2003). *A longitudinal investigation of emotional health among first-year college students: Comparisons of men and women.* Los Angeles: Higher Education Research Institute, Graduate School of Education and Information Studies, University of California.

Schafer, P., Yost Hammer, E., & Bernsten, J. (2012). Using course portfolios to assess and improve teaching. In M. Kite (Ed.), *Effective evaluation of teaching: A guide for faculty and administrators.* Retrieved from the Society for the Teaching of Psychology Web site: http://teachpsych.org/ebooks/evals2012/index.php.

Scholl-Buckwald, S. (1985). The first meeting of the class. In J. Katz (Ed.), *Teaching as though students mattered: New directions for teaching and learning* (No. 21; pp. 13–21). San Francisco: Jossey-Bass.

Schreiner, L., Louis, M., & Nelson, D. (Eds.). (2012). *Thriving in transitions: A research-based approach to college student success.* Columbia, SC (University of South Carolina): National Resource Center for the First-Year Experience.

Schroeder, J., Stephens, R., & Williams, K. (2013). Managing the large(r) classroom. *APS Observer, 26*(3). Retrieved from www.psychologicalscience.org/index.php/publications/observer/2013/march-13/managing-the-larger-classroom.html.

Schuldt, B., Totten, J., Adrian, C., & Cox, S. (2012). Student rudeness & technology: Going beyond the business classroom. *Journal of Learning in Higher Education, 8*(1), 35–43.

Schwartz, B., Tatum, H., & Wells, J. (2012). The honor system: Influences on attitudes, behaviors, and pedagogy. In R. Landrum & M. McCarthy (Eds.), *Teaching ethically: Challenges and opportunities* (pp. 89–98). May also be found at http://psycnet.apa.org/bookcollections/13496/.

Schwartz, M. (1986). An experimental investigation of bad karma and its relationship to the grades of college students. *Journal of Polymorphous Perversity, 3,* 9–12.

Scott, K. (2012). Using the e-portfolio to validate student learning. *The Teaching Professor, 26*(1), 1.

Scott, S. (1997). Accommodating college students with learning disabilities: How much is enough? *Innovative Higher Education, 22*, 85–99.

Scott, S., McGuire, J., & Foley, T. (2003). Universal design for instruction: A framework for anticipating and responding to disability and other diverse learning needs in the college classroom. *Equity and Excellence in Education, 36*(1), 40–49.

Scott, S., McGuire, J., & Shaw, S. (2003). Universal design for instruction: A new paradigm for teaching adults in postsecondary education. *Remedial and Special Education, 24*(6), 369–379.

Scutter, S., Stupans, I., Sawyer, T., & King, S. (2010). How do students use podcasts to support learning? *Australasian Journal of Educational Technology, 26*(2), 180–191. Retrieved from www.ascilite.org.au/ajet/ajet26/scutter.pdf.

Seldin, P. (1991). *The teaching portfolio: A practical guide to improved performance and promotion/tenure decisions.* Bolton, MA: Anker.

Seldin, P. (1999a). Current practices—Good and bad—Nationally. In P. Seldin (Ed.), *Changing practices in evaluating teaching: A practical guide to improved faculty performance and promotion/tenure decisions* (pp. 1–24). Bolton, MA: Anker.

Seldin, P. (1999b). Self-evaluation: What works? What doesn't? In P. Seldin (Ed.), *Changing practices in evaluating teaching: A practical guide to improved faculty performance and promotion/tenure decisions* (pp. 97–115). Bolton, MA: Anker.

Seldin, P., & Miller, J. (2009). *The academic portfolio: A practical guide to documenting teaching, research, and service.* San Francisco: Jossey-Bass.

Şendağ, S., Duran, M., & Fraser, R. (2012). Surveying the extent of involvement in online academic dishonesty (e-dishonesty) related practices among university students and the rationale students provide: One university's experience. *Computers in Human Behavior, 28*(2012), 849–860.

Seward, L. (2002). A time for inclusion. *AAHE Bulletin, 54*, 3–6.

Shachar, M., & Neumann, Y. (2010). Twenty years of research on the academic performance differences between traditional and distance learning: Summative meta-analysis and trend examination. *MERLOT Journal of Online Learning and Teaching, 6*(2), 318–334.

Shadiow, L. (2013). *What our stories teach us.* San Francisco: Jossey-Bass.

Sherer, P., & Shea, T. (2011). Using online video to support student learning and engagement. *College Teaching, 59*, 56–59.

Shimoff, E., & Catania, A. (2001). Effects of recording attendance on grades in introductory psychology. *Teaching of Psychology, 28*, 192–195.

Short, F., & Martin, J. (2011). Presentation vs performance: Effects of lecturing style in higher education on student preference and student learning. *Psychology Teaching Review, 17*(2), 71–82.

Shu, L, Gino, F., & Bazerman, M. (2011). Dishonest deed, clear conscience: When cheating leads to moral disengagement and motivated forgetting. *Personality and Social Psychology Bulletin, 17*(3), 330–349.

Shulman, L. (2003, January). *Lamarck's revenge: Teaching and learning among the scholarships.* University of Illinois Faculty Retreat presentation, Urbana, IL.

Silberman, M. (1996). *Active learning: 101 strategies to teach any subject.* Boston: Allyn & Bacon.

Silverman, R., & Welty, W. (1990). Teaching with cases. *Journal on Excellence in College Teaching, 1*, 88–97.

Silvestri, M., & Buskist, W. (2012). Conflict in the college classroom: Understanding, preventing, and dealing with classroom incivilities. In W. Buskist & V. Benassi (Eds.), *Effective college and university teaching: Strategies and tactics for the new professoriate* (pp. 135–143). Los Angeles: Sage. May also be found at www.sagepub.com/upm-data/43586_14.pdf.

Silvestri, M., Cox, B., Buskist, W., & Keeley, J. (2012). Preparing for the transition from graduate school to the academy: An exemplar from psychology. In W. Buskist & V. Benassi (Eds.), *Effective college and university teaching: Strategies and tactics for the new professoriate* (pp. 27–37). Thousand Oaks, CA: Sage.

Simons, H., Bosworth, C., Fujita, S., & Jensen, M. (2007). The athlete stigma in higher education. *College Student Journal, 41*(2), 251–273.

Singham, M. (2007). Death to the syllabus! *Liberal Education, 93*, 52–56.

Singleton-Jackson, J., Jackson, D., & Reinhardt, J. (2010). Students as consumers of knowledge: Are they buying what we are selling? *Innovative Higher Education, 35*, 343–358.

Skinner, B. (1954). The science of learning and the art of teaching. *Harvard Educational Review, 24*, 86–97.

Skinner, B. (1968). *The technology of teaching.* New York: Appleton-CenturyCrofts.

Slattery, J. & Carlson, J. (2005). Preparing an effective syllabus: Current best practices. *College Teaching, 53*(4), 159–164.

Slay, J. (2005). No extra credit for you. *Chronicle of Higher Education.* Retrieved from http://chronicle.com/article/No-Extra-Credit-For-You/44956.

Sleigh, M., McCann, L., & Kadah-Ammeter, T. (2012). Creating student interest. *APS Observer, 25*(4), 47–50.

Sleigh, M., & Ritzer, D. (2001). Encouraging student attendance. *APS Observer, 14*, 19–20, 32–33.

Sleigh, M., Ritzer, D., & Casey, M. (2002). Student versus faculty perceptions of missing class. *Teaching of Psychology, 29*, 53–56.

Slife, B. (2001). *Taking sides: Clashing views on controversial psychological issues.* Guilford, CT: Dushkin/McGraw-Hill.

Smit, D. (2010). Strategies to improve student writing. *The Idea Center.* Retrieved from www.theideacenter.org/sites/default/files/IDEA_Paper_48.pdf.

Smith, B., & MacGregor, J. (1998). What is collaborative learning? In K. Feldman & M. Paulsen (Eds.), *Teaching and learning in college classrooms* (2nd ed., pp. 585–596). Boston: Pearson Custom Publishing.

Smith, D., & Valentine, T. (2012). The use and perceived effectiveness of instructional practices in two-year technical colleges. *Journal on Excellence in College Teaching, 23*(1), 133–161.

Smith, J. C. (Ed.). (2000). *ABC relaxation training: A practical guide for health professionals.* New York: Springer.

Smith, K. (2000). Going deeper: Formal small-group learning in large classes. In J. MacGregor, J. Cooper, K. Smith, & P. Robinson (Eds.), Strategies for energizing large classes: From small groups to learning communities. *New Directions for Teaching and Learning, 81*, 25–46.

Smith, L. (2008). Grading written projects: What approaches do students find most helpful? *Journal of Education for Business,* July/August, 325–330.

Snyder, M. (2012). Much ado about MOOCs. *Academe, 98*(6), 55.

Sojka, J., Gupta, A., & Deiter-Schmelz, D. (2002). Student and faculty perceptions of student evaluations of teaching: A study of similarities and differences. *College Teaching, 50*, 44–49.

Soysa, C., Dunn, D., Dottolo, A., Burns-Gover, A., & Gurung, R. (2013). Orchestrating authorship: Teaching writing across the psychology curriculum. *Teaching of Psychology, 40*(2), 88–97.

Stevens, D., & Levi, A. (2005). *Introduction to rubrics.* Sterling, VA: Stylus.

Stevenson, M. (1989). Creating a connected classroom: Two projects that work! *Teaching of Psychology, 16,* 212–214.

Storch, E., & Storch, J. (2002). Fraternities, sororities, and academic dishonesty. *College Student Journal, 36*(2), 247–252.

Stork, E., & Hartley, N. (2009). Classroom incivilities: Students' perceptions about professors' behaviors. *Contemporary Issues in Education Research, 2*(4), 13–24.

Strayer, D., Watson, J., & Drews, F. (2011). Cognitive distraction while multitasking in the automobile. *Psychology of Learning and Motivation, 54,* 29–58.

Stuber-McEwen, D., Wisely, P., & Hoggatt, S. (2009). *Point, click, and cheat: Frequency and type of academic dishonesty in the virtual classroom.* Retrieved from www.westga.edu/~distance/ojdla/fall123/stuber123.html.

Sturtridge, J. (2012). Too many papers: Two solutions. *The Teaching Professor, 26*(6), 8.

Suskie, L. (2000). *Fair assessment practices* (American Association for Higher Education Bulletin). Retrieved from www.aahebulletin.com/ archive/may2.asp.

Suskie, L. (2009). *Assessing student learning: A common sense guide* (2nd ed.). San Francisco: Jossey-Bass.

Suskie, L. (2011). Writing good multiple-choice items. *Tomorrow's Professor e-mail Newsletter, #1108.* Retrieved from http://derekbruff.org/blogs/tomprof/2011/06/10/tp-msg-1108-writing-good-multiple-choice-items/.

Svinicki, M. (1998). Helping students understand grades. *College Teaching, 46,* 101–105.

Svinicki, M. (2013). MOOCs: What part of learning goes on where and how? *Tomorrow's Professor Blog, TP#1229.* Retrieved from http://derekbruff.org/blogs/tomprof/2013/02/14/tp-msg-1229-moocs-what-part-of-learning-goes-on-where-and-how/.

Svinicki, M., Hagen, A., & Meyer, D. (1996). How research on learning strengthens instruction. In R. Menges & M. Weimer (Eds.), *Teaching on solid ground: Using scholarship to improve practice* (pp. 257–288). San Francisco: Jossey-Bass.

Svinicki, M., & McKeachie, W. (2014). *McKeachie's teaching tips: Strategies, research & theory for college and university teachers* (14th ed.). Belmont, CA: Wadsworth, Cengage Learning.

Taylor, L., & Parsons, J. (2011). Improving student engagement. *Current Issues in Education, 14*(1). Retrieved from cie.asu.edu/ojs/index.php/cieatasu/article/download/745/162.

Teven, J., & McCroskey, J. (1996). The relationship of perceived teacher caring with student learning and teacher evaluation. *Communication Education, 46,* 1–9.

Theall, M. (2010). Evaluating teaching: From reliability to accountability. *New Directions for Teaching and Learning, 123,* 85–95.

Theall, M., & Feldman, K. (2007). Commentary and update on Feldman's (1997) "Identifying exemplary teachers and teaching: Evidence from student ratings." In R. Perry & J. Smart (Eds.), *The scholarship of teaching and learning in higher education: An evidence-based perspective* (pp. 130–143). New York: Springer.

Thompson, B. (2007). The syllabus as a communication document: Constructing and presenting the syllabus. *Communication Education, 56*, 54–71.

Thormann, J., & Zimmerman, I. (2012). *The complete step-by-step guide to designing and teaching online courses.* New York: Columbia Teachers College Press.

Tiberius, R., & Flak, E. (1999). Incivility in dyadic teaching and learning. *New Directions for Teaching and Learning, 77*, 3–12.

Timpson, W, & Bendel-Simso, P. (1996). *Concepts and choices for teaching: Meeting the challenges in higher education.* Madison, WI: Magna.

Tindell, D., & Bohlander, R. (2012). The use and abuse of cell phones and text messaging in the classroom: A survey of college students. *College Teaching, 60*(1), 1–9.

Tobin, K. (1987). The role of wait time in higher cognitive level learning. *Review of Educational Research, 57*, 69–95.

Tozer, S. (1992, August). *Effective lecturing,* Presentation to University of Illinois, Urbana-Champaign, Teaching Assistants Orientation.

Tracey, M. (2005). Why do you want to teach? Experts offer tips on writing a philosophy of teaching statement. *gradPSYCH* (American Psychological Association). Retrieved from www.apa.org/gradpsych/2005/11/teach.aspx.

Trudeau, G., & Barnes, K. (2002). Shared expectations: Identifying similarities and differences between student and faculty teaching values based on student evaluation of faculty classroom performance. *International Business & Economics Research Journal, 1*(7), 67–79.

Trzesniewski, K. & Donnellan, M. (2010). Rethinking 'Generation Me': A study of cohort effects from 1976–2006. *Perspectives on Psychological Science, 5*(1), 58–75.

Tufte, E. (2003a). *The cognitive style of PowerPoint.* Cheshire, CT: Graphic Press.

Tufte, E. (2003b, September). Powerpoint is evil. *Wired Magazine.* Retrieved from www.wired.com/wired/archive/IL09/ppt2.html.

Twale, D., & DeLuca, B. (2008). *Faculty incivility: The rise of the academic bully culture.* San Francisco: Jossey Bass.

Twenge, J. (2009). Generational changes and their impact in the classroom: Teaching generation me. *Medical Education, 43*, 398–405.

Twenge, J. (2013). Teaching generation me. *Teaching of Psychology, 40*(1), 66–69.

Twenge, J. & Campbell, W. (2001). Age and birth cohort differences in self-esteem: A cross-temporal meta-analysis. *Personality and Social Psychology Review, 5*, 321–344.

University of Illinois Campus Resources for Faculty. (2013). Video retrieved at http://mooc.illinois.edu/resources/.

University of Illinois Center for Teaching Excellence (formerly Office of Instructional Resources). (1999, February). University of Illinois Faculty Retreat, Urbana, IL.

University of Illinois Guide to Massive Open Online Courses (MOOCs). (2013). Retrieved at http://mooc.illinois.edu/docs/moocs-at-illinois-guide.pdf.

University of Iowa. (2013). *Teaching Goals Inventory.* Retrieved from http://fm.iowa.uiowa.edu/fmi/xsl/tgi/data_entry.xsl?-db=tgi_data&-lay=Layout01&-view.

University of Texas, El Paso. (2013). *Selecting textbooks for efficient comprehension.* www.txprofdev.org/apps/reading/module14/module_html.html.

Upcraft, M. L. (1996). Teaching and today's college students. In R. Menges & M. Weimer (Eds.), *Teaching on solid ground: Using scholarship to improve practice* (pp. 21–41). San Francisco: Jossey-Bass.

U.S. Census Bureau. (2012). *The 2012 Statistical Abstract: The National Data Book*. Retrieved from www.census.gov/compendia/statab/cats/education/higher_education_institutions_and_enrollment.html.

Van Gyn, G. (2013). It's the little assignment with the big impact: Reading, writing, critical reflection, and meaningful discussion. *Faculty Focus*, May 6. Retrieved from www.facultyfocus.com/articles/instructional-design/the-little-assignment-with-the-big-impact-reading-writing-critical-reflection-and-meaningful-discussion/.

Vickers, M. (2010). Accommodating college students with learning disabilities: ADD, ADHD, and dyslexia. *Pope Center on Higher Education*. Retrieved from www.popecenter.org/acrobat/vickers-mar2010.pdf.

Wade, C. (1988, April). *Thinking critically about critical thinking in psychology*. Paper presented at the annual meeting of the Western Psychological Association, San Francisco, CA.

Walck, C. (1997). A teaching life. *Journal of Management Education, 21*, 473–482.

Walvoord, B. (2010). Explaining the reasons for criticisms of students' academic performance. *Tomorrow's Professor E-mail Newsletter #989*. Retrieved from http://cgi.stanford.edu/~dept-ctl/tomprof/posting.php.

Walvoord, B., & Anderson, V.J. (1998). *Effective grading: A tool for learning and assessment*. San Francisco: Jossey-Bass.

Walvoord, B., & Anderson, V.J. (2010). *Effective grading: A tool for learning and assessment in college* (2nd ed.). San Francisco, CA: Jossey-Bass.

Ward, A., & Jenkins, A. (1992). The problems of learning and teaching in large classes. In G. Gibbs & A. Jenkins (Eds.), *Teaching large classes in higher education: How to maintain quality with reduced resources* (pp. 23–36). London: Kogan Page.

Ward, M., Peters, G., & Shelley, K. (2010). Student and faculty perceptions of the quality of online learning experiences. *The International Review of Research in Open and Distance Learning, 11*(3), 57–77.

Ware, J., & Williams, R. (1975). The Dr. Fox effect: A study of lecturer effectiveness and ratings of instruction. *Journal of Medical Education, 50*(2), 149–156.

Ware, M., & Johnson, R. (Eds.). (2000a). *Handbook of demonstrations and activities in the teaching of psychology: Vol. 1. Introductory, statistics, research methods, and history* (2nd ed.). Mahwah, NJ: Lawrence Erlbaum Associates.

Ware, M., & Johnson, R. (Eds.). (2000b). *Handbook of demonstrations and activities in the teaching of psychology; Vol. 2. Physiological-comparative, perception, learning, cognitive, and developmental* (2nd ed.). Mahwah, NJ: Lawrence Erlbaum Associates.

Ware, M., & Johnson, R. (Eds.). (2000c). *Handbook of demonstrations and activities in the teaching of psychology: Vol. 3. Personality, abnormal, clinical, counseling, and social* (2nd ed.). Mahwah, NJ: Lawrence Erlbaum Associates.

Warren Trufant, L. (2003). Move over Socrates: Online discussion is here. *Educause*. Retrieved from http://net.educause.edu/ir/library/pdf/ncp0330.pdf.

Watkins, D. (1994). Student evaluations of teaching effectiveness: A cross-cultural perspective. *Research in Higher Education, 35*, 251–266.

Weimer, M. (Ed.). (1987). *Teaching large classes well: New directions for teaching and learning*. San Francisco: Jossey-Bass.

Weimer, M. (1988). Reading your way to better teaching. *College Teaching, 36*(2), 48–51.

Weimer, M. (1989). Research summary: Professors part of the problem? In R. Neff & M. Weimer (Eds.), *Classroom communication: Collected readings for effective discussion and questioning* (pp. 67–71). Madison, WI: Magna.

Weimer, M. (1996). *Improving your classroom teaching*. Newbury Park, CA: Sage. (Volume 1 of a 10-volume series collectively titled Survival Skills for Scholars.)

Weimer, M. (2010). *Inspired college teaching: A career-long resource for professional growth*. San Francisco: John Wiley & Sons.

Weimer, M. (2011). Revisiting extra credit policies. *Faculty Focus*. Retrieved from www.facultyfocus.com/articles/teaching-professor-blog/revisiting-extra-credit-policies.

Weimer, M. (2012a). End-of-course evaluations: Making sense of student comments. *Faculty Focus*, November 28. Retrieved from www.facultyfocus.com/articles/teaching-professor-blog/end-of-course-evaluations-making-sense-of-student-comments/.

Weimer, M. (2012b). Getting students to act on our feedback. *Faculty Focus*, March 5. Retrieved from www.facultyfocus.com/articles/teaching-professor-blog/getting-students-to-act-on-our-feedback/.

Weimer, M. (2012c). Student self-assessment: A sample assignment. *Faculty Focus*, February 1. Retrieved from www.facultyfocus.com/articles/teaching-professor-blog/student-self-assessment-a-sample-assignment/.

Weimer, M. (2013a). Defining teaching effectiveness. *Faculty Focus*, February 6. Retrieved from www.facultyfocus.com/articles/teaching-professor-blog/defining-teaching-effectiveness/.

Weimer, M. (2013b). Exams: Maximizing their potential. *Faculty Focus*. Retrieved from www.facultyfocus.com/articles/educational-assessment/exams-maximizing-their-learning-potential/.

Weimer, M. (2013c). First day of class activities that create a climate for learning. *The Teaching Professor Blog*. Retrieved from www.facultyfocus.com/articles/teaching-professor-blog/first-day-of-class-activities-that-create-a-climate-for-learning/.

Weimer, M. (2013d). Six steps to making positive changes in your teaching. *Faculty Focus*, January 23. Retrieved from www.facultyfocus.com/articles/teaching-professor-blog/six-steps-to-making-positive-changes-in-your-teaching/.

Weimer, M., & Lenze, L. (1997). Instructional interventions: A review of the literature on efforts to improve instruction. In R. Perry & J. Smart (Eds.), *Effective teaching in higher education: Research and practice* (pp. 205–240). New York: Agathon.

Wiggins, G., & McTighe, J. (1998). *Understanding by design*. Alexandria, VA: Association for Supervision and Curriculum Development.

Willingham, D. (2008). Critical thinking: Why is it so hard to teach? *Arts Education Policy Review, 109*(4), 21–29.

Willyard, C. (2010). The benefits of pop quizzes. *Science Now*. Retrieved from http://news.sciencemag.org/sciencenow/2010/10/the-benefits-of-pop-quizzes.html.

Wilson, J., & Ryan, R. (2012). Developing student teacher rapport in the undergraduate classroom. In W. Buskist & V. Benassi (Eds.), *Effective college and university teaching: Strategies and tactics for the new professoriate* (pp. 81–89). Los Angeles: Sage. May also be found at www.sagepub.com/upm-data/43586_14.pdf.

Wilson, J., & Ryan, R. (2013). Professor-student rapport scale: Six items predict student outcomes. *Teaching of Psychology, 40*(2), 130–133.

Wilson, J., Smalley, B., & Yancey, T. (2012). Building relationships with students and maintaining ethical boundaries. In R. Landrum & M. McCarthy (Eds.), *Teaching ethically: Challenges and opportunities.* May also be found at http://psycnet.apa.org/bookcollections/13496/.

Wilson, K., & Korn, J. (2007). Attention during lectures: Beyond ten minutes. *Teaching of Psychology, 34,* 85–89.

Wilson, S. (2013). The flipped class: A method to address the challenges of an undergraduate statistics course. *Teaching of Psychology, 40*(3), 193–199.

Wilson, S., & Florell, D. (2012). What can we do about student e-mails? *Association for Psychological Sciences, 25*(5), 47–50.

Wilson, V. (1999). From "zzz's" to "As": Using rubrics to improve student presentations. *The Teaching Professor, 13,* 3.

Witte, J., & Mock, J. (2013). MOOCs@Illinois: First Year Report. Presented at a *Teaching with Technology Brown Bag Series.* University of Illinois at Urbana-Champaign, November 20.

Woody, W., Daniel, D., & Baker, C. (2010). E-books or textbooks: Students prefer textbooks. *Computers & Education, 55,* 945–948.

Wright, D. (2012). *The most important day: Starting well.* Retrieved from www2.honolulu.hawaii.edu/facdev/guidebk/teachtip/dayone.htm.

Xu, D., & Jaggars, S. (2011). *Online and hybrid course enrollment and performance in Washington state community and technical colleges: CCRC Working Paper No. 31.* Retrieved from http://ccrc.tc.columbia.edu/media/k2/attachments/online-hybrid-performance-washington.pdf.

Yardley, J., Rodriguez, M., Bates, S., & Nelson, J. (2009). True confessions?: Alumni's retrospective reports on undergraduate cheating behaviors. *Ethics & Behavior, 19*(1), 1–14.

Yeager, D., & Dweck, C. (2012). Mindsets that promote resilience: When students believe that personal characteristics can be developed. *Educational Psychologist, 47*(4), 302–314.

Yew, E., & Schmidt, H. (2012). What students learn in problem-based learning: A process analysis. *Instructional Science, 40,* 371–395.

Young, J. (2010). To save students money, colleges may force a switch to E-textbooks. *Chronicle of Higher Education.* Retrieved from http://chronicle.com/article/The-End-of-the-Textbook-as-We/125044/.

Zakrajsek, T. (1998). Developing effective lectures. *APS Observer, 11,* 24–26.

Zax, D. (2009, October). Learning in 140-character bites: Twitter can improve teacher–student communication, in and out of class. *ASEE PRISM.* Retrieved from www.prism-magazine.org/oct09/tt_01.cfm.

Zepke, N., & Leach, L. (2010). Improving student engagement: Ten proposals for action. *Active Learning in Higher Education, 11*(3), 167–177.

Zlokovich, M. (2001). Grading for optimal student learning. *APS Observer, 14,* 12–13, 20–21.

Zlokovich, M. (2004). Grading for optimal student learning. In B. Perlman, L. McCann, & S. McFadden (Eds.), *Lessons learned: Practical advice for the teaching of psychology* (pp. 255–264). Washington, DC: American Psychological Association.

Zubizarreta, J. (1999). Evaluating teaching through portfolios. In P. Seldin (Ed.), *Changing practices in evaluating teaching: A practical guide to improved faculty performance and promotion/tenure decisions* (pp. 162–181). Bolton, MA: Anker.

Index ●●●●●

Page numbers in italics indicate figures and tables.